WORKSHOPS IN COMPUTING
Series edited by C. J. van Rijsbergen

Also in this series

ALPUK91, Proceedings of the 3rd UK
Annual Conference on Logic Programming,
Edinburgh, 10–12 April 1991
Geraint A.Wiggins, Chris Mellish and
Tim Duncan (Eds.)

Specifications of Database Systems
International Workshop on Specifications of
Database Systems, Glasgow, 3–5 July 1991
David J. Harper and Moira C. Norrie (Eds.)

**7th UK Computer and Telecommunications
Performance Engineering Workshop**
Edinburgh, 22–23 July 1991
J. Hillston, P.J.B. King and R.J. Pooley (Eds.)

Logic Program Synthesis and Transformation
Proceedings of LOPSTR 91, International
Workshop on Logic Program Synthesis and
Transformation, University of Manchester,
4–5 July 1991
T.P. Clement and K.-K. Lau (Eds.)

Declarative Programming, Sasbachwalden 1991
PHOENIX Seminar and Workshop on Declarative
Programming, Sasbachwalden, Black Forest,
Germany, 18–22 November 1991
John Darlington and Roland Dietrich (Eds.)

**Building Interactive Systems:
Architectures and Tools**
Philip Gray and Roger Took (Eds.)

Functional Programming, Glasgow 1991
Proceedings of the 1991 Glasgow Workshop on
Functional Programming, Portree, Isle of Skye,
12–14 August 1991
Rogardt Heldal, Carsten Kehler Holst and
Philip Wadler (Eds.)

Object Orientation in Z
Susan Stepney, Rosalind Barden and
David Cooper (Eds.)

Code Generation – Concepts, Tools, Techniques
Proceedings of the International Workshop on Code
Generation, Dagstuhl, Germany, 20–24 May 1991
Robert Giegerich and Susan L. Graham (Eds.)

Z User Workshop, York 1991, Proceedings of the
Sixth Annual Z User Meeting, York,
16–17 December 1991
J.E. Nicholls (Ed.)

Formal Aspects of Measurement
Proceedings of the BCS-FACS Workshop on
Formal Aspects of Measurement, South Bank
University, London, 5 May 1991
Tim Denvir, Ros Herman and R.W. Whitty (Eds.)

AI and Cognitive Science '91
University College, Cork, 19–20 September 1991
Humphrey Sorensen (Ed.)

5th Refinement Workshop, Proceedings of the 5th
Refinement Workshop, organised by BCS-FACS,
London, 8–10 January 1992
Cliff B. Jones, Roger C. Shaw and
Tim Denvir (Eds.)

**Algebraic Methodology and Software
Technology (AMAST'91)**
Proceedings of the Second International Conference
on Algebraic Methodology and Software
Technology, Iowa City, USA, 22–25 May 1991
M. Nivat, C. Rattray, T. Rus and G. Scollo (Eds.)

ALPUK92, Proceedings of the 4th UK
Conference on Logic Programming,
London, 30 March–1 April 1992
Krysia Broda (Ed.)

continued on back page...

Kung-Kiu Lau and Tim Clement (Eds.)

Logic Program Synthesis and Transformation

Proceedings of LOPSTR 92,
International Workshop on Logic
Program Synthesis and Transformation,
University of Manchester, 2–3 July 1992

Sponsored by the Association for Logic
Programming and ALPUK

Springer-Verlag London Ltd.

Kung-Kiu Lau, BSc, PhD
Department of Computer Science
The University
Manchester M13 9PL, UK

Timothy Paul Clement, MA, DPhil
Department of Computer Science
The University
Manchester M13 9PL, UK

ISBN 978-3-540-19806-2

British Library Cataloguing in Publication Data
Logic Program Synthesis and
Transformation: Proceedings of LOPSTR 92,
International Workshop on Logic Program
Synthesis and Transformation, University
of Manchester, 2-3 July 1992. -
(Workshops in Computing Series)
  I. Lau, K-.K. II. Clement, T.P.
  III. Series
  005.1
ISBN 978-3-540-19806-2   ISBN 978-1-4471-3560-9 (eBook)
DOI 10.1007/978-1-4471-3560-9

Library of Congress Cataloging-in-Publication Data
A catalog record for this book is available from the Library of Congress

Typesetting: Camera ready by contributors
34/3830-543210 Printed on acid-free paper

Foreword

This volume consists of extended versions of selected papers originally presented at the LOPSTR 92 workshop held in Manchester in July 1992. The workshop followed LOPSTR 91 in what promises to be a very successful series, ably organised by Kung-Kiu Lau and his colleagues.

The topic of both workshops (and hence this volume) was the synthesis and transformation of logic programs. This is a topic of central importance for the software industry. The demand for software can not be met by the current supply, in volume, in complexity or in reliability. The most promising solution to this multi-faceted problem is the increased automation of software production. Machine assisted program development can help us improve programmer productivity, take care of book-keeping, and apply mathematical methods to ensure correctness. Machine assistance is most effective when used to develop declarative programs, e.g. logic programs. The mathematical foundations of logic programs lend themselves to the use of mathematical methods of program development, and hence to automation.

This volume describes some of the most recent advances in machine assisted development of logic programs. Among the new techniques described here are some for the transformation of an inefficient program into an equivalent, but more efficient, program, the synthesis of a program from a formal specification of its required behaviour, and the proof that a program terminates. As these techniques begin to leave the laboratory and become standard practice they promise to revolutionise the software industry.

Edinburgh   Alan Bundy
August 1992

Preface

Organising the second of a series of workshops brings its own particular concerns: those who attended the first workshop have made encouraging noises about another, but will this translate into submissions and attendance when the time comes, or is the field insufficiently active to support an annual event? In the event, we had eighteen talks, of which seventeen appear as papers in these proceedings and one as an extended abstract. What the proceedings can not show is the active discussion which went on around the formal presentations.

The papers cover a broad range, from abstract models of logics to the details of register allocation in Prolog implementations, and including equational logics and database languages as well as the traditional Horn clauses of logic programming. The theme of partial deduction guided by abstract interpretation recurs in many different settings. Less clear is where the boundary between synthesis and transformation lies. A panel discussion at the end of the workshop addressed itself to this question, and resulted in not one but several equally convincing characterisations of the distinction.

Once again, we should like to thank the Association for Logic Programming for supporting student travel to the workshop, ALPUK for their financial support for the workshop itself, and Lynn Howarth for her help with the organisation of the workshop.

We should also like to thank the other Programme Committee members for their invaluable contribution and cooperation without which the workshop would not have been possible. We thank them and the other referees for their detailed and timely refereeing of the papers submitted to the workshop.

LOPSTR 93 will take place in Louvain-la-Neuve, Belgium on 7–9 July. See you there!

Manchester
September 1992

Kung-Kiu Lau and Tim Clement

Programme Committee

Tim Clement
University of Manchester, UK

Danny De Schreye
Katholieke Universiteit Leuven, Belgium

Yves Deville
Université Catholique de Louvain, Belgium

John Gallagher
University of Bristol, UK

Kung-Kiu Lau
University of Manchester, UK (Chair)

Referees

Behnam Bani-Eqbal
Dmitri Boulanger
Maurice Bruynooghe
Tim Clement
Nicoletta Cocco
Danny De Schreye
Bart Demoen
Philippe Devienne
Yves Deville
Pierre Flener
John Gallagher
Pat Hill
Kung-Kiu Lau
Bern Martens
Maurizio Proietti
Harold Simmons
Geraint Wiggins

Contents

Logic Program Synthesis via Proof Planning

Ina Kraan

Department of Artificial Intelligence
University of Edinburgh
Edinburgh, Scotland, U.K.
inak@ai.ed.ac.uk

David Basin *

Max-Planck-Institut für Informatik
Saarbrücken, Germany
basin@mpi-sb.mpg.de

Alan Bundy †

Department of Artificial Intelligence
University of Edinburgh
Edinburgh, Scotland, U.K.
bundy@ai.ed.ac.uk

Abstract

We propose a novel approach to automating the synthesis of logic programs: Logic programs are synthesized as a by-product of the planning of a verification proof. The approach is a two-level one: At the object level, we prove program verification conjectures in a sorted, first-order theory. The conjectures are of the form $\forall \overline{args}.\ prog(\overline{args}) \leftrightarrow spec(\overline{args})$. At the meta-level, we plan the object-level verification with an unspecified program definition. The definition is represented with a (second-order) meta-level variable, which becomes instantiated in the course of the planning.

This technique is an application of the Clam proof planning system [Bundy *et al* 90c]. Clam is currently powerful enough to plan verification proofs for given programs. We show that, if Clam's use of middle-out reasoning is extended, it will also be able to synthesize programs.

1 Introduction

The aim of the work presented here is to automate the synthesis of logic programs. This is done by adapting techniques from areas such as *middle-out reasoning* in *explicit proof plans* [Bundy 88, Bundy *et al* 90a], *proofs-as-programs*

---

*Supported by the German Ministry for Research and Technology (BMFT) under grant ITS 9102. Responsibility for the contents of this publication lies with the authors.

†Supported by SERC grant GR/E/44598, Esprit BRA grant 3012, Esprit BRA grant 3245, and an SERC Senior Fellowship.

[Bates & Constable 85] and *deductive synthesis* [Bibel 80]. We synthesize *pure logic programs* [Bundy *et al* 90b] from specifications in sorted, first-order theories. The approach encompasses two levels of reasoning: An object level, which is a sorted, first-order predicate logic with equality, and a meta-level, which reasons explicitly with object-level proofs. At the object level, we prove that the specification and the program are logically equivalent, which ensures the partial correctness and completeness of the program [Hogger 81]. At the meta-level, we construct a plan for the object-level proof. While planning, we represent the body of the program we are synthesizing with a meta-level variable. The use of meta-level variables in proof planning is called *middle-out reasoning*. Synthesis takes place when, in the course of planning, the meta-level variable representing the body of the program is instantiated to an object-level term. However, this term may not always correspond to a pure logic program. If it does not, an auxiliary synthesis is required.

The approach is embedded within the framework of the Clam proof planner [Bundy *et al* 90c]. Clam is currently powerful enough to conduct verification proofs for conjectures containing no meta-level variables. To synthesize programs in the way we are proposing here, however, Clam's use of middle-out reasoning will have to be extended.

The remainder of this paper is organized as follows: Section 2 discusses related work. Section 3 contains a definition of pure logic programs. Section 4 provides a brief introduction to proof planning, middle-out reasoning and rippling. Section 5 shows how verification proofs for a given specification and a given program can be planned, and Section 6 shows how programs can be synthesized by leaving the program unspecified when planning a verification proof. Section 7 contains a summary and suggestions for future work.

2   Related Work

In program synthesis from specifications[1], there are two main approachs, i.e., *proofs-as-programs* [Bates & Constable 85] and *deductive synthesis* [Bibel 80, Biundo 88].

Proofs-as-programs is based on what is known as the *Curry-Howard isomorphism* [Howard 80], whereby a proposition is identified with a type of terms in the λ-calculus that represent evidence for its truth. Under this isomorphism, a proposition is true if and only if the corresponding type has members. A proof of a proposition will construct such a member. Since terms in the λ-calculus may be evaluated, proofs give rise to functional programs. For example, given the proposition[2]

$$\forall \overrightarrow{input}.\exists output.\ spec(\overrightarrow{input}, output)$$

a proof of the proposition will construct a program f such that, for all inputs, f yields an output that satisfies the specification, i.e., $spec(\overrightarrow{input}, f(\overrightarrow{input}))$ holds. These ideas underlie the Nuprl system [Constable *et al* 86] and its Edinburgh reimplementation Oyster [Bundy *et al* 90c], which are interactive proof development systems for a variant of Martin-Löf type theory[Martin-Löf 79].

---

[1] As opposed to synthesis from input-output tuples, for example.

[2] Here, and in the following, we often omit sort or type information to avoid notational clutter.

Adapting proofs-as-programs to logic program synthesis is not straightforward. The main problem is that proofs-as-programs synthesizes total functions. Logic programs, however, are partial and multivalued [Bundy *et al* 90b]. They may return no value, i.e., fail, or they may return more than one value on backtracking. Moreover, they may not terminate.

One adaptation of proofs-as-programs to logic program synthesis is presented in [Fribourg 90]. Fribourg synthesizes programs from Prolog-style proofs. He extends standard Prolog goals to goals of the form $\forall \overline{x}.\exists \overline{y}.\ q(\overline{x}, \overline{y}) \Leftarrow r(\overline{x})$, where $q(\overline{x}, \overline{y})$ and $r(\overline{x})$ are conjunctions of atoms, and he extends standard Prolog SLD-resolution to the rules of *definite clause inference*, *simplification* and *restricted structural induction*, each of which is associated with a program construction rule. Given an appropriate specification, extended Prolog execution returns a program to compute $\overline{y}$ in terms of $\overline{x}$. However, the program is only correct if it is called with the variables $\overline{x}$ ground and the variables $\overline{y}$ unbound. Also, it will return exactly one answer. It is thus a functional program in the guise of a logic program.

To overcome these disadvantages, [Bundy *et al* 90b] suggests viewing logic programs in all-ground mode as functions returning a boolean value. A specification of a logic program is then:

$$\forall \overline{args}.\exists boole.\ spec(\overline{args}) = boole$$

If such specification theorems are proved in type theory, e.g., with the Oyster system, the programs are higher-order and functional. Such programs are difficult to translate into equivalent logic programs. Therefore, [Bundy *et al* 90b] suggests working with a constructive first-order logic in which the extract terms are pure logic programs.

This idea was pursued in [Wiggins *et al* 91] and has been implemented in Whelk, an interactive proof editor for logic program synthesis. The Whelk system distinguishes between the logic of the specification and the logic of the program. The two are related by a mapping from the program logic to the specification logic. Each inference rule in the specification logic corresponds to a program construction rule in the program logic. A major concern is proving the correctness of the rules [Wiggins 92].

In *deductive synthesis*, a set of transformation rules is applied to a given specification to derive a program. For instance, [Biundo 88] starts with a specification formula $\forall \overline{x}.\exists y.\forall \overline{z}.\ \Phi[\overline{x}, y, \overline{z}]$, where Φ is a quantifier-free first-order formula. Biundo Skolemizes the formula to $\forall \overline{x}.\forall \overline{z}.\ \Phi[\overline{x}, f(\overline{x}), \overline{z}]$ and applies transformation rules to the Skolemized specification until a program is obtained that computes the Skolem function $f(\overline{x})$. Her rules include *evaluation*, *substitution*, *case analysis* and *induction*. Transformation rules must be proved sound if the correctness of the program is to be guaranteed.

Our approach to synthesis can be related both to proof-as-programs and deductive synthesis. On one hand, we are proving

$$\forall \overline{args}.\ prog(\overline{args}) \leftrightarrow spec(\overline{args})$$

where the definition of *prog* is unknown. This is similar to proving the (higher-order) specification

$$\forall \overline{args}.\exists prog.\ prog(\overline{args}) \leftrightarrow spec(\overline{args})$$

constructively, since a constructive proof requires showing how a witness for an existentially quantified variable can be constructed. Thus our approach can be seen as proofs-as-programs. On the other hand, proof planning consists of the successive application of methods to a conjecture, where each method transforms the conjecture into another one. Each method can thus be perceived as a transformation rule.

3 Pure Logic Programs

Our notion of pure logic programs is similar to pure logic programs as defined in [Bundy *et al* 90b] and to logic descriptions as defined in [Deville 90]. In Deville's approach, logic program development is a two-stage process. First, a pure logic description is obtained from a specification in a subset of natural language. Then, the program is derived from the logic description. Deville's reasons for choosing logic descriptions as an intermediate representation are the same as ours for synthesizing pure logic programs. Pure logic programs are a subset of first-order predicate logic and thus share its purely declarative semantics. Pure logic programs are not meant to be directly executed, yet their syntax is sufficiently restricted that they are straightforward to translate into executable programs in logic programming languages, e.g., Prolog or Gödel [Hill & Lloyd 91]. We are thus not restricted to any particular logic programming language.

For the purpose of this paper, pure logic programs are collections of sentences of the form

$$\forall x_1 : t_1, \ldots, x_n : t_n. \, pred(x_1, \ldots, x_n) \leftrightarrow body$$

where *pred* is a predicate symbol, the x_i are distinct variables of sorts t_i and *body* is a pure logic program body. Only one definition per predicate symbol is allowed. Pure logic program bodies are defined recursively:

- The predicates *true* and *false* are pure logic program bodies.

- A member of a predefined set of decidable atomic relations is a pure logic program body[3].

- A call to a previously defined predicate is a pure logic program body.

- If P and Q are pure logic program bodies, then

    - $P \wedge Q$
    - $P \vee Q$
    - $\exists x. \, P$

  are pure logic program bodies.

Other connectives such as negation or implication can be added. Avoiding those, however, largely eliminates floundering, without restricting the expressive power of the language.

---

[3]For the purpose of this paper, the set consists of equality ($=$) and inequality ($\neq$).

An example of a pure logic program is:

$$\forall x, l.\ member(x, l) \quad \leftrightarrow \quad \exists h, t.\ l = [h|t] \wedge (x = h \vee member(x, t))$$
$$\forall i, j.\ subset(i, j) \quad \leftrightarrow \quad i = [\,] \vee$$
$$\exists h, t.\ i = [h|t] \wedge member(h, j) \wedge subset(t, j)$$

The predicate $member(x, l)$ is true if x is a member of the list l, the predicate $subset(i, j)$ is true if i is a subset of j. Translated into Prolog, for instance, they become:

$$member(X, [X|\_]).$$
$$member(X, [\_|T]) \leftarrow member(X, T).$$

$$subset([\,], \_).$$
$$subset([H|T], J) \leftarrow member(H, J), subset(T, J).$$

The pure logic program is the completion of the Prolog program.

4 Proof Planning

The central problem of automated theorem proving is the enormous search space for proofs. Some theorem provers, e.g., NQTHM [Boyer & Moore 88], use heuristics to decide when to apply which inference rule. These heuristics are often built-in, which makes them inflexible and difficult to understand. To avoid this, [Bundy 88] suggests using a meta-logic to reason about and to plan proofs. Proof plans are combinations of *methods*, which are specifications of *tactics*. A tactic is a program that applies a number of object-level inference rules to a goal formula. A method is a specification of a tactic in the sense of the assertion: If a goal formula matches the input pattern and if the preconditions are met, the tactic is applicable, and, if the tactic succeeds, the output conditions (or effects) will be true of the resulting goal formulae. These ideas are the basis of the proof planner Clam [Bundy *et al* 90c]. Clam constructs proof plans that can be executed in Oyster.

Middle-out reasoning [Bundy *et al* 90a] extends the meta-level reasoning of proof planning in that it allows the meta-level representation of object-level entities to contain meta-level variables. This allows proof planning to proceed even though an object-level entity is not fully specified. Thus, it is possible to postpone a decision about the entity's real identity. Clam currently uses middle-out reasoning to synthesize tail-recursive programs from non-tail-recursive specifications and to generalize inductive theorems. We will extend Clam's use of middle-out reasoning significantly. In particular, we will use meta-level variables to represent unspecified parts of logic programs.

Clam is particularly good at proving theorems by induction. Its power stems from the *rippling* method, which is central to proving the step case(s) of inductive proofs. In the step case, the overall strategy is to manipulate the induction conclusion in such a way that it is possible to exploit the induction hypothesis. Rippling does this by keeping track of the differences between the induction hypothesis and the induction conclusion and applying rewrites to the induction conclusion to reduce these differences.

Rippling is best illustrated by an example. Clam would represent the step case of the proof of the associativity of plus as

$$(x + y) + z = x + (y + z)$$
$$\vdash$$
$$\left(\boxed{s(\underline{x})}^{\uparrow} + y\right) + z = \boxed{s(\underline{x})}^{\uparrow} + (y + z)$$

where s represents the successor function. The boxes and underlining are meta-level annotations. The non-underlined parts in the boxes are *wave fronts*—they do not appear in the induction hypothesis. The underlined parts in the boxes are *wave holes*. The wave holes and the remaining parts of the induction conclusion are called the skeleton—strung together they form the induction hypothesis. The arrows indicate the direction in which the wave fronts are moving, in this case up the term tree of the induction conclusion. Rippling is the exhaustive application of a set of rewrite rules called *wave rules*. Wave rules are also annotated. They are applied only if the wave rule and a subexpression of the induction conclusion match, including annotations. The annotation on the wave rule ensures that applying it will move the wave front up in the term tree of the induction conclusion. Often, all wave fronts can be rippled to the top of the term tree of the induction conclusion, which means that the induction hypothesis can be exploited. The wave rules required for our example proof are

$$\boxed{s(\underline{M})}^{\uparrow} + N \;\Rightarrow\; \boxed{s(\underline{M + N})}^{\uparrow} \tag{1}$$

$$\boxed{s(\underline{M})}^{\uparrow} = \boxed{s(\underline{N})}^{\uparrow} \;\Rightarrow\; M = N \tag{2}$$

where M and N are free variables. Clam generates these wave rules automatically from the definition of $+$ and the substitution axiom for s. The rippling of the example consists of three applications of wave rule (1) (two on the left- and one on the right-hand side) and one of wave rule (2):

$$
\begin{array}{rcl}
\left(\boxed{s(\underline{x})}^{\uparrow} + y\right) + z & = & \boxed{s(\underline{x})}^{\uparrow} + (y + z) \\[2mm]
\boxed{s(\underline{x + y})}^{\uparrow} + z & = & \boxed{s(\underline{x})}^{\uparrow} + (y + z) \\[2mm]
\boxed{s(\underline{(x + y) + z})}^{\uparrow} & = & \boxed{s(\underline{x})}^{\uparrow} + (y + z) \\[2mm]
\boxed{s(\underline{(x + y) + z})}^{\uparrow} & = & \boxed{s(\underline{x + (y + z)})}^{\uparrow} \\[2mm]
(x + y) + z & = & x + (y + z)
\end{array}
$$

Not only has the wave front moved to the top of the induction conclusion, but it has also disappeared. The induction conclusion is now identical to the induction hypothesis, and the step case is complete. This final step is called *strong fertilization*.

Rippling will be the key method in planning the step cases of the verifications proofs. Other methods we will use in the following sections are induction, symbolic evaluation, tautology checking and unblocking. What these methods do will become apparent in the discussion of the proofs.

5 Verification

In this section, we show how Clam's existing methods can be used to plan the verification proof for a given program. Our verification conjectures, which we prove classically, are first-order sentences of the form:

$$\forall \overline{args}.\ prog(\overline{args}) \leftrightarrow spec(\overline{args})$$

The logical equivalence of the specification and the program guarantees the partial correctness and completeness of the program with respect to the specification [Hogger 81].

We show how Clam plans proofs for such conjectures using the example conjecture

$$\forall i, j.\ subset(i, j) \quad \leftrightarrow \quad (\forall x.\ member(x, i) \to member(x, j)) \tag{3}$$

where the program *subset* is defined as

$$\forall i, j.\ subset(i, j) \quad \leftrightarrow \quad i = [\,]\ \lor$$
$$\exists h, t.\ i = [h|t] \land member(h, j) \land subset(t, j)$$

and *member* in the program and the specification is defined as:

$$\forall x, l.\ member(x, l) \quad \leftrightarrow \quad \exists h, t.\ l = [h|t] \land (x = h \lor member(x, t))$$

The definitions of *subset* and *member* give rise to the following wave rules:

$$subset(\boxed{[H|\underline{T}]}^{\uparrow}, J) \quad \Rightarrow \quad \boxed{member(H, J) \land \underline{subset(T, J)}}^{\uparrow} \tag{4}$$

$$member(X, \boxed{[H|\underline{T}]}^{\uparrow}) \quad \Rightarrow \quad \boxed{X = H \lor \underline{member(X, T)}}^{\uparrow} \tag{5}$$

We also need the following wave rules, which are derived from lemmas:

$$\boxed{P \lor \underline{Q}}^{\uparrow} \to R \quad \Rightarrow \quad \boxed{P \to R \land \underline{Q \to R}}^{\uparrow} \tag{6}$$

$$\forall x. \boxed{P \land \underline{Q}}^{\uparrow} \quad \Rightarrow \quad \boxed{\forall x.\ P \land \underline{\forall x.\ Q}}^{\uparrow} \tag{7}$$

$$\boxed{P \land \underline{Q}}^{\uparrow} \leftrightarrow \boxed{P \land \underline{R}}^{\uparrow} \quad \Rightarrow \quad Q \leftrightarrow R \tag{8}$$

Wave rules such as (6)–(8) that are stated in terms of logical connectives only are called *propositional* wave rules.

For conjecture (3), based on wave rules (4)–(8), Clam suggests one-step structural induction on the list i[4]. The annotated step case is then:

$$subset(t, j) \leftrightarrow \forall x.\ member(x, t) \to member(x, j)$$
$$\vdash$$
$$subset(\boxed{[h|\underline{t}]}^{\uparrow}, j) \leftrightarrow \forall x.\ member(x, \boxed{[h|\underline{t}]}^{\uparrow}) \to member(x, j)$$

---

[4] Clam uses a technique called recursion analysis [Bundy *et al* 89] to choose an induction schema. Explaining recursion analysis is beyond the scope of this paper.

Rippling with wave rules (4) and (5) on the left and right, respectively, gives us:

$$\boxed{member(h,j) \wedge \underline{subset(t,j)}}^{\uparrow} \leftrightarrow$$

$$\forall x.\, \boxed{x = h \vee \underline{member(x,t)}}^{\uparrow} \rightarrow member(x,j)$$

Rippling with wave rule (6) on the right results in:

$$\boxed{member(h,j) \wedge \underline{subset(t,j)}}^{\uparrow} \leftrightarrow$$

$$\forall x.\, \boxed{x = h \rightarrow member(x,j) \wedge \underline{member(x,t) \rightarrow member(x,j)}}^{\uparrow}$$

Rippling with wave rule (7) on the right gives us:

$$\boxed{member(h,j) \wedge \underline{subset(t,j)}}^{\uparrow} \leftrightarrow$$

$$\boxed{\forall x.\, x = h \rightarrow member(x,j) \wedge \forall x.\, member(x,t) \rightarrow member(x,j)}^{\uparrow}$$

Now, we cannot continue rippling because none of the wave rules applies, but we cannot yet exploit the induction hypothesis either. We say that the rippling is *blocked*. We can unblock the rippling by simplifying the wave front on the right-hand side, i.e., by rewriting $\forall x.\, x = h \rightarrow member(x,j)$ to $member(h,j)$:

$$\boxed{member(h,j) \wedge \underline{subset(t,j)}}^{\uparrow} \leftrightarrow$$

$$\boxed{member(h,j) \wedge \underline{\forall x.\, member(x,t) \rightarrow member(x,j)}}^{\uparrow}$$

Wave rule (8) applies and yields:

$$subset(t,j) \leftrightarrow \forall x.\, member(x,t) \rightarrow member(x,j)$$

We strong fertilize to complete the step case. The base case is:

$$\vdash subset([],j) \leftrightarrow \forall x.\, member(x,[]) \rightarrow member(x,j)$$

Symbolic evaluation of $subset([],j)$ and $member(x,\lfloor\rfloor)$ gives us:

$$\vdash true \leftrightarrow \forall x.\, false \rightarrow member(x,j)$$

which further simplifies to the tautology:

$$\vdash true$$

Our proof plan is thus complete. It is identical to the proof plan that Clam produces automatically, except that Clam does the base case before the step case.

In the following section, we will show how the planning of verification proofs carries over to the synthesis of logic programs.

6 Synthesis

Verification can be extended to synthesis by introducing middle-out reasoning in the proof planning. Middle-out reasoning involves representing object-level entities with meta-level variables, thus enabling the proof planning to continue even though the identity of the object-level entity is unknown. We will represent the body of the program to be synthesized with a meta-level variable. One might expect that middle-out reasoning would significantly increase the amount of search in planning, but we will show that this is not case, due to the tight control that rippling provide.

If we inspect the planning of Section 5 to determine which steps depend directly on the definition of the program, we see that there are only two: The application of wave rule (4), since the rule was derived from the program, and the symbolic evaluation of $subset([], j)$. Not having wave rule (4) means that, in the step case, the rippling would be blocked after the application of wave rules (5)–(7). It is precisely the use of middle-out reasoning which will allow us to continue planning even though we do not have wave rule (4).

We begin our synthesis with the same conjecture, wave rules (5)–(8), and with a program whose body is undefined, i.e.,

$$\forall i, j. \; subset(i, j) \leftrightarrow \mathcal{P}(i, j)$$

($\mathcal{P}$ is a second-order meta-level variable representing the program body). As before, we proceed by one-step structural induction on the list i. Because of the duality between induction and recursion, we know what the recursive structure of the body of the program will be: A base case where the list i will be empty, and a step case where the list i consists of a head and a tail and which may contain a recursive call. Thus $\mathcal{P}(i, j)$ can already be partially instantiated such that

$$\forall i, j. \; subset(i, j) \quad \leftrightarrow \quad \begin{aligned} & i = [] \wedge \mathcal{B}(j) \vee \\ & \exists h, t. \; i = [h|t] \wedge \mathcal{S}(h, t, j, subset(t, j)) \end{aligned}$$

($\mathcal{B}$ and $\mathcal{S}$ are again second-order meta-level variables). Moreover, if the step case contains a recursive call, there will be a wave rule for $subset$ of the form:

$$subset(\boxed{[H|\underline{T}]}^{\uparrow}, J) \Rightarrow \boxed{\mathcal{S}(H, T, J, \underline{subset(T, J)})}^{\uparrow} \tag{9}$$

The rippling proceeds as in Section 5 using wave rule (9) instead of (4). Applying wave rules (5) and (9) yields:

$$\boxed{\mathcal{S}(h, t, j, \underline{subset(t, j)})}^{\uparrow} \leftrightarrow$$

$$\forall x. \boxed{x = h \vee \underline{member(x, t)}}^{\uparrow} \rightarrow member(x, j)$$

Applying wave rules (6), (7) and the unblocking step to the right-hand side of the equivalence as before gives:

$$\boxed{\mathcal{S}(h, t, j, \underline{subset(t, j)})}^{\uparrow} \leftrightarrow$$

$$\boxed{member(h, j) \wedge \forall x. \; member(x, t) \rightarrow member(x, j)}^{\uparrow}$$

We now apply wave rule (8), which instantiates

$$\mathcal{S}(h,t,j,subset(t,j))$$

with:

$$member(h,j) \wedge \mathcal{S}'(h,t,j,subset(t,j))$$

We obtain the subgoal:

$$\boxed{\mathcal{S}'(h,t,j,\underline{subset(t,j)})}^\uparrow \leftrightarrow \forall x.\ member(x,t) \rightarrow member(x,j)$$

Finally, strong fertilization, which is now applicable, matches the conclusion with the induction hypothesis, which was

$$subset(t,j) \leftrightarrow \forall x.\ member(x,t) \rightarrow member(x,j)$$

thus instantiating $\mathcal{S}'(h,t,j,subset(t,j))$ with $subset(t,j)$.

To complete the proof plan, we need to deal with the base case:

$$\vdash subset([],j) \leftrightarrow \forall x.\ member(x,[]) \rightarrow member(x,j)$$

Symbolic evaluation of $subset([],j)$ and $member(x,[])$ gives us

$$\vdash \mathcal{B}(j) \leftrightarrow \forall x.\ false \rightarrow member(x,j)$$

which simplifies to:

$$\vdash \mathcal{B}(j) \leftrightarrow true$$

This is a tautology if we take $\mathcal{B}(j)$ to be $true$.

The proof plan is complete, and the fully instantiated $subset$ program is:

$$\forall i,j.\ subset(i,j) \quad \leftrightarrow \quad i = [] \wedge true \vee$$
$$\exists h,t.\ i = [h|t] \wedge member(h,j) \wedge subset(t,j)$$

To summarize the synthesis process, we can say that synthesis equals planning verification proofs using middle-out reasoning. Whether we are doing verification or synthesis, the schema of the proof plan is the same:

1. Choosing an induction schema

2. Base case(s): Symbolic evaluation and tautology checking

3. Step case(s): Rippling and strong fertilization

In the $subset$ example, the instantiation of the initial meta-level variable representing the program body met the definition of a pure logic program in Section 3. However, this is not necessarily true of all instantiations in general. We discuss this problem briefly in the following.

Auxiliary Syntheses In the course of planning, a meta-level variable may become instantiated with a program body that violates the definition of pure logic programs of Section 3. Thus, we must check the synthesized program. We need to run an auxiliary synthesis for any part of the program that constitutes a violation; the part itself becomes the specification. We replace any part for which we run an auxiliary synthesis with a call to the auxiliary predicate, and we add the auxiliary predicate to our program.

An example where an auxiliary synthesis is necessary is the specification:

$$\forall m, l. \ max(m, l) \leftrightarrow m \in l \wedge (\forall x. \ x \in l \rightarrow x \leq m)$$

The element m is the maximum element of the list l. The initial synthesized program is:

$$\forall m, l. \ max(m, l) \quad \leftrightarrow \quad l = [] \wedge false \vee \\ \exists h, t. \ l = [h|t] \wedge ((m = h \wedge \forall x. \ x \in t \rightarrow x \leq m) \vee \\ (h \leq m \wedge max(m, t)))$$

The part $\forall x. \ x \in t \rightarrow x \leq m$ in the program body violates the definition of pure logic program bodies, since it contains a universal quantifier and an implication. We therefore run the auxiliary synthesis:

$$\forall m, l. \ aux(m, l) \leftrightarrow (\forall x. \ x \in l \rightarrow x \leq m)$$

The auxiliary specification states that m is greater than any element of the list l. Unlike the original max specification, however, m does not have to be an element of l. The final program with the auxiliary predicate is:

$$\forall m, l. \quad max(m, l) \leftrightarrow \\ l = [] \wedge false \vee \\ \exists h, t. \ l = [h|t] \wedge ((m = h \wedge aux(m, t)) \vee (h \leq m \wedge max(m, t))) \\ \forall m, l. \quad aux(m, l) \leftrightarrow \\ l = [] \wedge true \vee \\ \exists h, t. \ l = [h|t] \wedge h \leq m \wedge aux(m, t)$$

7 Summary and Future Work

We have shown how pure logic programs can be synthesized by using middle-out reasoning in the planning of verification proofs. The approach provides a basis for the automatic synthesis of partially correct and complete programs from specifications in sorted, first-order predicate logic. The only synthesis step that lies outside of the proof planning proper is the syntactic check whether the instantiation of the body of the program is acceptable as a pure logic program.

The current methods of the proof planner Clam are a solid foundation to start with. A version of Clam which works with sorted first-order predicate logic with equality (the original Clam was written for a variant of Martin-Löf type theory) is able to verify the *subset* and *max* programs in Sections 5 and 6. The main change to Clam to enable the corresponding syntheses is the extension of middle-out reasoning.

There are other extensions to Clam which are needed to cope with problems that arise in synthesis proofs. One problem is posed by nested quantifiers in

the body of the specification. This occurs, for example, in the proof planning
for:

$$\forall k.\ no\_duplicates(k) \leftrightarrow (\forall l, m.\ append(l, m) = k \rightarrow (\forall x.\ x \in l \rightarrow x \notin m))$$

The annotated induction conclusion is:

$$no\_duplicates(\boxed{[h|\underline{t}]}^{\uparrow}) \leftrightarrow$$

$$(\forall l, m.\ append(l, m) = \boxed{[h|\underline{t}]}^{\uparrow} \rightarrow (\forall x.\ x \in l \rightarrow x \notin m))$$

Here, the rippling on the right-hand side of the equivalence is immediately
blocked. The wave rule we would like to apply is

$$\boxed{[H1|\underline{T1}]}^{\uparrow} = \boxed{[H2|\underline{T2}]}^{\uparrow} \Rightarrow \boxed{H1 = H2 \wedge \underline{T1 = T2}}^{\uparrow}$$

but in order to do so we need to unfold the *append* first. This is obstructed
by the universal quantification of l. Clam's current unblocking techniques will
have to be extended to deal with such cases.

Another difficult problem arises, for example, in the proof planning for:

$$\forall x.\ even(x) \leftrightarrow (\exists y.\ y \cdot s(s(0)) = x)$$

Here, the problem is that Clam is unable to suggest the appropriate type of
induction, namely two-step induction on x. Clam's technique to choose an
induction schema, i.e., recursion analysis [Bundy *et al* 89], works well for conjectures containing universal quantifiers only, but breaks down in the presence
of existential quantifiers. The alternative to recursion analysis is again to use
middle-out reasoning, this time to postpone the choice of induction schema
until the rippling in the step case determines the type of induction.

Finally, in Sections 5 and 6, we assumed that Clam had available the lemmas
necessary to derive the propositional wave rules (6)–(8). Given the large number of conceivable propositional wave rules, Clam should be able to generate
the lemmas and wave rules on demand.

References

[Bates & Constable 85] Joseph L. Bates and Robert L. Constable. Proofs as
programs. *ACM Transactions on Programming Lan-
guages and Systems*, 7(1):113–136, January 1985.

[Bibel 80] W. Bibel. Syntax-directed, semantics-supported program synthesis. *Artificial Intelligence*, 14:243–261,
1980.

[Biundo 88] S. Biundo. Automated synthesis of recursive algorithms as a theorem proving tool. In Y. Kodratoff,
editor, *Eighth European Conference on Artificial Intelligence*, pages 553–8. Pitman, 1988.

[Boyer & Moore 88]   R.S. Boyer and J.S. Moore. *A Computational Logic Handbook*. Academic Press, 1988. Perspectives in Computing, Vol 23.

[Bundy 88]   A. Bundy. The use of explicit plans to guide inductive proofs. In R. Lusk and R. Overbeek, editors, *9th Conference on Automated Deduction*, pages 111–120. Springer-Verlag, 1988. Longer version available from Edinburgh as DAI Research Paper No. 349.

[Bundy *et al* 89]   A. Bundy, F. van Harmelen, J. Hesketh, A. Smaill, and A. Stevens. A rational reconstruction and extension of recursion analysis. In N.S. Sridharan, editor, *Proceedings of the Eleventh International Joint Conference on Artificial Intelligence*, pages 359–365. Morgan Kaufmann, 1989. Also available from Edinburgh as DAI Research Paper 419.

[Bundy *et al* 90a]   A. Bundy, A. Smaill, and J. Hesketh. Turning eureka steps into calculations in automatic program synthesis. In S.L.H. Clarke, editor, *Proceedings of UK IT 90*, pages 221–6, 1990. Also available from Edinburgh as DAI Research Paper 448.

[Bundy *et al* 90b]   A. Bundy, A. Smaill, and G. A. Wiggins. The synthesis of logic programs from inductive proofs. In J. Lloyd, editor, *Computational Logic*, pages 135–149. Springer-Verlag, 1990. Esprit Basic Research Series. Also available from Edinburgh as DAI Research Paper 501.

[Bundy *et al* 90c]   A. Bundy, F. van Harmelen, C. Horn, and A. Smaill. The Oyster-Clam system. In M.E. Stickel, editor, *10th International Conference on Automated Deduction*, pages 647–648. Springer-Verlag, 1990. Lecture Notes in Artificial Intelligence No. 449. Also available from Edinburgh as DAI Research Paper 507.

[Constable *et al* 86]   R.L. Constable, S.F. Allen, H.M. Bromley, *et al*. *Implementing Mathematics with the Nuprl Proof Development System*. Prentice Hall, 1986.

[Deville 90]   Y. Deville. *Logic Programming. Systematic Program Development*. International Series in Logic Programming. Addision-Wesley, 1990.

[Fribourg 90]   L. Fribourg. Extracting logic programs from proofs that use extended Prolog execution and induction. In *Proceedings of Eighth International Conference on Logic Programming*, pages 685 – 699. MIT Press, June 1990.

[Hill & Lloyd 91]   P. Hill and J. Lloyd. The Gödel Report. Technical Report TR-91-02, Department of Computer Science,

University of Bristol, March 1991. Revised in September 1991.

[Hogger 81]   C.J. Hogger. Derivation of logic programs. *JACM*, 28(2):372–392, April 1981.

[Howard 80]   W.A. Howard. The formulae-as-types notion of construction. In J.P. Seldin and J.R. Hindley, editors, *To H.B. Curry; Essays on Combinatory Logic, Lambda Calculus and Formalism*, pages 479–490. Academic Press, 1980.

[Martin-Löf 79]   Per Martin-Löf. Constructive mathematics and computer programming. In *6th International Congress for Logic, Methodology and Philosophy of Science*, pages 153–175, Hanover, August 1979. Published by North Holland, Amsterdam. 1982.

[Wiggins 92]   G. A. Wiggins. Synthesis and transformation of logic programs in the Whelk proof development system. In K. R. Apt, editor, *Proceedings of JICSLP-92*, 1992.

[Wiggins *et al* 91]   G. A. Wiggins, A. Bundy, H. C. Kraan, and J. Hesketh. Synthesis and transformation of logic programs through constructive, inductive proof. In K-K. Lau and T. Clement, editors, *Proceedings of LoPSTr-91*, pages 27–45. Springer Verlag, 1991. Workshops in Computing Series.

Deductive Synthesis of Programs for Query Answering

Daniele Nardi, Riccardo Rosati

Dipartimento di Informatica e Sistemistica

Università di Roma "La Sapienza"

Via Salaria 113, 00198 Roma, Italia

nardi@assi.ing.uniroma1.it

Abstract

In this paper we discuss the application of the deductive-tableau method for program synthesis to the generation of programs for computing the answers to the queries posed to a relational database. The input-output specification for the synthesis is directly extracted from the expressions of relational calculus. The synthesis is then divided into two steps: the first one produces programs implementing the operators of relational algebra in an applicative, side-effect free language; the second one translates the queries expressed in relational calculus into equivalent expressions of relational algebra. The syntheses have been machine checked using the Deductive Tableau System[1]. The work follows a previous application of the deductive-tableau method to the synthesis of programs for data base transactions and aims at developing a test of practical significance for program synthesis.

1 Introduction

In this paper we discuss the synthesis of programs for computing the answer to queries posed to relational data bases. The syntheses are accomplished within the framework of the deductive-tableau method developed by Manna and Waldinger [6, 8]. This method for program synthesis is based on theorem proving, using non-clausal resolution as the basic deductive apparatus. The synthesized program is expressed in an applicative, side-effect free language.

Our aim in studying the synthesis of query answering programs is to identify a framework where current techniques for automatic programming and in particular the deductive-tableau method can be successfully applied. The difficulties in automating program synthesis of large, real world applications are well-known, and there is now an interest in finding frameworks that are suitable for experimentation with program synthesis techniques. The conceptual simplicity of the relational model provides the basis for our study, which complements the work reported in [12, 13], describing the synthesis of programs for data base transactions using the deductive-tableau method.

In data base management systems one can consider the use of relational calculus for querying the data base as a form of automatic programming, since the user simply provides the specification of the desired output. However, the synthesis of programs for query evaluation could be relevant to the following

---

[1] The Deductive Tableau System is a Trademark of Tableau Deductive Systems.

practical purposes in the field of data bases. First of all, as a tool for generating user-defined query answering procedures, which could be useful for improving the performance of a specific set of queries. Secondly, as a tool for data base system design, which could support the verification of the critical parts of the implementation, such as the implementation of the operators of relational algebra.

Such practical achievements are still outside the scope of the present work, whose aim is rather to provide a serious test for program synthesis, and specifically for the deductive-tableau method. In particular, we would like program synthesis methods to be capable of supporting the synthesis of programs from simple specification languages such as relational calculus. Moreover, in this simple framework, we aim at identifying parts of the synthesis process that can be realized fully automatically, namely without human intervention in the synthesis.

Our synthesis starts from a specification directly obtained from queries expressed in relational calculus. In particular we always refer to safe formulas of tuple relational calculus [15]. We then split the process into two steps: (1) find the programs corresponding to the operators of relational algebra; (2) translate expressions of relational calculus into equivalent expressions of relational algebra. The first step does not depend on the form of the query and can be thought of as an extension of the basic theory of relations, which is introduced to describe relational data bases. In the terminology of deductive-tableaux this step corresponds to the synthesis of auxiliary procedures. The second step starts from the queries and outputs expressions containing the operators synthesized in the first step. This step is simpler because it does not need to deal with recursive calls, and in fact it can be performed mechanically if the deductive system is sufficiently powerful.

Proofs have been machine checked using the Deductive Tableau System, an interactive environment for theorem proving with the deductive-tableau method [1].

The paper is organized as follows. In Section 2 we provide a quick overview of the deductive-tableau method. Section 3 describes the basic theory of relations and Section 4 discusses the input-output specification. The two steps of the synthesis are presented in Section 5 and 6, respectively. Section 7 reports on the actual derivations done within the Deductive Tableau System. The final section presents some concluding remarks.

2   The Deductive-Tableau method

In this section we give a short and informal presentation of the deductive-tableau method, in particular we focus on the aspects that are relevant to the present paper. The reader is referred to [6, 8] for a complete account on the method.

The deductive-tableau method is a formal apparatus for program synthesis. The approach is based on theorem proving: starting from a specification, a program is obtained by proving the validity of the specification. The program thus derived is guaranteed to be correct with respect to the initial specification. A specification has the form

$$f(a) \Leftarrow \text{find } z \text{ such that } R[a, z] \text{ where } P[a]$$

$R[a, z]$ specifies the output condition, and $P[a]$ specifies the input condition; $f(a)$ is the program obtained at the end of the derivation, and is expressed as a set of mutually recursive expressions written in a side-effect free applicative language.

The input-output behavior of the target program is described by the following sentence in the language of first order logic:

$$(\forall a)[\text{if } P[a] \text{ then } (\exists z)[R[a, z]]]$$

The proof of the validity of the input-output condition leads to the synthesis of the program. The tableau associated with a specification is represented by

Assertions	Goals	$f(a)$
An $P(a)$		
Gn	$R[a, z]$	z

An and Gn are the labels that we use to refer to a particular row of the tableau. The meaning of the tableau can be characterized in terms of the *associated sentence*. Let $\mathcal{A}_1 \ldots \mathcal{A}_m$ be the sentences of the assertions of a tableau, and $\mathcal{G}_1 \ldots \mathcal{G}_n$ the sentences of its goals, the associated sentence of the tableau is

$$\text{if } [(\forall*)\mathcal{A}_1 \wedge \ldots \wedge (\forall*)\mathcal{A}_m] \text{ then } [(\exists*)\mathcal{G}_1 \vee \ldots \vee (\exists*)\mathcal{G}_n]$$

where $(\forall*)$ and $(\exists*)$ denote universal and existential closure, respectively. Under a given intepretation, the truth of the tableau is defined as the truth of its associated sentence.

The distinction between assertions and goals is done only for methodological reasons; in fact, given the meaning of the tableau, any sentence in the goal column can be moved into the assertion column by simply negating it (and viceversa). This property is called *duality*.

The output (usually associated with the goals) is said to be *suitable* if it satisfies the input-output condition whenever the corresponding instance of the goal (assertion) is true (false).

A deduction consists of adding new rows to the tableau without changing its meaning, so if the old tableau is true under a certain interpretation, then the new tableau is true under the same interpretation, and if the output of the old tableau is suitable, then the output of the new tableau is suitable as well. The deduction terminates when either a *true* goal or a *false* assertion is derived: the associated output contains the desired program.

The deduction is essentially based on nonclausal resolution, which has been proved complete in [10], combined with well-founded induction, which is necessary to obtain the recursive calls in the programs. Below we briefly describe the rules used in the present work.

Splitting rules allow one to split a row of the tableau. According to the meaning of the tableau, a disjunctive goal can be split onto several rows, each with the same output as the original goal ($\vee$-rule). A dual $\wedge$-rule exists for the assertions.

Transformation rules allow one to replace equivalent or equal subexpressions within assertions, goals and outputs. In particular, the simplifications of propositional logic formulas are expressed as transformation rules (e.g. $P \wedge false \equiv false$).

The *resolution rule* allows one to derive a new line of a tableau if it is possible to unify two subsentences of two rows of the tableau. In the ground case the rule is expressed by the following tableau.

Assertions	Goals	$f(a)$
	$F[P]$	s
	$G[P]$	t
	$F[true] \wedge G[false]$	if P then s else t

If a subsentence P occurs both in the goal F and in the goal G, then by applying the resolution rule a new goal is derived as the conjunction of the initial goals, where the subsentence P has been substituted by *true* in one formula and *false* in the other one. This rule represents a generalization of the standard resolution step on ground terms, which allows collapse of two clauses containing P and $\neg P$ respectively. The output of the new goal contains a conditional whose test-part is the eliminated subsentence, the then-part corresponds to the case of a *true* P and the else-part to the case of a *false* P. The application of the resolution rule usually leads to sentences that can be simplified using the transformation rules. The use of the polarity strategy (see [8]) guarantees that the resolution step is applied successfully, i.e. that it is possible to simplify the result of the resolution. The resolution rule works in the above form when it is applied to goals. According to the duality between assertions and goals, analogous rules are defined for the resolution between two assertions and between a goal and an assertion. The resolution rule is generalized to the non-ground case by applying it when two subsentences unify: the result is then obtained as in the ground case, but the most general unifier is applied to the sentences as well as to the output. We use boxes in the tableaux to surround the expressions that are unified at each step. In this way, the unifiers of the steps of the proof should be easily understandable from the context.

The *induction rule* consists of the introduction of an induction hypothesis and makes it possible to obtain a recursive call in the final program. If the induction rule is applied to the initial tableau, it allows for the introduction of the following assertion

if $x \prec_w a$ then if $P[x]$ then $R[x, f(x)]$		

This assertion, on the assumption that a well-founded relation $\prec_w$ exists, states that the program f applied on input x will satisfy the input-output condition, provided that $x \prec_w a$. If during the proof the resolution rule can be applied between the induction hypothesis and a derived goal by unifying a subexpression containing $f(x)$, the resulting goal has a recursive call in the output. In such a goal a conjunct involving the $\prec_w$ relation occurs, which represents the termination condition for the program and can be specified later in the proof by finding an appropriate well-founded relation. A more general version of this rule allows for the synthesis of auxiliary procedures.

The *equivalence rule* is used as simplified form of two applications of the resolution rule, whenever the equivalence operator occurs in one of the tableau rows. Below we present the ground *GG-equivalence rule, left to right*; all the extensions are defined as for the resolution rule, and the right to left form is obtained by applying the rule to the right side of the equivalence.

Assertions	Goals	$f(a)$
	$A_1[P \equiv Q]$	
	$A_2 < P >$	
	$A_1[false] \wedge A_2 < Q >$	

The notation $A_2 < P >$ is used for partial substitution as defined in [7]. In this case, one or more occurrences of the subsentence P of A_2 can be substituted by Q.

Other deduction rules that allow for the treatment of equality (see again [8]) are the *equality replacement rule*, also known as paramodulation and the *equality matching rule*, also known as E-resolution [9]. They are not reported here, since they are not used in the derivations presented in the paper.

3 The theory of relations

We first define the theory, i.e. the formalism we use to describe relational data bases: we call it the "theory of relations", since it is based on the concept of relation. A relation is defined as a pair composed of a set of attributes and a set of tuples; a tuple is defined as a set of pairs, each composed of an attribute and a value. More precisely, the data types defined in the theory of relations are:

atoms: the elementary values composing the tuples (i.e. the values in the "fields" of the tuples). *atom* is the unary predicate which is true if its argument is an atom and false otherwise;

attributes: the values constituting the schemata of tuples and relations (i.e. the field names of tuples and relations); *attr* is the unary predicate which is true if its argument is an attribute and false otherwise;

relation schemata: sets of attributes. Sets are finite collections of elements, in which we disregard the order of occurrence of the elements and their multiplicity ([7]). *sch* is the unary predicate which is true if its argument is a relation schema and false otherwise. CH stands for choice and RE for rest. $\subseteq, \in_s, \cup, \cap$ are used to denote subset, membership, union and intersection, respectively.

tuples: a tuple is a set of pairs, each composed of an attribute and an atom. Every atom represents the value of the corresponding field of that tuple. [] is the constant defining the empty tuple; $tup(x, y)$ is the predicate which is true if x is a tuple with schema y and false otherwise; $\varphi(x, y)$ is the function which returns the projection of the tuple x on the schema y; $\varphi_1(x, u)$ is the function which returns the value of the tuple x corresponding to the attribute u.

relation instances: a relation instance is a set of tuples, all having the same schema (the schema of the given relation).

relations: a relation is a pair composed by a schema and an instance. $A(r)$ is the function which returns the schema of relation r, while $T(r)$ returns the instance of r; $\Phi(x)$ is the function which returns the empty relation with schema x; *rel* is the predicate which is true if its argument is a relation (i.e. a pair <schema, instance>) and false otherwise; $y \circ x$ is the function which returns the relation in which the tuple y has been added to the relation x. Φ, *rel* and $\circ$ are defined by the axioms[2]:

- $(\forall sch\ x)\ (rel(\Phi(x)))$

- $(\forall sch\ x)\ (A(\Phi(x)) = x)$

- $(\forall rel\ x)(\forall tup(u, A(x)))\ (rel(u \circ x) \wedge A(u \circ x) = A(x))$

- $(\forall tup(u, A(x)))(\forall rel\ x)\ (u \circ (u \circ x) = u \circ x)$

- $(\forall tup(u, A(x)))(\forall tup(v, A(x)))(\forall rel\ x)\ (u \circ (v \circ x) = v \circ (u \circ x))$

- $(\forall rel\ x)(\forall rel\ y)$
  $[\ x = y \equiv A(x) = A(y) \wedge (\forall tup(u, A(x)))(u \in x \equiv u \in y)\ ]$

ch and *re* again stand for choice and rest; $x \in y$ is the predicate which is true if the tuple x belongs to the relation y and false otherwise. It is defined by the axioms:

- $(\forall sch\ u)(\forall sch\ v)(\forall tup(t, v))\ (t \notin \Phi(u))$

- $(\forall tup(t, A(r)))(\forall tup(v, A(r)))(\forall rel\ r)\ (t \in v \circ x \equiv t = v \vee t \in r)$

4 The input-output specification

The first step to be accomplished in order to obtain programs for computing answers to queries formulated as expressions of relational calculus is to extract the input-output specification from the queries.

An expression of relational calculus is of the form:

$\{t(a) \mid f(t)\}$

---

[2]We adopt the notation of *relativized quantifiers* ([7]) to shorten first-order logic formulas. In this notation the quantifiers can vary only over a particular subset of a domain, rather than on the entire domain. We abuse this notation for the predicate *tup*, which is not a unary predicate, but only its first argument is a free variable.

which is interpreted as follows: compute all the tuples t, with schema a, such that $f(t)$ is true. This can be phrased in the theory of relations as: find the relation z, with schema a, whose tuples t satisfy $f(t)$. The input-output specification takes the following form:

> find z
> such that $rel(z) \wedge A(z) = a \wedge (\forall t)\,(t \in z \equiv tup(t, a) \wedge \mathcal{F}(t))$
> where $P(r_i, a_i)$,

where r_i and a_i denote the input relations and their attributes, respectively, and the input condition $P(r_i, a_i)$ is a conjunction of formulae obtained by applying the following rules:

1. For every relation r occurring in the expression, $rel(r)$ is in the input condition;

2. For every term $x(a)$ occurring in the expression, if a is a schema then $a \subseteq a_1$ (where a_1 is the schema associated with x) is the input condition, and if a is an attribute then $a \in_s a_1$ is in the input condition;

and $\mathcal{F}(t) = \Gamma[f(t)]$, where the transformation Γ is defined by the following rules:

1. $\Gamma[r(x)] = x \in r$

2. $\Gamma[t_1(a) = t_2(a)] = (\varphi(t_1, a) = \varphi(t_2, a))$

3. $\Gamma[t(a) = v] = (\varphi_1(t, a) = v)$

4. $\Gamma[(\exists x(a_1))\,(p(x, t))] = (\exists x)\,(tup(x, a_1) \wedge \Gamma[p(x, t)])$,

5. $\Gamma[(\forall x(a_1))\,(p(x, t))] = (\forall x)\,(\text{ if } tup(x, a_1) \text{ then } \Gamma[p(x, t)])$

Notice that the input condition specifies the structure of the relations of the data base. The synthesis process does not address the verification of the correctness of the query with respect to a given data base. However, if the requirements expressed by the input condition are met by the data base, then the synthesized program will always compute an answer, possibly an empty relation if there are no instances satisfying the query.

5 Synthesizing the operators of relational algebra

In this section we discuss how to synthesize programs implementing the basic operators of relational algebra. Their syntheses rely on the theory of relations as specified in the previous section, and start from an input-output specification obtained by applying the transformation defined above to the definition of the operator in relational calculus. For example, selection, denoted in relational algebra as $\sigma(r, a, v)$, is expressed in relational calculus as

$$\{t(a_r) \mid r(t) \wedge t(a) = v\}$$

(where a_r is a constant corresponding to the schema of relation r), and the corresponding input-output specification is given by:

$\sigma(r, a, v) \Leftarrow$ find z

such that $rel(z) \wedge A(z) = A(r) \wedge$
$(\forall t) [t \in z \equiv tup(t, A(r)) \wedge t \in r \wedge \varphi_1(t, a) = v]$
where $rel(r) \wedge a \in_s A(r)$.

The initial deductive-tableau is the following one, where the goal and the assertion contain the output and the input condition, respectively, and $f_s(z)$ is introduced by the skolemization of the universal quantifier (see [8]).

Assertions	Goals	$\sigma(r, a, v)$
G1.	$rel(z) \wedge A(z) = A(r) \wedge$ $[f_s(z) \in z \equiv tup(f_s(z), A(r)) \wedge$ $f_s(z) \in r \wedge \varphi_1(f_s(z), a) = v]$	z

A2. $rel(r) \wedge a \in_s A(r)$		

The synthesis follows the schema of inductive proofs: first one develops the base case, then the inductive case by introducing the induction hypothesis. Finally, the different cases are combined together by application of the resolution rule. Given the lack of space we do not report here all the details of the synthesis process (see [14]). The base case for the selection operator deals with the empty relation. We start from goal G1, and then perform a few steps using the properties of empty relations, in particular the assertion stating that there are no tuples in the empty relation. The result is given by the following tableau:

G9.	$r = \Phi(A(r))$	$\Phi(A(r))$

Notice that the equality in the goal column specifies the condition that r is an empty relation; the expression in the output column has been obtained by substituting the output variable z with the empty relation. Therefore, goal G9 says that when the input relation is empty the program must return the empty relation.

The inductive case is dealt with by introducing the following assertion, corresponding to the induction hypothesis:

A21. if $rel(r') \wedge a' \in_s A(r') \wedge r' \prec_w r$ then $rel(\sigma(r', a, v)) \wedge A(\sigma(r', a, v)) = A(r') \wedge$ $[x \in \sigma(r', a, v) \equiv tup(x, A(r')) \wedge$ $x \in r' \wedge \varphi_1(x, a) = v]$		

where $r' \prec_w r$ is interpreted as set containment since relations are defined in terms of sets of tuples. In order to make the induction hypothesis applicable one has to reason on the structure of relations, and obtain starting from G1 a goal that can be resolved with assertion A21. In particular, when non-empty, the input relation takes the form $ch(r) \circ re(r)$, and one can split the deduction into two branches, depending on whether the value of the attribute a of r is equal to v or not. The first branch, developing the case $\varphi_1(ch(r), a) = v$, after resolution with the induction hypothesis, leads to goal G41:

G41.	$r \neq \Phi(A(r)) \wedge \varphi_1(ch(r), a) = v$	$ch(r)\circ$ $\sigma(re(r), a, v)$

Notice that the output of goal G41 contains the expression to be returned when the tuple $ch(r)$ must be added to the result, because the value of its attribute a is equal to v. $\sigma(re(r), a, v)$ denotes a recursive call to the selection function and is introduced by the resolution with the induction hypothesis.

The second branch, developing the case $\varphi_1(ch(r), a) \neq v$, terminates with goal G51:

G51.	$r \neq \Phi(A(r)) \wedge \varphi_1(ch(r), a) \neq v$	$\sigma(re(r), a, v)$

In this case the output expression simply contains the recursive call because the tuple considered does not match the condition for the selection.

The last part of the synthesis combines the partial results obtained by analyzing different cases for the input relation We first apply the resolution rule to goals G41 and G51:

G41.	$r \neq \Phi(A(r)) \wedge$ $\boxed{\varphi_1(ch(r), a) = v}$	$ch(r) \circ \sigma(re(r), a, v)$
G51.	$r \neq \Phi(A(r)) \wedge$ $\boxed{\varphi_1(ch(r), a) \neq v}$	$\sigma(re(r), a, v)$
G52.	$r \neq \Phi(A(r))$	if $\varphi_1(ch(r), a) = v$ then $ch(r) \circ \sigma(re(r), a, v)$ else $\sigma(re(r), a, v)$

The if-then-else expression in the output is the result of the application of the resolution rule between two goals with different output. The test of the conditional is given by the unifying subsentence $\varphi_1(ch(r), a) = v$. In fact, whenever r is non-empty, if $\varphi_1(ch(r), a) = v$ then goal G41 is true, and the output must be $ch(r) \circ \sigma(re(r), a, v)$. Conversely, if $\varphi_1(ch(r), a) \neq v$, then goal G51 is true and the output espression is $\sigma(re(r), a, v)$.

Finally we apply the resolution rule to goals G9 and G52, thus obtaining the goal true whose output is the synthesized program.

G9.	$\boxed{r = \Phi(A(r))}$	$\Phi(A(r))$
G52.	$\boxed{r \neq \Phi(A(r))}$	if $\varphi_1(ch(r), a) = v$ then $ch(r) \circ \sigma(re(r), a, v)$ else $\sigma(re(r), a, v)$

G53.	*true*	if $r = \Phi(A(r))$
		then $\Phi(A(r))$
		else if $\varphi_1(ch(r), a) = v$
		    then $ch(r) \circ \sigma(re(r), a, v)$
		    else $\sigma(re(r), a, v)$

The synthesis of join and difference requires the introduction of auxiliary procedures [14]; below we show the program obtained for the join operator, where U_t denotes the union operator for tuples:

$\bowtie (r_1, r_2) \Leftarrow$ if $r_1 = \Phi(A(r_1))$
$\qquad$ then $\Phi(A(r_1) \cup A(r_2))$
$\qquad$ else $U(\bowtie_{aux} (ch(r_1), A(r_1), r_2), \bowtie (re(r_1), r_2))$

$\bowtie_{aux} (a, s, r) \Leftarrow$ if $r = \Phi(A(r))$
$\qquad$ then $\Phi(s \cup A(r))$
$\qquad$ else if $\varphi(ch(r), s \cap A(r)) = \varphi(a, s \cap A(r))$
$\qquad\quad$ then $U_t(a, ch(r)) \circ \bowtie_{aux} (a, s, re(r))$
$\qquad\quad$ else $\bowtie_{aux} (a, s, re(r))$

6   From calculus to algebra

In order to synthesize programs for evaluating queries formulated as safe expressions of relational calculus (see [15]), we now apply the deductive-tableau method for generating equivalent expressions in relational algebra. The synthesis process is very similar to the one considered for the operators of relational algebra, in that it starts from a specification expressed in the theory of relations and generates a side-effect free applicative expression. However, in this case the initial specification is obtained from a query and the background theory includes the assertions concerning the algebra operators to be used in the synthesis so that they will appear in the resulting program. In this way the synthesis never requires the application of the induction rule and can be performed mechanically. This aspect is considered in the next section; here we give an example of synthesis by considering the following query:

$$\{t(a_0) \mid (\exists x(s))(r_1(x(a_{r_1})) \land x(a_1) = v \land r_2(x(a_{r_2})) \land t = x(a_0))\},$$

where s is equal to $a_{r_1} \cup a_{r_2}$.

First, we translate this expression into an input-output specification in the theory of relations, obtaining the following result:

find z
such that $rel(z) \land A(z) = a_0 \land$
  $(\forall t)(\exists x)[t \in z \equiv t = \varphi(x, a_0) \land tup(x, A(r_1) \cup A(r_2)) \land$
  $\varphi(x, A(r_1)) \in r_1 \land \varphi_1(x, a_1) = v \land \varphi(x, A(r_2)) \in r_2]$
where $rel(r_1) \land rel(r_2) \land a_0 \subseteq A(r_1) \cup A(r_2) \land a_1 \in_s A(r_1) \cup A(r_2)$

which corresponds to the initial tableau

G1.	$rel(z) \land A(z) = a_0 \land$ $[f_s(z) \in z \equiv f_s(z) = \varphi(x, a_0) \land$ $tup(x, A(r_1) \cup A(r_2)) \land$ $\varphi(x, A(r_1)) \in r_1 \land \varphi_1(x, a_1) = v \land$ $\varphi(x, A(r_2)) \in r_2]$	z

A2. $rel(r_1) \land rel(r_2) \land a_0 \subseteq A(r_1) \cup A(r_2) \land$ $a_1 \in_s A(r_1) \cup A(r_2)$		

where f_s is a skolem function which replaces the universally quantified variable t. We have that the boxed subformula of G1 unifies with the right hand side of the equivalence occurring in assertion A3 (obtained from the join operator axiom), so we can apply the equivalence rule to G1 and A3:

G1.	$rel(z) \land A(z) = a_0 \land$ $[f_s(z) \in z \equiv f_s(z) = \varphi(x, a_0) \land$ $\boxed{tup(x, A(r_1) \cup A(r_2)) \land}$ $\boxed{\varphi(x, A(r_1)) \in r_1 \land} \varphi_1(x, a_1) = v \land$ $\boxed{\varphi(x, A(r_2)) \in r_2}]$	z

A3. if $rel(r') \land rel(r'')$
   then $[x' \in\bowtie (r', r'') \equiv \boxed{tup(x', A(r') \cup A(r'')) \land}$
   $\boxed{\varphi(x', A(r')) \in r' \land \varphi(x', A(r'')) \in r''}]$		

G4.	$rel(r_1) \land rel(r_2) \land$ $rel(z) \land A(z) = a_0 \land$ $[f_s(z) \in z \equiv f_s(z) = \varphi(x, a_0) \land$ $x \in\bowtie (r_1, r_2) \land \varphi_1(x, a_1) = v]$	z

The unifier of this step is $\{x' \leftarrow x, r' \leftarrow r_1, r'' \leftarrow r_2\}$. The result of this deduction step consists of a replacement in the right hand side of the equivalence of goal G1, by applying the definition of join given by assertion A3. More specifically, the formula $x \in \bowtie (r_1, r_2)$ replaces $tup(x, A(r_1) \cup A(r_2)) \wedge \varphi(x, A(r_1)) \in r_1 \wedge \varphi(x, A(r_2)) \in r_2$. Moreover, the conjunction $rel(r_1) \wedge rel(r_2)$ is added to the goal, as an additional condition to be verified. No modifications occur in the output expression.

Now we can again apply the equivalence rule to goal G4 and assertion A5, which is obtained from the selection operator axiom:

G4.	$rel(r_1) \wedge rel(r_2) \wedge$ $rel(z) \wedge A(z) = a_0 \wedge$ $[f_s(z) \in z \equiv f_s(z) = \varphi(x, a_0) \wedge$ $\boxed{x \in \bowtie (r_1, r_2) \wedge \varphi_1(x, a_1) = v}]$		z

A5. if $rel(r') \wedge a' \in_s A(r')$
    then $[x' \in \sigma(r', a', v') \equiv \boxed{x' \in r' \wedge}$
    $\boxed{\varphi_1(x', a') = v'}]$		

G6.	$rel(r_1) \wedge rel(r_2) \wedge$ $rel(\bowtie (r_1, r_2)) \wedge a_1 \in_s A(r_1) \cup A(r_2) \wedge$ $rel(z) \wedge A(z) = a_0 \wedge$ $[f_s(z) \in z \equiv f_s(z) = \varphi(x, a_0) \wedge$ $x \in \sigma(\bowtie (r_1, r_2), a_1, v)]$		z

The unifier of this step is $\{x' \leftarrow x, r' \leftarrow \bowtie (r_1, r_2), a' \leftarrow a_1, v' \leftarrow v\}$. Again we have a replacement in the right hand side of the equivalence of the initial goal, in this case obtained from the definition of selection given in assertion A5. In particular, $x \in \sigma(\bowtie (r_1, r_2), a_1, v)$ replaces the conjuncts $x \in \bowtie (r_1, r_2) \wedge \varphi_1(x, a_1) = v$. Two conditions on the input, $rel(\bowtie (r_1, r_2))$ and $a_1 \in_s A(r_1) \cup A(r_2)$, are introduced, the former simply requiring the result of the join to be a relation, and the latter requiring a_1 to be an attribute belonging to the union of the schemata of r_1 and r_2. No modifications occur in the output expression.

We now apply the resolution rule between the current goal and assertion A7 (obtained from the projection operator axiom).

G6.	$rel(r_1) \wedge rel(r_2) \wedge$ $rel(\bowtie (r_1, r_2)) \wedge a_1 \in_s A(r_1) \cup A(r_2) \wedge$ $\boxed{rel(z) \wedge A(z) = a_0 \wedge}$ $\boxed{[f_s(z) \in z \equiv f_s(z) = \varphi(x, a_0) \wedge}$ $\boxed{x \in \sigma(\bowtie (r_1, r_2), a_1, v)]}$		z

A7. if $rel(r') \wedge a' \subseteq A(r')$		
then $\boxed{rel(\pi(r',a')) \wedge}$		
$\boxed{A(\pi(r',a')) = a' \wedge}$		
$\boxed{[x' \in \pi(r',a') \equiv x' = \varphi(t_1,a') \wedge}$		
$\boxed{t_1 \in r']}$		

G8.	$rel(r_1) \wedge rel(r_2) \wedge$ $rel(\bowtie (r_1,r_2)) \wedge$ $a_1 \in_s A(r_1) \cup A(r_2) \wedge$ $rel(\sigma(\bowtie (r_1,r_2),a_1,v)) \wedge$ $a_0 \subseteq A(\sigma(\bowtie (r_1,r_2),a_1,v))$	$\pi(\sigma(\bowtie (r_1,r_2),a_1,v),a_0)$

The unifier of this step is $\{x \leftarrow t_1, a' \leftarrow a_0, r' \leftarrow \sigma(\bowtie (r_1,r_2),a_1,v), x' \leftarrow f_s(\pi(\sigma(\bowtie (r_1,r_2),a_1,v),a_0)), z \leftarrow \pi(\sigma(\bowtie (r_1,r_2),a_1,v),a_0)\}$. This substitution modifies the output expression; moreover, the equivalence formula is eliminated from the resulting goal G8, which now can be proved through simple deduction steps, i.e. resolutions with the assertions concerning the selection and join operators and with the input condition A2. Our final output is therefore $\pi(\sigma(\bowtie (r_1,r_2),a_1,v),a_0)$, which is the translation into relational algebra of the query initially expressed in relational calculus.

7 Using the Deductive Tableau System

The proofs for the syntheses of the programs outlined in the previous sections have been machine checked using the Deductive Tableau System [1], which is an interactive implementation of the deductive tableau method for Apple Macintosh computers. This system does not allow the user to associate an output expression with the rows of the tableau, so one has to keep track by hand of the transformations of the output expressions. The proofs are conducted in an interactive way, i.e. at every step the deduction rule to be applied is selected by the user.

The syntheses of the operators of relational algebra are rather involved. The length of the syntheses ranges from 100 to 200 steps. In addition, as remarked elsewhere [11], the deduction is mainly driven by the expected form of the output. Therefore, one may envisage the use of the deductive-tableau method as a tool for verifying those aspects of the system that are most critical in the implementation, such as the programs implementing the operators of relational algebra. However, this would require a much more detailed description of the data structures used in the implementation, in particular the introduction of memory structures with destructive operations.

Conversely, the translation from relational calculus to relational algebra can be done through much simpler proofs, which do not require the application of the induction rule. The analysis of these proofs has outlined the following

28

procedure for making the derivation of the expressions in relational algebra fully mechanical.

Let G be the initial goal corresponding to the output condition of the specification obtained from the relational calculus expression $\{t(a)|f(t)\}$; let E be the formula $t \in z \equiv (tup(t,a) \wedge \mathcal{F}(t))$ occurring in G; let A denote assertions about the operators of relational algebra, which all contain an equivalence subexpression, which is denoted as $A[L \equiv R]$.

WHILE E does not unify with any A
DO BEGIN
    find a subexpression E' of E and an assertion $A[L \equiv R]$
        such that E' unifies with R;
    apply the equivalence rule between E' and $A[L \equiv R]$;
END;
apply the resolution rule to E and the assertion A which unifies with E;

The resulting goal is composed of subformulas of the form $rel(r), A(r) = s, a \in_s A(r)$ and $A(r) \subseteq s$. Therefore, it is easily proved by applying the resolution rule with the input condition and with the assertions about the operators of relational algebra. Since the Deductive Tableau System does not provide support to the design of automatic proof strategies, this procedure for automating the synthesis could not be implemented.

8 Conclusions

In this paper we have presented an application of the deductive-tableau method for synthesizing programs that compute answers to queries posed to relational data bases. Our study complements the work on data base transactions reported in [12, 13], addressing other aspects of data base systems, in particular query evaluation.

Our syntheses of programs for query evaluation start from specifications directly obtained from the expressions of relational calculus. In this way, we use a logic program (in this case represented by expressions of relational calculus) as the specification and not as the target of the synthesis process. This seems appropriate if one considers logic programming as a specification language, different from the implementation language. In this respect we aim at extending our work to include a more powerful specification language, such as for example recursive DATALOG, while maintaining the goal of identifying strategies for making the synthesis fully automatic.

References

[1] R. Burback, S.A. Frazer, H. McGuire, J. Smith, M. Winstandley. Using the Deductive Tableau System. Chariot Software Group, 1990.

[2] J. Freytag, N. Goodman. On the translation of relational queries into iterative programs. ACM Transactions on Database Systems 14:1, 1989, pp. 1-27.

[3] G. Gardarin, P. Valduriez. Relational Databases and Knowledge Bases. Addison Wesley, 1989.

[4] M. Jarke, J. Koch. Query optimization in Database Systems. ACM Computing Surveys, 16, 2 (June 1984), pp. 111-152.

[5] D. Maier. The theory of relational databases. Computer Science Press, 1983.

[6] Z. Manna, R. Waldinger. A deductive approach to program synthesis, ACM Transaction on Programming Languages and Systems, 2:1980,pp.90-121.

[7] Z. Manna, R. Waldinger. The logical basis for computer programming. Vol.1: Deductive reasoning. Addison Wesley, 1985.

[8] Z. Manna, R. Waldinger. The logical basis for computer programming. Vol.2: Deductive systems. Addison Wesley, 1990.

[9] J.B. Morris. E-resolution: extension of resolution to include the equality relation. Proceedings of the 1st IJCAI, 1969, 394-402.

[10] N.W. Murray. Completely nonclausal theorem proving. Art. Int. 18: pp.67-85, 1982.

[11] D. Nardi. Formal synthesis of a unification algorithm by the Deductive-Tableau method. Journal of Logic Programming, 1989:7: pp. 1-43.

[12] X. Qian. Synthesizing database transactions. Proc. of 16th VLDB Conf., Brisbane, Australia, 1990, 552-565.

[13] X. Qian. The deductive synthesis of database transactions. Ph.D. dissertation, technical report STAN-CS-89-1291. Dept. of Computer Science, Stanford University, 1989.

[14] R. Rosati. Sintesi di programmi con il metodo dei tableaux deduttivi per il calcolo della risposta ad una interrogazione ad una base di dati. Tesi di Laurea, Univ. Roma "La Sapienza", (in Italian) 1991.

[15] J. Ullman. Principles of database and knowledge-base systems. Computer Science Press, 1988.

Synthesis of Narrowing Programs

Carlos Loría-Sáenz

Universität Kaiserslautern

Fachbereich Informatik (AG Avenhaus)

Postfach 3049

6750 Kaiserslautern (Germany)

E-mail address: `loria@informatik.uni-kl.de`

Abstract

In this paper, we present a method for synthesis of programs whose specifications are given by *term-rewriting systems* and *goals* (set of equations). The rule system specifies the operations which we use to compute. The goal represents the program requirements, denoting relations between input-output variables. Our method demonstrates how program synthesis techniques can be used to optimize narrowing. The synthesis method is formulated as an *inference system* for extracting a rewrite program from the so-called *input-output narrowing trees* of the goal. We define operations to manipulate these trees and to derive the programs from them. Our formulation is very natural, permitting the easy implementation of prototypes based on our ideas. It also allows theoretical reasoning about properties of the programs we derive. For instance, we can give sufficient conditions guaranteeing the correctness, completeness and improvement of the transformations.

1 Introduction

Term-rewriting systems ([DO90]) are an important model for investigating basic computational problems and mechanical theorem-proving by means of equational reasoning (i.e. representing problems through equations). This includes in particular functional languages (with semantics based on reduction) and logic programming languages (with semantics based on equation solving) as well as integrations of both paradigms ([BL86])[1]. With such languages, we can generally obtain more 'expressive power' by specifying programs using both relations and functions ([Red86]). Such combinations represent an important aid for computing with abstract data types and for symbolic program evaluation. Using a typical rule system for instance, we are able to specify the usual arithmetic operations such as *plus* (+) over natural numbers and an *append* operation to concatenate lists as follows:

$$0 + y \rightarrow y \quad (1) \qquad\qquad append([], Y) \rightarrow Y \quad (3)$$
$$s(x) + y \rightarrow s(x + y) \quad (2) \qquad append(x :: L, M) \rightarrow x :: append(L, M) \quad (4)$$

where s is the *successor* operation, :: stands for the *cons* operation and $[]$ is the empty list.

---

[1]By 'semantics' we will mean operational semantics throughout this paper.

Furthermore, we can define useful properties for proving and deduction, such as the associativity of append

$$append(L, append(M, N)) \rightarrow append((append(L, M), N) \qquad (5)$$

Using such a class of rules, we *compute* by matching terms (expressions) with the left-hand sides of the rules, testing the validity of the rule conditions if there are any and appropriately replacing them by the corresponding right-hand sides (assuming that right sides and conditions of rules contain no *free variables*). This general procedure corresponds to a semantics by reduction or *rewriting* (as in functional languages).

However, we can also *compute* in the sense of Prolog by solving sets of equations (goals) in order to produce values or answers for *free variables* ([Llo87]). The semantics necessary to achieve that - *narrowing* - is an extension of the standard SLD-resolution procedure for handling equality (see [Hul80]). This method demands in general more computational effort than rewriting (which motivates this work) but offers powerful alternatives for implementing deductive program transformation (which we use in our approach).

When computing with narrowing, we may need to try all applicable rules and unifiers for the equations of a goal (in order to avoid losing answers). The set of valid answers can be infinite and should be systematically generated. Therefore, implementations of narrowing in general require backtracking algorithms. Different classes of strategies can be used (normalizing, innermost, outermost, basic, etc.) to reduce and select narrowing-redexes or to restrict them ([Hol89]) making naïve narrowing more efficient (the rule systems must satisfy certain theoretical conditions in order to guarantee *soundness* and *completeness*).

In this work, we consider *rewrite systems* as an abstract specification (programming) language[2] and use **program synthesis techniques as an approach to optimize narrowing** (in contrast to the strategies mentioned above). In order to perform this, we construct a formal *inference system* to transform some classes of program specifications. This system can be considered as a method of transforming programs which use narrowing into programs that use rewriting. The advantage of such a transformation is that we can replace the basic operation *unification* by *matching* and (in some cases) we are able to avoid non-determinism in the computation process. However, the system can also be used to perform other typical and more general algorithm transformations. In addition to that, we give sufficient conditions in order to guarantee the correctness, completeness and improvement of the transformations.

The rest of this paper is structured in the following way. In the next section we present the principles of our ideas. We illustrate some problems with narrowing which we intend to avoid using our approach. Some necessary basic definitions and concepts of the term-rewriting systems theory are given in section 3[3]. This includes the definition of input-output goals as well as relations used to compute (rewriting and narrowing). In section 4 we define the basic operations over input-output goals needed to construct the corresponding

---

[2]This means that our 'programs' are rewrite rule systems

[3]However, this background is not self-contained due to the space. The quotes can be consulted for more details.

trees. We also show by an example how we use them to derive programs. Then in section 5, we formulate our inference system for synthesis. The theoretical properties of the system (equivalence and improvement of programs) are formally investigated in section 6 and we conclude by discussing certain practical aspects of our formulation in section 7.

2 The Problem and a Sketch of the Method

In this section, we present the concepts and the class of problems we want to consider and sketch the principles on which we base our solution to these problems. We illustrate the explanation by means of a simple example.

Suppose we have a rule system R like the one above (rules 1 to 4). The rules of R represent the specification of operations which are available to compute (e.g. *plus* and *append*). Suppose also, we have a goal E (set of equations) specifying an input-output relation between the variables of the goal. For instance, E might be the goal containing only the equation:

$$append(Z, [z]) = X. \tag{6}$$

By interpreting the variable X as known (i.e. an input variable) in E, we want to find values for the remaining (output) variables (Z and z)[4].

These values can be found by instantiating X in goal 6 and then using narrowing to produce values for z and Z as we can see in figure 1 for the case $X = [1, 2, 3]$. The tree in this figure shows all the possible derivations that we can obtain by applying narrowing or unification steps to the root and recursively to newly generated goals. As an example, node 3 is produced by unifying the left-hand side of rule 4 and the term $app(Z, [z])$ of goal 1 and immediately applying this rule. We call this operation a **narrow** step. On the other hand, node 6 leads to the empty node after unifying the equation in the goal. We call that a **unify** step. In both cases (narrow and unify), we use **most general unifiers** (denoted mgu). The aim of **narrowing** (the combination of narrow and unify steps) is to produce derivation paths leading to the empty goal. In such a case, we can obtain an **answer** to the goal occurring at the root by composing the substitutions over the path(s) leading to the empty goal. An answer is a substitution which makes the equations of the goal *valid* with respect to the rules of a rule system. For instance, the only answer in this case is obtained over the path 1, 3, 5, 6 of the tree shown in figure 1[5].

In this figure, we can also observe that narrowing is trying to 'guess' the length of the list $app(Z, [z])$ and to do that it needs to generate the *failure* nodes (2 and 4) at the left side of the answer path to the goal (because narrowing has no way to know this length a priori). In general if the list X contains $n + 1$ elements, then narrowing will produce n of these failure nodes.

Expecting to avoid this kind of inefficiency, we are interested in synthesizing a program by analyzing the *'behavior'* of narrowing when E is solved by trying

---

[4]We can interpret the problem as optimizing a frequent query E for some fixed but arbitrary values of X. Note that the relation 6 specifies a program for computing the last element (z) and the list of elements without the last element (Z) of a given list X.

[5]Note in figure 1 that the path 5,7 can be detected as failure by considering that the symbols '[]' and '::' are different *free* constructors. Otherwise, we obtain an infinite branch. It is worth remarking that this problem can also be avoided after transforming the goal.

to discover some class of 'regularities'. An example of regularity can be observed in the tree of figure 1: the subtrees beginning with roots 3 and 5 are practically 'equivalent' to the initial tree (note that after eliminating the heads of the two lists represented in the equation of node 3, we obtain $app(Z, [z]) = [2, 3]$. As we can observe, this equation has the same 'form' as the equation in node 1. The same applies to node 5.).

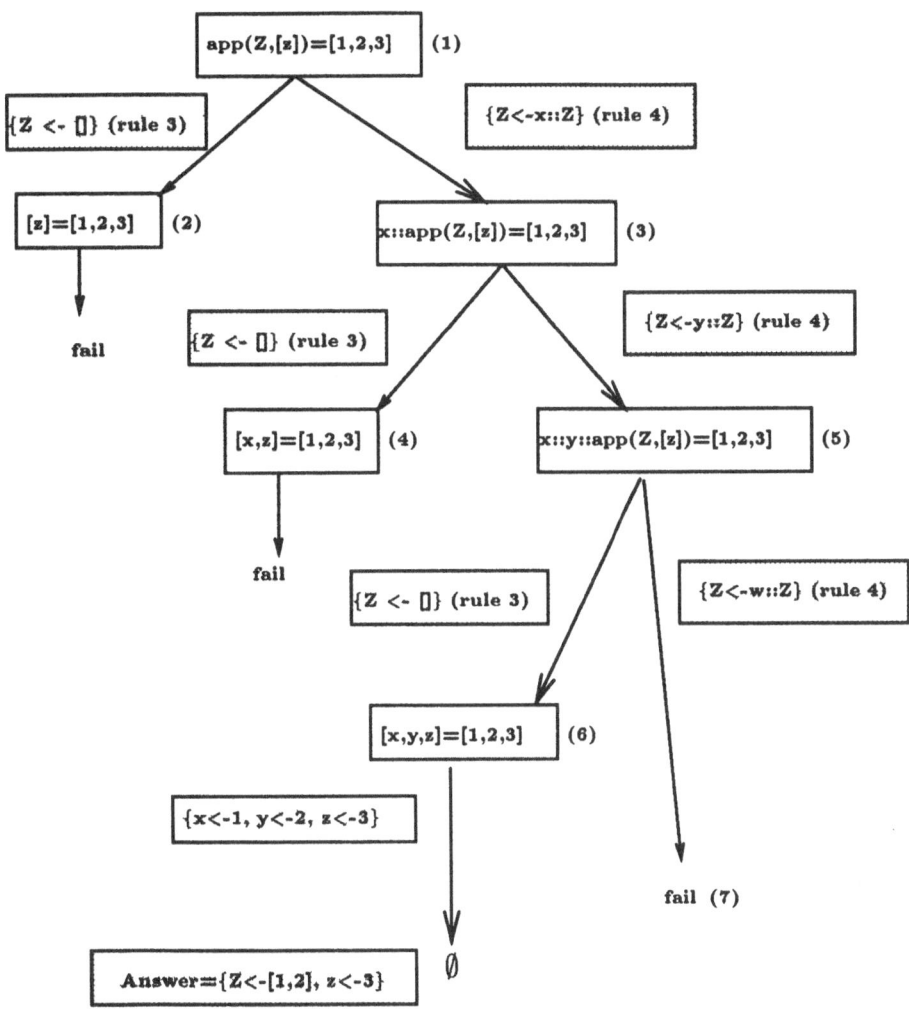

Figure 1

To discover regularities, we define operations to manipulate the so-called **input-output narrowing tree** associated with the goal E (e.g. figure 3). Input-output trees are extensions of narrowing trees containing information about inputs and outputs. Suitable applications of our operations can be used to extract a finite (regular) tree from the (usually infinite) input-output narrowing tree, essentially by expanding (unfolding), contracting (folding) or splitting (subgoaling) the nodes of the tree. From such a regular tree we directly derive a program[6].

Our transformations take into account which variables of the goals are inputs or outputs for newly generated nodes of the tree (directionality)[7]. We can also make use of some other rules to guide the expansion of the tree because this expansion is non-deterministic, in general.

For instance, we are able to extract the following two rules using our transformations in the way we will explain later in this paper in detail[8]:

$$lastWithoutlast([x]) \rightarrow (x, []) \tag{7}$$
$$lastWithoutlast(x :: R) \rightarrow (z, x :: M) \, if \, lastWithoutlast(R) = (z, M) \tag{8}$$

By comparing trees, it can be verified that the failing subgoals like those appearing in figure 1 can be eliminated by computing

$$lastWithoutlast([1, 2, 3]) = (z, Z)$$

with the new rules 7 and 8. Therefore, we can produce the solutions in a more efficient way by performing the transformation of the goal 6.

The synthesis problem is sketched in figure 2.

3 Basic Notations and Definitions

In this section we introduce general concepts and notations needed for the specification of our inference system (sections 4 and 5). These concepts are commonly used in the field of term rewriting systems and particularly of narrowing. In the latter case, we essentially base our work on [Hol89]. The contents of this section are unavoidably technical. However, it is particularly necessary for understanding the technical definitions of this work and for the formalization of properties of our system (section 6). The reader not very interested in such technical details may skip this section in a first reading of the paper.

Syntactic Objects

$\mathcal{F}$ is the set of *operators* (function symbols) and $\mathcal{V}$ the set of *variables*. $\mathcal{F}$ can be partitioned in the disjunct sets $\mathcal{C}$ of *constructor symbols* and $\mathcal{D}$ of *defined symbols*. A ground term (GT) is an element of $T(C,\emptyset)$. A term not belonging to $\mathcal{V}$ is a non-variable term. A **constructor term (C-term)** is an element of $T(C,V)$. A **basic** term is a term of the form $f(s_1, \ldots, s_n)$ where s_i is a C-term for all $i(1 \leq i \leq n)$.

An *equation* is a pair (s, t) (denoted by $s = t$) of terms. In order to avoid any confusion with the symbol '=', we use the symbol $\equiv$ for denoting 'syntactically equal' and $:\equiv$ for 'defined as'. An equation $s = t$ is a C-equation if s and t are C-terms.

---

[6]Prolog programs, query patterns and symbolic trace trees for deriving programs were already used in [BSK89] and [SB89]. However our input-output narrowing trees are different from the symbolic trace trees used in these works.

[7]A method for transformation of implicative goals containing 'undecided' (output) variables into logic programs were presented in [Fri90]. In contrast to our method (based on narrowing trees, only), they use a restricted form from structural induction over data types. They extract the program from the inductive proof of the goal.

[8]For the sake of clarity, we have used a suitable name here for the generated function.

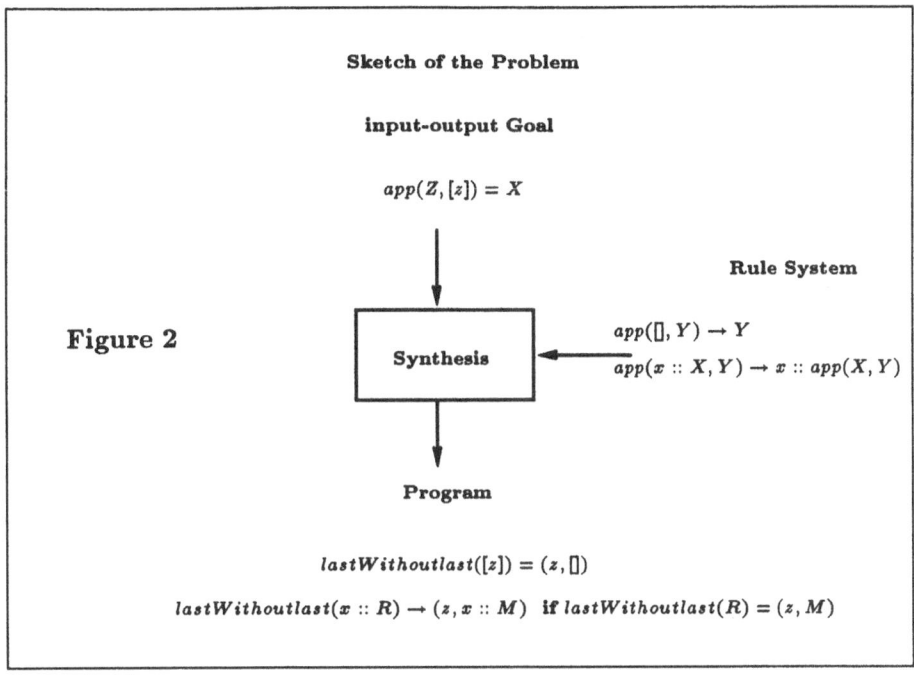

Figure 2

Sketch of the Problem

input-output Goal

$$app(Z, [z]) = X$$

Rule System

Synthesis

$$app([], Y) \rightarrow Y$$
$$app(x :: X, Y) \rightarrow x :: app(X, Y)$$

Program

$$lastWithoutlast([z]) = (z, [])$$
$$lastWithoutlast(x :: R) \rightarrow (z, x :: M) \text{ if } lastWithoutlast(R) = (z, M)$$

For a term t (equation e) $s|_p$ ($e|_p$) is the subterm of t (of e) at position p. A *goal* is a set of equations. For a goal E, $E|_p$ denotes the subterm at position p of an equation $e \in E$. $t[p]_s$ ($e[p]_s$, $E[p]_s$) denotes the result of replacing the subterm at position p by the term s.

A conditional equation is a pair (e, B) of an equation e and a goal B (denoted 'e if B'). Similarly, we define *rule* and *conditional rule* denoted by $s \rightarrow t$ and '$s \rightarrow t$ if B' respectively ($s = t$ is the *head* and E are the *conditions* of the rule). A *(conditional) rule system* is a set of (conditional) rules. A conditional rule $s \rightarrow t$ if B is called *basic* if s is basic. A rule system is *basic* if each rule of the system is *basic*.

For a *substitution* σ, $\mathcal{D}om(\sigma)$ is its domain. σ is a **C-substitution** (ground) if $\sigma(x)$ is a C-term (ground) for all $x \in \mathcal{D}om(\sigma)$. The operator $\mathcal{V}ar(o)$ denotes the set of variables appearing in the object o. The symbol $\geq_R$ denotes the *subsumption ordering modulo a set of rules* ($\sigma \geq_R \mu$ means that σ is a particular case of μ with respect to the rule system R).

An **input-output goal** is a triple (X, Z, E) where X and Z are sets of terms and E is a goal. An input-output goal will be graphically represented in the following way:

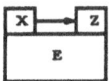

The set X contains subterms of the goal E which are considered to be inputs during the transformation. Similarly Z contains the output terms. An input-output goal (X, Z, E) can be directly transformed into a conditional rule $f(X) = Z$ if E where f is a new function symbol, which gives name to the arrow in its graphical representation. An **input-output tree** is a tree of input-output goals (e.g. figure 3).

The following list contains the formal description of all the relations we use to transform goals. For this description let R be a conditional rule system. The list includes the definition and the notation of the mentioned *narrow* and *unify* steps as well as *narrowing* (the union of these both). Note the definition of *flatten* for converting subterms of an equation into new equations (introducing new variables). This operation simulates a generalization or abstraction of a goal. The operation $\leadsto\Rightarrow_R$ combines *rewriting* with *unification*. It will be used in section 6. It represents an intermediate relation between $\Rightarrow_R$ and $\leadsto_R$. The operations for *rewriting* and *deleting* are used to simplify goals. Note that $\Rightarrow_R$ uses matching in contrast to $\leadsto_R$ which requires unification.

List of Relations

$\Rightarrow_{rewrite(R)}$ (**Rewrite step**):

$$E \Rightarrow_{rewrite(R)} E[p]_{\sigma(r)} \cup \sigma(B) \text{ if}$$
$$\begin{cases} \exists (l \to r \text{ if } B) \in R \text{ with } E|_p \equiv \sigma(l) \\ \text{and} \\ \mathcal{D}om(\sigma) \subseteq \mathcal{V}ar(l) \end{cases}$$

$\Rightarrow_{delete}$ (**Delete step**):

$$\{s = s\} \cup E \Rightarrow_{delete} E$$

$\Rightarrow_R$ (**Rewriting and deleting**):

$$\Rightarrow_R :\equiv \Rightarrow_{rewrite(R)} \cup \Rightarrow_{delete}$$

$\leadsto_{narrow(R)}$ (**Narrow step**):

$$E \leadsto_{narrow(R),\mu} \mu(E[p]_r \cup B) \text{ if}$$
$$\begin{cases} \exists (l \to r \text{ if } B) \in R \text{ with } \mu \equiv mgu(E|_p, l) \\ \text{for } E|_p \text{ a non-variable term} \end{cases}$$

$\leadsto_{unify}$ (**Unify step**):

$$\{s = t\} \cup E \leadsto_{unify,\mu} \mu(E) \text{ if}$$
$$\mu \equiv mgu(s, t)$$

$\leadsto_R$ (**Narrowing**):

$$\leadsto_R :\equiv \leadsto_{narrow(R)} \cup \leadsto_{unify}$$

$\leadsto\Rightarrow_R$ (**Rewriting and unifying**):

$$\leadsto\Rightarrow_R :\equiv \Rightarrow_R \cup \leadsto_{unify}$$

$\leadsto_{flatten}$ (**Flatten step**):

$$E \leadsto_{flatten} \{x = E|_p\} \cup E[p]_x$$
$$\text{if}$$
$$\begin{cases} x \text{ is a new variable} \\ \text{and} \\ E|_p \text{ a non-variable term} \end{cases}$$

4 Operations over Input-Output Goals

We can extend the narrowing operations over simple goals to input-output goals by taking into account the input and ouputs of the set of equations. Additionally, we need other complementary operations in order to manipulate input-output trees. Formally, we define the operations **narrow (unify)**, **fold**, **subgoal** and **transform** as follows:

Narrow:

$$(f(X) = Z \text{ if } E) \leadsto_{narrow(R)} (f(X') = Z' \text{ if } E') \quad \text{if} \quad \begin{cases} E \leadsto_{narrow(R),\sigma} E' \\ \text{and} \\ (X', Z') \equiv \sigma(X, Z) \end{cases}$$

Fold:

$$(f(X) = Z \text{ if } E) \leadsto_{fold(B)} (f(X) = Z \text{ if } \{g(V) = W\})$$

$$\text{if} \quad \begin{cases} \exists \, (g(V') = W' \text{ if } E') \in B \\ \quad \text{such that } E \equiv \delta(E') \text{ for some substitution } \delta \\ \text{and} \\ (V, W) \equiv \delta(V', W') \end{cases}$$

Subgoal:

$$(f(X) = Z \text{ if } ES \cup ER) \leadsto_{subgoal} (f(X) = Z \text{ if } \{g(V) = W\} \cup ER), (g(V) = W \text{ if } ES)$$

where 'g' is a new symbol

Transform:

$$(f(X) = Z \text{ if } E) \leadsto_{transform} (f(X) = Z \text{ if } E')$$

Note that **narrow** corresponds to the application of a narrowing step (using the rule system R) over the conditions E of an input-output goal $(f(X) = Z \text{ if } E)$ (the **unify** operation is defined analogously). The only difference is that we need to update the inputs and outputs X, Z appropriately using the corresponding narrowing substitution and producing the input-outputs X', Z' of the new goal.

The **fold** operation makes use of a parameter B, representing a set of input-output goals to perform the fold step. We will explain later how we select the set B but the idea is that the goals of B represent 'problems' which we have solved (transformed). When we apply this operation over a goal, say $G \equiv (f(X) = Z \text{ if } E)$, then we try to find a goal $G' \equiv (g(V') = W' \text{ if } E')$ belonging to B and such that E is an instance of E' (meaning the goal G is only a particular case of G'). In such a situation, we generate a new goal by replacing E by the instance of the head of G'.

The operation **subgoal** can be employed to produce new goals representing 'subproblems' of a goal we prefer to solve independently (subprograms). Note that the operation generates two new goals. In the formulation of this rule, it can be seen that the subproblem we want to separate is given by the subset of equations ES (V and W are the corresponding input-output terms of ES). The rule then creates a new input-output goal associated with ES with head $g(V) = W$ and substitutes this head for ES in the old goal.

Finally, with the transformation **transform**, we really specify a class of operations over the equations of a goal. Among others for instance, we admit

38

rewriting and *flatten* steps[9] into this class (naturally it is intended that the application of **transform** does not affect the solutions of a goal).

As an example using these transformations, figure 3 shows the input-output tree associated with our goal E (equation 6).

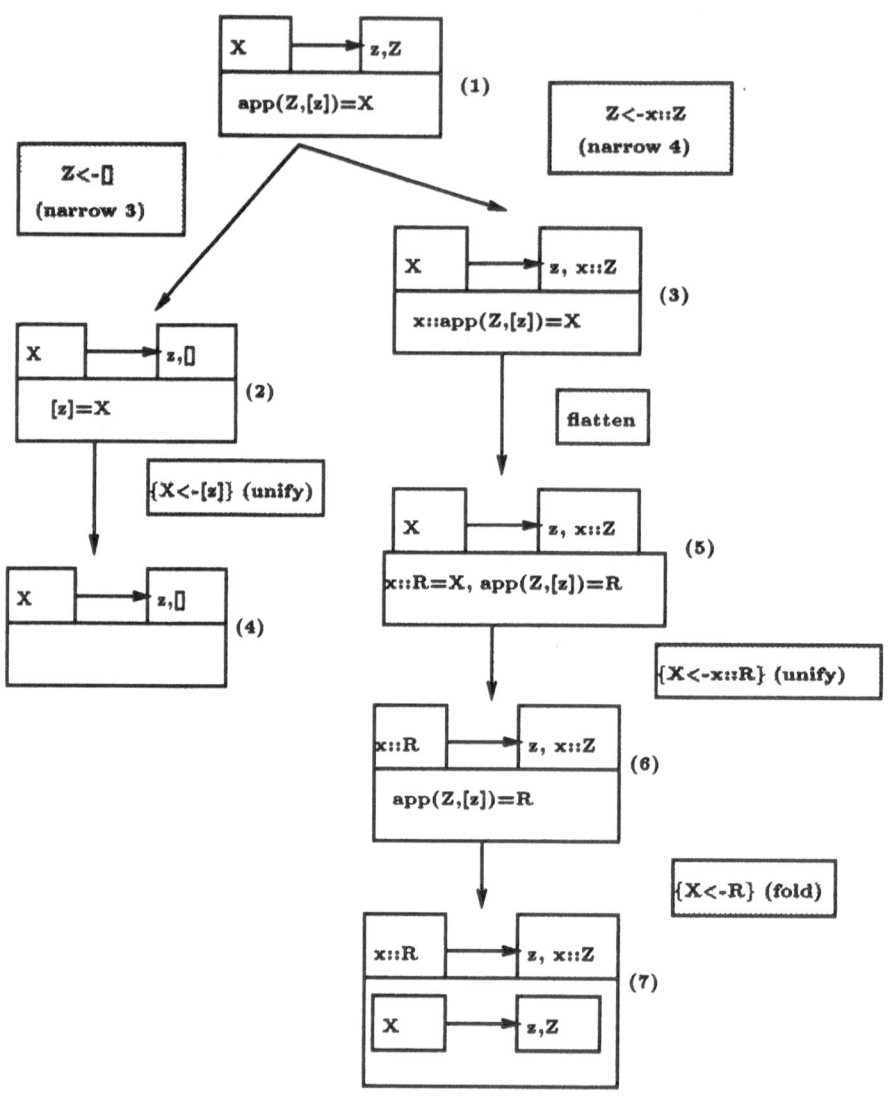

Figure 3.

This figure illustrates how we generate the program *lastWithoutlast* defined by equations 7 and 8. For example, the terminal nodes 4 and 7 represent in this case the generated rules of the program.

---

[9] For instance path 3,5 in figure 2.

To extract the equations 7 and 8, we only need to interpret the goals as conditional rules giving the name *lastWithoutlast* to the arrow of the input-output-goal of the root. With respect to the construction of the tree, note that node 4 is generated after applying a *narrow* and a *unify* step. The resulting node 4 can be *admitted* as goal of the program because it has no more conditions.[10]

On the other side, node 3 is transformed into node 5 by applying a *flatten* step introducing a new variable R which replaces the subterm $app(Z, [z])$. Now, the condition of node 6 is only an instance of the condition of the root node (characterizing in this case the regularity of the tree). Therefore, a *fold* operation using node 1 can take place yielding node 7[11]. No more transformations are possible at node 7, therefore it belongs to the program. The tree generation is finished because there are no pending goals to transform. A *regular tree* is obtained in this way.

5 Inference System

By means of the above definitions and principles, we are able to define the inference system to transform input-output trees into programs. First, we formulate it in a non-restricted form. Later, we are going to incorporate some technical conditions on its application in order to guarantee that the synthesized programs satisfy some requirements described below.

Actually, our system can be considered to be the formal description of a **state machine** for transforming input-output goals into programs. The states of the machine represent a description of the computation (inference) performed. The highest-level operations of this machine are the inference rules we will describe below. These inference rules make use of lower-level operations, like *narrow*, *fold(B)* or *subgoal*. At the lowest level of this machine we have, for example, *unification* and other usual operations for manipulation of expressions.

So, an **inference state** of the system is given by a triple of the form

$$(T, B, P)$$

where T, B and P are sets of input-output goals. The first component T contains the (remaining) goals we intend to transform using the system (i.e. a part of the input-output tree). The component B contains the goals we have already transformed during the inference process. And finally, P contains the rules already belonging to the program we are trying to synthesize. The inference rules have the general form:

$$\frac{(T, B, P)}{(T', B', P')} \quad \text{(inference rule)}$$

---

[10] This is the simplest criterion for admitting goals into the program. In general different criteria are possible depending on the aim of the transformation. To be flexible, we have parameterized these criteria in our transformation system (see below).

[11] As in this example, we already use transformed nodes to construct the *fold set* (parameter B of the definition of *fold*). The selection of the goal in B to perform the *fold* could be non deterministic and represent a quite difficult problem which can only be solved in an 'intelligent' way (i.e using heuristics or by the user). The efficiency of the generated program depends on this selection.

defining a transition from the inference state (T, B, P) to the (T', B', P') produced by the named rule. If we denote by $\vdash$ the corresponding **inference relation** generated by the inference rules, then the **aim** of the system can be described in the following way: Given an input-output goal G_0 which we want to transform, we first form the **initial state** (T_0, B_0, P_0) to this goal by setting:

$$(T_0, B_0, P_0) :\equiv (G_0, \emptyset, \emptyset)$$

Now using the inference rules, we try to produce a sequence of inference states

$$\{ (T_i, B_i, P_i) \}_{i=0}^n$$

such that the following conditions hold:

- $(T_i, B_i, P_i) \vdash (T_{i+1}, B_{i+1}, P_{i+1})$ for $i \equiv 0, \dots n-1$ and

- $T_n \equiv \emptyset$

We call such a derivation a **successful derivation** for the goal G_0 and call its last (nth) state a **final state**. The synthesized program becomes the input-output goals which remain in the third component P_n of the final state of a successful derivation $\{ (T_i, B_i, P_i) \}_{i=0}^n$.

We also indicate that the system is parameterized by the rule system R. In addition to R, we make use of other parameters to operate. For instance, the system needs to know the so-called **admission criteria** for accepting goals as part of the program (see the *accept* rule below). We also need parameters for *splitting* goals (see the *split* rule). Other parameters we eventually utilize are (Eureka) Lemmas representing rules or conditional equations we use for simplification (not for unfolding), only. The application of such Lemmas represents an example of the *transform* rule.

The list of inference rules is the following:

Inference Rules

$$\frac{(\{G\} \cup T, B, P)}{(T \cup NG, B \cup \{G\}, P)} \quad (unfold)$$

where $\quad NG \equiv \{ G' : G \rightsquigarrow_{narrow(R)} G' \}$

$$\frac{(\{G\} \cup T, B, P)}{(T \cup \{G'\}, B, P)} \quad (fold)$$

if $G \rightsquigarrow_{fold(B)} G'$

$$\frac{(\{G\} \cup T, B, P)}{(T \cup \{G', G''\}, B, P)} \quad (split)$$

if $G \rightsquigarrow_{subgoal} G' \; G''$

$$\frac{(\{G\} \cup T, B, P)}{(T, B, P \cup \{G\})} \quad (accept)$$

if G satisfies the *admission criteria*

$$\frac{(\{G\} \cup T, B, P)}{(T \cup \{G'\}, B, P)} \quad (transform)$$

if $G \rightsquigarrow_{transform} G'$

In order to explain briefly how the rules work, let us consider the *unfold* rule. The transition selects an input-output goal G from the first component of the state and replaces it by the set NG of goals derivable using narrowing (the sons G in the input-output tree). The goal G is then moved to the component B

of the resulting state, indicating that it is already transformed. The component P remains the same in this case. Note that this transformation simulates a decomposition by cases of the problem G into the set given by the goals in NG (the narrowing substitutions representing conditions for the cases) as can be seen in figure 3. This illustrates part of the deductive power of narrowing.

In the case of the *fold* transition, we can observe the use of the component B (containing the already transformed goals). In this way we avoid the expansion of the same goal (up to a substitution) and produce 'recursive calls'. The transition *accept* moves goals from the component T to the component P accepting them into the program according to the **admission parameters**. The rule *split* just replaces a goal of the component T by two new goals generated by the *subgoal* operation. Again, we need parameters in order to specify the partition of goals (i.e. how to generate the partition $(ES \cup ER)$ of the operation $subgoal)^{12}$.

6 Properties of the Transformations

In this section we investigate some theoretical properties of our transformation system. In particular, we are interested in analyzing some kind of *equivalence* between the goals we transformed and the resulting programs in a formal way. **Equivalence preservation** is our first requirement from our system. The basic aim is to formulate conditions which permit us to guarantee this property. In order to solve this problem, we proceed in the following way.

First, we define *equivalence* in terms of the answers we can obtain by solving the initial goal using narrowing and the answers we can compute using the synthesized programs[13]. This requirement has two directions: whether the answers we produce using the program are answers to the goal (*soundness*), and whether each answer to the goal can be generated using the program (*completeness*). Then, we give some restrictions on the application of the inference rules and are able to show that **we achieve equivalence** under these conditions.

In addition to equivalence, we want a second requirement from our system. Although the benefits of employing program transformation techniques are rather evident in many particular cases, we want to analyze whether some kind of **improvement** can be guaranteed in the general case. That is, whether the generated programs are 'better' in some sense than the narrowing solution.

As we can surely expect, verifying this class of requirement can become very complicated because concepts like 'efficiency' or 'improvement' are extremely difficult to capture in a formal sense. In spite of that, we select a particular criterion for improvement and are able to prove that the produced programs satisfy it whenever some special conditions are guaranteed during the inference process. We are going to present these conditions formally but informally the result is the following: the programs we generate use a simpler reduction relation to compute values for the output variables. This means more exactly,

---

[12] For instance, a frequent criterion is to group in ER equations containing only operators we do not want to transform. The list of operators we want to transform can be a parameter of the system. This list can also be used by the accept transformation.

[13] Clearly, this definition of equivalence is very natural because we intend to replace narrowing by the synthesized programs.

that *narrow steps* between goals and rules of the rule system or program are **not necessary**. Only *matching* is needed to reduce goals. In other words, synthesis replaces certain unification steps by matching steps (a cheaper operation).

In the following, we give the formalization of both mentioned requirements. This formulation is a technical translation of the ideas explained above. The proof of the claims are omitted due to the lack of space. They can be found in [LS92]. Our principal aim in the rest of this section is to illustrate how our system admits the analysis of theoretical properties of the derived programs.

First, we need to introduce a special narrowing strategy, which we will use for restricting the unfolding of goals. It can be seen that this strategy is a restriction of the **innermost** strategy.

Definition 6.1 (SLD-strict) *A step $E \rightsquigarrow E'$ is called* **SLD** *if the selected equation in E is leftmost. A SLD-narrow step is called* **strict** *if the narrowed term is basic. A SLD-unify step is also called* **strict** *when the unified equation is a C-equation. We write $E \rightsquigarrow_{narrow(R)} E'$ (SLD-strict) or $E \rightsquigarrow_{unify} E'$ (SLD-strict) respectively. We define* **SLD-strict narrowing** *to be the combination of SLD-strict narrow and SLD-strict unify. We write $E \rightsquigarrow_R E'$ (SLD-strict) to denote one step of SLD-strict narrowing.*

A relevant property of SLD-narrowing in this work is given by the following result

Proposition 6.1 (SLD-strict answers are CS) *Let R be a basic rule system and E be a equation set. For each derivation $E \rightsquigarrow^*_\mu \emptyset$ (SLD-strict) the answer μ is a C-substitution.*

This result guarantees that the generated programs are *basic* rule systems. In addition to that, we can prove that SLD-strict is correct and complete under the following conditions for the rule system.

Theorem 6.1 (soundness and completeness of SLD-strict narrowing) *Let R be (ground) convergent, regular, basic and completely defined. For all sets of equations E, we have:*

1. *If $E \rightsquigarrow^*_{R,\mu} \emptyset$ then $\mu(E) \Rightarrow^*_R \emptyset$ (soundness) and*

2. *For all σ ground substitution: if $\sigma(E) \Rightarrow^*_R \emptyset$ then there exists $E \rightsquigarrow^*_{R,\mu} \emptyset$ (SLD-strict) such that $\sigma \geq_R \mu$ (completeness)*

The result 6.1 guarantees that the answers of E produced by *SLD-strict narrowing* are correct (part 1) and that we are able to generate any answer of E using *SLD-strict narrowing* (part 2). Now we define three properties which we will employ to guarantee the requirements of equivalence and improvement mentioned above.

Definition 6.2 (Rewrite-solvable and well-behaved properties) *Let G be an input-output goal of the form $(f(X) = Z$ if $E)$. We say that:*

1. *G is* **rewrite-solvable** *in R if the following property holds: $\forall \delta$ C-substitution such that $Dom(\delta) \equiv Var(X)$: $\exists(\delta(E) \rightsquigarrow^*_{R,\sigma} \emptyset$ (SLD-strict)) if and only if $\exists(\delta(E) \rightsquigarrow\Rightarrow^*_{R,\sigma} \emptyset)$ and*

2. G *is* **well-behaved in** R *if* $(E \leadsto_{R,\sigma}^{*} \emptyset$ *(SLD-strict))* **implies**
   $(Var(Z) \subseteq Var(X))$

The *rewrite-solvability* of a goal G means that the conditions E of G can always be solved in rule system R without using any *narrow operation*. Only rewriting and unification are necessary (reduction $\leadsto\Rightarrow$). On the other hand, *well-behavedness* guarantees that the outputs of the goal can never become 'independent' of the inputs for any solution (σ) of the conditions E of the goal G. As can be shown, this property particularly implies that the outputs are already ground when the inputs are ground too.

For example, $(lastWithoutlast(X) = (z, Z)$ if $app(Z, [z]) = X)$ is well-behaved but not rewrite-solvable with respect to the rules 3 and 4. On the other hand, $(foo(X) = (A, B)$ if $app(X, A) = B)$ is rewrite-solvable but not well-behaved with to respect to the same rule system[14].

The third special property we need is employed to restrict the *fold* operation.

Definition 6.3 (Input-output preserving) *Consider a fold step* $(f(X) = Z$ if $E) \leadsto_{fold(B)} (f(X) = Z$ if $\{g(V) = W\})$ *and let us suppose that a substitution* δ *is used by this operation. Then, we say that the fold step is* **input-output preserving** *if the following conditions hold:*

1. $Var(Z) \subseteq (Var(X) \cup Var(W))$ *and*

2. $Var(V) \subseteq Var(X)$

Part 1 of the above definition implies that the outputs of the goal $(f(X) = Z$ if $E)$ can be generated if we compute using $(f(X) = Z$ if $\{g(V) = W\})$ (each output can be produced). Part 2 guarantees that all the inputs $Var(V)$ needed to solve the conditions of the generated goal, are available in $Var(X)$ (no input need to be generated).

Now, we are able to postulate the restrictions on our inference system.

Definition 6.4 (Restrictions) *Let* G_0 *be an input-output goal and consider a successful derivation* $\{ (T_i, B_i, P_i) \}_{i=0}^{n}$ *for* G_0. *The derivation is called* **restricted** *if the goal* G_0 *and each operation or inference rule used to produce the derivation satisfy the following restrictions:*

- G_0 *is well-behaved*
- *Narrow and unify are always SLD-strict*
- *Only C-substitutions are used by fold*
- *Fold steps are input-output preserving*
- *Accept admits only rewrite-solvable goals*
- *Split produces only well-behaved goals*

Using that, we postulate the following result:

Theorem 6.2 (Equivalence and Improvement) *Let* R *be (ground) convergent, regular, basic and completely defined and* $G_0 \equiv (f_0(X_0) = Z_0$ if $E_0)$ *be an input-output goal. Then, for each* $\{ (T_i, B_i, P_i) \}_{i=0}^{n}$ *restricted successful derivation for* G_0, *we have:*

---

[14] We are able to give some sufficient criteria for testing these properties.

1. *If* $\{f_0(X_0) = Z_0\}$ *(SLD-strict)* $\leadsto^*_{R \cup P_n, \mu} \emptyset$ *then* $\mu(E_0) \Rightarrow^*_R \emptyset$

2. *For all* σ *ground substitution:*
   if $\sigma(E_0) \Rightarrow^*_R \emptyset$ *then there exists* $\{f_0(X_0) = Z_0\} \leadsto_{R,\mu} \emptyset$ *(SLD-strict)*
   such that $\sigma \geq_R \mu$

3. *For all* δ *ground C-substitution s.t.* $\mathcal{D}om(\delta) \equiv \mathcal{V}ar(X_0)$:
   if $(\delta(E_0) \leadsto^*_{R,\sigma} \emptyset$ *(SLD-strict))* *then there exists* $(\delta(\{f_0(X_0) = Z_0\})$
   $\leadsto \Rightarrow^*_{R \cup P_n, \sigma} \emptyset)$

Note that parts 1 and 2 constitute the *equivalence property*. Part 3 is the *improvement*. Therefore, we are able to achieve these properties and in this way the aim of this section is reached.

As an simple illustration of theorem 6.2, let us consider figure 1. We can see that $E_0 \equiv \{app(Z, z) = [1, 2, 3]\}$ can only be solved using *narrow-steps* (rules 3 and 4). However, using our synthesized program given by rules 7 and 8, we do not require any *narrow-steps* for solving $\{lastWithoutlast([1, 2, 3]) = (z, Z)\}$ as we can easily verify. (Note that in this example $f_0 \equiv$ 'lastWithoutlast', $\delta \equiv \{X \leftarrow [1, 2, 3]\}$ and $X_0, Z_0 \equiv X, (z, Z)$ in relation to the parameters of theorem 6.2).

7 Conclusions

In this work, we demonstrate how deductive synthesis can be employed to optimize narrowing. Our synthesis method is presented as an inference system for extracting rewrite programs from their input-output narrowing trees. The formulation that we use is new as is the analysis of the results about properties (equivalence and improvement) of the programs we can infer. Our approach has two major advantages which we briefly want to discuss. On the one hand, the formulation we present in this paper is very *natural* because the proposed inference rules simulate the process of systematic program derivation. Our representation using narrowing trees permits orienting the synthesis to a 'problem-solving' activity. Our rules decompose by cases and create subgoals or discover recursive problems making use of the deductive power of narrowing. This characteristic makes it possible to implement prototypes based on our ideas in a very fast and simple way. Of course such implementations need the incorporation of strategies and heuristics in order to guide the program derivations. Nevertheless, many known (toy) examples can be derived automatically using a relatively small set of strategies.

On the other hand, our formulation allows the theoretical treatment of the synthesis making possible by this means the investigation of properties of the programs, as we have done in this paper. In particular, we have shown how an improvement property could be analyzed in a general case. We conjecture that similar techniques can be used to reason about particular classes of inefficiencies of narrowing.

Acknowledgements

I wish to express special thanks to Prof. Dr. Jürgen Avenhaus, Dipl.-Inform Roland Fettig and MSc. Ignacio Trejos for the support and the many valuable suggestions. Also, I am very grateful to Dipl.-Inform Joachim Steinbach, Dipl.-Inform Thomas Deiss and Dipl.-Inform Bernhard Gramlich for technical support. This work was supported by the group 'PROGRESS' of Kaiserslautern and by a scholarship from the 'Deutschen Akademischen Austauschdienst' (DAAD) and the 'Instituto Tecnológico de Costa Rica' (ITCR)

References

[BL86]   M. Bellia and G. Levi. The Relation between Logic and Functional Languages. A survey. *J. of Logic Programming*, 3:217–236, 1986.

[BSK89] M. Bruynooge, D. De Schreye, and B. Krekels. Compiling Control. *J. of Logic Programming*, 5:135–162, 1989.

[DO90]   N. Dershowitz and M. Okada. A Rationale for Conditional Equational Programming. *Theo. Comp. Sci*, 75:111–138, 1990.

[Fri90]   L. Fribourg. Extracting Logic Programs from Proofs that use Extended Prolog and Induction. In *7th Intl. Conf. and Symp. on Logic Programming*, pages 683–699, 1990.

[Hol89]   S. Hölldobler. *Foundations of Equational Logic Programming*. LNCS 353 Springer, 1989.

[Hul80]   J. Hullot. Canonical Forms and Unification. In *CADE*, pages 318–334. LNCS 306 Springer, 1980.

[Llo87]   J. W. Lloyd. *Foundations of Logic Programming*. Springer, 2 edition, 1987.

[LS92]   C. Loría Sáenz. Synthese von Narrowingprogrammen (in German). Technical report, Uni. Kaiserslautern (Germany), 1992.

[Red86]   U.S. Reddy. On the Relation between Logic and Functional Languages. In DeGroot/Lindstrom, editor, *Logic Programming. Functions, Relations and Equations*, pages 3–36. Prentice-Hall, 1986.

[SB89]   D. De Schreye and M. Bruynooge. On the Transformation of Logic Programs with Instantiation Based Computation Rules. *J. of Logic Programming*, 7:125–154, 1989.

A Unifying View of Structural Induction and Computation Induction for Logic Programs

Laurent Fribourg

L.I.E.N.S.

URA 1327 C.N.R.S.

45 rue d'Ulm, 75005 Paris France

fribourg@dmi.ens.fr

Hans Olsén

Dept. of Information Science

Linköping University

S-581 83 Linköping Sweden

hanol@ida.liu.se

Abstract

In the framework of Extended Prolog Execution [K&S 86] a rule of Structural Induction is presented. For the induction step the new rule takes advantage of a Prolog program synthesized through Proof-Extraction techniques, and rests on extensive use of Negation as Failure Inference for exploiting the information contained in the extracted program. A comparison is made between the new rule and the rules of Restricted Structural Induction [Fri 90] and Computation Induction [Cla 79], and we note that by an uncomplicated preprocessing of the goal formula and the program the new rule subsumes the two latter rules.

1 Introduction

Consider the predicate $p(X)$ defined by the Prolog program P, where X is a vector of variables. Suppose we want to prove that some relation $Q(X)$ holds between the values of the computation. This can be expressed by the formula $\forall X Q(X) \Leftarrow p(X)$, and is usually proved by applying some form of induction.

One of the problems with inductive reasoning is that the size of the formulas to be proved grows rapidly with the number of applications of induction. In this paper a rule of Structural Induction is presented, which splits the induction step into two formulas. One of these two formulas corresponds to the only-if part of the Clark completion of the program [Cla 78]. The inference rule is defined in the framework of the Extended Execution proof system of Kanamori and Seki [K&S 86] and takes advantage of a Prolog program synthesized through Proof-Extraction techniques [Fri 90]. The rule makes extensive use of Negation as Failure Inference (NFI) [K&S 86], for exploiting the information contained in the extracted program. For this reason the rule is called *NFI-driven Induction*.

The plan is as follows. In section 2 we review some formal notions of Extended Prolog Execution and of classical induction rules. In section 3 we introduce the rule of NFI-driven Induction. We compare this rule with Structural Induction (section 4) and with Computation Induction (section 5). We then indicate a preprocessing of goal formulas and programs in order to enhance NFI-driven Induction (section 6) and conclude with final remarks.

2 Background

In this section a subset of the Extended Execution of Prolog [K&S 86] is informally reviewed and we briefly explain the main concepts of Proof-Extraction. Because of limited space we will not explain how to synthesize programs during proofs using the rules mentioned in this section. The reader should consult [Fri 90] for details. Familiarity with notions such as atoms, predicates, substitutions, most general unifiers (mgu) and definite clause programs is assumed.

2.1 Extended Execution of Prolog

We consider sentences G of the form $\forall X \exists Y G^+(X, Y) \Leftarrow G^-(X)$ where $G^+(X, Y)$ and $G^-(X)$ are conjunctions of atoms, and X and Y are vectors of variables. No variable of Y is allowed to occur in $G^-(X)$. The formula $G' : G^+(X, ?Y) \Leftarrow G^-(X)$ obtained from G by replacing the existentially quantified variables Y by $?Y$ and dropping the quantifiers, is called an *implicative goal* where $G^-(X)$ is the *hypothesis* and $G^+(X, ?Y)$ is the *conclusion*. The variables of X are called *free* and those of $?Y$ are called *undecided*. We use lower case Greek letters to denote substitutions. $G\sigma$ denotes the formula that results from applying the substitution σ to the formula G. A substitution instantiating only undecided variables is called a *deciding substitution*. A goal, the conclusion of which is empty, is said to be a *trivial goal*. A goal which is a conjunction of the form $G^+(X, ?Y)$ is an implicative goal with an empty hypothesis. In order to distinguish definite clauses of Prolog programs from implicative goals, we will write definite clauses using the C-Prolog convention (i.e. we will use ':-' instead of '$\Leftarrow$', and ',' instead of '$\wedge$'.)

The predicates appearing in a goal are defined by a definite clause program and we prove the goal in a backward fashion by applying the rules of Extended Execution. Given a program P defining the predicates occurring in a goal G, an inference rule *generates* or *yields* a set S of goals $H1, \ldots, Hn$ such that the conjunction of the goals of S implies G in the least Herbrand model of P.

With every goal $G : G^+(X, ?Y) \Leftarrow G^-(X)$ we associate a Prolog atom, $io_G(X, Y)$, called an *io-atom*, often abbreviated as $IO_G(Y)$ or simply as IO_G. The io-atom is intended to have the same meaning, or define the same relation between the variables as the goal G, and is defined by a definite clause program, the *io-program*, synthesized during the proof of G. With each rule of inference there is associated a rule of construction for a set of definite clauses, an *io-procedure*, to add to the synthesized program when the rule is applied. For example, if the inference rule applied to G yields the goals $H1, \ldots, Hn$, the associated io-procedure will define IO_G in terms of $IO_{H1}, \ldots, IO_{Hn}$. The intention that the io-atom should have the same meaning as the goal is formalized by the notions of *partial correctness* and *termination*. Given a goal $G : G^+(X, ?Y) \Leftarrow G^-(X)$ the io-program Q defining the associated io-atom $io_G(X, Y)$ is said to be partially correct w.r.t. G iff $\forall XY G^+(X, Y) \Leftarrow G^-(X) \wedge io_G(X, Y)$. The io-atom

$io_G(X, Y)$ is said to be terminating w.r.t. G iff $\forall X \exists Y\, io_G(X, Y) \Leftarrow G^-(X)$. In case G is a trivial goal we take the io-procedure defining IO_G to be the clause $io_G(X) \Leftarrow G^-(X)$ which obviously is terminating and partially correct. The io-procedures associated with applications of inference rules preserve partial correctness and termination, therefore programs synthesized using this scheme are guaranteed to possess these properties.

In this paper we make use of three of the inference rules of Extended Execution applied to the set of implicative goals: DCI, Simplification and NFI. The rules of Restricted Structural Induction and Computation Induction are reviewed in subsections 2.2 and 2.3 respectively.

DCI is an extension of SLD-resolution to implicative goals. By this rule, an atom of the conclusion of a goal that unifies with the head of a program clause via a deciding mgu, may be replaced by the body of the program clause. All new variables introduced are treated as undecided.

Example 2.1: Let the predicate $*(x, y, z)$ (whose intended meaning is that z equals x times y) be defined by the program

    $*(0,y,0)$.
    $*(\text{succ}(x),y,z) :- *(x,y,w)\,,\,+(y,w,z)$.

Consider the goal

    G: $*(\text{succ}(x),y,?z) \Leftarrow *(x,y,v)$.

DCI generates the new goal

    H: $*(x,y,?w) \wedge +(y,?w,?z) \Leftarrow *(x,y,v)$.

By the rule of Simplification an atom of the conclusion of a goal that unifies with an atom of the hypothesis via a deciding mgu, may be deleted. Optionally the atom of the hypothesis may be deleted as well.

Example 2.2: Consider the goal

    G: $*(x,y,?w) \wedge +(y,?w,?z) \Leftarrow *(x,y,v)$.

Simplification via the substitution $\{v/w\}$ yields

    H: $+(y,v,?z)$.

Let A be an atom occurring in the hypothesis of a goal G, and $C_1, ..., C_n$ the clauses of the program whose head unifies with A. The rule of NFI will generate a set of n goals $H_1, ..., H_n$ obtained by replacement of A with the body of the clauses $C_1, ..., C_n$ and by corresponding instantiation. All new variables introduced are treated as free.

Example 2.3: Consider the goal

    G: $+(x,?v,z) \Leftarrow *(\text{succ}(x),y,z)$.

NFI yields the new goal

    H: $+(y,?v,z) \Leftarrow *(x,y,w) \wedge +(y,w,z)$.

2.2 Restricted Structural Induction

The general rule of Structural Induction was introduced by Burstall (in the framework of functional programming) [Bur 69]. When applied to implicative goals, the rule introduces a second level of implication connectives and thus goes beyond our class of implicative goals. In order to stay within the framework of implicative goals, we consider a restricted form of the rule. Rules of Structural Induction assumes that the variables are typed, and there has to be one instance of the rule for every datatype. We present the rule of Restricted Structural Induction for the case the induction variable is of type natural number.

Definition 2.1: Consider the goal $G : G^+(x, ?Y) \Leftarrow G^-$ where x is a free variable of type natural number, not occurring in G^-, and Y is a vector of undecided variables. *Restricted Structural Induction* w.r.t. x yields the new goals

> H1: $G^+(0, ?Y) \Leftarrow G^-$.
> H2: $G^+(\text{succ}(w), ?Y) \Leftarrow G^+(w, Y') \wedge G^-$

where w is a new free variable of type natural number and Y' is a vector of free variables that is a renaming of Y.
The free variables other than x are all frozen and treated as constants. (This is why the rule is said to be "restricted".)

Example 2.4: Let the predicate $+(x, y, z)$ (whose intended meaning is that z equals x plus y) be defined by the program

> +(0,y,y).
> +(succ(x),y,succ(z)) :- +(x,y,z).

Consider the goal expressing the termination of +

> G: +(x,y,?z).

Restricted Structural Induction w.r.t. x yields the new goals

> H1: +(0,y,?z).
> H2: +(succ(x),y,?z) $\Leftarrow$ +(x,y,z_1).

2.3 Computation Induction

The rule of Computation Induction has been defined by Clark for logic programs [Cla 79]. Roughly speaking, when applied to a goal of the form $G^+ \Leftarrow A$ where A is an atom defined by a program P, it generates the induction scheme obtained by replacing all occurrences of A in P by the corresponding instances of G^+. Formally we have:

Definition 2.2: Let P be a definite clause program. Consider the goal $G :$ $G^+(?Y) \Leftarrow A$ where A is an atom of the form $a(T(X))$, a is a predicate symbol, $T(X)$ a vector of terms and X a vector of variables. Let $D1, \ldots, Dn$ be all clauses

D1: $A_1 :- A_{11} , \ldots, A_{1m_1} , R_1.$

$\ldots$

Dn: $A_n :- A_{n1} , \ldots, A_{nm_n} , R_n.$

in P the heads of which unify with A by a mgu $\sigma_i \cup \tau_i$ $(1 \leq i \leq n)$ such that $A\sigma_i \equiv A_i\tau_i$. Let R_i be a possibly empty conjunction of atoms containing no instance of the predicate a. It may be that $m_i = 0$. Then, if all instantiated atoms $A_{ij}\tau_i$ $(1 \leq j \leq m_i)$ are instances of the atom A by a substitution θ_{ij} so that $A_{ij}\tau_i \equiv A\theta_{ij}$, *Computation Induction* applies and yields the new goals

H1: $G^+(?Y)\sigma_1 \Leftarrow G^+(Y_{11})\theta_{11} \wedge \ldots \wedge G^+(Y_{1m_1})\theta_{1m_1} \wedge R_1\tau_1.$

$\ldots$

Hn: $G^+(?Y)\sigma_n \Leftarrow G^+(Y_{n1})\theta_{n1} \wedge \ldots \wedge G^+(Y_{nm_n})\theta_{nm_n} \wedge R_n\tau_n.$

where Y_{ij} are distinct renamings of Y as new vectors of free variables.

Example 2.5:   Consider again the goal expressing commutativity of $+$

G: $+(y,x,z) \Leftarrow +(x,y,z).$

Computation Induction yields

H1: $+(y,0,y).$
H2: $+(y,\text{succ}(x_0),\text{succ}(z_0)) \Leftarrow +(y,x_0,z_0).$

3   NFI-driven Induction

We have pointed out that general Structural Induction does not preserve the class of implicative goals. On the other hand, Restricted Structural Induction preserves this class but does not allow the induction variable to occur in the hypothesis of the goal. We now introduce a form of Structural Induction, called "NFI-driven Induction", that at once preserves the class of implicative goals and allows induction variables to occur in goal hypotheses. The inference rule is derived by examining the formulas resulting from general Structural Induction. We consider the case when the induction variable is of type natural number, and following this example it is straightforward to apply the line of reasoning to any data structure.
Consider the sentence

S: $\forall x,z \; \exists y \; C(x,z,y) \Leftarrow A(x,z)$

A proof of S by general structural induction w.r.t. x (where x is a natural number) will result in the induction step formula

I: $\forall x \; (\forall z \; \exists y \; C(\text{succ}(x),z,y) \Leftarrow A(\text{succ}(x),z)) \Leftarrow$
$(\forall z \; \exists y \; C(x,z,y) \Leftarrow A(x,z))$

Transformed to prenex form, I becomes

I': $\forall x,z,y' \; \exists y,z' \; (C(\text{succ}(x),z,y) \Leftarrow A(\text{succ}(x),z)) \Leftarrow$
$(C(x,z',y') \Leftarrow A(x,z'))$

A natural attempt to prove I' would be to assume $A(succ(x), z)$, prove $A(x, z')$, apply the induction hypothesis to get $C(x, z', y')$ and finally prove $C(succ(x), z, y)$. Formally, this is achieved by proving the sentences

I2: $\forall x, z \; \exists z' \; A(x,z') \Leftarrow A(succ(x),z)$.

I3: $\forall x, z, z', y' \; \exists y \; C(succ(x),z,y) \Leftarrow C(x,z',y') \wedge Q(x,z,z')$

where $Q(x, z, z')$ satisfies the conditions

(Term): $\forall x, z \; \exists z' \; Q(x,z,z') \Leftarrow A(succ(x),z)$

(Corr): $\forall x, z, z' \; A(x,z') \Leftarrow Q(x,z,z') \wedge A(succ(x),z)$

It is straightforward to verify that these conditions are sufficient and, indeed, necessary for $I2$ and $I3$ to guarantee that I' holds. Now we may transform the sentences A and B to the implicative goals

I2': $A(x,?z') \Leftarrow A(succ(x),z)$

I3': $C(succ(x),z,?y) \Leftarrow C(x,z'',y') \wedge Q(x,z,z'')$

Letting the expression $Q(x, z, z')$ be the io-atom $io_{I2'}(x, z, z')$ associated with the goal $I2'$, the conditions $(Term)$ and $(Corr)$ express termination and partial correctness of $io_{I2'}(x, z, z')$ w.r.t. $I2'$. The goal $I2'$ states the existence of a recursion scheme for $A(x, z)$ according to the structure of x. We will say that such a goal is an *assumption of structural recursion* of A w.r.t. x. Actually, $I2'$ is an induction axiom stating that every vector (x, z) of variables such that $A(x, z)$ holds, is either of the form $(0, z)$ or of the form $(succ(x'), z)$ where $io_{I2'}(x', z, z')$ and $A(x', z')$ holds. Thus, $IO_{I2'}$ induces a well-founded ordering relation $<$ on the data so that $(x', z') < (succ(x'), z)$ iff $io_{I2'}(x', z, z')$.

Typically, a proof of $I3'$ starts with some applications of NFI to the atom $IO_{I2'}$ in order to communicate the substitutions done during the proof of the assumption of structural recursion of A. This is why we call the induction rule "NFI-driven Induction". The proof of the assumption $I2'$ of structural recursion also usually starts by applying NFI. We present the rule of NFI-driven Induction for the case when the induction variable is of type natural number.

Definition 3.1: Let G be the goal $G^+(x, Z, ?Y) \Leftarrow G^-(x, Z)$ where x is a free variable of type natural number. Then *NFI-driven Induction* w.r.t. x yields the new goals

H1: $G^+(0,Z,?Y) \Leftarrow G^-(0,Z)$.

H2: $G^-(w,?Z') \Leftarrow G^-(succ(w),Z)$.

H3: $G^+(succ(w),Z,?Y) \Leftarrow G^+(w,Z'',Y') \wedge IO_{H2}(w,Z,Z'')$.

where $IO_{H2}(w, Z, Z')$ is the io-atom associated with the goal $H2$ and w is a new free variable of type natural number, Z' and Z'' are renamings of Z as new vectors of variables, and Y' is a renaming of Y as a new vector of free variables.

The io-procedure defining the io-atom $IO_G(x, Z, Y)$ associated with the goal G is shown in appendix A.

Example 3.1: Consider once more the goal expressing commutativity of $+$.

G: $+(y,x,z) \Leftarrow +(x,y,z)$.

By NFI-driven Induction w.r.t. x, we get

H1: $+(y,0,z) \Leftarrow +(0,y,z)$.
H2: $+(x,?y_0,?z_0) \Leftarrow +(succ(x),y,z)$.
H3: $+(y,succ(x),z) \Leftarrow +(y_0,x,z_0) \wedge io_{H2}(x,y,z,y_0,z_0)$.

NFI applied to $H1$ by $\{y/z\}$ yields

I1: $+(y,0,y)$.

This may be easily proved by induction w.r.t. y. NFI applied to $H2$ by $\{succ(z_1)/z\}$ yields

I2: $+(x,?y_0,?z_0) \Leftarrow +(x,y,z_1)$.

Simplification on $I2$ by $\{y/y_0, z_1/z_0\}$ yields the trivial goal. The io-program defining $IO_{H2}(x,y,z,z_0,y_0)$ becomes

$io_{H2}(x,y,succ(z_1),z_0,y_0)$:- $io_{I2}(x,y,z_1,y_0,z_0)$.

$io_{I2}(x,y,z_1,y,z_1)$.

Two applications of NFI to $H3$ w.r.t. IO_{H2} by $\{succ(z_1)/z, y/y_0, z_1/z_0\}$ yields

I3: $+(y,succ(x),succ(z_1)) \Leftarrow +(y,x,z_1)$.

NFI-driven Induction w.r.t. y yields

J3: $+(0,succ(x),succ(z_1)) \Leftarrow +(0,x,z_1)$.
J4: $+(y,?x_0,?z_2) \Leftarrow +(succ(y),x,z_1)$.
J5: $+(succ(y),succ(x),succ(z_1)) \Leftarrow +(y,succ(x_0),succ(z_2))\wedge$
$io_{J4}(x,y,z_1,x_0,z_2)$.

The goal $J3$ is proved by an application of NFI followed by an application of Simplification. NFI on $J4$ by $\{succ(z_3)/z_1\}$ yields

K4: $+(y,?x_0,?z_2) \Leftarrow +(y,x,z_3)$.

Simplification by $\{x/x_0, z_3/z_2\}$ yields the trivial goal. The io-atom $io_{J4}(x,y,z_1,x_0,z_2)$ is defined by the io-program

$io_{J4}(x,y,succ(z_3),x_0,z_2)$:- $io_{K4}(x,y,z_3,x_0,z_2)$.
$io_{K4}(x,y,z_3,x,z_3)$.

Consider the goal $J5$. Two applications of NFI w.r.t. the atom IO_{J4} by $\{succ(z_3)/z_1\}$ followed by $\{x/x_0, z_3/z_2\}$ yields

K5: $+(succ(y),succ(x),succ(succ(z_3))) \Leftarrow +(y,succ(x),succ(z_3))$

DCI followed by Simplification yields the trivial goal.

4 NFI-driven Induction vs. Restricted Structural Induction

Restricted Structural Induction is a special case of NFI-driven Induction since when the induction variable does not occur in the hypothesis of the goal, the assumption of structural recursion generated by NFI-driven Induction is always true and can be proved by at most some applications of Simplification. The following example shows that NFI-driven Induction is actually a *proper* extension of the rule of Restricted Structural Induction.

Example 4.1: Commutativity of $+$ expressed as $+(x, y, z) \Leftarrow +(y, x, z)$ cannot be proved by Restricted Structural Induction since all free variables occur in the hypothesis. It does not solve the problem reformulating the goal as $+(x, y, ?z) \wedge +(y, x, ?z)$. Consider the goal

G: $+(x,y,?z) \wedge +(y,x,?z)$.

Restricted Structural Induction w.r.t. x yields

H1: $+(0,y,?z) \wedge +(y,0,?z)$.
H2: $+(succ(x),y,?z) \wedge +(y,succ(x),?z) \Leftarrow +(x,y,z_0) \wedge +(y,x,z_0)$.

DCI on $H2$ w.r.t. the atom $+(succ(x), y, ?z)$ by $\{succ(z_1)/z\}$ yields

I2: $+(x,y,?z_1) \wedge +(y,succ(x),succ(?z_1)) \Leftarrow +(x,y,z_0) \wedge +(y,x,z_0)$.

Simplification by $\{z_0/z_1\}$ yields

J2: $+(y,succ(x),succ(z_0)) \Leftarrow +(y,x,z_0)$.

While true, the goal $J2$ would have to be proved by induction on y, but y occurs in the hypothesis so Restricted Structural Induction does not apply. However, the goal $J2$ can be proved by NFI-driven Induction (see example 3.1).

5 NFI-driven Induction vs. Computation Induction

Though introduced as a generalization of Restricted Structural Induction, NFI-driven Induction sometimes behaves as Computation Induction. Consider the goal G : $G^+(x, Z, ?Y) \Leftarrow a(x, Z)$ where a is recursively defined as

a(0,Z) :- B(Z).
a(succ(x),Z) :- a(x,Z') , R(x,Z,Z').

NFI-driven Induction and Computation Induction yields essentially the same goals and io-programs (compare examples 2.5 and 3.1 where the goals $H1$ and $H2$ of example 2.5 are identical, up to renaming of variables, to the goals $I1$ and $I3$ of example 3.1).

The similarity between Computation Induction and NFI-driven Induction stems from the coincidence between the recursion scheme of a and the recursive structure of the datum x. In such a case the assumption of structural recursion of $a(x, Z)$ trivially holds. In general, when the recursion scheme of a differs from the recursion scheme of x, the rule of NFI-driven Induction w.r.t. x behaves differently from Computation Induction. Actually, in such cases NFI-driven Induction often fails, as illustrated by the following example.

Example 5.1: Let the predicates $odd(x)$ and $even(x)$ be defined by the program P

    odd(succ(0)).
    odd(succ(succ(x))) :- odd(x).
    even(0).
    even(succ(succ(x))) :- even(x).

Consider the goal

    G: odd(succ(x)) ⇐ even(x).

Computation Induction yields

    H1: odd(succ(0)).
    H2: odd(succ(succ(succ(x)))) ⇐ odd(succ(x)).

DCI on $H1$ yields the trivial goal and DCI on $H2$ yields

    I2: odd(succ(x)) ⇐ odd(succ(x)).

Simplification yields the trivial goal. Let us see what happens when we try to prove the goal G by NFI-driven Induction. NFI-driven Induction on G yields

    H1: odd(succ(0)) ⇐ even(0).
    H2: even(x) ⇐ even(succ(x)).
    H3: odd(succ(succ(x))) ⇐ odd(succ(x)) ∧ io_{H2}(x).

The goal $H2$ corresponds to the assumption of structural recursion of $even(x)$ w.r.t. x. This assumption is false here and NFI-driven Induction fails.

In order to make NFI-driven Induction behave as Computation Induction (and succeed) even in case a is not recursively defined according to the structure of x, we need a preprocessing of the goal G that will be explained in the next section.

6 NFI-driven Induction As a Simulation of Computation Induction

Structural Induction is in a way a special case of Computation Induction [Bur 69]. Since any data structure can be defined by a program, every proof by Structural Induction can be turned into a proof by Computation Induction (for example, natural numbers can be defined by the clauses $nat(0)$ and $nat(succ(x)) :- nat(x)$, see [K&S 86]). In this section we take the opposite point of view to the effect that Computation Induction is a special case of Structural Induction. Instead of saying that every data type is defined by a program, we say that every program defines a data type. Consider the program P defining the atom $a(x)$

a(x) :- B_1(x).

. . .

a(x) :- B_n(x).

a(x) :- a(x_1) , ..., a(x_{k_1}) , R_1(x,x_1, ..., x_{k_1}).

. . .

a(x) :- a(x_1) , ..., a(x_{k_m}) , R_m(x,x_1, ..., x_{k_m}).

where $B_1, \ldots, B_n, R_1, \ldots, R_m$ are conjunctions of atoms not containing any occurrences of a or any atom defined (even indirectly) in terms of a. We introduce the data type $comp_a$ associated with the atom a, consisting of n constant symbols $b_1, \ldots, b_n$ and m functors $c_1, \ldots, c_m$ of arity $k_i, 1 \leq i \leq m$, where b_j and c_i are new symbols. We extend the predicate $a(x)$ to the associated predicate $a'(x^a, x)$ defined by the program $P' \cup P$ where P' is

a'(b_1,x) :- B_1(x).

. . .

a'(b_n,x) :- B_n(x).

a'(c_1($x^a_1, \ldots, x^a_{k_1}$),x) :- a'(x^a_1,x_1) , ..., a'($x^a_{k_1}$,x_{k_1}) ,
$\qquad\qquad$ R_1(x,x_1, ..., x_{k_1}).

. . .

a'(c_m($x^a_1, \ldots, x^a_{k_m}$),x) :- a'(x^a_1,x_1) , ..., a'($x^a_{k_m}$,x_{k_m}),
$\qquad\qquad$ R_m(x,x_1, ..., x_{k_m}).

It is clear that for any x, $a(x)$ is true in the least Herbrand model of P iff $a'(x^a, x)$ is true for some x^a in the least Herbrand model of $P' \cup P$. Thus, any goal $G : G^+(x) \Leftarrow G^-(x) \wedge a(x)$ is true in the least Herbrand model of P iff the goal $G' : G^+(x) \Leftarrow G^-(x) \wedge a'(x^a, x)$ is true in the least Herbrand model of $P' \cup P$. This is a generalisation of the program transformation process described in [E&McA 88]. A proof by Structural Induction w.r.t. the variable x^a will be identical to a proof by induction w.r.t. the depth of recursion. In particular, NFI-driven Induction w.r.t. x^a will generate goals and io-programs that are equivalent to those generated by Computation Induction.

Example 6.1: Consider the goal $G : odd(succ(x)) \Leftarrow even(x)$ in example 5.1. The atoms $even(x)$ and $odd(x)$ are defined by the program P

odd(succ(0)).
odd(succ(succ(x))) :- odd(x).
even(0).
even(succ(succ(x))) :- even(x).

The extended program becomes $P' \cup P$ where P' defines the predicate $even'$
(x^{even}, x)

even'(b,0).
even'(c(x^{even}),succ(succ(x))) :- even'(x^{even},x).

Consider the goal G'

$\qquad$ G': odd(succ(x)) $\Leftarrow$ even'(x^{even},x).

NFI-driven Induction w.r.t. x^{even} yields the new goals

H1:   odd(succ(x)) $\Leftarrow$ even'(b,x).
H2:   even'(x^{even},?x_0) $\Leftarrow$ even'(c(x^{even}),x).
H3:   odd(succ(x)) $\Leftarrow$ odd(succ(x_0)) $\wedge$ io$_{H2}$(x^{even},x,x_0).

The goal $H1$ is easily proved by NFI followed by DCI. NFI applied to $H2$ by $\{succ(succ(x_1))/x\}$ yields

I2:   even'(x^{even},?x_0) $\Leftarrow$ even'(x^{even},x_1).

Simplification by $\{x_1/x_0\}$ yields the trivial goal. The io-program that defines the associated io-atom $io_{H2}(x^{even}, x, x_0)$ is

io$_{H2}$(x^{even},succ(succ(x_1)),x_1).

NFI applied to $H3$ w.r.t. to the atom IO_{H2} by $\{succ(succ(x_1))/x,\ x_1/x_0\}$ yields

I3:   odd(succ(succ(succ(x_1)))) $\Leftarrow$ odd(succ(x_1)).

DCI followed by simplification yields the trivial goal.

We see that by extending the predicate with a recursion variable, NFI-driven Induction subsumes Computation Induction.

7   Final Remarks

We have introduced the rule of NFI-driven Induction, a new method for inductive reasoning that merges the principles of Structural Induction and Computation Induction by assuming that the recursion is made w.r.t. the structure of the data. NFI-driven Induction is a generalization of the rule of Restricted Structural Induction, and we have noted that by extending the recursively defined predicates with a recursion variable NFI-driven Induction subsumes Computation Induction.

Implicative goals that contain two (or more) atoms in the hypothesis are generally hard to prove by induction without the use of lemmas. This remains true with NFI-driven Induction. The difficulty is there to make the assumption of structural recursion true for such goals. There are some simple cases where this can be done: The proof of goal $H2$ in example 5.1 succeeds because the two atoms of the hypothesis are defined according to two independent recursion schemes. The proof of goal $J6$ in appendix B succeeds as well because the two atoms of the hypothesis are defined according to the same recursion scheme. But in general the recursive definitions of the atoms interfere in a nontrivial way, and we have either to discover a nontrivial scheme of induction or to make use of lemmas. For example $(x*y)*z = (x*z)*y$, "right commutativity of times" [Fri 91], expressed as the goal $G : *(x, y, u) \wedge *(u, z, w) \Leftarrow *(x, z, v) \wedge *(v, y, w)$ is not provable by NFI-driven Induction. We should not expect to find a general solution to this problem, but NFI-driven Induction may perhaps be refined to deal with commonly appearing simple cases: e.g., the assumption of structural recursion is always provable when the predicates are compatible for composition or tupling [Bou 91].

Appendix A: Proof of Correctness

Consider the goal G in the definition of NFI-driven Induction, (definition 3.1). The io-atom $IO_G(x, Z, Y)$ associated with the goal G is defined by

$$IO_G(0,Z,Y) :\text{-} IO_{H1}(Z,Y).$$
$$IO_G(succ(w),Z,Y) :\text{-} IO_{H2}(w,Z,Z'') , IO_G(w,Z'',Y') ,$$
$$IO_{H3}(w,Z,Y',Z'',Y).$$

Theorem 1: The io-procedure associated with the rule of NFI-driven Induction preserves partial correctness and termination.
Proof of partial correctness: We have to show that if

(Corr1): $\forall Z,Y \ G^+(0,Z,Y) \Leftarrow G^-(0,Z) \wedge IO_{H1}(Z,Y)$

(Corr2): $\forall x,Z \ Z' \ G^-(x,Z') \Leftarrow G^-(succ(x),Z) \wedge IO_{H2}(x,Z,Z')$

(Corr3): $\forall x,Y,Y' \ Z \ Z'' \ G^+(succ(x),Z'',Y) \Leftarrow G^+(x,Z'',Y')$
$\wedge IO_{H2}(x,Z,Z'') \wedge IO_{H3}(x,Z,Y',Z'',Y)$

hold, then

(Corrx): $\forall x,Y,Z \ G^+(x,Z,Y) \Leftarrow G^-(x,Z) \wedge IO_G(x,Z,Y)$

holds. Suppose $(Corr1)$, $(Corr2)$ and $(Corr3)$ hold. We prove $(Corrx)$ by induction w.r.t. x.

Base case ($x = 0$). Assume $G^-(0, Z)$ and $IO_G(0, Z, Y)$. By the only-if part of the io-procedure $IO_G(0, Z, Y)$ yields $IO_{H1}(Z, Y)$, which together with $(Corr1)$ yields $G^+(0, Z, Y)$. So the base case holds.

Induction step ($x = succ(w)$). Assume

(ind. hyp.): $\forall Z,Y \ G^+(w,Z,Y) \Leftarrow G^-(w,Z) \wedge IO_G(w,Z,Y)$

Suppose $G^-(succ(w), Z)$ and $IO_G(succ(w), Z, Y)$ hold. By the only-if part of the io-procedure, $IO_G(succ(w), Z, Y)$ gives us $IO_G(w, Z'', Y')$, $IO_{H2}(w, Z, Z'')$ and $IO_{H3}(w, Z, Y', Z'', Y)$, for some Y' and Z''. By $(Corr2)$, $G^-(succ(w), Z)$ and $IO_{H2}(w, Z, Z'')$ we get $G^-(w, Z'')$. Now, by the induction hypothesis, $G^-(w, Z'')$ and $IO_G(w, Z'', Y')$ give us $G^+(w, Z'', Y')$. And finally, $(Corr3)$, $G^+(w, Z'', Y')$, $IO_{H2}(w, Z, Z'')$ and $IO_{H3}(w, Z, Y', Z'', Y)$ yield $G^+(succ(w), Z'', Y)$. This concludes the proof of partial correctness.
Proof of termination: We have to show that if

(Term1): $\forall Z \ \exists Y \ IO_{H1}(Z,Y) \Leftarrow G^-(0,Z)$

(Term2): $\forall x,Z \ \exists Z' \ IO_{H2}(x,Z,Z') \Leftarrow G^-(succ(x),Z)$

(Term3): $\forall x,Y' \ Z,Z'' \ \exists Y \ IO_{H3}(x,Z,Y',Z'',Y) \Leftarrow G^+(x,Z'',Y')\wedge$
$IO_{H2}(x,Z,Z'')$

hold, then

(Termx): $\forall x,Z \ \exists Y \ IO_G(x,Z,Y) \Leftarrow G^-(x,Z)$

holds. Suppose $(Term1)$, $(Term2)$ and $(Term3)$ holds. We prove $(Termx)$ by induction w.r.t. x.

Base case ($x = 0$). Assume $G^-(0, Z)$. By $(Term1)$ $IO_{H1}(Z, Y)$ holds for some Y. By the io-procedure we get $IO_G(0, Z, Y)$, so the base case holds.

Induction step ($x = succ(w)$). Assume

(ind. hyp.): $\forall Z \exists Y \, IO_G(w,Z,Y) \Leftarrow G^-(w,Z)$

Suppose $G^-(succ(w), Z)$ holds. By $(Term2)$ we get $IO_{H2}(w, Z, Z')$ for some Z'. $G^-(succ(w), Z)$, $IO_{H2}(w, Z, Z')$ and $(Corr2)$ yield $G^-(w, Z')$ which by the induction hypothesis gives us $IO_G(w, Z', Y)$ for some Y. From $(Corrx)$, $IO_G(w, Z', Y)$ and $G^-(w, Z')$ we get $G^+(w, Z', Y)$. Now $IO_{H2}(p, w, Z, Z')$, $G^+(w, Z', Y)$ and $(Term3)$ give us, for some Y', $IO_{H3}(w, Z, Y, Z', Y')$. Then finally by the io-procedure we have $IO_G(succ(w), Z, Y')$. This concludes the proof of termination.

Appendix B: Commutativity of Times

Let the predicates $*(x, y, z)$ and $+(x, y, z)$ be defined by the program

```
+(0,y,y).
+(succ(x),y,succ(z)) :- +(x,y,z).
*(0,y,0).
*(succ(x),y,z) :- *(x,y,w) , +(y,w,z).
```

Consider the goal G expressing the commutativity of times

G: $*(x,y,z) \Leftarrow *(y,x,z).$

NFI-driven Induction w.r.t. y yields

H1: $*(x,0,z) \Leftarrow *(0,x,z).$
H2: $*(y,?x_0,?z_0) \Leftarrow *(succ(y),x,z).$
H3: $*(x,succ(y),z) \Leftarrow *(x_0,y,z_0) \wedge io_{H2}(y,x,z,x_0,z_0).$

By some applications of NFI and Simplification these three goals yield the two new goals

I1: $*(x,0,0).$
I3: $*(x,succ(y),z) \Leftarrow *(x,y,w_0) \wedge +(x,w_0,z).$

NFI-driven Induction applied to $I1$ yields the new goals

J1: $*(0,0,0).$
J4: $*(succ(x),0,0) \Leftarrow *(x,0,0).$

which are easily proved. NFI-driven Induction w.r.t. x applied to $I3$ yields

J5: $*(0,succ(y),z) \Leftarrow *(0,y,w_0) \wedge +(0,w_0,z).$
J6: $*(x,?y_1,?w_1) \wedge +(x,?w_1,?z_1) \Leftarrow *(succ(x),y,w_0) \wedge$
$\qquad\qquad\qquad\qquad\qquad\qquad\qquad +(succ(x),w_0,z).$
J7: $*(succ(x),succ(y),z) \Leftarrow *(x,succ(y_1),z_1) \wedge$
$\qquad\qquad\qquad\qquad\qquad\quad io_{J6}(x,y,z,w_0,y_1,z_1,w_1).$

$J5$ is proved by two applications of NFI and one application of DCI. Now, the assumption $J6$ will have to be proved by induction and this will reappear in the proof of the goal $J7$, so let us look at this part of the proof in more detail. Two applications of NFI applied to the goal $J6$ by $\{succ(z_2)/z\}$ yields

K6: $*(x,?y_1,?w_1) \wedge +(x,?w_1,?z_1) \Leftarrow *(x,y,w_2) \wedge +(y,w_2,w_0)\wedge$
$$+(x,w_0,z_2).$$

Simplification by $\{y/y_1, w_2/w_1\}$ yields

L6: $+(x,w_2,?z_1) \Leftarrow +(y,w_2,w_0) \wedge +(x,w_0,z_2).$

NFI-driven induction w.r.t. x yields

M8: $+(0,w_2,?z_1) \Leftarrow +(y,w_2,w_0) \wedge +(0,w_0,z_2).$
M9: $+(?y_3,?w_3,?w_4) \wedge +(x,?w_4,?z_3) \Leftarrow +(y,w_2,w_0) \wedge$
$$+(succ(x),w_0,z_2).$$
M10: $+(succ(x),w_2,?z_1) \Leftarrow +(x,w_3,z_4) \wedge$
$$io_{M9}(x,y,z_2,w_0,w_2,w_3,w_4,z_3).$$

DCI on $M8$ yields the trivial goal. NFI on $M9$ by $\{succ(z_5)/z_2\}$ yields

N9: $+(?y_3,?w_3,?w_4) \wedge +(x,?w_4,?z_3) \Leftarrow +(y,w_2,w_0) \wedge +(x,w_0,z_5).$

Two applications of Simplification by $\{y/y_3, w_2/w_3, w_0/w_4, z_5/z_3\}$ will yield the trivial goal. Three applications of NFI on $M10$ w.r.t. the atom IO_{M9} yield the goal

N10: $+(succ(x),w_2,?z_1) \Leftarrow +(x,w_2,z_4).$

Applying DCI by $\{succ(z_6)/z_1\}$ and Simplification by $\{z_4/z_6\}$ we get the trivial goal. The atom $io_{J6}(x, y, z, w_0, y_1, z_1, w_1)$ is defined by

$io_{J6}(x,y,succ(z_2),w_0,y,z_1,w_2)$:- $io_{L6}(x,w_0,w_2,y,z_2,z_1).$
$io_{L6}(0,w_0,w_2,y,w_0,w_2)$:- $+(y,w_2,w_0).$
$io_{L6}(succ(x),w_0,w_2,y,succ(z_5),succ(z_4))$:- $io_{L6}(x,w_0,w_2,y,z_5,z_4).$

Consider the goal $J7$. NFI by $\{succ(z_2)/z\}$ yields

K7: $*(succ(x),succ(y),succ(z_2)) \Leftarrow *(x,succ(y),z_1) \wedge$
$$io_{L6}(x,w_0,w_2,y,z_2,z_1).$$

Two applications of DCI followed by Simplification yield

L7: $+(y,z_1,z_2) \Leftarrow io_{L6}(x,w_0,w_2,y,z_2,z_1).$

Now we apply NFI-driven Induction w.r.t. x

M11: $+(y,z_1,z_2) \Leftarrow io_{L6}(0,w_0,w_2,y,z_2,z_1).$
M12: $io_{L6}(x,?w_7,?w_8,?y_7,?z_8,?z_7) \Leftarrow io_{L6}(succ(x),w_0,w_2,y,z_2,z_1).$
M13: $+(y,z_1,z_2) \Leftarrow +(y_7,z_7,z_8) \wedge io_{M12}(x,w_0,w_2,y,z_1,z_2,w_7,w_8,y_7,z_7,z_8).$

NFI on $M11$ yields

N11: $+(y,z_1,z_2) \Leftarrow +(y,z_1,z_2).$

Simplification yields the trivial goal. NFI applied to $M12$ by $\{succ(z_5)/z_2,$ $succ(z_4)/z_1\}$ yields

N12: $io_{L6}(x,?w_7,?w_8,?y_7,?z_8,?z_7) \Leftarrow io_{L6}(x,w_0,w_2,y,z_5,z_4).$

Simplification by $\{w_0/w_7, w_2/w_8, y/y_7, z_4/z_7, z_5/z_8\}$ will result in the trivial goal. Now, NFI on $M13$ w.r.t. IO_{M12} yields

N13: $+(y,succ(z_4),succ(z_5)) \Leftarrow +(y,z_4,z_5).$

N13 is easily proved by one application of NFI-driven Induction (see example 3.1).

References

[Bou 91]   Bouverot A., *Extracting and Transforming Logic Programs*. Technical Report LIENS-91-4, Laboratoire d'Informatique de l'Ecole Normale Supérieure, Paris, 1991.

[Bur 69]   Burstall R. M., *Proving Properties of Programs by Structural Induction*. Comput. J., vol. 12, February 1969, pp. 41-48.

[Cla 78]   Clark K. L., *Negation As Failure*. In Logic and Databases, H. Gallaire and J. Minker (Eds.), Plenum Press, New York, 1978, pp. 293-322.

[Cla 79]   Clark K. L., *Predicate Logic as a Computational Formalism*. Research Monograph 79/59, TOC, Imperial College, 1979.

[E&McA 88] Elkan C. and McAllester D., *Automated Inductive Reasoning about Logic Programs*. Proc. 5th Intl. Conf. and Symp. on Logic Programming, Seatle, 1988, pp. 876-892.

[Fri 90]   Fribourg L., *Extracting Logic Programs from Proofs that use Extended Prolog Execution and Induction*. Proc. 7th Intl. Conf. on Logic Programming, Jerusalem, 1990, pp. 685-699.

[Fri 91]   Fribourg L., *Automatic Generation of Simplification Lemmas for Inductive Proofs*. Proc. Intl. Symp. on Logic Programming, San Diego, 1991, pp. 103-116.

[K&S 86]   Kanamori T. and Seki H., *Verification of Prolog Programs Using an Extension of Execution*. In (Shapiro E., ed.) 3rd International Conference on Logic Programming, Lecture Notes in Computer Science 225, 1986, pp. 475-489.

[M&V 72]   Manna Z. and Vuillemin J., *Fixpoint Approach to the Theory of Computation*. Commun. Ass. Comput. Mach., vol. 15, no. 7, 1972, pp. 528-536

[R&Y 76]   Reynolds C. and Yeh R. T., *Induction as the Basis for Program Verification*. In IEEE Transactions on Software Enginering, vol. SE-2, no. 4, December 1976.

[Rog 67]   Rogers H.R., *Theory of Recursive Functions and Effective Computability*. N.Y., McGraw-Hill. th IEEE Symp. on Logic Programming, San Fransisco, 1967, pp. 215-223.

Proof Nets.

Mario Ornaghi
Dipartimento di Scienze dell'Informazione
Via Comelico 39/41
MILANO (Italy)

Abstract.

Constructive logic has been proposed as a frame to formalize program synthesis according to the paradigm "constructive proofs = programs". To obtain a *natural interpretation* of proofs as programs, adequate representations of proofs are required. In this paper we propose to represent proofs by a kind of Predicate Transition Petri Nets. Net representation gives rise to an immediate reading of the computational aspects of proofs and allows to treat various logics in an uniform way.

1. Introduction

Constructive logic has been proposed by many authors as a frame to model program synthesis (e.g. [Nep, BaC, Nuprl, Goad, Gir, Hy, Nor, MO]). The idea is that a *logical formula* represents a *program specification* and a *constructive proof* implicitly represents a *correct program*. The problem is to extract this program from the proof. A way to solve this problem is to *directly interpret proofs as programs*.

The possibility of interpreting *proofs as programs* depends both on the kind of logic and on the formalism to represent proofs. Here we propose a formalism where proofs are represented by a kind of Petri Nets, we call proof-nets. Proof-nets have an *immediate* computational meaning. Other kinds of proof nets have been proposed by [Gir, Nep].

The computational interpretation of proof-nets is based on Predicate-Transitions Petri Nets [PTN], with the following additional features. Data worked out by proof-nets are *evaluations* of formulas, where, intuitively, an evaluation of a formula is an "explanation of its truth". *Places* are labelled by *formulas* or by *terms,* and *transitions* by *rules*. A place labelled by a formula F may contain an evaluation of F, and a place labelled by a term T may contain a value of T. Rules state how transitions transform evaluations of their preset into evaluations of their postset. Computations are defined as in usual Predicate-Transition Nets.

Net systems, i.e. proof systems based on proof-nets, have the following characteristics. In a proof net, formulas labelling input places (i.e. without incoming arcs) represent *assumptions,* and formulas labelling output places (i.e. without outcoming arcs) represent *consequences*. To prove that B is a consequence of $A_1, .., A_n, ...,$ one has to build up a proof net with assumptions in $A_1, .., A_n, ...$ and consequence B. Proof nets are built up according to suitable *"logical rules"*, which are not inference rules of the usual kind, but rules defining the "geometry" of nets. Only an inference rule, called *procedure introduction,* is needed for implication and universal quantification.

In this paper we treat the computational aspects of proof-nets and the related correctness and validity aspects. We *don't treat completness problems*. We present different net systems. Each of them is characterized by some minimal properties of evaluations, needed to obtain *correct* proof-nets. We say that a set of evaluations satisfying these minimal properties is an *admissible evaluation space*. We use admissible evaluation spaces to state validity of net systems with respect to any logical or mathematical system for which there are suitable admissible evaluation spaces, and to put together different net systems.

In Section 2 we explain the computation model of *nets*. Then, in Section 3, we explain the general features of propositional net systems and we show how some well known constructive logical systems can be obtained. Most of the general characteristics of propositional net systems holds for predicate net systems, which are introduced in Section 4. Finally, in Section 5, we give a brief conclusion and discuss the application of net systems to program synthesis.

2. The Basic Computation Model

Here we present the computational features of our nets. They are Predicate/Transition Nets, with some modifications. We distinguish the *structure* of a net from its *interpretations*. Net structures are defined as follows.

Definition 1. A net-structure is a quadruple $<P, T, pre, post>$, where:
- P and T are disjoint sets. P is called the set of the *places* and T the set of the *transitions*;
- pre : $T \to 2^P$ is a function associating to every transition t its *preset* pre(t);
- post : $T \to 2^P$ is a function associating to every transition t its *postset* post(t);
- for every transition t, pre(t) $\cap$ post(t) = $\emptyset$.

We say that p is an *input place* of a net structure if, for every transition t, p $\notin$ post(t); p is an *output place* if, for every transition t, p $\notin$ pre(t)

Interpretations of net structures are based on markings (see e.g. [PTN]). In proof nets, there are different types of marks and every place p has an associated set D_p of admitted marks. Markings are defined as follows.

Let $N = <P, T, pre, post>$ be a net structure and $D = \{D_p / p \in P\}$ be a P indexed family of sets. For every $Q \subseteq P$, a D-*based marking* of Q is any function m defined on Q such that, for every $q \in Q$, m(q) is a finite (possibly empty) subset of D_q; the domain Q of m will be indicated by dom(m)

We have the following partial ordering on markings

$n \subseteq m$ iff dom(n) $\subseteq$ dom(m) and, for every p $\in$ dom(n), n(p) $\subseteq$ m(p) ;

we can define:

$\perp$ =$_{def}$ the least element (dom($\perp$) = $\emptyset$) ;
$\emptyset$ =$_{def}$ the empty marking (dom($\emptyset$)=P and $\emptyset$(p)=$\emptyset$, for every place p);
$m \cap n$ =$_{def}$ the greatest m' such that m' $\subseteq$ m and m' $\subseteq$ n ;
$m \cup n$ =$_{def}$ the least m' such that m $\subseteq$ m' and n $\subseteq$ m' ;
m|P =$_{def}$ the restriction of m on P ;
$m - n$ =$_{def}$ the marking m' with dom(m')=dom(m), such that: m'(p) = m(p)-n(p)
    if p $\in$ dom(m) $\cap$ dom(n) and m'(p) = m(p) otherwise

By $\mathbb{M}(\mathcal{P},D)$ we indicate the set of D-based markings with domain $\mathcal{P}$. Interpreted nets are defined as follows.

Definition 2. A net is a triple $\mathcal{N} = <N, \mathfrak{I}, D>$, where $N=<\mathbb{P}, T, \text{pre, post}>$ is a net structure, D is a $\mathbb{P}$-indexed family of sets and $\mathfrak{I}$ is the interpretation of T. $\mathfrak{I}$ associates to every transition t a relation $\mathfrak{I}(t) \subseteq \mathbb{M}(\text{pre}(t),D) \times \mathbb{M}(\text{post}(t),D)$, called the *relation computed by* t. $\mathcal{N}$ will be called an *interpretation* of N.

Let $\mathcal{N} = <N, \mathfrak{I}, D>$ be an interpretation of $N=<\mathbb{P}, T, \text{pre, post}>$. A *marking of* $\mathcal{N}$ is any marking $m \in \mathbb{M}(\mathbb{P},D)$. Transitions transform markings of $\mathcal{N}$ into markings of $\mathcal{N}$, according to the following definition.

Definition 3. Let $\mathcal{N} = <N, \mathfrak{I}, D>$ be a net. Each transition t computes the binary relation [t> on markings of $\mathcal{N}$ so defined.
  For every $m, m' \in \mathbb{M}(\mathbb{P},D)$, m [t> m' iff:
  a) $m|\text{post}(t) = \emptyset|\text{post}(t)$
  b) there is $< m_{in}, m_{out} > \in \mathfrak{I}(t)$ such that $m_{in} \subseteq m$
  c) $m' = (m - m_{in}) \cup m_{out}$.

In the following, we say that a transition t is *enabled* by m if a), b) of Definition 3 hold, and that m' is the result of the *firing* of t. We define computations as follows.
  By $m > m'$ we indicate that there is a transition t such that m [t> m'. We call $m > m'$ a *computation step*. An *execution sequence* is a sequence $m_0 > m_1 >...> m_k$ of computation steps.
  An *input marking* is any marking m such that $m(p) \neq \emptyset$ for every input place p and $m(q) = \emptyset$ for every other place q. An *output marking* is any marking n such that $n(u) \neq \emptyset$, for at least an output place u.
  A *computation* is an execution sequence $m_0 > m_1 >...> m_k$, where m_0 is an input marking and m_k is an output marking.
  In the following, we will use only interpretations such that, for every transition t,

$$\mathfrak{I}(t) \subseteq \mathbb{M}_1(\text{pre}(t),D) \times \mathbb{M}_1(\text{post}(t),D)$$

where $\mathbb{M}_1(\mathcal{P},D)$ indicates the set of the D-based markings m with domain $\mathcal{P}$ such that, for every $p \in \mathcal{P}$, $m(\mathcal{P})$ has cardinality 1. With this kind of interpretations, every computation, starting from an input marking assigning one mark to the input places, will reach only markings where each place is empty or contains one mark.

3. Propositional Net Systems

3.1 General Aspects

A propositional *net system* is a propositional system where proofs are represented by suitable *labelled* net structures, we call *proof nets*.

In a proof net N, places are labelled by formulas and transitions by "logical rules". By t:R we indicate a transition t labelled by a logical rule R, and by p:F we indicate a place p labelled by a formula F. If p:F is an input place of N, we call F an *assumption* of N; if p:F is an output place of N, we call F a *consequence* of N.

The logical rules of a net system $\mathfrak{N}$ state the set of the *labelled net structures of* $\mathfrak{N}$, as follows. Every rule R has an associated family of pre and post sets:

$$\text{PrePost}(R) \subseteq \{ <\mathcal{P}, \mathcal{Q}> / \mathcal{P}, \mathcal{Q} \text{ are sets of labelled places} \}$$

The *net structures of* $\mathfrak{N}$ are the <u>finite acyclic</u> labelled net structures N such that, for every transition t:R of N, $<\text{pre}(t:R), \text{post}(t:R)> \in \text{PrePost}(R)$.

Example 1. The logical rule $\wedge i$ ($\wedge$-introduction) is so defined:

$$\text{PrePost}(\wedge i) = \{ \langle \{p:A, q:B\}, \{r:A\wedge B\} \rangle / p,q,r \text{ are places and } A,B \text{ formulas} \}$$

Hence a possible net structure using $\wedge i$-transitions is:

$N1 = < \{0:A, 1:B, 2:C, 3:A\wedge B, 4:C\wedge(A\wedge B)\}, \{t1:\wedge i, t2:\wedge i\}, \text{pre, post}>$ with
$\text{pre}(t1:\wedge i) = \{0:A, 1:B\}$ and $\text{post}(t1:\wedge i) = \{3:A\wedge B\}$,
$\text{pre}(t2:\wedge i) = \{2:C, 3:A\wedge B\}$ and $\text{post}(t2:\wedge i) = \{4:C\wedge(A\wedge B)\}$.

N1 can be drawn as in FIG.1. The assumptions of N1 are A, B, C; there is one conclusion, namely $C\wedge(A\wedge B)$.

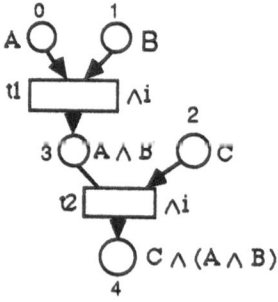

FIG. 1.

Now we introduce the interpretations of our net structures. First of all, every net sysyem $\mathfrak{N}$ has an associated class $\mathcal{A}_\mathfrak{N}$ of *admissible evaluation spaces*, and every evaluation space $\pounds \in \mathcal{A}_\mathfrak{N}$ assigns to every formula F a set $\pounds(F)$ of *possible evaluations* and a (possibly empty) set $\mathcal{V}(F) \subseteq \pounds(F)$ of *valid evaluations*

Hence, for every set $\mathcal{P}$ of labelled places, we have a corresponding $\mathcal{P}$-indexed family of sets, defined by:

$D_{\mathcal{E}}(\mathcal{P}) =_{def} \{ D_{p:L} \ / \ p:L \in \mathcal{P} \text{ and } D_{p:L} = \mathcal{E}(L) \}$

An $\mathcal{E}$-*marking* (with domain $\mathcal{P}$) is any marking based on $D_{\mathcal{E}}(\mathcal{P})$. We say that an $\mathcal{E}$-marking m is *valid in* $\mathcal{E}$ iff, for every $p:F$ and ϕ, $m(p:F) = \{\phi\}$ implies that ϕ is a valid evaluation of F.

Every rule R is interpreted in $\mathcal{E}$ by a family of relations $R_{\mathcal{E}}$. For every $<\mathcal{P},\mathcal{Q}> \in \text{PrePost}(R)$, $R_{\mathcal{E}}$ contains a relation $R_{\mathcal{E}}(\mathcal{P},\mathcal{Q})$ such that:

$R_{\mathcal{E}}(\mathcal{P},\mathcal{Q}) \subseteq M_1(\mathcal{P}, D_{\mathcal{E}}(\mathcal{P})) \times M_1(\mathcal{Q}, D_{\mathcal{E}}(\mathcal{Q}))$

We require that the interpretation of rules is *valid* in $\mathcal{E}$, i.e. that, for every $<m,n> \in R_{\mathcal{E}}(\mathcal{P},\mathcal{Q})$, if m is a valid $\mathcal{E}$-marking, then n is valid too.

Starting from the interpretation of rules, we can interpret every labelled net structure $N = <\mathcal{P}, T, \text{pre}, \text{post}>$ by the net $N_{\mathcal{E}} = <N, \mathcal{I}_{\mathcal{E}}, D_{\mathcal{E}}>$ such that $D_{\mathcal{E}} = D_{\mathcal{E}}(\mathbb{P})$, and $\mathcal{I}_{\mathcal{E}}(t:R) = R_{\mathcal{E}}(\text{pre}(t:R), \text{post}(t:R))$, for every $t:R \in T$. We call $N_{\mathcal{E}}$ the $\mathcal{E}$-*interpretation* of N.

We say that N is *valid* in $\mathcal{E}$ iff, for every step $m > m'$ of $N_{\mathcal{E}}$, if m is valid in $\mathcal{E}$, then m' is valid in $\mathcal{E}$ (i.e., *validity of markings* is preserved). One easily sees that, if the interpretation of rules is valid in $\mathcal{E}$, then N is *valid* in $\mathcal{E}$.

Example 1 (continued)

The interpretation of the rule $\wedge i$ is given by the following interpretation scheme:

$\wedge i((\{p:A,q:B\},\{r:A\wedge B\})) = \{ \langle m,n \rangle \ / \ m(p:A)=\{\alpha\}, \ m(q:B)=\{\beta\}, \ n(r:A\wedge B)=\{P(\alpha,\beta)\} \}$

where P is a binary operation defined in every admissible evaluation space for the logical symbol $\wedge$. P takes an evaluation α of A and an evaluation β of B and builds up an evaluation $P(\alpha,\beta)$ of $A\wedge B$. $P(\alpha,\beta)$ is valid iff α and β are. Hence the interpretation scheme of $\wedge i$ is valid. It can be drawn as follows (where we inscribe in the rectangle the relation to be computed, and use the labels x, y, z to indicate the incoming and outcoming data).

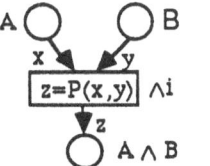

FIG. 2

By the above interpretation, a computation of the net N1 of FIG.1 is the sequence of steps $m_0 \ [t1:\wedge i> m_1 \ [t2:\wedge i> m_2$ such that:

$m_0(0:A) = \{\alpha\}$, $m_0(1:B) = \{\beta\}$, $m_0(2:C) = \{\chi\}$ (the other places are empty)
$m_1(3:A\wedge B) = \{P(\alpha, \beta)\}$, $m_1(2:C) = \{\chi\}$ (the other places are empty)
$m_2(4:C\wedge(A\wedge B)) = \{P(\chi,P(\alpha, \beta))\}$ (the other places are empty)

Now we discuss the *computational properties* of our nets. First of all, the following definition characterizes the input output relation computed by a net.

Definition 4. Let $\mathcal{E}$ be an admissible evaluation space and $\mathbb{N}$ be a net structure with assumptions $A_1,...,A_n$ and consequences $C_1,...,C_k$. We say that $\mathbb{N}_\mathcal{E}$ *computes an output evaluation* $\chi \in \mathcal{E}(C_h)$, *starting from the input evaluations* $\alpha_1 \in \mathcal{E}(A_1), ..., \alpha_n \in \mathcal{E}(A_n)$, iff there is a computation $m_0 > .... > m_k$ such that:
- m_0 is an input marking and $m_0(p:A_i) = \{\alpha_i\}$, for every input place $p:A_i$;
- m_k is an output marking and $m_k(q:C_h) = \{\chi\}$.

In the following, to indicate that $\mathbb{N}_\mathcal{E}$ computes $\chi \in \mathcal{E}(C_h)$ starting from $\alpha_1 \in \mathcal{E}(A_1), ..., \alpha_n \in \mathcal{E}(A_n)$, we will write:

$\chi:C_h \in \mathbb{N}_\mathcal{E}(\alpha_1:A_1,...,\alpha_n:A_n)$.

Since every net structure is locally valid in every admissible evaluation space $\mathcal{E}$, if $\alpha_1 \in \mathcal{E}(A_1), ..., \alpha_n \in \mathcal{E}(A_n)$ are valid, then $\chi \in \mathcal{E}(C_h)$ is valid. But it might be that no execution sequence $m_0 > .... > m_h$ reaches an output marking, i.e. that the set $\mathbb{N}_\mathcal{E}(\alpha_1:A_1,...,\alpha_n:A_n)$ is empty. Then we require the following reachability property.

Definition 5. A net structure $\mathbb{N}$ with assumptions $A_1,..., A_n$ is *reachable* in a class $\mathcal{A}$ of evaluation spaces iff, for every $\mathcal{E} \in \mathcal{A}$ and every $\alpha_1 \in \mathcal{E}(A_1), ..., \alpha_n \in \mathcal{E}(A_n)$, $\mathbb{N}_\mathcal{E}(\alpha_1:A_1,...,\alpha_n:A_n)$ is not empty.

Reachability implies the following correctness property.

Correctness Property. Let $\mathbb{N}$ be a net structure of a net system $\mathfrak{N}$, with assumptions $A_1, ..., A_n$ and consequences $C_1, ..., C_m$. If $\mathbb{N}$ is *reachable* in $\mathcal{A}_\mathfrak{N}$, then, for every $\mathcal{E} \in \mathcal{A}_\mathfrak{N}$ and every valid $\alpha_1 \in \mathcal{E}(A_1), ..., \alpha_n \in \mathcal{E}(A_n)$, the following properties hold:
(CP1) $\mathbb{N}_\mathcal{E}(\alpha_1:A_1,...,\alpha_n:A_n)$ is not empty;
(CP2) every $\chi:C_j \in \mathbb{N}_\mathcal{E}(\alpha_1:A_1,..., \alpha_n:A_n)$ is a valid evaluation of C_j.

Correctness Property shows that we can interpret a reachable net as a computational device transforming input evaluations into output evaluations. Validity of evaluations is preserved, because the interpretation of the rules of a net system must be *valid*. Correctness allows to treat the validity aspects of net systems, considered as a proof systems, as we briefly explain in next subsection.

3.2. Net Systems as Proof Systems.

We define the *proof nets* and the *provability relation* of a net system $\mathfrak{N}$, with class $\mathcal{A}_\mathfrak{N}$ of admissible evaluation spaces, as follows.

The *proof nets* of $\mathfrak{N}$ are the net structures of $\mathfrak{N}$ which are reachable in $\mathcal{A}_\mathfrak{N}$, and a formula C is a *consequence* of a set of formulas $\mathcal{C}$ in $\mathfrak{N}$, written:

$\mathcal{C} \vdash_\mathfrak{N} C$

iff there is a proof net of $\mathfrak{N}$ with assumptions contained in $\mathcal{C}$ and consequence C.

We remark that "logical rules" of a net system don't work as usual inference rules. They only state the admitted labels of pre and post sets, and reachability is required for proof nets. The only connective for which we need a kind of inference rule is constructive implication, as we will explain in Section 3.5.

Of course, we are interested in net systems with a *decidable set of proof nets* (in a formal system the set of the formal proofs should be decidable). This means that reachability should be a decidable property. In this paper we will present propositional net systems $\mathcal{N}$ where reachability in $\mathcal{A}_\mathcal{N}$ holds iff it holds in a suitable *reachability space,* and reachability in the reachability space is decidable.

Correctness Property gives our interpretation of proof nets as programs. Moreover, it allows to compare any net system $\mathcal{N}$ with other propositional systems, such as, e.g., minimal or intuitionistic logic, in the following way.

Let $\mathcal{S}$ be any propositional system; we say that $\mathcal{S}$ *is valid in a class of evaluation spaces* $\mathcal{A}_\mathcal{S}$ iff the following Validity Property holds:

(VP)   If there is a relation among evaluations of $A_1, ..., A_n$ and evaluations of C satisfying (CP1) and (CP2) (see Correctness Property) for every $\mathcal{E} \in \mathcal{A}_\mathcal{S}$, then $\{A_1, ..., A_n\} \vdash_\mathcal{S} C$".

If there is an $\mathcal{A}_\mathcal{S} \subseteq \mathcal{A}_\mathcal{N}$, such that $\mathcal{S}$ is valid in $\mathcal{A}_\mathcal{S}$, then $\mathcal{C} \vdash_\mathcal{N} C$ implies $\mathcal{C} \vdash_\mathcal{S} C$; indeed, if $\mathcal{C} \vdash_\mathcal{N} C$, then there is a proof net computing the relation required by (VP). We say that $\mathcal{N}$ is *valid with respect to* $\mathcal{S}$. Hence, a general method to state validity of net systems with respect to other formal systems $\mathcal{S}$ is to build up suitable classes $\mathcal{A}_\mathcal{S}$ of evaluation spaces, using formal proofs of $\mathcal{S}$ as evaluations.

3.3 The And-Or System $\mathcal{N}(\wedge, \vee)$

3.3.1 Properties of admissible evaluation spaces

Admissible evaluation spaces satisfy the following minimal properties.

(1) The set of the evaluations is closed under the operations P binary, C1 and C2 unary.
(2) If ξ is an evaluation of a formula $A \wedge B$, then we can compute α, β such that $\xi = P(\alpha, \beta)$. Moreover, for every α, β, $P(\alpha, \beta)$ is a valid evaluation of $A \wedge B$ iff α is a valid evaluation of A and β of B.
(3) If ξ is an evaluation of a formula $A \vee B$, then we can compute a η such that $\xi = C1(\eta)$ or $\xi = C2(\eta)$. Moreover, $C1(\eta)$ is a valid evaluation of $A \vee B$ iff η is a valid evaluation of A and $C2(\eta)$ is a valid evaluation of $A \vee B$ iff η is a valid evaluation of B.

3.3.2 Rules

and-introduction ($\wedge$i), *and-elimination* ($\wedge$e1, $\wedge$e2)

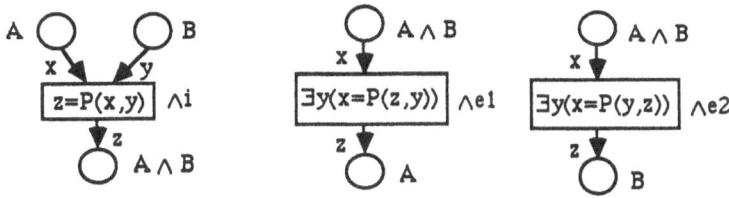

68

or-introduction ($\lor i1$, $\lor i2$), *or-elimination* ($\lor e1$, $\lor e2$)

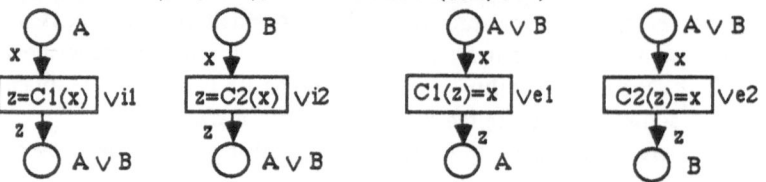

The above rules are valid, as one can easily prove.

3.3.3 The reachability space $\mathcal{R}_{\land\lor}$

Every formula F built up by $\land, \lor$ has a finite set $\mathcal{R}_{\land\lor}(F)$ of evaluations, so inductively defined:

$\mathcal{R}_{\land\lor}(F) = \{x\}$, if F is atomic (x stands for a generic evaluation);
$\mathcal{R}_{\land\lor}(A \land B) = \{ P(\alpha,\beta) \,/\, \alpha \in \mathcal{R}_{\land\lor}(A)$ and $\beta \in \mathcal{R}_{\land\lor}(B) \}$
$\mathcal{R}_{\land\lor}(A \lor B) = \{ C1(\alpha) \,/\, \alpha \in \mathcal{R}_{\land\lor}(A) \} \cup \{ C2(\beta) \,/\, \beta \in \mathcal{R}_{\land\lor}(B) \}$
One easily sees that a net structure N is reachable in every evaluation space of $\mathfrak{N}(\land, \lor)$ iff it is reachable in the reachability space $\mathcal{R}_{\land\lor}$.

Example 2

    (I) A proof net:
                                          (II) A non reachable net

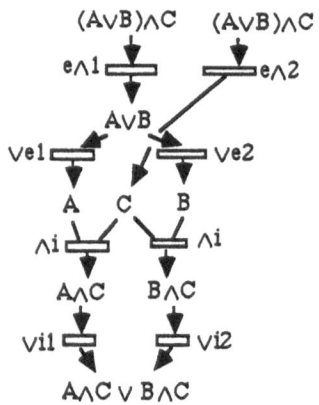

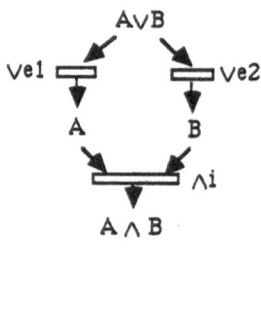

                                                                       FIG. 3

    In FIG.3, circles representing places are omitted for the sake of simplicity. The net structure (I) is a proof net, since it is reachable in $\mathcal{R}_{\land\lor}$. Indeed, $\mathcal{R}_{\land\lor}((A \lor B) \land C) =$ $\{P(C1(x),x), P(C2(x),x)\}$, and the following holds:
with the input marking assigning $P(C1(x),x)$ to the input places, the result $C1(P(x,x))$ is reached, and, with the input marking assigning $P(C2(x),x)$, the result $C2(P(x,x))$ is reached. The net structure (I) proves:

$$(A \lor B) \land C \,\vdash_{\mathfrak{N}(\land,\lor)} A \land C \lor B \land C.$$

The net structure (II) is not reachable.

3.4 The Strong Negation System $\mathcal{R}(\wedge, \vee, \neg)$.

3.4.1 Minimal properties of admissible evaluation spaces

(1') The set of the evaluations is closed under the operations P binary, C1, C2, N unary, and P, C1, C2 satisfy properties 2), 3) of $\mathcal{R}(\wedge, \vee)$.

(2') If ξ is an evaluation of $\neg(A \vee B)$, then we can compute α, β such that $\xi = P(\alpha, \beta)$. Moreover, for every α, β, $P(\alpha, \beta)$ is a valid evaluation of $\neg(A \vee B)$ iff α is a valid evaluation of $\neg A$ and β of $\neg B$.

(3') If ξ is an evaluation of $\neg(A \wedge B)$, then we can compute a η such that $\xi = C1(\eta)$ or $\xi = C2(\eta)$. Moreover, $C1(\eta)$ is a valid evaluation of $\neg(A \wedge B)$ iff η is a valid evaluation of $\neg A$ and $C2(\eta)$ is a valid evaluation of $\neg(A \wedge B)$ iff η is a valid evaluation of $\neg B$.

(4') If ξ is an evaluation of $\neg\neg A$, then we can compute a η such that $\xi = N(\eta)$. Moreover, $N(\eta)$ is a valid evaluation of $\neg\neg A$ iff η is a valid evaluation of A.

3.4.2 Rules

The rules are the ones of $\mathcal{R}(\wedge, \vee)$, and the following ones (which are valid, as one easily sees).

notor-introduction ($\neg\vee$i), notor-elimination ($\neg\vee$e1, $\neg\vee$e2)

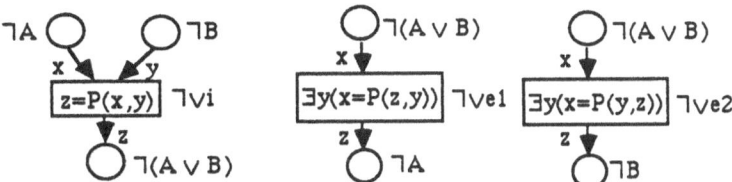

notand-introduction ($\neg\wedge$i1, $\neg\wedge$i2), notand elimination ($\neg\wedge$e1, $\neg\wedge$e2)

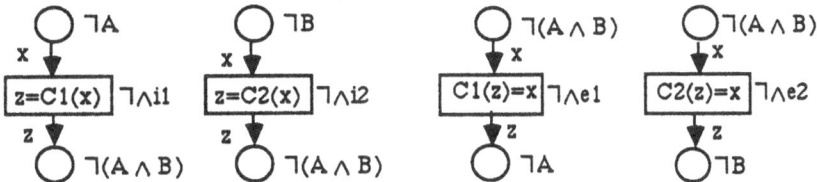

notnot-introduction ($\neg\neg$i), notnot-elimination ($\neg\neg$e)

3.4.3 Reachability space $\mathcal{R}_{\wedge\vee\neg}$

One has to add, to the clauses defining $\mathcal{R}_{\wedge\vee}$, the following ones:

$\mathcal{R}_{\wedge\vee\neg}(\neg(A \vee B)) = \{ P(\alpha, \beta) \ / \ \alpha \in \mathcal{R}_{\wedge\vee\neg}(\neg A) \text{ and } \beta \in \mathcal{R}_{\wedge\vee\neg}(\neg B) \}$

$\mathcal{R}_{\wedge\vee\neg}(\neg(A \wedge B)) = \{ C1(\alpha) \ / \ \alpha \in \mathcal{R}_{\wedge\vee\neg}(\neg A) \} \cup \{ C2(\beta) \ / \ \beta \in \mathcal{R}_{\wedge\vee\neg}(\neg B) \}$

$\mathcal{R}_{\wedge\vee\neg}(\neg\neg A) = \{ N(\alpha) \ / \ \alpha \in \mathcal{R}_{\wedge\vee\neg}(A) \}$

3.5. Net Systems containing Constructive Implication.

The interpretation of constructive implication is related to the notion of procedure. Hence, evaluations of formulas such as A→B are "input output relations" (from inputs of type A to outputs of type B), and we treat rules for implication as rules to call or create procedures.

Here we define three formal systems containing implication, indicated by $\mathfrak{N}(\rightarrow)$, $\mathfrak{N}(\wedge, \vee, \rightarrow)$ and $\mathfrak{N}(\wedge, \vee, \neg, \rightarrow)$.

3.5.1 Properties of admissible evaluation spaces.

For $\mathfrak{N}(\rightarrow)$ the minimal properties to be satisfied are:

1") An evaluation $\rho \in E(A \rightarrow B)$ is an input output relation $\rho \subseteq E(A) \times E(B)$; by $\beta \in \rho(\alpha)$ we indicate that $<\alpha,\beta> \in \rho$, i.e. that β is an output for the input α.
2") If ρ is a valid evaluation of A→B and α a valid evaluation of A, then $\rho(\alpha)$ is not empty and, for every $\beta \in \rho(\alpha,\beta)$, β is a valid evaluation of B.
3") The set of the evaluations is "closed under net realizability", as we will explain.

For $\mathfrak{N}(\wedge, \vee, \rightarrow)$, we add the properties of $\mathfrak{N}(\wedge, \vee)$.

For $\mathfrak{N}(\wedge, \vee, \neg, \rightarrow)$, we add the properties of $\mathfrak{N}(\wedge, \vee, \neg)$ and the further property:

4") for every evaluation ξ of $\neg(A \rightarrow B)$ we can compute an evaluation α of A and an evaluation β of $\neg B$ such that $\xi = P(\alpha,\beta)$. Moreover, ξ is a valid evaluation of $\neg(A \rightarrow B)$ iff α is a valid evaluation of A and β of $\neg B$.

3.5.2 Rules of $\mathfrak{N}(\rightarrow)$.

I) *procedure call*

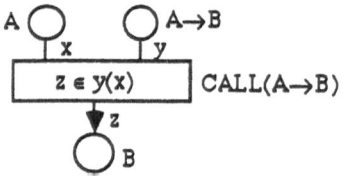

II) *procedure creation*

Let N be a proof net with assumptions $H_1, .., H_n$, A and consequence B; then PROC($H_1, .., H_n$, A→B, N) is a *procedure creation rule*. Its pre and post sets and its interpretation are defined according to the following scheme:

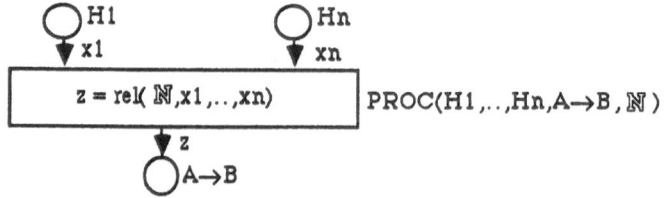

In the above scheme, for every evaluation space $\mathcal{E}$ and every $\eta_1 \in \mathcal{E}(H_1)$, ..., $\eta_n \in \mathcal{E}(H_n)$, $\text{rel}(N, \eta_1, .., \eta_n)$ indicates the evaluation $\rho \in \mathcal{E}(A \to B)$ so defined:

for every evaluation α of A, $\beta \in \rho(\alpha)$ iff $\beta:B \in \mathcal{N}_{\mathcal{E}}(\eta_1:H_1,...,\eta_n:H_n,\alpha:A)$

ρ is the evaluation assigned to the output place by the transition, when the inputs are $\eta_1, ..., \eta_n$.

Procedure creation transitions have no meaning if the considered evaluation space is not closed under net realizability, i.e. if $\text{rel}(N,\eta_1,..,\eta_n)$ is not an evaluation of $A \to B$. Closure under net realizability in admissible evaluation space $\mathcal{E}$ means that we can represent $\text{rel}(N,\eta_1,...,\eta_n)$ by a pair (N, p), where p is the *partial input marking* such that $p(p:H_i) = \{\eta_i\}$, for every input place $p:H_i$ of N with a label H_i different from A, and $p(q:A) = \emptyset$ for every input place of N with label A. (N, p) realizes an evaluation $\rho \in \mathcal{E}(A \to B)$ as follows: for every evaluation α of A, we complete p into an input marking and start a computation of $\mathcal{N}_{\mathcal{E}}$. The results are the evaluations of $\rho(\alpha)$.

To obtain a well founded introduction of procedure creation rules, one builds up "derivations" of the following kind:

$$\text{PROC}(\text{PRE}_0,C_0,N_0), \quad ..., \quad \text{PROC}(\text{PRE}_k,C_k,N_k), \quad N_{k+1}$$

where N_0 is a proof net *not containing procedure-creation transitions* and, for $0 < i \le k+1$, N_i is a proof net which may contain transitions $t:\text{PROC}(\text{PRE}_m,C_m,N_m)$, for some $m < i$. In this sense, procedure creation works as an inference rule.

The meaning of derivations could be explained by the following analogy. A rule $\text{PROC}(\text{PRE}_m,C_m,N_m)$ introduced in a derivation can be seen as a definition of a *class of procedures* (namely, the ones which can be obtained from the possible evaluations of the preset PRE_m). A procedure creation transition operates a dinamic creation of a procedure of the corresponding class, in a way similar to the operation "new" used in many object oriented languages. A call transition operates a call to a dinamically created procedure.

3.5.3 Rules of $\mathcal{N}(\wedge, \vee, \to)$.

The rules of $\mathcal{N}(\wedge, \vee, \to)$ are the ones of $\mathcal{N}(\wedge, \vee)$ and of $\mathcal{N}(\to)$.

3.5.4 Rules of $\mathcal{N}(\wedge, \vee, \neg, \to)$.

The rules of $\mathcal{N}(\wedge, \vee, \neg, \to)$ are the ones of $\mathcal{N}(\wedge, \vee, \neg)$, $\mathcal{N}(\to)$, and the following

notimp-rules.

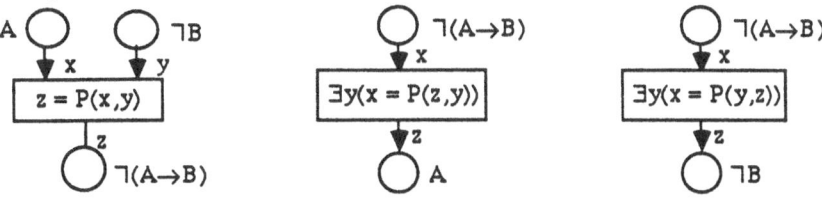

3.5.5 Reachability spaces

For $\mathfrak{n}(\rightarrow)$, $\mathcal{R}_\rightarrow(F) = \{x\}$, for every formula F. For $\mathfrak{n}(\wedge, \vee, \rightarrow)$, add $\mathcal{R}_{\wedge\vee\rightarrow}(A{\rightarrow}B) = \mathcal{R}_{\wedge\vee\rightarrow}(A) \times \mathcal{R}_{\wedge\vee\rightarrow}(B)$ to the clauses of $\mathcal{R}_{\wedge\vee}$. For $\mathfrak{n}(\wedge, \vee, \neg, \rightarrow)$, add $\mathcal{R}_{\wedge\vee\neg\rightarrow}(A{\rightarrow}B) = \mathcal{R}_{\wedge\vee\neg\rightarrow}(A) \times \mathcal{R}_{\wedge\vee\neg\rightarrow}(B)$ to the clauses of $\mathcal{R}_{\wedge\vee\neg}$.

3.6. Some Net Systems for Some Constructive Logics

We extend the propositional language by a constant $\wedge$, representing *absurdum*. We require that there is no valid evaluation of $\wedge$.

In this language, $\mathfrak{n}(\wedge, \vee, \rightarrow)$ is deductively equivalent to *minimal propositional logic* $\mathfrak{X}_{min}$ and $\mathfrak{n}(\wedge, \vee, \neg, \rightarrow)$ is equivalent to *minimal logic with strong negation* $\mathfrak{X}_{min\neg}$ (for strong negation see [Nel]).

If we add the further elementary nets of the form:

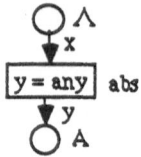

where "any" is any evaluation of A

we obtain $\mathfrak{n}(\wedge, \vee, \rightarrow, \wedge)$, equivalent to *intuitionistic propositional logic* $\mathfrak{X}_{int}$ and $\mathfrak{n}(\wedge, \vee, \neg, \rightarrow, \wedge)$, equivalent to *intuitionistic logic with strong negation* $\mathfrak{X}_{int\neg}$.

$\mathfrak{X}_{min}$, $\mathfrak{X}_{int}$, $\mathfrak{X}_{min\neg}$, $\mathfrak{X}_{int\neg}$ are valid in *suitable classes* of admissible evaluation spaces of the corresponding net systems, whence the corresponding net systems are valid (see Section 3.2). In such classes, evaluations are built up starting from formal proofs of any presentation of the inferential apparatus of the logic (e.g. in natural calculus). Completeness can be stated by showing that proofs of $\mathfrak{X}_{min}$, $\mathfrak{X}_{int}$, $\mathfrak{X}_{min\neg}$, $\mathfrak{X}_{int\neg}$ can be translated into proof nets of the corresponding net system.

4. Predicate Systems.

4.1. General Aspects.

Predicate proof nets are finite acyclic labelled net structures, where labels of places are formulas or terms, and labels of transitions are logical rules. The label of an input place may be a formula, called an *assumption*, or a variable, called an *input variable*. As for the propositional case, a *consequence* is a formula labelling some output place.

The set of the *net structures* of a predicate net system $\mathfrak{n}$ and the *interpretation* of the net structures of $\mathfrak{n}$ are defined by the rules of $\mathfrak{n}$, in the way explained for propositional net systems.

Validity aspects are treated in a different way, since the properties of predicate evaluation spaces are different and nets may contain places labelled by terms. We have the following points.

4.1.1. General properties of evaluation spaces

An evaluation space $\mathcal{E}$ for a first order language $\mathbb{L}$ is based on a class $\mathcal{L}$ of *individual evaluations*. To simplify notations, we consider "substitutions" of variables by "mixed terms", where a mixed term is a term of $\mathbb{L}$, or an individual evaluation, or a term where some variables have been substituted by individual evaluations. By S we indicate the substitution of a list of variables by a corresponding list of mixed terms. By F·S we indicate the application of the substitution S to a formula F. A substitution S of a list of variables by a list of *individual evaluations* will be called an *assignment*.

Admissible evaluation spaces must satisfy the following *General Properties* (GP):

- For every formula F and every assignment S of its free variables, there is a corresponding set of *possible evaluations* $\mathcal{E}(F·S)$ and a (possibly empty) set of *valid evaluations* $\mathcal{V}(F·S) \subseteq \mathcal{E}(F·S)$.
- For every n-ary function symbol f of the language $\mathbb{L}$, there is a corresponding function $F : \mathcal{L}^n \to \mathcal{L}$. Hence, for every term T of $\mathbb{L}$ and every assignment S substituting all the variables of T by individual evaluations, the value $val_{\mathcal{E}}(T, S)$ can be recursively defined in the usual way.
- Let T be a term of $\mathbb{L}$ and $\mathbb{W} = val_{\mathcal{E}}(T, S)$; α is a valid evaluation of A(T)·S iff it is a valid evaluation of A(y)·S[y/$\mathbb{W}$], where S[y/$\mathbb{W}$] assigns $\mathbb{W}$ to y and is identical to S for the other variables.

4.1.2 Validity

We say that a marking m is *consistent* with respect to an evaluation space $\mathcal{E}$ and an assignment S iff the following properties are satisfied:

a) for every place p:T labelled by a term, if $m(p:T) = \{\mathbb{W}\}$, then $\mathbb{W} = val_{\mathcal{E}}(T,S)$;
b) for every place p:F labelled by a formula, if $m(p:F) = \{\phi\}$, then $\phi \in \mathcal{E}(F·S)$.

If, in point b), ϕ is a valid evaluation of F·S, we say that m is *valid* (with respect to $\mathcal{E}$, S).

The interpretations $R_{\mathcal{E}}(\mathcal{P},\mathcal{Q})$ of a rule R are defined as in propositional case. For *validity*, we require that, for every $<m,n> \in R_{\mathcal{E}}(\mathcal{P},\mathcal{Q})$, consistency of m implies consistency of n and validity of m implies validity of n.

To introduce validity and correctness of computations, some preliminary definitions are needed, explaining the role of variables occurring in the labels of a net structure N.

If a variable x is the label of a place p:x of the postset of a transition t, this means that the firing of t assigns a value to x (i.e., a mark is placed in p:x). We say that x is *assigned (or bounded) in* N.

If x occurs free in the label of some place of N and is not assigned in N, we say that x is *free in* N

In a proof net N, the *input variables must be free in* N. At the beginning of a computation, the values of input variables are assigned by the input marking and may be used, but not modified. On the contrary, assigned variables assume a value during the computation, and this value may change.

Validity of predicate nets is different from the one of propositional nets, since assignments are involved. It is defined as follows.

We say that a net N is *valid* in an evaluation space E iff, for every assignment S_0 of the variables free in N, every input marking m_0 valid with respect to S_0, and every computation $m_0>m_1>...>m_k$, there is a corresponding sequence of assignments $S_0, S_1, ..., S_k$ such that the following two properties hold:

1) m_i is valid with respect to S_i, for $0<i\le k$;
2) $S_0, S_1, ..., S_k$ assign the same values to the variables free in N.

The sequence $S_0, S_1, ..., S_k$ keep trace of the assignments to variables. For predicate nets, validity of rules is not sufficient to guarantee validity, as shown by the following example.

Example 2.

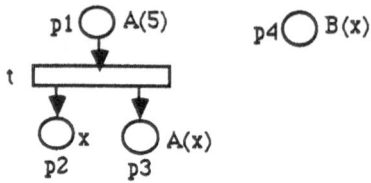

Let t be interpreted as follows: for every marking $m(p1:A(5)) = \{\alpha\}$, t builds up the marking $n(p2:x) = \{5\}, n(p3:A(x)) = \{\alpha\}$. If α is a valid evaluation of $A(5)$, then the output marking is valid for the assignment $[x/5]$. Hence the interpretation of t is valid. But validity of t holds only for its pre and post-set. For example, let $m_0(p1:A(5)) = \{\alpha\}, m_0(p4:B(x)) = \{\beta\}$ be a marking valid (e.g.) with respect to $[x/3]$, but not with respect to $[x/5]$. By firing t, we obtain $m_1(p2:x) = \{5\}$, $m_1(p3:A(x)) = \{\alpha\}, m_1(p4:B(x)) = \{\beta\}$. For $p2, p3$, m_1 is valid with respect to $[x/5]$, but for $p4$ it is valid with respect to $[x/3]$. Hence there is no assignment for which m_1 is valid.

To avoid situations as the one shown in Example 2, our nets must be *sound* with respect to assignments, according to the following definition.

Definition 6. Let N be a net structure, E be an evaluation space, and N_E be the E-interpretation of N. We say that:
(I) A marking m is *sound* iff, for every transition $t:R$, if $t:R$ is *enabled* by m and there is $q:u \in post(t:R)$ labelled by a variable u, then every place $r:L(u) \in post(t:R)$ (where $L(u)$ is a term or a formula containing u free) is such that $m(r:L(u)) = \emptyset$.
(II) N is *sound* in E iff, for every input marking m_0 and every execution sequence $m_0>m_1>...>m_k$ of N_E, m_i is sound (for $1\le i\le k$).

Now, we define the proof nets of a predicate net system Π with a class A_Π of admissible evaluation spaces. First of all, we say that a net structure N is sound and reachable in Π iff it is sound and reachable in every $E \in A_\Pi$ (reachability is defined as in the case of propositional nets).

The *proof nets* of $\mathcal{N}$ are the finite and acyclic net structures N of $\mathcal{N}$ which are *sound and reachable in* $\mathcal{N}$ and satisfy the requirement that *all the variables occurring free in the labels of the input and output places of* N *are free in* N.

Now we explain correctness of proof nets. Let N be a proof net with assumptions $A_1, ..., A_n$ and input variables $v_1, ..., v_m$, and $\mathcal{E}$ be an evaluation space. By

$$\chi:C \in \mathcal{N}_{\mathcal{E}}(\alpha_1:A_1,..., \alpha_n:A_n, \upsilon_1:v_1,...,\upsilon_n:v_m)$$

we indicate that $\chi:C$ is *a result computed by* $\mathcal{N}_{\mathcal{E}}$ *with inputs* $\alpha_1:A_1, ..., \alpha_n:A_n$, $\upsilon_1:v_1, ..., \upsilon_m:v_m$. One can prove that proof nets of $\mathcal{N}$ satisfy the following:

Correctness property. For every evaluation space $\mathcal{E}$ of $\mathcal{A}_{\mathcal{N}}$, and for every assignment S of the free variables of N such that $\alpha_k \in \mathcal{E}(A_k \cdot S)$ (for $1 \le k \le n$) and $S(v_h) = \upsilon_h$ (for $1 \le h \le m$), the following properties hold:
a) $\mathcal{N}_{\mathcal{E}}(\alpha_1:A_1,..., \alpha_n:A_n, \upsilon_1:v_1,...,\upsilon_n:v_m)$ is not empty;
b) for every $\chi:C \in \mathcal{N}_{\mathcal{E}}(\alpha_1:A_1,...,\alpha_n:A_n,\upsilon_1:v_1,...,\upsilon_n:v_m)$, $\chi:C \in \mathcal{E}(C \cdot S)$ and if, for $1 \le i \le n$, α_i is a valid evaluation of $A_i \cdot S$, then χ is a valid evaluation of $C \cdot S$.

Correctness property explains the computational meaning of proof nets. Moreover (as we have explained for propositional systems), it can be used to state validity of a first order net system with respect to other first order formal systems.

4.1.3 Reachability spaces

As for the propositional case, here we will use particular evaluation spaces, we call *reachability spaces*. Since proof nets must satisfy both reachability and soundness, the reachability space of a net system $\mathcal{N}$ will satisfy the following property:
a net structure will be sound and reachable in $\mathcal{N}$ iff its interpretation in the reachability space will be sound and reachable, and this latter property will be decidable.

4.2 Net systems containing $\exists$

4.2.1 Admissible evaluation spaces of $\mathcal{N}(\exists)$

Admissible evaluation spaces satisfy (GP) and the following properties:

(E1) The class of formula-evaluations is closed under a binary operation $C3(\alpha,\upsilon)$ defined for every individual evaluation υ and formula evaluation α.
(E2) For every evaluation ε of $\exists y A(y) \cdot S$ there are an individual evaluation υ and an evaluation α of $A(y) \cdot S[y/\underline{\upsilon}]$ such that $\varepsilon = C3(\alpha,\upsilon)$. Moreover, ε is a valid evaluation of $\exists y A(y) \cdot S$ iff α is a valid evaluation of $A(y) \cdot S[y/\underline{\upsilon}]$.

4.2.2 Rules of $\mathcal{N}(\exists)$.

Each function symbol has a corresponding *function evaluation rule*. Evaluation rules compose functions to evaluate terms, and give rise to *term evaluation nets* of the kind shown in the example of FIG.4.

76

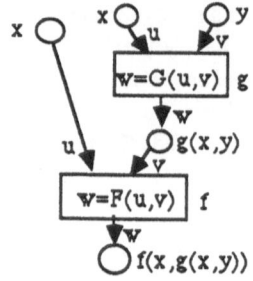

FIG. 4

Moreover we have the following ∃-*introduction* (∃i) and ∃-*elimination* (∃e) rules:

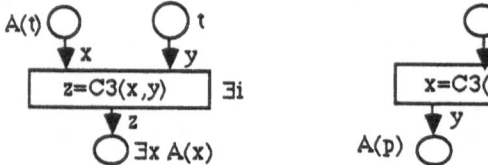

4.2.3 Reachability space $\mathcal{R}$

In this space evaluations don't depend on assignments and are so defined:
$\mathcal{R}(F) = \{x\}$ for every F atomic, and
$\mathcal{R}(\exists xF) = \{C3(\aleph,f) \ / \ f \in R(F)\}$ (where $\aleph$ stands for a generic value).

4.2.4 Other net systems containing ∃

We can merge $\mathcal{R}(\exists)$ and propositional net systems without strong negation (to add strong negation, we need universal quantifier). It is sufficient to consider evaluation spaces and reachability spaces satisfying all the properties of the systems we merge.

We don't enter into details. FIG.5 shows an example of two net structures of $\mathcal{R}(\exists, \wedge, \vee)$. The first net is sound and reachable. Hence it proves:

$\exists xA(x) \vee \exists yB(y) \vdash \exists x(A(x) \vee B(x))$

The second one is reachable, but not sound.

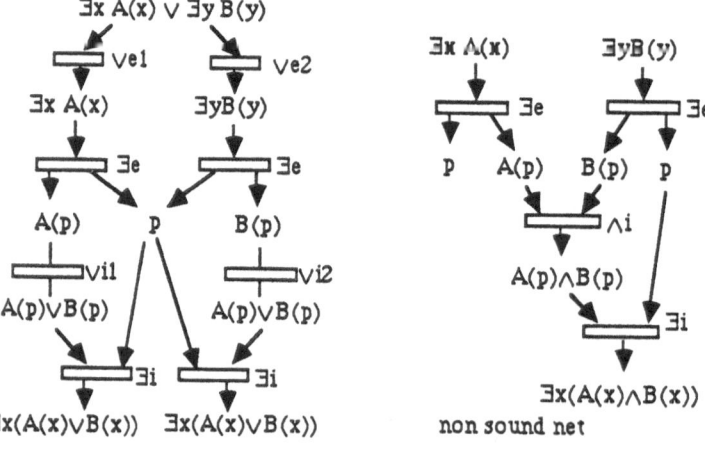

FIG.5

4.3 The system $\mathfrak{N}(\forall)$

4.3.1 Admissible evaluation spaces.

Universal quantification has a procedural meaning, and is treated in a way similar to implication. Admissible evaluation spaces satisfy (GP) and the following properties.

(Q1) Let $[z/\mathbf{w}]$ be an assignment of the free variables z of $\forall x\, A(x)$. An evaluation of $\forall x\, A(x) \cdot [z/\mathbf{w}]$ is an input output relation $\rho(\mathbf{v})$ such that, for every individual evaluation $\mathbf{v}, ... \rho(\mathbf{v})$ is not empty. Moreover, for every $\alpha \in \rho(\mathbf{v})$, α is an evaluation of $A(x) \cdot [x,z/\mathbf{v},\mathbf{w}]$. ρ is valid iff, for every $\mathbf{v}$ and $\alpha \in \rho(\mathbf{v})$, α is a valid evaluation of $A(x) \cdot [x,z/\mathbf{v},\mathbf{w}]$.

(Q2) As in propositional case, we require closure under net realizability.

4.3.2 Rules

procedure call

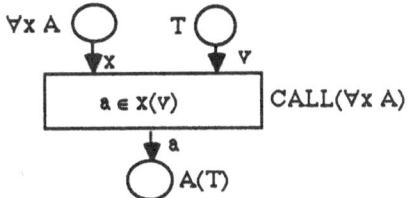

procedure introduction

Let N be a net with *assumptions* $H_1, ..., H_n$, *unique consequence* $A(x)$, and *input variables* $z_1,..., z_m$, and (possibly) x, such that x is not free in the assumptions. We can introduce the following procedure introduction rule:

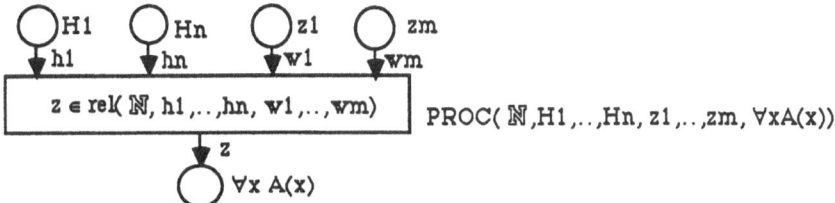

In the above figure, for every E, $\eta_1 \in E(H_1)$, .., $\eta_n \in E(H_n)$ and $\mathbf{w}_1,..., \mathbf{w}_m \in \mathcal{L}$, $\mathrm{rel}(N, \eta_1,...,\eta_n,\mathbf{w}_1, ..., \mathbf{w}_m)$ indicates the evaluation ρ of $\forall x A(x)$ so defined:
$\alpha \in \rho(\mathbf{v})$ iff $\alpha : A(x) \in N_E(\eta_1 : H_1, ..,\eta_n : H_n, \mathbf{w}_1 : z_1,...,\mathbf{w}_m : z_m, \mathbf{v} : x)$.
As in propositional case, $\mathrm{rel}(N, \eta_1,...,\eta_n,\mathbf{w}_1,..,\mathbf{w}_m)$ can be realized by N itself.

5. Conclusion and perspectives.

$\mathfrak{N}(\forall)$ and $\mathfrak{N}(\exists)$ can be merged into a net system $\mathfrak{N}(\forall, \exists)$, built up by the combination of the evaluation and reachability spaces and the union of the rules. $\mathfrak{N}(\forall, \exists)$ can be combined with $\mathfrak{N}(\wedge, \vee, \rightarrow)$ without significant modifications. One has only to redefine propositional evaluations and their validity, taking into account that now they depend on assignments. In this way we obtain the system $\mathfrak{n}(\wedge, \vee, \forall, \rightarrow, \exists)$. If we add the atomic formula $\wedge$ to the considered language, $\mathfrak{n}(\wedge, \vee, \forall, \rightarrow, \exists)$ becomes equivalent to minimal predicate logic, and $\mathfrak{n}(\wedge, \vee, \wedge, \forall, \rightarrow, \exists)$ (where the abs-elementary-nets are introduced) becomes equivalent to intuitionistic predicate logic. To add strong negation, we have to introduce the dual rules for not-exist and not-every.

The possibility of combining different net systems without changing the computational interpretation of rules shows that we have a very general and open model of computation, which can be used in many different situations where one works with the paradigm *proofs as programs*. The study of net systems is at the beginning. The next steps will be the following.

Stronger proof net-systems. We will consider both stronger constructive logical rules and extralogical rules representing properties of mathematical structures (e.g. the axioms needed to introduce abstract data types). In particular, we are interested in the possibility of representing induction.

Structural transformations and linear logic. The structure of a proof net can be transformed, preserving soundness and reachability, by the following transformation rules (TR1) and (TR2).

(TR1) Two or more output places with the same label can be unified.

(TR2) Two or more input places with the same label can be grouped into a unique input place by introducing a transition of the following form:

Structural transformations correspond to the structural rules of sequent calculi. They may be omitted, without modifying the deductive power of net systems. They are implicit in the following two facts. (1) Nets are built up according to transitions in a free way, so that (TR1) can be omitted. (2) In procedure introduction rules, assumptions and consequences with the same label are taken as labels of single places, even if in the net used to introduce a rule they occurr in many input or output places.

If we give a more rigid geometry of nets and if in procedure introduction rules we count how many times a formula occurs as an assumption or as a consequence, we have a situation similar to linear logic. A comparison with linear logic will be one of the next steps in the study of proof-nets.

Program synthesis. The computation model of proof nets is meaningful for program synthesis, in the frame of specific first order theories axiomatizing the properties of the considered data structures and of the problem to be solved. In this frame, one has the logical rules and suitable specific rules corresponding to the axioms of the considered theory. The more important specific rules are related to induction principles, and we are studying their interpretations by proof nets.

By the use of induction principles, net systems become programming systems, where proof nets directly work as a programs. Moreover, it is possible to use the computational informations of nets to synthesise programs in some other language, as the example of FIG.6 shows. BASIS and STEP are the basis and the induction step of an induction proof on natural numbers. $f(i,z)$ means: "z is fibonacci number of place i". We assume "true" as the unique possible evaluation of atomic formulas ("true" is a valid evaluation of an atomic F for an assignment s iff F·s is true).

By BASIS, we obtain the final mark P(C3(s 0, true), C3(s 0, true)). By STEP, from P(C3(X,true), C3(Y,true)) we obtain P(C3(Y,true),C3(X+Y,true)). Since i is the induction variable, we can extract the following prolog-like program:

rec(p(c3(s(0), true),c3(s(0), true)), 0).
rec(p(c3(Y,true), c3(X+Y,true)), s(I)) :- rec(p(c3(X,true),c3(Y,true)), I)

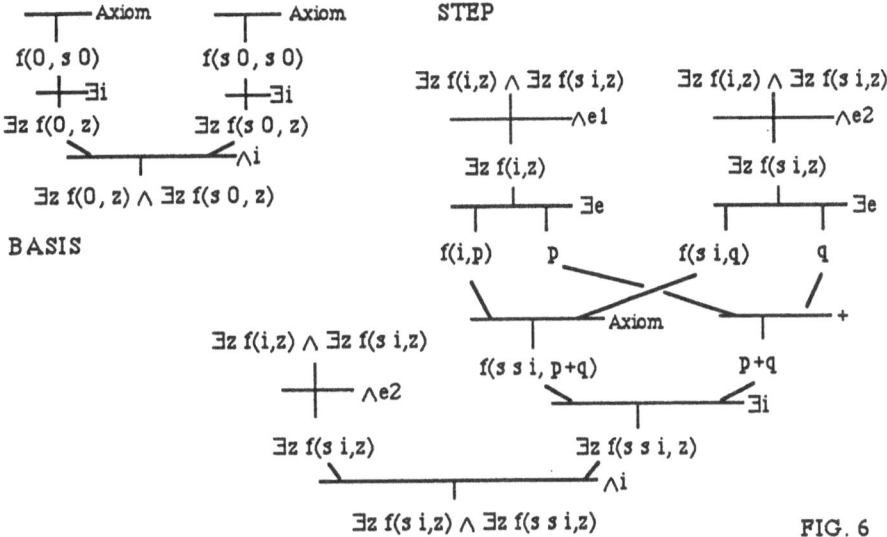

FIG. 6

REFERENCES

[BaC] Bates J., Constable R. - Proofs as programs - *ACM Transaction on Programming Languages and Systems*, vol. 7, n.1, 1985, pp. 113-136.

[PTN] Brauer W., Reisig W., Rozenberg G. (ed.) - Petri Nets: Central Models and Their Properties - LNCS n. 254, Springer Verlag, 1987.

[Nuprl] Constable R. et al. - *Implementing Mathematics with the Nuprl Development System* - N. J., Prentice-Hall, 1986.

[Goad] Goad C. - *Computational uses of the manipulation of formal proofs* - Rep. STAN-CS-80-819, Stanford University, 1980.

[Gir] Girard, J.Y. - Linear Logic - Theoretical Computer Science, 50 (1987), pp.1-102.

[Hy] Hayashi S., Nakano H. - *PX: A computational logic* - MIT Press, Cambridge, 1988.

[MO] Miglioli P., Ornaghi M. - A logically justified model of computation I,II - *Fundamenta Informaticae*, IV.1,2, 1981.

[Nel] Nelson D. - Constructible falsity - *Journal of Symbolic Logic*, vol 14, pag. 16-26

[Nep] Nepejvoda N. - Proofs as Graphs - *Semiotics and Informatics*, vol. 26, 1986 (known by title)

[Nor] Nordstrom B., Smith J.M. - Propositions, Types and Specifications of Programs in Martin-Löf's Type Theory - *BIT*, vol. 24, n.3, 1984, pp.288-301.

The LOPS Approach:
A Transformational Point of View

Gerd Neugebauer

Intellektik, Informatik
Technische Hochschule Darmstadt
D-6100 Darmstadt, Germany
Net: gerd@intellektik.informatik.th-darmstadt.de

Extended Abstract

Program synthesis can be seen from different points of view. One possibility is the proof-based synthesis like the classical [5]. Another one is the transformational synthesis in the spirit of [4].

The LOPS approach to program synthesis has been described in the spirit of the proof-based approach [1, 3, 2]. Now we review the LOPS approach in terms of the transformational point of view.

The central idea of the LOPS approach is to apply a small set of heuristics in a fixed sequence to control the synthesis process. The first step is a normalization and preparation step. The second step is the application of the GUESS/DOMAIN heuristic. This heuristic implements the idea that candidates for a desired output can be guessed within a domain. This domain may be found as part of the prepared specification. The guess can be right or wrong. If it is right we have found an output value. If it is wrong we can reduce the domain.

The third step is the introduction of recursion (GET-REC). Usually this is applied to the failure case of GUESS/DOMAIN. Finally the remaining parts of the specification have to be made evaluable in the fourth step (GET-EVAL).

As we can imagine the distinction of input and output values is rather important especially for GUESS/DOMAIN. Since we want to use an transformational approach to program synthesis the specification reads

$$\forall inputs\, \forall outputs\, (precondition(inputs, outputs) \rightarrow$$
$$spec(inputs, outputs) \leftrightarrow postcondition(inputs, outputs))$$

In this specification *spec* is the predicate to be synthesized. This predicate is defined for all *inputs* and *outputs* satisfying *precondition* by the formula *postcondition*.

Within the logical formulation of the specification given above we can not distinguish between input and output values. Thus we are forced to introduce modes to allow this distinction.

The transformation based LOPS has been enhanced by reasoning about modes. This combination allows a formalization of several ideas informally given in earlier papers on LOPS. As another consequence we have overcome some restrictions lying in a trivial treatment of proof-based specifications.

The full integration of modes throughout the LOPS heuristics has been proven fruitful. Several lines of argumentation which have been present formerly as vague meta-control of heuristics are now fixed and formally specified. Here we can name at first hand the test of executability of formulae. Those tests are hidden in several heuristics of LOPS. Especially the final step (GET-EVAL) heavily uses those tests.

The formulation of the LOPS approach in terms of a transformational approach turned out to be surprisingly simple. All ideas could easily be transfered. Additionally examples which might pose problems can now be easily formulated and solved.

The modes have also been used to guide an algorithm implementation module transforming the algorithm obtained from LOPS into a programming language.

For a detailed description we refer to [6].

References

[1] Wolfgang Bibel. Syntax-directed, semantics-supported program synthesis. *Artificial Intelligence*, 14:243–261, 1980.

[2] Wolfgang Bibel. Concurrent software production. In Michael R. Lowry and Robert McCartney, editors, *Automating Software Design*. AAAI Press, Menlo Park CA, 1991.

[3] Wolfgang Bibel and K.M. Hörnig. LOPS — A system based on a strategical approach to program synthesis. In Alan W. Biermann, Gérard Guiho, and Yves Kodratoff, editors, *Automatic Program Construction Techniques*, chapter 3, pages 69–89. MacMillan, New York, 1984.

[4] R.M. Burstall and John Darlington. A transformation system for developing recursive programs. *Journal of the Association for Computing Machinery*, 24(1):44–67, 1977.

[5] Zohar Manna and Richard J. Waldinger. Synthesis: Dreams ⇒ programs. *IEEE Transactions on Software Engeneering*, SE-5(4):294–328, July 1979.

[6] Gerd Neugebauer. *Pragmatische Programmsynthese*. DISKI. Infix Verlag, 1992. To appear.

Best-first Strategies for Incremental Transformations of Logic Programs*

Maurizio Proietti

IASI-CNR

Viale Manzoni 30

00185 Roma (Italy)

proietti@iasi.rm.cnr.it

Alberto Pettorossi

Electronics Department

University of Roma II

00133 Roma (Italy)

adp@iasi.rm.cnr.it

Abstract

We propose some techniques for mechanizing a class of rule-based transformations of logic programs. Analogous techniques can be applied also in the case of functional programs for which the program transformation methodology was first introduced [4].

We consider the following abstract *Transformation Problem*: given a program P and a property Φ, we are required to find a program, say *TransfP*, equivalent to P such that Φ holds for *TransfP*. The property Φ characterizes the desired 'shape' of the program to be derived (for instance, linear recursive, tail recursive, without intermediate variables, etc.).

We propose some restrictions on the property Φ which make it possible to perform the desired transformation in an incremental way, in the sense that, if a clause which does not satisfy Φ is transformed into clauses which do satisfy Φ, then these resulting clauses need not be considered again during the transformation process.

The core of our technique is a procedure, called *Incremental Transformation*, which is a generalization of the procedure for eliminating unnecessary variables introduced in [13]. The generalization basically consists in the fact that we have parametrized our transformation procedure w.r.t. the property Φ which the transformed program is required to satisfy.

The proposed procedure is nondeterministic and it generates a possibly infinite tree of programs which are all derivable from the given program P. We study the use of *best-first* search strategies for traversing this tree of programs. We finally provide a sufficient condition for solving a given transformation problem by using a best-first strategy, in case our Incremental Transformation procedure can find a solution by using any other strategy.

1 Preliminary Definitions

We consider *definite logic programs* [8]. Given a clause C we denote its head by $hd(C)$ and its body by $bd(C)$. Given a term t, we denote by $vars(t)$ the set of variables occurring in t. Similar notation will be used for variables occurring in atoms, goals, and clauses.

*This work has been partially supported by the 'Progetto Finalizzato Sistemi Informatici e Calcolo Parallelo' of the CNR and MURST 40%, Italy under grant n. 89.00026.69.

We denote by $\mathcal{M}(P,p)$ the set of all atoms with predicate p belonging to the least Herbrand model of P, and we say that two programs P_1 and P_2 are *equivalent* w.r.t. the predicate p iff $\mathcal{M}(P_1,p) = \mathcal{M}(P_2,p)$.

In this paper we will make use of the Definition, Unfolding, Folding, Goal Replacement, and Clause Deletion rules defined in [16]. These rules preserve total correctness, in the sense that if we derive program P_2 from program P_1 then for each predicate p in P_1 we have that: $\mathcal{M}(P_1,p) = \mathcal{M}(P_2,p)$.

For our purposes we need to further restrict the use of the Definition rule as follows.

Definition Rule. Let P be a program and D a clause (belonging or not to P) of the form: $newp(X_1,\ldots,X_m) \leftarrow A_1,\ldots,A_n$, such that: i) $\{X_1,,X_m\} \subseteq vars(\{A_1,\ldots,A_n\})$, ii) $newp$ does not occur in $P-\{D\}$, and iii) every predicate occurring in $bd(D)$ occurs in $P \rightarrow \{D\}$ as well.

D is said to be a *definition clause (for P)*.

We say that a definition clause D_1 is a *synonym* of a definition clause D_2 iff there exists a renaming substitution ρ such that $vars(hd(D_1)) = vars(hd(D_2\rho))$ and $bd(D_1) = bd(D_2\rho)$.

Given a program P and a definition clause D (not occurring in P) we may derive a new program by adding D to P. □

According to Tamaki and Sato's rules, we assume that a clause can be used for folding only if it is a definition clause occurring either in the current or in an earlier version of the program.

As far as the application of the Goal Replacement rule is concerned, we associate with every program a set of goal equivalences, called *Replacement Laws*. We assume that the Replacement Laws are *directed*, in the sense that we can only replace an instance of the left-hand side of a goal equivalence by the corresponding right-hand side, and not viceversa. We also assume that the replacement is correct even if combined with applications of the other transformation rules (see [16] for some suitable proof-theoretic conditions).

The Clause Deletion rule will be applied only when a clause $\dot{C}$ of a program P is a *failing clause*, that is, $bd(C)$ contains an atom which is *not* unifiable with the head of any clause in P.

The extension of our techniques to more general cases in which the deletion of a clause can be performed (see, for instance, [6]) is straightforward, and we leave it to the reader.

For simplicity reasons, we will not discuss here the use of our transformation techniques in the case of other logic languages and/or different program semantics (see, for instance, [14,6,12,15,1]). We will rather focus our attention on the problem of mechanizing a class of strategies for an effective use of the transformation rules we have indicated above. We believe that the techniques we will introduce, can easily be extended to more sophisticated logic languages and more complex transformation rules.

2 Program Transformation Problems

We formalize the class of program transformation problems which we study in this paper as instances of the following

Transformation Problem: given a program P and a property Φ ranging over logic programs, we are required to find a program, say *TransfP*, such that: i) P is equivalent to *TransfP* w.r.t. every predicate occurring in P and ii) $\Phi(\textit{TransfP})$ holds. □

We look for strategies to solve instances of the Transformation Problem. It will be shown that by imposing some restrictions on the form of the property Φ which is required to hold for the transformed program *TransfP*, we can indeed provide a general strategy for dealing with a large class of instances of the Transformation Problem.

Our strategy is an enhancement of the one presented in [13] for avoiding unnecessary variables. We will now see an example of application of this strategy, which will motivate the restriction on Φ presented in Section 3.

Example 1. (*Common Left-Embedded Trees*) We say that a variable X in a clause C is *unnecessary* iff either X occurs twice in $bd(C)$ or it does not occur in $hd(C)$. Unnecessary variables may cause inefficiency because they may force redundant computations.

Let us consider the *common_left_embed* relation defined by the following logic program, called *Common*:

1. $common\_left\_embed(T, U, V) \leftarrow left\_embed(T, U), left\_embed(T, V).$
2. $left\_embed(leaf, U).$
3. $left\_embed(tree(TL, TR), tree(UL, UR)) \leftarrow left\_embed(TL, UL),$
    $\qquad\qquad\qquad\qquad\qquad\qquad\qquad\qquad\qquad left\_embed(TR, UR).$
4. $left\_embed(tree(TL, TR), tree(UL, UR)) \leftarrow left\_embed(tree(TL, TR), UL).$

Variable T in clause 1 is unnecessary because it occurs twice in the body of that clause. We would like to find a program which computes the relation *common_left_embed* without using any unnecessary variable.

Thus, we would like to solve an instance of the Transformation Problem where the property Φ is defined as follows: $\Phi(\textit{Prog})$ holds iff for every clause C in *Prog* no unnecessary variable occurs in C.

We will now see how the procedure for avoiding unnecessary variables works in this case. We partition the initial version of program *Common* into two sets of clauses: *TransfCommon* and *RestofCommon*. We collect in *TransfCommon* all clauses without unnecessary variables and in *RestofCommon* all other clauses which contain unnecessary variables and need to be processed. Thus, initially *TransfCommon* consists of clauses 2, 3, and 4, while *RestofCommon* consists of clause 1 only.

Before showing our derivation, we notice that, according to our Definition rule, clause 1 is a definition clause and it can be used for performing folding steps.

We now unfold clause 1 w.r.t. the atom $left\_embed(T, U)$, and we get the following three clauses:

5. $common\_left\_embed(leaf, U, V) \leftarrow left\_embed(leaf, V).$
6. $common\_left\_embed(tree(TL, TR), tree(UL, UR), V) \leftarrow$
    $\qquad\qquad\qquad left\_embed(TL, UL), left\_embed(TR, UR),$
    $\qquad\qquad\qquad left\_embed(tree(TL, TR), V).$

7. $common\_left\_embed(tree(TL, TR), tree(UL, UR), V) \leftarrow$
    $\qquad left\_embed(tree(TL, TR), UL), left\_embed(tree(TL, TR), V).$

We add clause 5 to *TransfCommon* because it does not contain any unnecessary variable, while clauses 6 and 7 still contain unnecessary variables and need to be processed. Thus, we replace clause 1 in *RestofCommon* by clauses 6 and 7. By the correctness of the Unfolding rule we have that the initial program *Common* is equivalent to *TransfCommon* ∪ *RestofCommon*.

Now, each clause of *RestofCommon* can be transformed into one without unnecessary variables by means of some definition and folding steps. This property holds in general, that is, given any clause C we can always consider some (possibly new) definition clauses so that by folding C using those definition clauses, we get a clause without unnecessary variables. In our case we introduce the following new definition clause:

8. $new(TL, TR, UL, UR, V) \leftarrow left\_embed(TL, UL), left\_embed(TR, UR),$
    $\qquad left\_embed(tree(TL, TR), V).$

Then we fold clauses 6 and 7 using clauses 8 and 1 (recall that clause 1 is a definition clause), thereby getting the following two clauses which do not contain any unnecessary variables:

9. $common\_left\_embed(tree(TL, TR), tree(UL, UR), V) \leftarrow$
    $\qquad new(TL, TR, UL, UR, V).$
10. $common\_left\_embed(tree(TL, TR), tree(UL, UR), V) \leftarrow$
    $\qquad common\_left\_embed(tree(TL, TR), UL, V).$

Clauses 9 and 10 are added to *TransfCommon*, while according to the Folding rule clauses 6 and 7 are removed from *RestofCommon*. On the other hand, clause 8 contains unnecessary variables and it is added to *RestofCommon*.

At this point of the derivation process *TransfCommon* is made out of clauses 2, 3, 4, 5, 9, and 10, while *RestofCommon* contains clause 8 which is the only clause with unnecessary variables. By the correctness of the Definition and Folding rules *Common* is equivalent to the current value of *TransfCommon* ∪ *RestofCommon*.

We proceed our transformation by unfolding clause 8 w.r.t. the third atom of its body, and we get:

11. $new(TL, TR, UL, UR, tree(VL, VR)) \leftarrow$
    $\qquad left\_embed(TL, UL), left\_embed(TR, UR),$
    $\qquad left\_embed(TL, VL), left\_embed(TR, VR).$
12. $new(TL, TR, UL, UR, tree(VL, VR)) \leftarrow$
    $\qquad left\_embed(TL, UL), left\_embed(TR, UR),$
    $\qquad left\_embed(tree(TL, TR), VL).$

Clauses 11 and 12 can be folded using clauses 1 and 8, respectively, and we get:

13. $new(TL, TR, UL, UR, tree(VL, VR)) \leftarrow$
    $\qquad common\_left\_embed(TL, UL, VL),$
    $\qquad common\_left\_embed(TR, UR, VR).$
14. $new(TL, TR, UL, UR, tree(VL, VR)) \leftarrow new(TL, TR, UL, UR, VL).$

Clause 13 and 14 do not contain unnecessary variables, and they are added to *TransfCommon*. Clause 8 which defines the predicate *new* can be discarded from *RestofCommon*, which thus becomes empty.

The initial program is equivalent to the final program *TransfCommon*, which does not contain any unnecessary variables and it is a solution of our instance of the Transformation Problem.

The current clauses of *TransfCommon* are: 2, 3, 4, 5, 9, 10, 13, and 14. □

The transformation presented in the above Example 1 can be seen as an instance of the following general transformation process:

- We partition the initial program P into two sets of clauses: *TransfP* and *RestofP*. A clause is in *TransfP* iff it does not contain any unnecessary variable.

- We then repeat one or more times the sequence of the following two transformations until *RestofP* is empty:

  1. a Definition & Folding transformation, where we consider possibly new definition clauses to be used for folding *all* clauses in *RestofP* and generating clauses without unnecessary variables, and

  2. an Unfolding transformation, where we unfold each clause of *RestofP*.

After each transformation we add the clauses without unnecessary variables to *TransfP* and all other clauses are left in *RestofP*.

Some transformation step of point 1 may sometimes be skipped. In particular, if all clauses in *RestofP* are definition clauses then no new definition is introduced. Furthermore, we do not introduce a new definition clause if it is a synonym of an already existing one, and for the folding steps we will use the old one instead. For instance, in Example 1 we fold clause 7 using clause 1, instead of introducing a new definition clause. The use of old definition clauses allows us to modify the recursive structure of the programs, and this is often desirable during program transformation.

Let us now point out some interesting features of the property of having no unnecessary variables.

i) The property of having no unnecessary variables is decidable.

ii) If we add a new clause to *TransfP*, the property of having no unnecessary variables continues to hold for the old clauses of *TransfP*. Thus, the elimination of unnecessary variables can be performed in an incremental way.

iii) If we delete a clause from a set of clauses having no unnecessary variables then the remaining clauses still have no unnecessary variables.

The properties at points ii) and iii) trivially hold because the property of having no unnecessary variables depends on the clause in hand only, and not on the other program clauses. However, in the next section we will consider the case of clause properties which depend on the program to which these clauses belong. In this case we will generalize the conditions of points i), ii), and iii) and we will introduce the notion of admissible properties.

3 Admissible Properties for Transformation Problems

The class of admissible properties which we now introduce is important because for solving transformation problems specified using properties in this class, we can provide a very simple and general transformation procedure (see the *Incremental Transformation* procedure in Section 4).

Definition 1. (*Admissible Properties*) Given a program P, a property $\Phi(P)$ is said to be *admissible* iff $\Phi(P)$ is of the form $\forall C \in P.\Psi(C, P)$ and Ψ satisfies the following conditions:

i) Ψ is a *decidable* property, and

ii) Ψ is *persistent* in the sense that for every clause D, for every program P, and for every clause C in P we have that:

$if\ \Psi(C, P)\ and\ \Psi(D, P \cup \{D\})\ then\ \Psi(C, P \cup \{D\})$ (*up-persistency*)

$if\ \Psi(C, P)\ then\ \Psi(C, P) - \{D\}$ (*down-persistency*) □

Example 2. (*Linear Recursive Programs*) Let us associate with each clause of the form: $q_0(\ldots) \leftarrow q_1(\ldots), \ldots, q_n(\ldots)$ the rewriting rule $Q_0 \rightarrow Q_1 \ldots Q_n$. Thus, with a program P we associate a set Rew_P of rewriting rules.

We consider the following two program properties, each of which expresses a notion of linear recursiveness of a clause C w.r.t. a given program P.

Let C be the clause $r_0(\ldots) \leftarrow r_1(\ldots), \ldots, r_m(\ldots)$ with associated rewriting rule $R_0 \rightarrow R_1 \ldots R_m$.

The property $\Psi_1(C, P)$ holds iff there exists at most one R_i for $1 \leq i \leq m$, such that it is possible to derive from R_i using Rew_P, a word with an occurrence of R_0.

The property $\Psi_2(C, P)$ holds iff it is not possible to derive from $R_1 \ldots R_m$ using Rew_P, a word with two occurrences of R_0.

Property Ψ_2 implies property Ψ_1. Indeed, if from both R_i and R_j with $1 \leq i < j \leq m$, we can derive a word with an occurrence of R_0 then from $R_1 \ldots R_m$ we can derive a word with two occurrences of R_0.

The following example shows that Ψ_1 does not imply Ψ_2. Let us consider the two clauses:

$F.\quad a \leftarrow b, a.$ and $G.\quad b \leftarrow a.$

The rewritings rules associated with F and G are: $A \rightarrow BA$ and $B \rightarrow A$, respectively. $\Psi_1(G, \{F, G\})$ holds because the r.h.s. of the rule $B \rightarrow A$ contains one symbol only, while $\Psi_2(G, \{F, G\})$ does not hold because from A we can produce BBA which has two occurrences of B.

We also have that: $\forall C \in P.\ \Psi_1(C, P)$ iff $\forall C \in P.\ \Psi_2(C, P)$. Since Ψ_2 implies property Ψ_1, it is enough to show that if $\forall C \in P.\ \Psi_1(C, P)$ then $\forall C \in P.\ \Psi_2(C, P)$. Indeed, suppose that for a given clause C in P, $\Psi_2(C, P)$ does not hold. Thus, there exists a derivation of the following form:

$$R_1 \ldots R_m \overset{*}{\rightarrow} X S_0 Z \rightarrow X S_1 Y S_2 Z \overset{*}{\rightarrow} X_1 A_1 R_0 B_1 Y_1 A_2 R_0 B_2 Z_1$$

where $S_1 \xrightarrow{*} A_1 R_0 B_1$ and $S_2 \xrightarrow{*} A_2 R_0 B_2$.

For the clause D associated with $S_0 \rightarrow S_1 Y S_2$, $\Psi_1(D, P)$ does not hold because $S_1 \xrightarrow{*} A_1 R_0 B_1 \rightarrow A_1 R_1 \ldots R_m B_1 \xrightarrow{*} A_1 X S_0 Z B_1$ and analogously, $S_2 \xrightarrow{*} A_2 X S_0 Z B_2$.

We have the following facts about Ψ_1 and Ψ_2.

Ψ_1 is decidable and down-persistent, but not up-persistent. Thus, $\forall C \in P$. $\Psi_1(C, P)$ is not admissible.

Indeed, consider again the clauses F and G above. $\Psi_1(F, \{F\})$ holds, $\Psi_1(G, \{F, G\})$ holds, and $\Psi_1(F, \{F, G\})$ does not hold. Notice that the above example is not a counterexample of the persistency of Ψ_2, because as already shown, $\Psi_2(G, \{F, G\})$ does not hold.

Ψ_2 is decidable and down-persistent. We now prove that it is also up-persistent, and thus we will have that $\forall C \in P$. $\Psi_2(C, P)$ is admissible.

Let us consider a program P and two clauses C and D with rewriting rules: $R_0 \rightarrow R_1 \ldots R_m$ and $S_0 \rightarrow S_1 \ldots S_n$, respectively. Suppose that $\Psi_2(C, P \cup \{D\})$ does not hold. Thus, we have:

$$R_1 \ldots R_m \xrightarrow{*} X R_0 Y R_0 Z \qquad\qquad (\alpha)$$

where $\xrightarrow{*}$ is relative to the rules of $P \cup \{D\}$.

Now there are two cases:

Case 1. During the derivation (α) we did not apply the rewriting rule associated with D. Hence, $\Psi_2(C, P)$ does not hold and we get the thesis.

Case 2. During the derivation (α) we have applied the rewriting rule associated with D.

Case 2.1 There exists a subderivation of (α) of the form:

$$S_0 \rightarrow S_1 \ldots S_k \xrightarrow{*} A R_0 B.$$

(A subderivation corresponds to a subtree of the derivation tree corresponding to (α), when we view the rewriting rules as context-free productions.) Thus we get:

$$S_1 \ldots S_k \xrightarrow{*} A R_0 B \rightarrow A R_1 \ldots R_m B \xrightarrow{*} A X R_0 Y R_0 Z B$$
$$\xrightarrow{*} A X R_1 \ldots R_m Y R_1 \ldots R_m Z B.$$

Since during the derivation (α) we have applied the rewriting rule associated with D, we have that:

$$R_1 \ldots R_m \xrightarrow{*} U S_0 V$$

and thus,

$$S_1 \ldots S_k \xrightarrow{*} A X U S_0 V Y U S_0 V Z B.$$

This means that $\Psi_2(D, P \cup \{D\}$ does not hold.

Case 2.2 For all subderivations of (α) of the form: $S_0 \xrightarrow{*} T$ we have that T does not contain R_0.

In this case it is possible to construct from the derivation (α) a new derivation such that:

$$R_1 \ldots R_m \xrightarrow{*} L R_0 M R_0 N$$

without using the rewriting rule associated with D. In order to so, it is enough to rearrange the rewriting steps in the derivation (α) by postponing as long as possible the application of the rewriting rule associated with D. If we then consider the word produced before the first application of this rule, we get the desired word with two occurrences of R_0. □

4 A General Strategy for Solving Transformation Problems

We now describe a general procedure for applying the transformation rules and solving transformation problems for admissible properties. This procedure, called *Incremental Transformation*, takes a program P and an admissible property Φ of the form $\forall C \in Prog. \; \Psi(C, Prog)$ as input and, if it terminates, returns a program *TransfP* satisfying Φ.

The Incremental Transformation procedure is a generalization of the transformation process described at the end of Section 2. It works as follows:

- The given program P is partitioned into two sets of clauses, *TransfP* and *RestofP*, such that for every clause C in *TransfP* the property $\Psi(C, P)$ holds.

- Then the sequence of the following three transformations is repeated until *RestofP* is empty:

  1. a Definition & Folding transformation, where some possibly new definition clauses are used for folding *some* clauses in *RestofP* and generating clauses which satisfy Ψ (if no clause satisfying Ψ can be obtained by performing Definition and Folding steps only then this transformation is skipped),

  2. an Unfolding transformation, where each clause of *RestofP* is unfolded, and

  3. a Replacement transformation, where the Replacement Laws are applied zero or more times to each clause in *RestofP*.

  All clauses satisfying Ψ produced by Folding, Unfolding, and Replacement transformation steps are added to *TransfP*, while the other clauses are left in *RestofP*. The hypothesis that Ψ is persistent ensures that, after adding to *TransfP* new clauses satisfying Ψ, property Ψ continues to hold for all clauses which were already present in *TransfP*.

We now present in a more formal way our general transformation strategy.

The Incremental Transformation Procedure

Input: A program P without failing clauses, a set R of Replacement Laws, and an admissible property Φ of the form $\forall C \in Prog. \; \Psi(C, Prog)$.

Output: a program *TransfP* such that: i) *TransfP* is equivalent to P w.r.t. every predicate occurring in P, and ii) *TransfP* satisfies Φ.

Initially, let *TransfP* be the set of clauses C in P such that $\Psi(C, P)$ holds, *RestofP* be the complement of *TransfP* in P, and *Defs* be the set of definition clauses in P (see the Definition rule in Section 1).

while $RestofP \neq \emptyset$ **do**

1. (*Definition & Folding*)

   consider a subset $\{C_1, \ldots, C_m\}$ of $RestofP - Defs$ and a set $\{D_1, \ldots, D_n\}$ of new definition clauses for $P \cup Defs$ such that for $j = 1, \ldots, m$ and $i = 1, \ldots, n$ the following conditions hold:

   i) in $Defs \cup \{D_1, \ldots, D_{i-1}, D_{i+1}, \ldots, D_n\}$ no clause is a synonym of D_i,

   ii) $bd(D_i)$ only contains predicate symbols occurring in P (and not in $Defs$),

   iii) C_j can be folded using clauses occurring in $Defs \cup \{D_1, \ldots, D_n\}$, thereby getting a clause F_j,

   iv) D_i is used at least once in the folding process of point iii), and

   v) $\Psi(F_j, TransfP \cup \{F_1, \ldots, F_m\})$ is true;

   $RestofP := (RestofP - \{C_1, \ldots, C_m\}) \cup \{D_1, \ldots, D_n\}$;

   $TransfP := TransfP \cup \{F_1, \ldots, F_m\}$;

   $Defs := Defs \cup \{D_1, \ldots, D_n\}$;

2. (*Unfolding*)

   for every clause C in $RestofP$ select an atom A in $bd(C)$ and consider the set C_{unfold} of all non-failing clauses which can be obtained by unfolding C w.r.t. A using clauses in the initial program P;

   consider the set $Unf = \bigcup_{C \in RestofP} C_{unfold}$;

   $RestofP := Unf - \{E \mid E \in Unf \text{ and } \neg\Psi(E, TransfP \cup Unf)\}$;

   $TransfP := TransfP \cup \{E \mid E \in Unf \text{ and } \Psi(E, TransfP \cup Unf)\}$;

3. (*Replacement*)

   for every clause C in $RestofP$ apply the Replacement rule zero or more times to C using laws in R, thereby obtaining the new clause C_R;

   consider the set $Repl$ of all new clauses C_R such that $C \in RestofP$ and C_R is a non-failing clause;

   $RostofP := Repl - \{E \mid E \in Repl \text{ and } \neg\Psi(E, TransfP \sqcup Repl)\}$;

   $TransfP := TransfP \cup \{E \mid E \in Repl \text{ and } \Psi(E, TransfP \cup Repl)\}$. □

The partial correctness of the above procedure can be shown as follows. We use a slight variant of the transformation rules of [16]. Indeed, we perform the unfolding steps using the clauses of the initial program P and not those of the current program. However, it is easy to see that our rules are correct, that is, after each transformation step we have that $TransfP \cup RestofP$ is equivalent to the initial program P w.r.t. all predicates in P.

For every clause C which is added to $TransfP$ we have that C belongs to some set of clauses S such that $\Psi(C, TransfP \cup S)$ holds. Then, by the down-persistency of Ψ we have that $\Psi(C, TransfP \cup \{C\})$ holds. Thus, by the up-persistency of Ψ we have that, after each update of $TransfP$, $\forall C \in TransfP$. $\Psi(C, TransfP)$ holds, that is, $TransfP$ satisfies Φ. If the procedure terminates then $RestofP = \emptyset$ and, therefore, the final version of $TransfP$ satisfies Φ and it is equivalent to P w.r.t. all predicates in P.

Example 3. (*Towers of Hanoi*) Consider the following program, called *Hanoi*, for solving the Towers of Hanoi problem:

1. $hanoi(0, A, B, C, [\,])$.
2. $hanoi(s(N), A, B, C, M) \leftarrow hanoi(N, A, C, B, M1), hanoi(N, C, B, A, M2),$
$$append(M1, [m(A, B) \mid M2], M).$$

$append([\,], L, L)$.
$append([H \mid T], L, [H \mid TL]) \leftarrow append(T, L, TL)$.

Suppose that we want to derive an equivalent program which is linear recursive. By definition we assume that a clause C in a given program $Prog$ is linear recursive if $\Psi_2(C, Prog)$ holds, where Ψ_2 is the decidable and persistent property considered in Example 2.

Thus, we need to solve an instance of the Transformation Problem where P is the *Hanoi* program and $\Phi(Prog)$ is $\forall C \in Prog$. $\Psi_2(C, Prog)$.

In order to solve this problem we apply the Incremental Transformation procedure to *Hanoi* and $\forall C \in Prog$. $\Psi_2(C, Prog)$. We also assume that we are given the Replacement Law which expresses the functionality of $hanoi(N, A, B, C, M)$ w.r.t. the first four arguments, that is, for any terms n, a, b, c, $m1$, and $m2$, we may replace the goal '$hanoi(n, a, b, c, m1), hanoi(n, a, b, c, m2)$' by the goal '$hanoi(n, a, b, c, m1), m1 = m2$'.

Initially *TransfHanoi* is made out of clause 1 together with the clauses for *append*, *RestofHanoi* contains clause 2, and *Defs* is empty.

(*Definition & Folding*) We consider the only clause in *RestofHanoi* (i.e. clause 2) and we introduce the following definition clause:

3. $new1(N, A, B, C, M1, M2) \leftarrow hanoi(N, A, C, B, M1),$
$$hanoi(N, C, B, A, M2).$$

By folding clause 2 using clause 3 we get:

2f. $hanoi(s(N), A, B, C, M) \leftarrow new1(N, A, B, C, M1, M2),$
$$append(M1, [m(A, B) \mid M2], M).$$

We have that $\Psi_2(2f, TransfHanoi \cup \{2f\})$ holds, that is, clause 2f is linear recursive if we restrict our attention to the clauses in $TransfHanoi \cup \{2f\}$ only. Thus, clause 2f is added to *TransfHanoi* and clause 2 is replaced by clause 3 in the set *RestofHanoi*. The definition clause 3 is added to *Defs*.

(*Unfolding*) We unfold clause 3 in *RestofHanoi* and we get:

4. $new1(0, A, B, C, [\,], M) \leftarrow hanoi(0, C, B, A, M)$.
5. $new1(s(N), A, B, C, M1, M2) \leftarrow hanoi(N, A, B, C, M11),$
$$hanoi(N, B, C, A, M12), hanoi(s(N), C, B, A, M2),$$
$$append(M11, [m(A, C) \mid M12], M1).$$

Clause 4 is linear recursive in *TransfHanoi* ∪ {clause 4} and it is added to *TransfHanoi*, while clause 5 is not linear recursive. Thus, we delete clause 3 from *RestofHanoi* and we add clause 5 to *RestofHanoi*.

(*Replacement*) The functionality rule *cannot* be applied to clause 5. Thus, no replacement is performed.

Since *RestofHanoi* is not empty we execute once more the body of the while-do loop of the Incremental Transformation procedure.

(*Definition & Folding*) We introduce the new predicate *new2* which is defined as follows:

6. $new2(N, A, B, C, M11, M12, M2) \leftarrow hanoi(N, A, B, C, M11),$
    $hanoi(N, B, C, A, M12), hanoi(s(N), C, B, A, M2).$

By folding clause 5 using clause 6 we get the following linear recursive clause:

7. $new1(s(N), A, B, C, M1, M2) \leftarrow new2(N, A, B, C, M11, M12, M2),$
    $append(M11, [m(A, C) \mid M12], M1).$

Clause 7 is added to *TransfHanoi* and clause 6 replaces clause 5 in the set *RestofHanoi*. The new definition clause 6 is added to *Defs*.

(*Unfolding*) By unfolding clause 6 we get:

8. $new2(N, A, B, C, M11, M12, M2) \leftarrow$
    $hanoi(N, A, B, C, M11), hanoi(N, B, C, A, M12),$
    $hanoi(N, C, A, B, M21), hanoi(N, A, B, C, M22),$
    $append(M21, [m(C, B) \mid M22], M2).$

(*Replacement*) By applying the functionality rule we get:

9. $new2(N, A, B, C, M11, M12, M2) \leftarrow$
    $hanoi(N, A, B, C, M11), hanoi(N, B, C, A, M12),$
    $hanoi(N, C, A, B, M21), M11 = M22,$
    $append(M21, [m(C, B) \mid M22], M2).$

Clause 9 is *not* linear recursive and it replaces clause 6 in *RestofHanoi*.

The reader may check that by executing some more times the body of the while-do loop of the Incremental Transformation procedure we add to *TransfHanoi* the following linear recursive clauses:

10. $new2(N, A, B, C, M11, M12, M2) \leftarrow$
    $new3(N, A, B, C, M11, M12, M21), M11 = M22,$
    $append(M21, [m(C, B) \mid M22], M2).$

11. $new3(0, A, B, C, [\,], M12, M21) \leftarrow new1(0, B, A, C, M12, M21).$

12. $new3(s(N), A, B, C, M11, M12, M21) \leftarrow$
    $new4(N, A, B, C, M111, M112, M12, M21),$
    $append(M111, [m(A, B) \mid M112], M11).$

13. $new4(N, A, B, C, M111, M112, M12, M21) \leftarrow$
    $new5(N, A, B, C, M111, M112, M121, M21),$
    $M111 = M122, append(M121, [m(B, C) \mid M122], M12).$

14. $new5(N, A, B, C, M111, M112, M121, M21) \leftarrow$
    $new3(N, A, C, B, M111, M112, M121), M211 = M112,$
    $M212 = M121, append(M211, [m(C, A) \mid M212], M21).$

The above clauses 10, 11, 12, 13, and 14, together with clauses 1, 2f, 4, 7, and the clauses for *append*, define a linear recursive program equivalent to *Hanoi*. The derived program can be further simplified by unfolding the equalities, the predicates *new1*, *new2*, *new4*, and *new5*, as well as some occurrences of the predicates *append* and *hanoi*. By doing so, we get the following program in which all clauses are linear recursive:

$$hanoi(0, A, B, C, [\,]).$$
$$hanoi(s(0), A, B, C, [m(A, B)]).$$
$$hanoi(s(s(N)), A, B, C, M) \leftarrow new3(N, A, B, C, M1, M2, M3),$$
$$append(M3, [m(C, B) \mid M1], M4),$$
$$append(M1, [m(A, C) \mid M2], M5),$$
$$append(M5, [m(A, B) \mid M4], M).$$
$$new3(0, A, B, C, [\,], [\,], [\,]).$$
$$new3(s(N), A, B, C, M1, M2, M3) \leftarrow new3(N, A, C, B, M4, M5, M6),$$
$$append(M5, [m(C, A) \mid M6], M3),$$
$$append(M6, [m(B, C) \mid M4], M2),$$
$$append(M4, [m(A, B) \mid M5], M1).$$

together with the clauses for *append*.   □

5   Applying Best-first Control Strategies to the Incremental Transformation Procedure

During the execution of the Incremental Transformation procedure the following actions are performed in a nondeterministic way:

i) the introduction of the set of definition clauses when executing the Definition & Folding steps,

ii) the selection of the atoms in the body of the clauses when executing the Unfolding steps, and

iii) the choice of the Replacement Laws to be applied.

Thus, the execution of the Incremental Transformation procedure for a program P and a property Φ generates a possibly infinite tree whose nodes are labelled by programs derivable from P. This tree is called *IT-tree* and it is constructed as follows.

The root is labelled by program P.

If a node N is labelled by a program Q and by using the Incremental Transformation procedure we may derive a program R from program Q then N has a son M labelled by R. (Since the Incremental Transformation procedure is nondeterministic, node N may have more than one son.)

The arc from N to M is labelled by the transformation step performed by the procedure for deriving R from Q. Thus, an arc may be labelled either by 'Definition & Folding', or 'Unfolding', or 'Replacement'. A node of the IT-tree is a leaf iff the corresponding program either i) satisfies Φ, or ii) it does *not* satisfy Φ and the transformation steps prescribed by the Incremental

Transformation procedure cannot be performed. In case i) the node is called a *success* leaf, while in case ii) it is called *failure* leaf.

For each node N of an IT-tree the program which labels N is partitioned into two subprograms, $Transf(N)$ and $Rest(N)$, which are the values of *TransfP* and *RestofP* corresponding to that node in the Incremental Transformation procedure.

We will now study the problem of traversing an IT-tree and searching for a program satisfying the given property Φ.

Let us first notice that strategies which do not use any heuristic information on our particular domain, such as depth-first and breadth-first strategies, are not feasible in our case. Indeed, a depth-first search may fail to find a success leaf of the IT-tree, because this tree may be infinite. On the other hand, a breadth-first search of the IT-tree will surely find a success leaf, if there exists one, because this tree has finite branching, but it will often construct too many nodes.

Thus, we will consider search strategies with heuristic information. We refer the reader to [11,3] for a general introduction to the use of this kind of search strategies. For our purposes we only need the following definitions.

Definition 2. (*Best-first Search Strategy*) Let T be a tree, $(L, \leq)$ a linear order, and ϵ a function from the set of nodes of T to L. The function ϵ is called an *evaluation function* for T.

Let S be a (possibly infinite) sequence of nodes of T. The set $Open(S)$ of open nodes of S is the set $\{M \mid M \text{ is a son of a node in } S \text{ and } M \text{ is not in } S\}$.

A *best-first* search of T *generated* by ϵ is a (possibly infinite) sequence $H(\epsilon) = N_0, \ldots, N_k, \ldots$ of nodes of T constructed as follows: N_0 is the root of T and for every $k \geq 0$, N_k is a node in $Open(N_0, \ldots, N_{k-1})$ for which the value of ϵ is minimal in L. $\qquad \Box$

Notice that a given evaluation function ϵ may generate more than one search, because for some $k \geq 0$ in $Open(N_0, \ldots, N_{k-1})$ there may be more than one node for which the value of ϵ is minimal in L.

Definiton 3. (*Adequate Best-first Strategies*) Let T be an IT-tree and ϵ an evaluation function for T. A best-first search $H(\epsilon)$ of T is *adequate* iff either T does not have any success leaf or $H(\epsilon)$ is a finite sequence of nodes with a success leaf as its last element. $\qquad \Box$

Definition 4. (*Divergent Nodes*) A node N of an IT-tree is said to be *divergent* iff N has an ancestor A such that i) $Rest(A) \subseteq Rest(N)$, and ii) an arc outgoing from N has a label equal to the one of the arc outgoing from A on the path from A to N. The inclusion of condition i) should be understood modulo renaming of variables in the clauses. $\qquad \Box$

We leave to the reader the proof of the following property of IT-trees.

Lemma 5. If an IT-tree T has a success leaf then in T there is a success leaf without divergent ancestors. $\qquad \Box$

For presenting the main result of this section we need the notion of predicate renaming of a program.

Definition 6. (*Predicate Renaming of a Program*) Let us consider the following equivalence relation ρ between programs: $P\rho Q$ iff either $P = Q$ or $P\rho R$, where R can be obtained from program Q by replacing all occurrences of a predicate symbol in Q by a different predicate symbol not in Q. Given a program P, we denote by $\rho(P)$ the equivalence class of P w.r.t. ρ. □

The following theorem enables us to construct adequate best-first strategies for traversing IT-trees.

Theorem 7. Let μ be a function from the set of all equivalence classes of programs w.r.t. ρ to a well-founded linear order $(L, \leq)$. Given an IT-tree T, let us suppose that for every x in L the set:
$$\{\rho(Rest(N)) \mid N \text{ is a node in } T \text{ and } \mu(\rho(Rest(N))) = x\}$$
is finite. Consider the evaluation function ϵ defined as follows: for every node N in T,
$$\epsilon(N) = \textit{if } N \text{ is divergent } \textit{then } \infty \textit{ else } \mu(\rho(Rest(N))),$$
where ∞ is an element not in L such that $x \leq \infty$ for every x in L. Then all best-first searches of T generated by ϵ are adequate.

Proof. We will reason by contradiction. Suppose that ϵ generates a best-first search $H(\epsilon)$ of T which is not adequate. Thus, T has a success leaf, say S, and $H(\epsilon)$ is an infinite sequence containing no success leaves.

Let K be the ϵ value of the ancestor A of S which belongs to $Open(H(\epsilon))$. Let F be the father of A and $H_F(\epsilon)$ the subsequence of all nodes which follow F in $H(\epsilon)$. By Lemma 5 we may assume that S has no divergent ancestors, and therefore, K is different from ∞. Every node in $H_F(\epsilon)$ has an ϵ value not larger than K, otherwise by definition of best-first search, node A would occur in $H_F(\epsilon)$. Thus, for every node N in $H_F(\epsilon)$, N is not divergent and $\mu(\rho(Rest(N)))$ is not larger than K. Since $(L, \leq)$ is a linear order $\mu(\rho(Rest(N))) \leq K$.

The set $\{\rho(Rest(N)) \mid N \text{ is a node in } T \text{ and } \mu(\rho(Rest(N))) \leq K\}$ is finite, by our hypotheses on μ and because $(L, \leq)$ is well-founded. Since the branching of the IT-tree is finite and the set of the labels of the arcs is finite, there exists an infinite subsequence $N_1, N_2, \ldots$ of $H_F(\epsilon)$ and an arc label V such that: i) $\rho(Rest(N_1)) = \rho(Rest(N_2)) = \ldots$, ii) N_i is an ancestor of N_j for any $i < j$, and iii) for every $i > 0$ the arc outgoing from N_i on the path from N_i to N_{i+1} has label V.

Since no divergent node occurs in $H_F(\epsilon)$, there must be an infinite number of different predicates in $H_F(\epsilon)$, otherwise there exist two nodes N_h and N_k in the above infinite subsequence such that $h < k$ and $Rest(N_h) = Rest(N_k)$ (and this entails that N_k is a divergent node). An infinite number of these predicates must have been introduced by adding new definition clauses during Definition & Folding steps of the Incremental Transformation procedure.

Let us consider the infinite set $\{DF_1, DF_2, \ldots\}$ of nodes corresponding to the programs derived by these Definition & Folding steps. Recalling that during the procedure no two synonym definition clauses are introduced and, by construction, the body of each definition clause contains only predicate symbols already occurring in the initial program P, we have that the set $\{\rho(Rest(DF_i)) \mid i > 0\}$ is infinite. Since, by hypothesis, for every x in L

the set $\{\rho(Rest(DF_i)) \mid i > 0 \text{ and } \mu(\rho(Rest(DF_i))) = x\}$ is finite, we have that the set $\{\mu(\rho(Rest(DF_i))) \mid i > 0\}$ is infinite. (Recall that every definition clause introduced when generating the program at node DF_i belongs to $Rest(DF_i)$). This contradicts the fact that for every $i > 0$ DF_i is in $H_F(\epsilon)$ and therefore for every $i > 0$ $\mu(\rho(Rest(DF_i))) \leq K$ because $(L, \leq)$ is well-founded. $\square$

Example 4. (*Maximal Clause Size*) Let us consider the function μ from the set of all equivalence classes of programs w.r.t. ρ to the set of natural numbers, defined as follows: for every program *Prog*,

$$\mu(\rho(Prog)) = max\{size(C) \mid C \text{ is a clause in } Prog\}$$

where $size(C)$ is the number of occurrences of symbols in C.

The function μ satisfies the hypotheses of Theorem 7. Indeed, no new function symbols are introduced during the construction of the IT-tree, and for a given natural number n, using a finite number of function symbols, we can construct only a finite number of ρ-equivalence classes of programs whose clauses have size not larger than n.

Thus, given any instance of the Transformation Problem we can solve it, if a solution exists, by generating a best-first search of the corresponding IT-tree where the evaluation function ϵ is defined as follows:

$$\epsilon(N) = \textit{if } N \text{ is divergent } \textit{then } \infty$$
$$\textit{else } max\{size(C) \mid C \text{ is a clause in } Rest(N)\}$$

$\square$

6 Conclusions

We have proposed a general strategy for solving instances of the following abstract Transformation Problem: given a program P and an *admissible* property Φ, we are required to find a program *TransfP* equivalent to P such that Φ holds for *TransfP*.

One of the distinguishing features of our strategy is that it is an incremental strategy, in the sense that if a clause satisfies Φ at some point of the transformation process then it will not be further transformed during subsequent transformation steps.

The proposed strategy is nondeterministic and it generates a possibly infinite tree of programs which are all derivable from the given program P. We have specialized the concept of *best-first* search to the problem of traversing that tree of programs, and we have provided a sufficient condition for the adequacy of a search strategy, that is, for the ability of finding a solution to the Transformation Problem in hand, if it is at all solvable using the proposed incremental strategy.

Obviously, a generic best-first search is not guaranteed to be more efficient than a breadth-first one. However, for each given application domain we may obtain an efficient best-first search by choosing an evaluation function which is suitable for that domain.

We did not establish any relationship between the success of our techniques and the increase of program efficiency. Since in various examples we observed that different instances of the property Φ generate programs with different time and space complexities, it would be interesting to analyze the relationships between the parameters of the Transformation Problem and the improvement of program efficiency.

The syntactical shape of the programs derived by transformation is a significant parameter and it is often very helpful for driving efficiency improving transformations. Indeed, in the transformation system for recursive equation programs described in [5], some steps are driven by the syntactic pattern of the equations to be derived.

Research areas related to ours include the definition of a suitable metalanguage for describing and manipulating the property Φ which expresses the desired program shape. Some experiments in this direction have already been performed (see, for instance, the use of λProlog for implementing program transformers [10]).

Our techniques have been developed in the case of definite logic programs. However, we believe that they do not depend in any significant way on the particular syntax and semantics of those programs and, therefore, their extension to more sophisticated logic languages and/or semantics does not seem hard.

One could strengthen our techniques by specializing them to particular domains. For instance, in some cases the unfolding process can be guided in an 'almost deterministic' way. This is the case for transformation techniques such as Compiling Control [2], Partial Deduction [7,9], and Eliminating Unnecessary Variables [13].

7   Acknowledgements

We would like to thank all participants in the LOPSTR '92 Workshop in Manchester for helpful and stimulating discussions on the topics of logic program synthesis and transformation. The IASI Institute of the National Research Council of Italy provided the necessary computing and financial facilities.

References

[1] A. Bossi, N. Cocco, and S. Etalle. Transforming normal programs by replacement. In A. Pettorossi, editor, *Proceedings of the Third International Workshop on Metaprogramming in Logic (Meta '92), Uppsala (Sweden)*, pages 204–220. Uppsala University, June 1992.

[2] M. Bruynooghe, D. D. Schreye, and B. Krekels. Compiling control. *Journal of Logic Programming*, 6:135–162, 1989.

[3] A. Bundy. *The Computer Modelling of Mathematical Reasoning*. Academic Press, 1983.

[4] R. M. Burstall and J. Darlington. A transformation system for developing recursive programs. *Journal of the ACM*, 24(1):44–67, January 1977.

[5] M. S. Feather. A system for assisting program transformation. *TOPLAS*, 4(1):1–20, January 1982.

[6] P. A. Gardner and J. C. Shepherdson. Unfold/fold transformations of logic programs. In J.-L. Lassez and G. Plotkin, editors, *Computational Logic, Essays in Honor of Alan Robinson*, pages 565–583. MIT Press, 1990.

[7] H. J. Komorowski. Partial evaluation as a means for inferencing data structures in an applicative language: A theory and implementation in the case of Prolog. In *Proceedings of the Ninth ACM Symposium on Principles of Programming Languages, Albuquerque, New Mexico (USA)*, pages 255–267, 1982.

[8] J. W. Lloyd. *Foundations of Logic Programming*. Springer-Verlag, Berlin, Second Edition, 1987.

[9] J. W. Lloyd and J. C. Shepherdson. Partial evaluation in logic programming. *Journal of Logic Programming*, 11:217–242, 1991.

[10] D. Miller and G. Nadathur. A logic programming approach to manipulating formulas and programs. In *Proceedings of the 1987 IEEE Symposium on Logic Programming, San Francisco, CA (USA)*, pages 379–388. IEEE Press, 1987.

[11] N. J. Nilsson. *Principles of Artificial Intelligence*. Springer-Verlag, 1982.

[12] M. Proietti and A. Pettorossi. Semantics preserving transformation rules for Prolog. In *Proceedings of the ACM Symposium on Partial Evaluation and Semantics Based Program Manipulation, PEPM '91, New Haven, CT (U.S.A.)*, pages 274–284. SIGPLAN NOTICES, 26, 9 (1991), 1991.

[13] M. Proietti and A. Pettorossi. Unfolding-definition-folding, in this order, for avoiding unnecessary variables in logic programs. In N. Jones, editor, *LNCS n. 528, Proceedings PLILP 91, Passau (Germany)*, pages 347–358. Springer-Verlag, 1991.

[14] T. Sato. An equivalence preserving first order unfold/fold transformation system. In *LNCS n. 463, Proceedings ALP 90, Nancy (France)*, pages 175–188. Springer-Verlag, 1990.

[15] H. Seki. Unfold/fold transformation of stratified programs. *Theoretical Computer Science*, 86:107–139, 1991.

[16] H. Tamaki and T. Sato. Unfold/fold transformation of logic programs. In S.-Å. Tärlund, editor, *Proceedings of the Second International Conference on Logic Programming, Uppsala (Sweden)*, pages 243–251. Uppsala University, 1984.

Deriving Transformations of Logic Programs Using Abstract Interpretation

Dmitri Boulanger[1]   Maurice Bruynooghe[2]

Department of Computer Science, Katholieke Universiteit Leuven
Celestijnenlaan 200 A, B-3001, Heverlee, Belgium
email: {dmitri, maurice}@cs.kuleuven.ac.be

Abstract. An extension of OLDT based abstract interpretation for definite logic programs is presented. The extension can abstract the behavior of programs under non standard computation rules, i.e. coroutining. The abstract behavior is captured in an EOLDT structure. It is shown that this EOLDT structure can guide an automatic equivalence preserving fold/unfold transformation. By making the appropriate choices during the abstract interpretation phase, one can obtain EOLDT structures which lead to a very broad range of transformations. It is argued that the approach provides a unifying framework for a large class of transformations.

1. Introduction

The operations of fold and unfold are the basis of lots of logic program transformation techniques [TaS84, PPe90, PPe91, BDK89, DMB91]. The unfold transformation corresponds to an evaluation step of SLD resolution and consists in having an atom substituted by its definition, namely by the bodies of the clauses that define it. Thus these transformations can be considered as a step in a partial evaluation procedure [LlS91], [BeL90]. The fold transformation is the inverse operation: a conjunction of atoms is substituted (folded) by an atom. Folding is used to terminate the unfolding process and to express recursion. The transformations have to be safe: the initial and final program should be equivalent wrt some semantics.

Fold/unfold based transformations and closely related techniques have been used to realize a large variety of program transformations. Well-known examples are partial evaluation [LlS91], the loop merging and elimination of intermediate data structures [BuD77], [Deb88], and compilation of non standard computation rules [BDK89].

Different versions of the residual program can be generated using different unfold/ fold transformations. To generate the most suitable version, we need a mechanism capable to produce different safe unfold/fold transformations of the source program. This class of transformations should be as large as possible. The main contribution of this paper is to develop a single technique which can cover a large *search space*. The

---

1. supported by the Belgian "Diensten voor Programmatie van Wetenschapsbeleid", under the contract AI/02/07 (AIXX666)
Permanent address: Institute for Informatics Problems (IPIAN), Russian Academy of Science, 30/4 Vavilov st., 117900 Moscow, Russia, Email: blng@sms.ccas.msk.su
2. supported by the Belgian National Fund for Scientific Research

technique can be equiped with different transformation strategies. Apart from using transformation strategies in the examples, the choice of strategies will not be discussed in this paper.

So, in this paper, we propose a general framework for deriving different fold/unfold transformations of definite logic programs. The transformation consists of two phases. Firstly, at the abstract interpretation phase, some properties of the global behavior of the source program are collected. This information includes the set of abstract call/ answer pairs of a set of abstract conjunctions of atoms. They cover the set of all the concrete pairs occurring during the real execution of the program. Also a finite tree-like structure used to represent the source program behavior is extracted during this phase. The particular conjunctions of atoms and the abstract representation of their call/exit patterns can be arbitrarily chosen and used to control the structure of the residual program. Secondly, the collected information is used to obtain new definition clauses and to generate the equivalent unfold/fold transformation sequence of the source program.

The basic mechanism for the abstract interpretation is extended abstract OLDT resolution. After some preliminaries, the extended OLDT resolution is described in section 2. Section 3 extends it to fit some requirements of abstract interpretation and of the subsequent fold/unfold transformation. Examples, as well as the transformation algorithm together with the proof of its correctness can also be found in Section 3.

2. Preliminaries

In the following the standard terminology and knowledge of the basic theory of logic programming, as can be found in [LLo87], is assumed. In the section below we give some basic notions, which slightly deviate from the standard ones.

We consider definite logic programs to be collections of definite clauses written as $c: H \leftarrow A_1, ..., A_n$, where $head(c)$ and $body(c)$ will denote the head atom H and the conjunction of the body atoms $A_1, ..., A_n$ of the clause c respectively. Throughout the paper logic programs are denoted by P, Q and R, while for atoms we use the letters A and H, and conjunctions of atoms are denoted by B and D. Expressions are denoted by E and idempotent substitutions are denoted by θ.

In the sequel we will deal with queried logic programs. A *queried logic program* is a logic program P having at least one clause of the form $c: \varepsilon (V_1, ..., V_m) \leftarrow B$, where ε / m is a predicate symbol of arity m not occurring in the bodies of the clauses of P and $V_1, ..., V_m$ are variables. This implies that any queried logic program will always have the standard initial query (goal) of the form $\leftarrow \varepsilon (...)$. The clauses defining the ε-predicate declare *all* the "entry points" of the program P. Given the queried logic program P and the initial goal $\leftarrow \varepsilon (V_1, ..., V_m)$, a computed answer substitution for the initial goal of P is obtained by restricting the composition of $\theta_1 ... \theta_k$ to the variables $V_1, ..., V_m$, where $\theta_1, ..., \theta_k$ is the sequence of mgu's used in an SLD refutation for the initial goal. Two queried logic programs P and R are said to be equivalent $P \sim R$ if and only if the set of computed answer substitutions of P is identical to that of R.

The transformation of a program P into a program R will be denoted by $P \Rightarrow R$. The unfold/fold transformations $P \Rightarrow R$ discussed below change the set of predicate symbols of P by introducing clauses defining completely new predicates.

The only predicate shared by P and R is ε/m. So it is convenient to consider the predicate symbol ε/m is not belonging to the alphabet of the queried logic program. This allows to freely modify the alphabet of the program during transformation and to check equivalence through the set of computed answer substitutions for ε/m.

3. Extended OLDT Resolution

OLDT resolution as introduced by Tamaki and Sato [Tas86] deviates from SLD resolution in two ways. Firstly, the computation rule is such that always a most recent literal is selected. Secondly, a so called extension table or solution table is used which stores atoms selected by the computation rule together with a list of answers. When an atom is selected which is a variant of an entry in the table, then the answers stored in the table are used. A second so called look up table provides some bookkeeping such that not only the currently available answers are used but also answers which become available at a later time.

Extended OLDT deviates from OLDT in the following ways:

- the keys of the entries in the solution table are not atoms but conjunctions of atoms
- the computation rule is more flexible

EOLDT resolution can be formalized by the following definitions which are adaptations of those by Plümer [Plü90]. An EOLDT structure is a partial tree (a leaf need not to be an empty goal or a failing goal) with two tables, a solution table Ts and a lookup table Tl. Every node contains a goal $\leftarrow A_1, ..., A_n$ represented as the ordered sequence $\langle B_1, ..., B_m \rangle$ of conjunctions of atoms (blocks) and is classified as a solution node, a lookup node, a failure node or a success node. *Block size* is the number of atoms in a block. The restriction upon the computation rule is that only an atom from the first block can be selected. A solution table is a set of entries. Each entry consists of a pair of a key and a list (called solution list) where the key is a block of atoms and the elements of the solution list are distinct instances of the key. The lookup table is a bookkeeping device which is used to keep track which members of a solution list have already been used in lookup nodes (more details in [Plü90, TaS86, KaK92]).

Definition 1. Initial EOLDT Structure
Given a program P and a standard query $\leftarrow \varepsilon(...)$ for a predicate not occurring in the body of the clauses of P, the initial EOLDT Structure is a triple (Tr_0, Ts_0, Tl_0), where Tr_0 is a partial EOLDT tree consisting of a single node (the root) with goal $\leftarrow \varepsilon(...)$ and represented as $\langle [\varepsilon(...)] \rangle$, Ts_0 is the empty solution table and Tl_0 the empty lookup table. The node is unclassified. ☐

Definition 2. Extension of an EOLDT Structure
Given a program P and an EOLDT structure $T = (Tr, Ts, Tl)$. An immediate extension of T by P is the result of applying (if possible) the following two operations.

1. Select a node v in Tr which is either a solution node and a leaf or a lookup node with unused elements on its solution list. Let $\langle B_1, ..., B_n \rangle$ be the goal at node v.
   - *SLD extension*: If v is a solution node and a leaf, then the computation rule

selects A_j from B_1. Let c_i, $1 \leq i \leq k$ be the clauses, such that $head(c_i)$ and A_j have the mgu θ_i. Then add k **unclassified new** child nodes. The i-th child k contains the goal $\langle B'_1, \ldots, B_n \rangle \theta$, where B'_1 is B_1 with A_j replaced by the body of c_i. The directed edge from v to its child is labeled by θ_i and by c_i. A v is a **failure** leaf node when no clause matching A_j exits. One or more sequential SLD extensions will be called an **SLD path** of the EOLDT tree.

● **Lookup extension**: If v is a lookup node with unused solutions (this can be checked using the lookup table), then B_1 has a permutation such that it is a variant of a key in the solution table. An **unclassified new** child is created for each unused element of the solution list. These child nodes are called **X-nodes**. The child contains the goal $\langle B_2, \ldots, B_n \rangle \theta_i$, where θ_i is the unifier of the permutation of B_1 and the element in the solution list. The lookup table is adjusted. The directed edge from v to its child is labeled by θ_i and by the corresponding element of the solution list. These edges are called **X-arcs** of the EOLDT tree.

2. For each unclassified new node v:
    ● If the first block of the goal of the node v is empty, then for every ancestor node w with a goal $\langle D, \ldots \rangle$ such that D is a key of the solution table and the path from w to v is a refutation for the conjunction of atoms in D labeled with substitutions $\theta_1, \ldots, \theta_k$, add $D\theta_1 \ldots \theta_k$ as a new element (if it is not a variant of an existing element) to the solution list of D. Remove the first block of the goal of the node v.
    ● If the sequence of blocks is empty ($[]$), it is a **success** node of the EOLDT tree.
    ● Else, if the sequence of blocks has the form $\langle B_1, \ldots, B_n \rangle$, $n \geq 1$, then partition B_1 into non empty parts $B_{11}, \ldots, B_{1m}$, $m \geq 1$ and replace the goal by $\langle B_{11}, \ldots, B_{1m}, B_2, \ldots, B_n \rangle$. If B_{11} is a permutation of a variant of a key in the solution table then classify the node as either a **lookup node** or a **solution node**. Else, create a new entry in the solution table with B_{11} as key and classify the node as a **solution node**. ☐

Definition 3. (Complete EOLDT tree).
An EOLDT tree is **complete**, if its corresponding EOLDT structure can not be extended. ☐

By always splitting the first block B_1 of an unclassified node in a set $B_{11}, \ldots, B_{1m}$ of singleton blocks with B_{1i} containing the i-th atom of the block and by classifying a node as a lookup node whenever possible, EOLDT reduces to OLDT. By always splitting the first block B_1 (if not a singleton block) of an unclassified node in a singleton block B_{11} and a remainder B_{12}, where the singleton can be any atom from B_1, EOLDT reduces to OLDT with *local selection function* [Vie89]. Our main extension is that the key of an entry in the solution table can be a conjunction of atoms (block), that these atoms can be executed in a "coroutining" mode and that the solutions are solutions to the block as a whole.

The following proposition summarizes the most important properties of the EOLDT resolution.

Proposition 1.
EOLDT resolution is sound and complete.

Proof follows from Soundness and Completeness of SLD resolution and OLDT resolution. ☐

By using a properly chosen algorithm (details in [TaS86]) a finite EOLDT structure can be constructed for any definite logic program having a finite extended minimal model (EMM) [FLM89]. This is not true for SLD resolution: there are function free logic programs (these programs have always a finite EMM), which have no finite SLD tree (see example in [Llo87]). Thus, it seems that OLDT-based static analysis could be much better than SLD-based as presented in [LlS91], [BeL90] because the former one has an advantage from the termination point of view.

In the sequel we will assume that an EOLDT structure is extended as follows:

1. Nodes of an EOLDT tree are identified by a unique number. The numbering starts from the root and has the following properties:
   - the root has number 0
   - if there is a directed path from node i to node j, then $i < j$.

2. Each entry in the solution table is associated with the number of the node, which triggered the creation of the entry.

3. Any lookup node i has a label *lookup(j)*, where j is the node associated to the entry of the solution table, which was used in the lookup extension of node i.

4. Some nodes have a ± label; they are the root (node 0) and all the nodes i for which there exists a lookup node labeled by *lookup(i)*.

Note that any leaf of a finite complete EOLDT tree is a success node, a failure node, or a *lookup(i)*-node with an empty solution list associated to the node i. The latter lookup nodes can be considered as failure nodes.

In the next section we will use the following technical definition:

Definition 4. (Set of Answer Nodes).
Suppose that there exists an element D of the solution list of the solution table entry associated with node i. Any refutation of the first block B of the goal of the node i (it is a variant of the entry key) is an EOLDT tree path from node i to some node j labeled by substitutions $\theta_1, ..., \theta_n$. Then the node j is in the set of answer nodes of the element D if and only if D can be represented as a variant of $B\theta_1...\theta_n$. ☐

An extensive example of an EOLDT tree structure is given in the next section.

4. A Transformation Using Abstract EOLDT Resolution

The main purpose of introducing EOLDT resolution is to suggest a flexible and powerful mechanism for the static analysis of the run-time program behavior. In general, analysis of real program execution cannot be done in all details, so we need abstraction to represent the program execution by some finite structure. A *Finite Complete* EOLDT tree can be used to represent the behavior of the program, but very often a finite EOLDT tree does not exist for a given program. Thus to obtain a finite representation of the program behavior we need to construct a sound abstract finite complete EOLDT tree.

An abstract Finite Complete EOLDT tree can be compiled into a sequence of primitive transformation operations such as definition, fold and unfold. The program obtained as a result of the transformations derived from a complete EOLDT tree will always be equivalent to the source program with respect to the set of answer substitutions for the variables of the initial goal. The main idea is the following: the SLD paths of the EOLDT tree can be transformed into sequences of corresponding unfold transformations, while the lookup nodes, for which the tabulation was used, should be used to introduce new definitions and to generate folding operations by using these new definitions as folding clauses. Note that using an abstract complete OLDT tree we can derive only unfolding and predicate renaming transformations (folding of singleton blocks) [Bou92], while tabulation applied to non singleton blocks of atoms produces folding transformations.

Interpreting a logic program by EOLDT resolution has a significant advantage compared to standard SLD resolution. The tabulation mechanism is capable of capturing loops, which can occur during execution of the program and represent them as a lookup extension. Moreover, using abstract tabulation we can always represent infinite loops by a finite solution list and safely approximate the real behavior.

In the section below we describe our framework for the construction of finite complete abstract EOLDT trees and an algorithm for compiling EOLDT trees into a sequence of primitive transformation operations. Correctness of the transformation of a program follows immediately from the completeness of the abstract EOLDT tree, which should be a safe approximation of the concrete one.

4.1. Abstract Interpretation Using Extended OLDT Resolution

Here we use a very simple abstraction mechanism based on the generalization of expressions. The clauses of the program P, the goals of the EOLDT tree and the elements of the solution table will be considered as expressions. Let E be an expression constructed using symbols from the alphabet of program P and some necessary special symbols not occurring in the alphabet of P. Then αE is an abstraction of E if there exists a substitution θ such that $\alpha E \theta = E$. Note that any substitution can only replace a variable by a term constructed from symbols of the alphabet of program P (more details in [Bou92, KeR90]).

EOLDT-based abstract interpretation deviates from the concrete one in the following:

1. The goal has to be abstracted when creating a new unclassified child node. The abstract goal is assigned to the new node. This means, that an abstract EOLDT tree can contain only abstracted atoms. Abstraction of a goal does not change the distribution of the atoms into blocks. Abstracting a goal means that the substitution labelling the arc is generalized. The most general substitution is the empty one. This limits the amount of abstraction possible for a goal.

2. Each new element of a solution list has to be abstracted before inserting it into the solution table.

3. Abstract EOLDT resolution can be started with an initial solution table. Entries in the initial table contain keys which *have to* be used for resolution of the corresponding blocks of atoms, i.e. if the first block of an unclassified node contains atoms, which correspond to the initial key, then this atoms *should be* isolated in the first block and resolved using the solution list. The solution lists for these entries should safely approximate the extended minimal model [FLM89] of the predicates. The corresponding arcs of the tree will be called *EMM extensions*. The EMM-extended nodes have a *lookup(i)* label, where i is the corresponding entry of the initial solution table.

4. Arbitrary different abstraction algorithms can be chosen for the source logic program, for the goals of the abstract EOLDT tree and for the elements of the solution table: the particular abstraction schema should be used to obtain the desired transformation of the source program P and should ensure finiteness of the abstract EOLDT structure.

The EMM-based mechanism can be used for predicates occurring in some closed module of the program, which should not be changed during transformation. The EMM solutions can be used to represent some predefined specialization of the predicates and to safely approximate the interference between the main part of the program and the module. In particular, this mechanism is useful for correctly abstracting the so called built-in predicates, which are often used in Prolog programs. If a built-in predicate has a global side-effect, then these algorithms should be applied very carefully (we will not discuss this).

Example 1. (Abstraction of the Text Processing Program).
Let us consider the following logic program for text processing [PPe90]:

c0: $\mathcal{E}(Char,Text,New\_Text)$:- *text_proc(Char,Text,New_Text).*

c1: *text_proc(Char,Text,New_Text)* :- *del_char(Char,Text,D), del_bcommas(D,New_Text).*

c2: *del_char(Char,[],[]).*

c3: *del_char(Char,[Char|Rest_Text],New_Text)* :- *del_char(Char,Rest_Text,New_Text).*

c4: *del_char(Char,[Char1|Rest_Text],[Char1|New_Text])* :-
         Char=/=Char1, del_char(Char,Rest_Text,New_Text).

c5: *del_bcommas([],[]).*

c6: *del_bcommas([Char|Rest_Text],[Char|New_Text])* :-
         Char=/=blank, del_bcommas(Rest_Text,New_Text).

c7: *del_bcommas([blank,comma|Rest_Text],[comma|New_Text])* :-
         del_bcommas(Rest_Text,New_Text).

c8: *del_bcommas([blank,Char|Rest_Text],[blank|New_Text])* :-
         Char=/=comma, del_bcommas([Char|Rest_Text],New_Text).

This program is processing the text *Text* given in the form of a list of characters by deleting a given character *Char* and by deleting all blank characters occurring immediately before commas. These operations are executed sequentially, i.e. during the first pass all occurrences of *Char* are deleted and an intermediate text D created; during the second pass the final version of the text, *New_Text* is created. The aim of the desired transformation is to run these two processes in parallel and to eliminate the intermediate variable D. For this purpose we use an abstraction αP of the source program P, which reflects the need to investigate how the intermediate text is processed:

$c0$: $\varepsilon(\_,\_,\_) :- tp(\_,\_,\_)$.

$c1$: $tp(\_,\_,\_) :- dc(\_,\_,D), db(D,\_)$.

$c2$: $dc(\_,\_,[])$.

$c3$: $dc(\_,\_,T) :- dc(\_,\_,T)$.

$c4$: $dc(\_,\_,[\_|T]) :- =/=(\_,\_), dc(\_,\_,T)$.

$c5$: $db([],\_)$.

$c6$: $db([\_|T],\_) :- =/=(\_,\_), db(T,\_)$.

$c7$: $db([b,c|T],\_) :- db(T,\_)$.

$c8$: $db([b,C|T],\_) :- =/=(\_,\_), db([C|T],\_)$.

The names of the predicate symbols have been abbreviated. The clauses of αP were obtained by abstracting each clause of the source program and for each $c_i \in P$ we have $c_i \in \alpha P$. Abstraction was used to factor out uninteresting properties of the concrete program. Note that the abstracted program has a larger EMM than the original. ☐

The abstraction of the goals and of the elements of the solution lists can be done during abstract interpretation in a similar way as it was shown for the clauses.

Example 2. (EOLDT-based Abstract Interpretation of Text Processing Program)

The abstract logic program of Example 1 contains one special system predicate $=/=$, which can be abstracted by the following abstract extended minimal model $EMM_{\neq} = \{Z_1 \neq Z_2\}$. Extension of corresponding atoms during abstract interpretation has to be done using its element as a solution from the initial part of the "extended solution table". Note that any predicate of the source program can be abstracted using some extended minimal model. Clauses defining such predicates as well as clauses defining predicates used in these defining clauses have to be preserved in the transformed program. In our example we only have one system predicate, which has no defining clauses.

The complete abstract finite EOLDT tree for the abstracted text processing program is shown in Fig.1. The first blocks are shown in rectangular frames and selected atoms are underlined. Extended blocks in lookup nodes are underlined by dashed lines. The solution table contains only abstracted answers which are variants of the corresponding key, while the goals are not abstracted. This ensures that the solution lists can contain no more than one element. Thus the EOLDT tree can contain only one child for each lookup node. The abstraction schema chosen for this example ensures, that if the block size is restricted, then *any* EOLDT structure for the abstracted Text Processing Program is finite. ☐

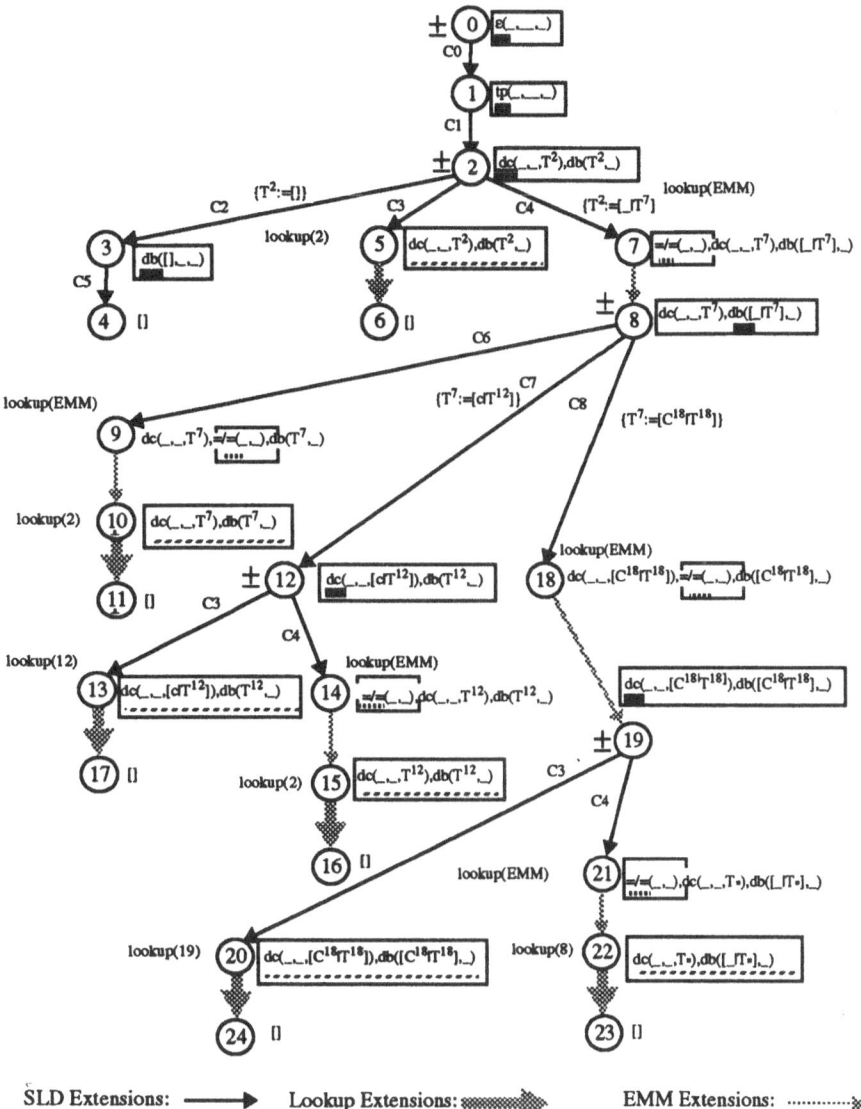

Fig 1: Abstract EOLDT tree for Text Processing Program

4.2. A Transformation Algorithm Guided by An Abstract EOLDT Structure

Below we describe the transformation of the source logic program P to some residual program R. The program R will be defined by a completely new set of predicate symbols. So we have to distinguish them: π and Π will denote respectively an atom and a conjunction of atoms constructed using (new) predicate symbols not occurring in P, while A and B will denote respectively an atom and a conjunction of atoms constructed using predicate symbols of P.

4.2.1. Primitive Transformation Operations

Our transformations consist of sequences of definition, unfolding and folding steps. Definitions for these primitive operations are given below.

Definition 5. (New Clause Definition)
A definition step introduces a new clause: $DEF(\ \pi/n\ ,\{V_1, V_2, ..., V_n\}, B) = \pi(V_1, V_2, ..., V_n) \leftarrow B$, where π/n is a new predicate symbol and each variable from the set $\{V_1, V_2, ..., V_n\}$ occurs in B. $\square$

Definition 6. (Unfolding an atom of a clause)
An unfolding step generates a set of new clauses: $UNFOLD((\pi \leftarrow A, B),$ $Unfolding\_Clauses) = New\_Unfolded\_Clauses$, where $\pi \leftarrow A, B$ is the clause being unfolded, A is the atom being unfolded by Unfolding_Clauses $=$ $\{c_1, c_2, ..., c_N\} \subseteq \{c \in P | mgu\,(head\,(c), A) \neq fail\,\}, N \geq 1$ and New_Unfolded_Clauses $=$
$\{\,(\pi \leftarrow B_k, B)\,\theta_k\big| k = 1, 2, ..., N, \theta_k = mgu\,(A, head\,(c_k)), B_k = body\,(c_k)\,\}$
$\square$

Definition 7. (Folding of atoms in a clause)
A folding step produces one folded new clause: $FOLD((\pi \leftarrow B, B'),\ \pi^f \leftarrow B^f\ )$ $=\ (\pi \leftarrow \pi^f, B')\,\theta$, where $\pi \leftarrow B, B'$ is the clause to be folded, B is the conjunction of the atoms to be folded using the folding clause $\pi^f \leftarrow B^f$ and $\theta = mgu\,(B, B^f) \neq fail$. $\square$

The algorithms below are using these primitive transformation operations.

4.2.2. Compiling an Abstract Finite EOLDT Tree Structure into a Residual Program

Given a finite complete abstract EOLDT structure for a logic program P and initial goal $\leftarrow \varepsilon\,(...)$, the compilation consists of two phases. In the *first phase* a set of definition clauses is generated. This set of definitions consists of two disjoint parts: the definitions to be unfolded *UDEF* and the definitions *FDEF* to be used as folding clauses.

The sets *UDEF* and *FDEF* are generated as follows. for every entry $i > 0$ of the solution table having a key B and a solution list $B\theta_1, ..., B\theta_k$ associated with ±-node i construct the unfold definition clause $udef(i) \in UDEF$ of the form $\pi_i\,(V_1, ..., V_n) \leftarrow B$ and the fold definition clauses $fdef(i, j) \in FDEF$, $j = 1, ..., k$ of the form $(\pi_i\,(V_1, ..., V_n) \leftarrow B)\,\theta_j$, where $\{V_1, ..., V_n\} = vars\,(B)$. Only one definition, $udef(0) \in UDEF$ of the form $\varepsilon\,(V_1, ..., V_m) \leftarrow \varepsilon\,(V_1, ..., V_m)$ is constructed for the entry associated with the root.

Example 3.
The set of unfolding/folding definitions generated from the abstract EOLDT structure

of the Text Processing Program is the following:

udef(0)			:	$\mathcal{E}(C,T, NT)$:- $\mathcal{E}(C,T, NT)$.
udef(2)	=	fdef(2,1)	:	p2(C,T,NT,D) :- del_char(C,T,D), del_bcommas(D,NT).
udef(8)	=	fdef(8,1)	:	p8(C,C1,T,NT,D) :- del_char(C,T,D), del_bcommas([C1|D],NT).
udef(12)	=	fdef(12,1)	:	p12(C,T,NT,D) :- del_char(C,T,[comma|D]), del_bcommas(D,NT).
udef(19)	=	fdef(19,1)	:	p19(C,C1,T,NT,D) :- del_char(C,T,[C1|D]), del_bcommas([C1|D], NT).

Note that we have pairs of identical unfold and fold definitions because the corresponding entries of the abstract solution table contain only one answer which is identical to the key.□

The *second phase* performs a sequence of fold/unfold transformations using definition clauses and the *concrete* clauses of program P. The transformations are guided by the abstract EOLDT tree. The transformation algorithm works on a set S of pairs $<c,i>$. The set S is initialized as follows: for each ±-node i we have the pair $<c,i>$, where $c=udef(i)$. Only these pairs will be involved in unfolding operations. The set *Final_Clauses* will contain clauses of the residual program R.

For a better understanding of the algorithm, it is useful to realize the relation between the pair $<c,i>$ and the goal at node i: the body of the clause c is of the form Π, B, where Π is a conjunction of new predicates and B is an instance of an initial segment of the goal at node i. This segment includes at least the first block (for the initial pairs, the part Π is empty while the segment is a renaming of the first block).

The algorithm is as follows:

> *Final_Clauses*:= $\varnothing$
> Mark all initial pairs

while $S \neq \varnothing$ **do**

begin

- Select and remove a pair $<c,i>$ from S
- If c is of the form $\pi \leftarrow \Pi$, then add c to *Final_Clauses*
- **Else if** i is a solution ±-node and the pair $<c,i>$ is not a marked initial pair, then c has the form $\pi \leftarrow \Pi, B, D$, where B corresponds to the first block of the goal of the node i. Perform folding of the atoms of B with $fdef(i,j), i = 1, ..., k$ generating clauses c'_j. The clause c'_j can be generated successfully if B and the body of $fdef(i,j)$ unify. For every clause c'_j add to S the pair $\langle c'_j, j_m \rangle$, where the node j_m is arbitrarily chosen from the set of answer nodes of the element j of the solution list associated with node i.
- **Else if** i is a solution node with the goal $\leftarrow A, B$ and selected atom A, we have that c is of the form $\pi \leftarrow \Pi, A', B'$, where A' is an instance of A and B' is instance of some initial segment of B. For every child j of the node i: let c_j be the

clause of program P labelling the corresponding arc; the clause c_j should be used to unfold A' in clause c, and if successful (A' and $head(c_j)$ unify) the clause c'_j is obtained and the pair $\langle c'_j, j \rangle$ is added to S

• Else i is a lookup node labeled by $lookup(m)$. Let $\pi \leftarrow \Pi, B, D$, where B corresponds to the marked atoms of the first block of the goal of the node i. Perform folding of atoms of B with $fdef(m,j)$, $j = 1, ..., k$ generating clauses c'_j and adding pairs $\langle c'_j, l_j \rangle$ for all child X-nodes l_j of the node i with incoming arc labeled by the element j of the solution list associated to node m. The clause c'_j can be generated successfully if B and the body of $fdef(m,j)$ unify.

end

Add defining clauses for the EMM-abstracted predicates to the set *Final_Clauses* using chosen naming conventions.◻

Failure nodes do not create any new pairs. SLD paths of the tree are compiled into sequences of unfolding operations, while X-arcs are used for extended folding operations. Note that the construction of the definition clauses is guided by the abstract solution table. These clauses define the structure of the residual program: the subset *UDEF* determines the predicates, which (after folding/unfolding) will appear in the residual program, while the subset *FDEF* determines the call patterns of the atoms in the bodies of clauses which define these predicates. Our folding operation deviates of that presented in [TaS84] by applying the type information [KaK92] collected in the answers of the solution table (abstract call/exit patterns extended to the blocks of atoms). The type information in the answers is controlled by the abstraction of the solution table, while the keys are determined by the goal abstraction. The number of different keys, which are allowed by the abstraction, determines the maximal number of predicates of the residual code. Thus the abstract solution table can be used to control the structure of the residual code.

Example 4.
The residual program R obtained from the source program P using the abstract EOLDT structure shown in Fig.1 is the following:

	Transformation Path	New Clauses of Compiled Text Processing Logic Program
c0:	$0{\longrightarrow}1{\longrightarrow}2{\longrightarrow}4$	$\mathcal{E}$(C,T, NT) :- p2(C, T, NT,D).
c1:	$2{\longrightarrow}3{\longrightarrow}4$	p2(C,[],[],[]).
c2:	$2{\longrightarrow}5{\longrightarrow}6$	p2(C, [C|T],NT,D) :- p2(C,T,NT,D).
c3:	$2{\longrightarrow}7{\longrightarrow}8{\longrightarrow}11$	p2(C,[C1|T],|NT,D) :- C=/=C1, p8(C,C1,T,NT,D).
c4:	$8{\longrightarrow}9{\longrightarrow}10{\longrightarrow}11$	p8(C,C1,T,[C1|NT],D) :- C1=/=blank, p2(C,T,NT,D)
c5:	$8{\longrightarrow}12{\longrightarrow}17$	p8(C,blank,T,[comma|NT],[comma|D]) :- p12(C,T,NT,D).
c6:	$8{\longrightarrow}18{\longrightarrow}19$	p8(C,blank,T,[blank|NT],[C1|D]) :- C1=/=comma, p19(C,C1,T,NT,D).
c7:	$12{\longrightarrow}13{\longrightarrow}17$	p12(C,[C|T],NT,D) :- p12(C,T,NT,D).
c8:	$12{\longrightarrow}14{\longrightarrow}15{\longrightarrow}16$	p12(C,[comma|T],NT,D) :- C=/=comma, p2(C,T,NT,D).

Transformation Path	New Clauses of Compiled Text Processing Logic Program
c9: $19\rightarrow20\rightarrow24$	p19(C,C1,[C|T],NT,D) :- p19(C,C1,T,NT,D).
c10: $19\rightarrow21\rightarrow22\rightarrow23$	p19(C,C1,[C1|T],NT,D) :- C=/=C1, p8(C,C1,T,NT,D).

Note that every clause of the program has a corresponding transformation path. This path is a subset of a corresponding EOLDT refutation of the first block of the goal at some $\pm$-node i. This node was assigned the unfold definition clause during initialization of the set of pairs S. The predicate name of the head of the clause was constructed using the node number i. Notice that for $c0$ we could extend the path $0\rightarrow1\rightarrow2$ with any node of the set $\{4, 6, 11, 17, 16, 24, 23\}$. In such cases we have selected the leftmost node. $\square$

Not all predicates of the program generated by the algorithm are necessary: some of them can be eliminated by auxiliary unfolding transformations. Moreover, some predicates can contain unnecessary variables, which should be eliminated [PPe90, PPe91]. These optimizations are discussed below.

4.2.3. Optimization of the Residual Program

In the sequel the residual program, which can be generated by the transformation algorithm, will be referred to as the *intermediate version* of the residual program. Optimization of the intermediate version includes elimination of some predicates by standard unfolding of the corresponding atoms and elimination of unnecessary variables.

For the predicates of the intermediate version of the residual program, the dependency graph DG can be defined, such that if a predicate q of the program occurs in the body of the clause defining p (p depends on q), then there is a directed arc from p to q. The nodes of DG are the $\pm$-nodes of the abstract EOLDT tree, and should be classified as + and - nodes with the following interpretation: predicates of the program with the + nodes can not be eliminated, while the others can be eliminated by unfolding all the occurrences of the atoms with - predicates in the bodies of the clauses of the residual program. Unfolding should be done using all the matching clauses of the program.

The label classification algorithm is the following:

Let $G := DG$ with node 0 having + label

while $G \neq \varnothing$ do

> • For all nodes i in G *do*
> begin
> *If* the node i has + label: delete the node together with all its incoming and outgoing arcs
> *If* node i has - label: for all the nodes j, k in G such that there exist the arcs $j \rightarrow i$, $i \rightarrow k$ add the arc $j \rightarrow k$ and delete the node i together with all its incoming and outgoing arcs

112

end
- For all the nodes i in G not occurring in any maximal strongly connected component of G: assign a - label
- For all the maximal strongly connected components of G: choose an arbitrary maximal subcomponent having a feedback node[1], assign a + label to the feedback node and assign - labels to the nodes from the remaining part of the chosen subcomponent

end

The definitions and the linear-time algorithms for finding all the maximal strongly connected components and all the feedback nodes can be found in [AHU74, GaT78]. The label classification algorithm ensures, that each node of the DG of the program will receive a + or - label. This algorithm is an extension of that suggested in [Plü90] for elimination of mutually recursive predicates.

Proposition 2.
The label classification algorithm ensures that all predicates with - labels can be successfully eliminated by unfolding corresponding atoms in the bodies using all the matching clauses, i.e. this transformation are finite and always generates a program equivalent to the source program with respect to the set of all computed answer substitutions of the initial goal.□

The proof can be obtained as an extension of that in [Plü90]. □

Example 5.
The dependency graph DG and the results of the label classification for the intermediate version of the Text Processing Program are shown in Fig.2. Thus the predicate *p8*

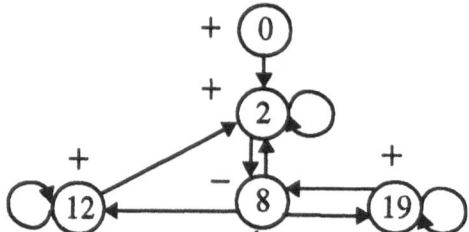

Fig. 2: Predicate Dependency Analysis for Intermediate Version of Text Processing Progra

can be eliminated by unfolding all the corresponding atoms in the bodies of the clauses of the program. □

The elimination of unnecessary variables, which can occur in the intermediate version after folding operations, can be done using the conditions presented in [Ppe90], [Ppe91], [TaS84]. These conditions can be incorporated in the definition clause gener-

1. A feedback vertex of a directed graph G is a vertex contained in *every* cycle of G.

ation algorithm by dropping some variables in the head of the definition clauses. Here we illustrate the variable elimination by an example.

Example 6. (Final Version of Residual Program)

Consider clause $c0$ of the intermediate version of the program. It contains the unnecessary variable D, because D does not occur in the head and has only one occurrence in one atom in the body. So it can be dropped. Starting from this atom and applying conditions of [PPe90, PPe91] we can derive that the predicate $p2$ has an unnecessary fourth argument. After that we obtain that the predicate $p8$ in the body of the clause $c3$ also has an unnecessary variable D. In a similar way we can conclude, that the predicates $p2$, $p8$, $p12$ and $p19$ of the intermediate version have unnecessary last arguments, which can be dropped. Thus the final version of the residual code of the Text Processing Program can be obtained by the eliminating the last argument of all the predicates of the intermediate version (except the initial goal predicate) and by unfolding in the bodies all atoms having the predicate symbol $p8$. The unfolding should be done using all the matching clauses. The final version has the form:

$c0$: $\mathcal{E}$(C,T, NT) :- p2(C, T, NT).

$c1$:   p2(C,[],[]).

$c2$:   p2(C, [C|T],NT) :- p2(C,T,NT).

$c3$:   p2(C,[C1|T],[C1|NT]) :- C=/=C1, C1=/=blank, p2(C,T,NT).

$c4$:   p2(C,[blank|T],[comma|NT]) :- C=/=blank, p12(C,T,NT).

$c5$:   p2(C,[blank|T],[blank|NT]) :- C=/=blank, C1=/=comma, p19(C,C1,T,NT).

$c6$:   p12(C,[C|T],NT):- p12(C,T,NT).

$c7$:   p12(C,[comma|T],NT) :- C=/=comma, p2(C,T,NT).

$c8$:   p19(C,C1,[C|T],NT) :- p19(C,C1,T,NT).

$c9$:   p19(C,C1,[C1|T],[C1|NT]) :- C=/=C1, C1=/=blank, p2(C,T,NT).

$c10$:   p19(C,blank,[blank|T],[comma|NT]) :- C=/=blank, p12(C,T,NT).

$c11$:   p19(C,blank,[blank|T],[blank|NT]) :- C=/=blank, C1=/=comma, p19(C,C1,T,NT).

Note that the final version of the program contains less clauses than the solution given in [Ppe90], and that the latter can be obtained from the intermediate version of the residual program by standard unfolding of some atoms in the bodies. The difference is due to the our algorithm, which applies a more natural procedure for synthesizing new predicates of the residual program, combined with the subsequent label classification procedure. Also notice, that we do not use the so called *Eureka*-algorithms to suggest new predicates. Instead, we have very natural criteria for this: only lookup nodes can "suggest" new predicates. It seems, that the use of *Eureka*-algorithms explains why the algorithms of [Ppe90] are less efficient than our. On the other hand, choosing the right strategy to obtain the adequate EOLDT structure is a kind of *Eureka*-step. ☐

4.2.4. Correctness of the Transformation Algorithm

It is clear, that the result of the optimization described above is always equivalent to the intermediate version of the residual program. So we have to explain the equivalence of the source program P and the program R generated by the transformation algorithm. Given the initial goal $\leftarrow \varepsilon\,(\dots)$ shared by P and R, our transformation of P into R can be represented as a sequence of four macro steps of the following form: $\quad P \Rightarrow Q_1 \Rightarrow Q_2 \Rightarrow Q_3 \Rightarrow R \quad$, where:

- $Q_1 = P \cup UDEF \cup FDEF$ was obtained as a result of introducing new definitions during the first phase of the transformation algorithm
- $Q_2 = \bar{P} \cup R_U \cup FDEF$ was obtained by unfolding some atoms in the bodies of the definition clauses of $UDEF$ (the set of unfolded definitions of $UDEF$ is denoted by R_U and $\bar{P}$ denotes the program P without clauses defining the ε-predicate).
- $Q_3 = \bar{P} \cup R \cup FDEF$ was obtained by folding all atoms in the bodies of the clauses of R_U using the definition of the clauses of $FDEF$ as the folding clauses

Our transformation is close to Tamaki-Sato's unfold/fold transformation for definite programs [TaS84], which was proved to preserve answer substitutions for any goal [KaK88] (here we are interested only in the computed answer substitutions for the initial goal $\leftarrow \varepsilon\,(\dots)$). It is clear, that $P \sim Q_1$ and that Q_1 satisfies the conditions of [TaS84] for the initial program of a standard transformation sequence (the definitions excluding $udef(0) \in UDEF$ introduced by the first phase of the transformation algorithm should be considered as the "new definition" part of the initial program [Sek91]). Moreover, $Q_1 \sim Q_2$ just because the abstract EOLDT tree always forces to use the standard unfolding rules of [TaS84] by choosing all the matching clauses for the atom to be unfolded (we have only one trivial exception for the clauses defining the ε-predicate: we unfold the single atom in the body of the definition clause $udef(0) \in UDEF$ of the form $\varepsilon\,(\dots) \leftarrow \varepsilon\,(\dots)$ by all the clauses of P defining the ε-predicate, immediately generating the same clauses for the ε-predicate of R_U, so after that these clauses can be dropped from P).

In the general case, our folding macro step $Q_2 \Rightarrow Q_3$ violates the conditions of [TaS84] and applies more general transformation rules than those of [PPe90, PPe91], i.e a clause $c = \pi \leftarrow B, D \in R_U$ is folded with a definition $\pi^f \leftarrow B^f$, where B^f and B unify, whereas the condition of [TaS84] states that B must be an instance of B^f. The reason is that the folding rule of [TaS84] is a *local* rule based on syntactical properties. To see that our folding preserves equivalence, one has to realize that it uses *global* type information collected during abstract interpretation. The instances $\pi^f \leftarrow B^f$ are obtained by applying *all* correct abstract exit patterns, and these patterns cover *all* the *concrete* exit patterns of some SLD tree for program P [KaK92]. So one can say that the clause to be folded $c = \pi \leftarrow B, D \in R_U$ is replaced by a set of clauses $c'_j = (\pi \leftarrow B, D)\,\theta_j$, where θ_j, $j = 1, \dots, k$ represent all correct abstract exit patterns. The folding of the appropriate element $(\pi \leftarrow B, D)\,\theta_j$ from this set with $\pi^f \leftarrow B^f$ from $FDEF$ obeys the folding rule of [TaS84].

To prove the equivalence $Q_3 \sim R$ of the transformation step $Q_3 \Rightarrow R$ it is sufficient to notice that the clauses of the subset $FDEF$ of the program Q_3 are no longer necessary, thus the clauses of $FDEF$ can be safely dropped. Also the clauses of $\bar{P}$ can be dropped, because they are only reachable through the clauses of $FDEF$.

5. Conclusion

We have presented a unified framework for deriving unfold/fold transformations of definite logic programs which is based on abstract EOLDT interpretation. The main purpose of the framework is to provide a "complete toolkit" for developing systems for complex logic program transformation. A particular transformation systems can be obtained by enriching the toolkit with a set of strategies for selecting blocks of atoms. The strategies and particular abstraction schemes should be chosen by taking into account the specific restrictions and properties of the problem at hand. The claim for completeness was supported by the examples. They were showing that lots of existing transformation algorithms [PPe90, PPe91, BDK89, DMB91, TaS84] can be explained by choosing appropriate abstraction schemes and strategies for the construction of the blocks of atoms during abstract EOLDT interpretation. This mainly is due to our algorithm for synthesizing the new predicates of the residual program. Choosing strategies and abstraction schemes is not a topic of this paper.

It is also important to note that we obtain equivalent transformations, which do not fit the standard conditions of [TaS84]. Our approach gives rise to the integration of the transformation techniques presented in [GCS88], [GaB90],[GaB91] by incorporating typing information collected during abstract interpretation, i.e the abstract set of solutions in the solution table. We expect that the latter feature of the framework will be very useful when compiling metainterpreters. For this class of transformation problems, when the logic program can be represented as *metainterpreter+object program*, the abstraction schema can be chosen to capture the structure of the object program in the abstract answers of the solution table and to force the EOLDT-driven transformations to penetrate very deeply into the metaprogram. The main idea of the abstraction schema can be the following: only stop abstract interpretation when processing data from the object program. This can be done by introducing fresh variables in the object level terms. This gives the possibility to factor out the syntactical analysis which is embedded in the metainterpreter. Some successful experiments were done using a weaker version of the transformation algorithms [Bou92].

The idea to use abstract OLDT resolution for logic program transformation was borrowed mainly from [GCS88]. In the correctness proof we have used some important results from [KaK92]. The examples and some motivations were found in [PPe90, PPe91, BDK89, DMB91].

6. Acknowledgment

The authors are grateful to Danny De Schreye for pointing out that the method presented in [Bou92] is unable to cope with several important applications and for many stimulating discussions which motivated the development of the EOLDT resolution algorithm.

7. References

[AHU74] Aho,A., Hopcroft,J., Ullman,J., The Design and Analysis of Computer Algorithms, Addison-Wesly, Reading, Mass., 1974.

[BeL90] Benkerimi,K., Lloyd,J., A Partial Evaluation Procedure for Logic Programs,

Proc. 1990 North American Conf. on Logic Programming, Austin, November 1990, 343-358.

[Bou92] Boulanger,D., Deep Logic Program Transformation Using Abstract Interpretation, Proc. 1st and 2nd Russian Conf. on Logic Programming, LNAI, Vol.592, Springer-Verlag, 1992, 79-101.

[BuD77] Burstall,R., Darlington,J., A Transformation System for Developing Recursive Programs, JACM, Jan.1977, Vol.24, No.1, 44-67

[BDK89] Bruynooghe,M., De Schreye,D., Krekels,B., Compiling Control, J. Logic Programming, 1989, Vol.6, Nos.2-3,135-162.

[Deb88] Debray,S., Unfold/Fold Transformations and Loop Optimization of Logic Programs, Proc. SIGPLAN'88 Conf. on Programming Language Design and Implementation, SIGPLAN Notices, July 1988, Vol.23, No.7, 297-307.

[DMB91] De Schreye,D., Martens,B., Sablon,G., Bruynooghe,M., Compiling Bottom-Up and Mixed Derivations into Top-Down Executable Logic Programs, J. Automated Reasoning, 1991, 337-358.

[FLM89] Falaschi,M., Levi,G., Martelli,M., Palamidessi,C., Declarative Modelling of the Operational Behavior of Logic Languages, Theoretical Computer Science, 1989, Vol.69, No.3, 289-318.

[Fut71] Futamura,Y., Partial Evaluation of Computation Process - An Approach to a Compiler-Compiler, Systems,Computers,Control, 1971,Vol.25, 45-50.

[GaB90] Gallagher,J., Bruynooghe,M., Some Low Level Transformations of Logic Programs, Proc. 2nd Workshop in Meta-Programming in Logic, Leuven, 1990, 229-244

[GaB91] Gallagher,J., Bruynooghe,M., The Derivation of an Algorithm for Program Specialization, New Generation Computing, 1991, Vol.9, 305-333.

[GaT78] Garey,M., Tarjan,R., A Linear-Time Algorithm for Finding all Feedback Vertices, Information Processing Letters, 1978, Vol.7, 274-276.

[GCS88] Gallagher, J., Codish M., Shapiro E., Specialization of Prolog and FCP Programs Using Abstract Interpretation, New Generation Computing, 1988, Vol.6, Nos.2-3, 159-186.

[KaK88] Kawamura, T., Kanamori, T., Preservation of Stronger Equivalence in Unfold/Fold Logic Program Transformation, Proc. 4th Int. Conf. on FGCS, Tokyo,1988.

[KaK92] Kanamori, T., Kawamura, T., Abstract Interpretation Based on OLDT Resolution, J. Logic Programming, 1992 (to appear).

[KeR90] Kemp,R., Ringwood,G., An Algebraic Framework for Abstract Interpretation of Definite Programs, Proc. 1990 North American Conf. on Logic Programming, Austin, Nov. 1990, 516-530.

[Lev91] Lever,J., Proving Program Properties by means of SLS-resolution, Proc. 8th

Int. Conf. on Logic Programming, Paris, June 1991, 614-628.

[LlS91] Lloyd,L., Shepherdson,J., Partial Evaluation in Logic Programming, J. Logic Programming, 1991, Vol.11, Nos.3-4, 217-242.

[Llo87] Lloyd,L., Foundations of logic Programming, Springer-Verlag, Berlin, 1987.

[Plu90] Plumer,L., Termination Proofs for Logic Programs, LNAI Vol.446, Springer-Verlag, 1990.

[PPe90] Proietti,M., Pettorossi,A., Construction of Efficient Logic Programs by Loop Absorption and Generalization, Proc. 2nd Workshop in Meta-Programming in Logic, Leuven, 1990, 57-81.

[PPe91] Proietti,M., Pettorossi,A., Unfolding - Definition - Folding, In this Order, For Avoiding Unnecessary Variables in Logic Programs, Proc. 3rd Int. Symp. on Programming Languages Implementation and Logic Programming, Aug. 1991, LNCS No.528, Springer-Verlag, 1991, 347-358.

[Sek91] Seki,H., Unfold/Fold Transformation of stratified programs, J. Theoretical Computer Science, 1991, Vol.86, 107-139.

[TaS84] Tamaki,H., Sato,T., Unfold/Fold Transformation of Logic Programs, Proc. 2nd International Conference on Logic Programming, Uppsala, 1984, 127-138.

[TaS86] Tamaki,H., Sato,T., OLD Resolution with Tabulation, Proc. 3rd Int. Conf. on Logic Programming, London, July 1986, 84-98.

[Vie89] Vielle,L., Recursive Query Processing: The power of Logic, Theoretical Computer Science, 1989, Vol.69, No.1, 1-53.

A Rationalisation of the ATMS in Terms of Partial Evaluation*

Evelina Lamma, Paola Mello

DEIS, Università di Bologna

Viale Risorgimento 2, 40136 Bologna, Italy

{evelina,paola}@deis33.cineca.it

Abstract

This work relates Assumption–based Truth Maintenance Systems (ATMS) to the transformation of logic programs. The ATMS representation, suitably extended to deal with the non–ground case, can be interpreted as an optimised version of a logic program, comparable to that obtained by applying source–to–source transformation techniques such as partial evaluation. Moreover, the ATMS algorithm can be interpreted as an incremental transformation scheme for logic programs whenever a new clause is added.

1 Introduction

Partial evaluation (PE, for short) has been devoted great attention during the last few years since it has been introduced in logic programming [12]. PE is a source–to–source transformation technique which, given a logic program P and a query G, produces a new program P', which is possibly more efficient than P. One technique extensively used in PE is the unfolding [21] of clauses.

This work relates Assumption–based Truth Maintenance Systems [6] to the transformation of logic programs and in particular to unfolding techniques.

Truth Maintenance Systems (TMS) [7] are a common tool in artificial intelligence for managing logical relationships between beliefs and statements. Assumption–based TMS (ATMS) [6] have been more recently proposed in order to maintain multiple sets of beliefs simultaneously, thus allowing inferences in multiple contexts at once. Given a set of clauses (*justifications*), the ATMS provides an efficient representation where each datum (*node*) is related to the minimal sets of atoms (*assumptions*) from which it logically follows. These sets (called *environments*) are reported in a *node label*. Inconsistent environments (i.e. environments which do not satisfy given *constraints* represented as denials) are automatically discarded from the node label. The main feature of the ATMS is incrementality. The addition of a justification initiates an incremental re–labelling of involved nodes, by applying a suitable label–updating algorithm (see [6]).

In this work, we show that the ATMS representation can be considered as the unfolded version of the logic program constituted by the current set of

---

*Work partially supported by CNR Progetto Finalizzato Sistemi Informatici e Calcolo Parallelo under grant n. 92.01606.PF69.

ATMS justifications, where "open" predicates (i.e. predicates subject to being dynamically extended with further definitions, see [2, 18]) correspond to ATMS assumptions. Even if node labels are computed in a bottom–up fashion, in practice they correspond to unresolved literals (viewed as assumptions) encountered during the unfolding process. Interpreting the ATMS as a transformation scheme for logic programs on one hand helps in understanding the ATMS, generally described in an algorithmic way only, and on the other hand can give some insights about partial evaluation techniques. In particular, the ATMS provides:

- A compact representation of the transformed logic program, thanks to the concept of *label minimality*, not considered in the standard partial evaluation scheme;

- An extended partial evaluation scheme also dealing with some form of *integrity constraints*;

- An *incremental* partial evaluation scheme, thanks to the label–updating algorithm that directly provides the updating of nodes when a justification is added.

The ATMS is a restricted reasoning maintenance system which handles propositional (or ground) Horn clauses only. For this reason, it can be interpreted as an incremental partial evaluation scheme for propositional logic programs only. In [15], we extend the basic ATMS to deal with Horn clauses possibly containing variables (hereinafter we call this extension NG–ATMS). In that paper this extension is mainly used for supporting hypothesis generation and intensional query answering in logic programming. In this work, instead, we show how NG–ATMS can be interpreted as an incremental transformation scheme for logic programs possibly containing variables.

When recursive justifications containing variables are added to the NG–ATMS, the termination of the label–updating algorithm is not guaranteed in some cases. The solutions we adopt in this work for loop detection are directly related to the ones defined in [19] for the case of partial evaluation, and can cope with recursion properly.

2   ATMS

We briefly recall the definition of Assumption-based Truth Maintenance Systems (ATMS), originally introduced by de Kleer in [6]. ATMS is a common tool in Artificial Intelligence for caching inferences coming from a problem solver. In particular, the ATMS records the dependencies among data by maintaining multiple contexts of beliefs simultaneously. Data are *believed* or *disbelieved* only with respect to a particular set of assumptions. This way, the reasoning may be carried on in multiple contexts at the same time.

An ATMS receives *justifications* from an associated problem solver, and records the dependencies between the premise and the conclusion of every inference. Justifications can be expressed in first order logic, as propositional definite clauses [22] of the form:

$$A \leftarrow B_1, \ldots, B_n$$

whose meaning is "if $B_1, \ldots, B_n$ are true then A is true". Constraints can be expressed by denials of the form:

$$\leftarrow B_1, \ldots, B_n$$

The reading of a such a constraint is "if $B_1, \ldots, B_n$ are all true then there is a contradiction". Denials correspond to definite clauses of the form:

$$false \leftarrow B_1, \ldots, B_n$$

Each datum (i.e. atomic formula) coming from the problem solver is associated with a *node* of the ATMS. Data corresponding to possible hypotheses are represented by special nodes, called *assumptions*. A set of assumptions is also called an *environment* of the ATMS. A *context* C contains the set of assumptions of an environment E along with the set of nodes which can be derived from those assumptions and from the set of justifications J.

The main task of ATMS is to determine whether a node datum holds in a certain context, given the current set of justifications J and the overall set of assumptions A. To this end, dependencies among data are explicitly represented by associating with each node a label, representative of the set of the environments in which the node datum holds.

The ATMS algorithm ensures that these labels satisfy some conditions. In particular, the label L of a node n is *sound*, i.e. n is derivable from every environment of L, *complete*, i.e. every (consistent) environment from which n is derivable is either an environment of L or a superset of an environment of L, and *minimal*, i.e. no environment of L is a superset of any other environment of L. A label is *consistent* if all its environments are consistent with respect to the constraints. A special node *false* is used to deal with consistency issues. The label of the node *false* contains the minimal sets of assumptions which lead to contradiction (also called *nogood sets*).

To sum up, every ATMS node is a triple of the form $\langle A, L, J \rangle$. The first element is the atomic formula A represented by the node. The second element is the set L of minimal, consistent environments in which A holds (i.e. the label). Finally, the third element is the set of justifications J having A as consequence.

Label environments uniquely characterise ATMS contexts. ATMS determines whether or not a given context/environment E is consistent by verifying that there is no environment E' of the node *false* such that $E' \subseteq E$. Moreover, operationally it determines whether a node n holds in an environment E and a set of justifications J by verifying if the label of n contains an environment E' such that $E' \subseteq E$.

When a new justification is added to the ATMS, node labels are possibly updated in a bottom–up way. Let us suppose that a new justification $C = A \leftarrow B_1, \ldots, B_n$ is added. Then the following steps are performed by the label–updating algorithm:

- A tentative label L' for A is computed. The tentative label for the node A is the union of all possible combinations obtained by choosing an environment from the label of each node B_i. Then subsumed and inconsistent environments are removed from L'.

- If the label of A has not changed, then return.

- If A is a contradiction node (*false*),

    1. Mark all the environments in L' as nogood.
    2. Remove all new nogoods from every node label in the ATMS representation.

- If A is not a contradiction node, then recursively update all consequences of A, by considering the justifications having A as antecedent.

3   Relation with partial evaluation

Partial evaluation (PE, for short) is a source–to–source transformation technique which, given a logic program P and a query G, produces a new program P', which is more efficient than P. As stated in [17] "the basic technique for obtaining P' from P is to construct a partial search tree for P and suitably chosen atoms as goals, and then extract the definitions — the *resultants* — associated with the leaves of the tree". The relevant case is when the query is atomic and therefore resultants are definite clauses. These clauses correspond to an unfolded version of the original ones, and replace the old definitions for the given query in the program. The equivalence between P and P' is guaranteed under an appropriate *closedness* condition on the transformed program and the goal to be evaluated (see [17]).

In this section, we show how the ATMS representation of a set of justifications J can be considered as the transformation of the corresponding logic program J, comparable to the one obtained by using unfolding and partial evaluation techniques. In fact, logically, the label of an ATMS node represents a set of propositional Horn clauses. In particular, the label of a node n:

$$\{\{A_1, A_2, \ldots\}, \{B_1, B_2 \ldots\}, \ldots\}$$

represents the set of Horn clauses:

$$n \leftarrow A_1, A_2, \ldots$$

$$n \leftarrow B_1, B_2, \ldots$$

$$\ldots$$

This ATMS representation can be considered as the unfolded version of the logic program represented by the current set of ATMS justifications, where "open" predicates (i.e. predicates subject to being dynamically extended with further definitions, and then suspended during the unfolding process) correspond to ATMS assumptions. Even if node labels are computed in a bottom–up fashion (see the algorithm in section 2), in practice they correspond to unresolved literals (viewed as assumptions) encountered during the unfolding process.

Example 3.1 *Let us consider the following program P:*

$$p \leftarrow q$$
$$q \leftarrow r$$

where r is open. The partial evaluation of P with respect to the query p produces the following program P':

$$p \leftarrow r$$
$$q \leftarrow r$$

which exactly corresponds to the ATMS representation for P. In fact, both node q and p have label $\{\{r\}\}$, and the environment $\{r\}$ corresponds to the bodies of clauses in P'. □

Distinguishing features of the transformation obtained through the ATMS are:

- A compact representation of the transformed logic program, thanks to the concept of minimality not considered in the standard partial evaluation scheme [17];

- An extended program transformation scheme also dealing with some form of integrity constraints, directly supported by the ATMS;

- An incremental partial evaluation scheme, since the current set of justifications can be dynamically augmented.

With reference to the first feature, thanks to the concept of label minimality, the ATMS produces a representation where subsumed clauses are deleted. A clause C' is subsumed by C if C and C' have the same head and each atom occurring in C's body also occurs in C''s body.

Example 3.2 *Let us consider the following program P:*

$$p \leftarrow q$$
$$p \leftarrow q, r$$
$$r \leftarrow t$$

where q and t are open. The partial evaluation of P with respect to the query p is the program P':

$$p \leftarrow q$$
$$p \leftarrow q, t$$
$$r \leftarrow t$$

The ATMS representation of P, instead, associates with node p only the environment $\{q\}$, by deleting $\{q,t\}$ since it is non minimal. In this way it exploits the fact that the second clause in P' is subsumed by the first one. Therefore, it corresponds in practice to the (minimal, equivalent) program:

$$p \leftarrow q$$
$$r \leftarrow t$$

□

Subsumption checking seems to be advantageous since it throws away unuseful computations which can be costly in some cases. However, performing subsumption checking might be expensive in the non–propositional case (see section 4), thus reducing its use in practice.

With reference to the second feature, whenever integrity constraints can be represented as denials, the ATMS can be seen as a transformation scheme which takes integrity checking into account.

Example 3.3 *Let us consider the following program P:*

$$a \leftarrow b, d$$
$$b \leftarrow c$$
$$b \leftarrow e$$

where c, d and e are "open" predicates, and the integrity constraint:

$$false \leftarrow d, c$$

The partial evaluation of P for the query a is:

$$a \leftarrow c, d$$
$$a \leftarrow e, d$$
$$b \leftarrow c$$
$$b \leftarrow e$$

whereas ATMS produces a representation which, for the node a, is:

$$\langle a, \{\{e, d\}\}, \{a \leftarrow b, d\} \rangle$$

and which corresponds to the clause:

$$a \leftarrow e, d$$

In fact, the first clause for a has been eliminated since it is supported by the inconsistent set of atoms $\{c, d\}$. □

With reference to the third feature, up to now partial evaluation has been applied to the case of a single logic programming theory [17, 19], and to a multi–theory framework [4], but not much work has been devoted to study *incremental* partial evaluation [13, 14, 20]. Adding some clause to the program in the first case, or dynamically changing the initial set of theories in the second one, requires, in principle, to apply again the partial evaluation scheme to the entire new program but that might be expensive. It is much more convenient to be able to transform parts of a program in an *incremental* fashion. The label–updating algorithm of the ATMS can be interpreted as an incremental partial evaluation scheme. It is worth noticing, however, that partial evaluation in logic programming is characterised by top–down computations which correspond to the execution of SLD–resolution steps, whereas the ATMS label–updating algorithm is bottom–up. In this sense our work is related to [1], where the authors show that the unfolding semantics of open logic programs is equivalent to a bottom–up transformation very similar to the one adopted in the ATMS label–updating algorithm.

Example 3.4 *Let us consider the program $P = \{r \leftarrow a, \ a \leftarrow b\}$, where b is an open predicate, i.e. it corresponds to an ATMS assumption. Its ATMS representation is:*

$$\langle r, \{\{b\}\}, \{r \leftarrow a\} \rangle$$
$$\langle a, \{\{b\}\}, \{a \leftarrow b\} \rangle$$
$$\langle b, \{\{b\}\}, \{\} \rangle$$

which corresponds to the unfolded program $PE(P)$:

$$r \leftarrow b$$
$$a \leftarrow b$$

When adding the clause $C = \{b \leftarrow c\}$ where c is an open predicate, the label–updating algorithm produces the following representation:

$$\langle r, \{\{b\}, \{c\}\}, \{r \leftarrow a\}\rangle$$
$$\langle a, \{\{b\}, \{c\}\}, \{a \leftarrow b\}\rangle$$
$$\langle b, \{\{b\}, \{c\}\}, \{b \leftarrow c\}\rangle$$
$$\langle c, \{\{c\}\}, \{\}\rangle$$

This representation corresponds to the program:

$$r \leftarrow b$$
$$r \leftarrow c$$
$$a \leftarrow b$$
$$a \leftarrow c$$
$$b \leftarrow c$$

Due to our definition of open predicates, predicates for which some definition is provided can still be considered open. This is the case for predicate b in the program above. An alternative could be to consider b closed as soon as a definition for it is provided. If this is the case, b is no longer an assumption and all the environments containing it are withdrawn from node labels. As a consequence the resulting program would be:

$$r \leftarrow c$$
$$a \leftarrow c$$
$$b \leftarrow c$$

The same program is obtained by applying unfolding to $PE(P) \cup C$. □

4 Dealing with variables

In [15], we extend the basic ATMS to deal with Horn clauses possibly containing variables for supporting hypothesis generation and intensional query answering (hereinafter we call this extension NG–ATMS). In NG–ATMS a new notion of minimality which subsumes the one given for the propositional case is introduced together with an extended label–updating algorithm. The main extensions concern the minimisation phase and the loop detection in the case of recursive justifications. In this section, we recall the basic ideas of how such an extension has been done, and we show how NG–ATMS can be interpreted as a transformation scheme for logic programs containing variables.

In NG–ATMS both justifications and assumptions can contain variables. More precisely, justifications are expressed by possibly *non-ground* definite clauses [16], and assumptions by possibly *non-ground* atomic formulae. In this setting, the label of a node n:

$$\{\{A_1, A_2, \ldots\}, \{B_1, B_2, \ldots\}, \ldots\}$$

represents the set of Horn clauses:

$$n \leftarrow A_1, A_2, \ldots$$

$$n \leftarrow B_1, B_2, \ldots$$

$$\ldots$$

where each clause is universally quantified. This representation corresponds to the partial evaluation of n with respect to the overall set of justifications.

The transformed program obtained through NG–ATMS is more efficient thanks to the minimality feature.

Example 4.1 *Let us consider the following program P:*

$$a(X) \leftarrow b(Y)$$
$$b(Y) \leftarrow c(Z)$$
$$a(X) \leftarrow c(Z), r(T)$$

where c and r are open predicates. The NG–ATMS representation of P is:

$$\langle a(X), \{\{c(Z)\}\}, \{a(X) \leftarrow b(Y), \quad a(X) \leftarrow c(Z), r(T)\}\rangle$$
$$\langle b(Y), \{\{c(Z)\}\}, \{b(Y) \leftarrow c(Z)\}\rangle$$

where the environment $\{c(Z), r(T)\}$ has been deleted from the label of $a(X)$ to maintain minimality. In fact, $\{c(Z)\} \subset \{c(Z), r(T)\}$. The representation above corresponds to the "unfolded" program:

$$a(X) \leftarrow c(Z)$$
$$b(Y) \leftarrow c(Z)$$

Notice that by partially evaluating P with respect to $a(X)$, we would also obtain the clause:

$$a(X) \leftarrow c(Z), r(T)$$

that could cause expensive, useless computations. In fact, if we add the clause:

$$r(T) \leftarrow a(X)$$

the partially evaluated program would generate for goal $\leftarrow a(X)$ an infinite branch, while this is not the case for the corresponding NG–ATMS representation. □

4.1 Minimality revised

When dealing with variables, the main problem is that set inclusion tests are no longer sufficient for determining minimal environments.

Example 4.2 *Let us consider the NG–ATMS node:*

$$\langle a(X), \{\{c(a)\}, \{c(Z)\}\}, \{\ldots\}\rangle$$

The environment $\{c(a)\}$ is somehow redundant since it is subsumed by the environment $\{c(Z)\}$. Thus, the node label is not minimal.

Simply introducing an ordering relationship between environments is not sufficient in some cases to deal with label minimality (see [15] for a deeper discussion). Thus, it is necessary to introduce an ordering relation which involves both the node environments and the datum. This ordering corresponds, in practice, to the notion of clause subsumption for definite clauses given in [8], and it is defined over pairs of the form $\langle A, E \rangle$, where A is an atomic formula and E is an environment. Notice that variables are not shared between different couples.

Definition 4.3 *Let A_1, A_2 be atomic formulae, E_1, E_2 environments, and ϑ a substitution:*

$$\langle A_1, E_1 \rangle \preceq \langle A_2, E_2 \rangle \ \equiv \ \exists \vartheta : \ (A_1)\vartheta = A_2 \wedge E_1 \vartheta \subseteq E_2$$

□

For the definition of an efficient procedure for determining clause subsumption see [9].

NG–ATMS and its extended label–updating algorithm (see [15] for details) guarantee that each couple $\langle A, E_i \rangle$ which can be built starting from any node A and some of its environments E_i is minimal under $\preceq$. This has practical advantages with respect to the usual application of unfolding.

Example 4.4 *Let us consider the following program P:*

$$a(X) \leftarrow b(Y)$$
$$b(Y) \leftarrow c(Z)$$
$$a(X) \leftarrow c(a)$$

where c is an open predicate. Partially evaluating P with respect to the atom $a(X)$ would produce the following program:

$$a(X) \leftarrow c(Z)$$
$$b(Y) \leftarrow c(Z)$$
$$a(X) \leftarrow c(a)$$

Thanks to the adoption of minimality under the $\preceq$ ordering relation, the NG–ATMS representation for $a(X)$ is instead:

$$\langle a(X), \{\{c(Z)\}\}, \{a(X) \leftarrow b(Y), a(X) \leftarrow c(a)\}\rangle$$

The environment $c(a)$ that was redundant (see example 4.2) has been deleted. This representation corresponds to the clause $a(X) \leftarrow c(Z)$. □

Some remarks are worth making here.

First of all, the representation produced by NG–ATMS for a set of justifications J corresponds to the program obtained by partially evaluating J with respect to the set of most general atoms. Thus, soundness and completeness properties are always guaranteed since the closedness condition defined in [17] cannot be violated.

Second, the equivalence between the original and transformed program we consider is with respect to the declarative semantics [22] (i.e., the original and the transformed program have the same success set). In fact, due to the minimality feature, it is not guaranteed that the two programs return the same computed answer substitutions for the same goal.

Example 4.5 *Let us consider the following program (set of justifications) P:*

$$p(X) \leftarrow q(X)$$
$$q(a) \leftarrow$$
$$q(X) \leftarrow$$

The NG–ATMS representation corresponds to the following program P^*:

$$p(X) \leftarrow$$
$$q(X) \leftarrow$$

For the query $p(X)$, in P we get the computed answer substitution X/a, whereas this substitution is not computed in P^*. Thus P and P^* are not equivalent with respect to the operational semantics. □

4.2 Recursive justifications and loop detection

When recursive justifications are added, unlike the propositional case, the termination of the NG–ATMS updating algorithm presented in [15] is not guaranteed in some cases. In fact, it can generate an infinite number of different nodes.

Example 4.6 *Let us consider the following clause:*

$$nat(0) \leftarrow$$

which corresponds to the NG-ATMS node:

$$N_1 = \langle nat(0), \{\{\}\}, \{nat(0) \leftarrow\}\rangle$$

and states that 0 is a natural number.
When the recursive clause:

$$nat(s(X)) \leftarrow nat(X)$$

is added, the algorithm (see [15]) firstly generates the node:

$$N_2 = \langle nat(s(0)), \{\{\}\}, \{nat(s(X)) \leftarrow nat(X)\}\rangle$$

Then, it recursively updates this node, and builds a new node:

$$N_3 = \langle nat(s(s(0))), \{\{\}\}, \{nat(s(X)) \leftarrow nat(X)\}\rangle$$

And so on, generating an infinite number of nodes of the kind:

$$N_m = \langle nat(s(s(s(\ldots(0))))), \{\{\}\}, \{nat(s(X)) \leftarrow nat(X)\}\rangle$$

□

To avoid the generation of an infinite number of nodes, a modification of the label–updating algorithm is required. The algorithm must be able to detect the looping situations and then suspend the updating. We provide some alternative loop detection strategies which can be applied within the NG–ATMS label–updating algorithm, inspired by the ones applied in partial evaluation [19] and in deductive databases for recursive queries (see [15] for a more detailed description).

Let N be the current node to be updated, and NS a node stack containing all the nodes added or updated because of the addition of a justification. A possible strategy could be to detect a loop if the number of nodes N' in node stack NS with $termsize(N) \geq termsize(N')$, where N' precedes N in the node stack, is at least k.

The function $termsize(X)$ is defined on terms as follows:

- 1, if X is a constant or variable;

- $1 + \sum_{i=1}^{arity(X)} termsize(argument(X, i))$ if X is a structured term, where $argument(X, i)$ returns the i–th argument of X.

This strategy is somewhat symmetric to the corresponding one applied in partial evaluation of logic programs. Partial evaluation, in fact, is characterised by top–down computations, whereas the label–updating algorithm of ATMS is bottom–up. Thus, in the case of partial evaluation we are interested in suspending the evaluation when the argument size grows from the head to the body of a clause (see [19]), whereas for NG–ATMS loops possibly arise when the argument size grows from the body to the head of a justification.

The loop detection strategy might become arbitrarily complex and it is easy to devise various extensions of the strategy presented above. For instance, it does not deal correctly with cases where one argument of a node datum grows during the (recursive) updating but some other argument gets smaller. More sophisticated strategies could be adopted to cope with this case also.

Whenever a loop is detected, the label–updating algorithm cannot simply terminate without performing any action, since in this case the completeness property could be lost.

Example 4.7 *Let us consider the example 4.6, and assume that the algorithm stops after detecting the loop (for example with $k = 2$). Thus, we have the following (incomplete) situation:*

$\langle nat(0), \{\{\}\}, \{nat(0) \leftarrow\} \rangle$
$\langle nat(s(0)), \{\{\}\}, \{nat(s(X)) \leftarrow nat(X)\} \rangle$
$\langle nat(s(s(0))), \{\{\}\}, \{nat(s(X)) \leftarrow nat(X)\} \rangle$

corresponding to the transformed program P^*:

$nat(0) \leftarrow$
$nat(s(0)) \leftarrow$
$nat(s(s(0))) \leftarrow$

which is not equivalent to the original program P:

$nat(0) \leftarrow$
$nat(s(X)) \leftarrow nat(X)$

In fact, $P \models nat(s(s(s(s(0)))))$, but $P^* \not\models nat(s(s(s(s(0)))))$ □

To solve this problem, it is sufficient to consider the predicates responsible for the possible loop as *open* (i.e., as ATMS assumptions).

Example 4.8 *Let us consider the example 4.7, and consider $nat(X)$ as an assumption (i.e. predicate nat is open). Now, the algorithm produces the following (complete) situation:*

$$\langle nat(0), \{\{\}\}, \{nat(0) \leftarrow\}\rangle$$
$$\langle nat(s(0)), \{\{\}\}, \{nat(s(X)) \leftarrow nat(X)\}\rangle$$
$$\langle nat(s(s(0))), \{\{\}\}, \{nat(s(X)) \leftarrow nat(X)\}\rangle$$
$$\langle nat(s(X)), \{\{nat(X)\}\}, \{nat(s(X)) \leftarrow nat(X)\}\rangle$$
$$\langle nat(s(s(X))), \{\{nat(X)\}\}, \{nat(s(X)) \leftarrow nat(X)\}\rangle$$
$$\langle nat(s(s(s(X)))), \{\{nat(X)\}\}, \{nat(s(X)) \leftarrow nat(X)\}\rangle$$

corresponding to the transformed program P^*:

$$nat(0) \leftarrow$$
$$nat(s(0)) \leftarrow$$
$$nat(s(s(0))) \leftarrow$$
$$nat(s(X)) \leftarrow nat(X)$$
$$nat(s(s(X))) \leftarrow nat(X)$$
$$nat(s(s(s(X)))) \leftarrow nat(X)$$

which is equivalent to the original one. The clauses:

C1	$nat(s(X)) \leftarrow nat(X)$
C2	$nat(s(s(X))) \leftarrow nat(X)$

are not redundant if predicate nat is considered open. In fact, if you extend the set of constants with zero, add the clause:

$$nat(zero) \leftarrow$$

and delete C1 and C2, you would get incompleteness, since:
$$P \models nat(s(zero)), \ but \ P^* \not\models nat(s(zero)). \qquad \square$$

5 Conclusions

We have shown that the ATMS representation of propositional justifications can be related to the one obtained by transforming logic programs through unfolding and partial evaluation techniques. Considering open predicates as assumptions suffices for obtaining transformed programs which are equivalent (with respect to the declarative semantics) to the original ones. This establishes a first link between program transformation in the logic programming field and reasoning maintenance systems.

In order to consider also non–propositional logic programs, we extend the ATMS to the case of variables (NG–ATMS), revising the minimality concept and the label–updating algorithm. NG–ATMS has been implemented in SIC-Stus Prolog running on a SUN SPARCstation 2. This implementation can be seen as an alternative implementation of a partial evaluator for logic programs, once the NG–ATMS representation of the program is suitably translated into clauses. However, this first prototype cannot be considered a real partial evaluator running system for Prolog since it is rather inefficient and does not deal with system predicates.

Some authors (see [3, 5, 10, 11, 15]) have pointed out the strict relationship existing between abduction and hypothesis generation in logic programming and the ATMS. We will investigate more deeply the relationship between program transformation and abduction in the near future.

References

[1] A. Bossi, M. Gabbrielli, G. Levi, and M.C. Meo. Contributions to the Semantics of Open Logic Programs. In *Proceedings Int. Conf. on Fifth Generation Computer Systems.* ICOT, Tokyo (J), pages 570–580, 1992.

[2] A. Brogi, E. Lamma, and P. Mello. Open Logic Theories. In L.-H. Eriksson, P. Krueger, and P. Schroeder-Heister, editors, *Proceedings of Second Workshop on Extensions of Logic Programming, Lectures Notes in Artificial Intelligence*, n. 596, pages 73–88, Springer-Verlag, 1992.

[3] A. Brogi, E. Lamma, and P. Mello. ATMS for Implementing Logic Programming. *Proceedings 10th European Conference on Artificial Intelligence*, B. Neumann, editor, Vienna, Austria, John Wiley & Sons, pages 114–118, 1992.

[4] M. Bugliesi, E. Lamma, and P. Mello. Partial Deduction for Structured Logic Programming. To appear in *Journal of Logic Programming*, North-Holland, Special issue on Partial Deduction and Partial Evaluation, J. Komorowski, editor.

[5] G. De Giacomo. Intensional Query Answering: An Application of Partial Evaluation. In *Proceedings LOPSTR92*, Manchester, UK, July 1992. To appear.

[6] J. de Kleer. An Assumption-based TMS. *Artificial Intelligence*, 28: 127–162,1986.

[7] J. Doyle. A Truth Maintenance System. *Artificial Intelligence*, 12: 231–272, 1979.

[8] H. Gaifman and E. Shapiro. Fully abstract compositional semantics for logic programs. In *Proc. sixteenth POPL*, pages 134–142, 1989.

[9] A.C. Kim, S.H. Lee, S.R. Maeng and J.W. Cho. A New Algorithm for Subsumption Test. In *Proceedings Int. Conf. on Fifth Generation Computer Systems.* ICOT, Tokyo (J), pages 643–649, 1992.

[10] A.C. Kakas and P. Mancarella. On the Relation between Truth Maintenance and Abduction. In *Proc. PRICAI*, pages 438–443, 1991.

[11] A.C. Kakas, R.A. Kowalski and F. Toni. Abductive Logic Programming. *Technical Report,* Imperial College, London, UK, 1992.

[12] H. J. Komorowski. A specification of an abstract Prolog machine and its application to Partial Evaluation. Technical Report Dissertation, Linkoping University, 1981.

[13] H. J. Komorowski. Towards a Programming Methodology Founded on Partial Deduction. In L. Carlucci Aiello, editor, *Proceedings 9th European Conference on Artificial Intelligence*, pages 404–409. Pitman Publishing, 1990.

[14] H.J. Kugler, K. Benkerimi and J. Shepherdson. Partial evaluation of dynamic programs. Technical Report CS-90-27, Department of Computer Science, University of Bristol, England, 1990.

[15] E. Lamma, and P. Mello. An Assumption-based Truth Maintenance System dealing with Non-ground Justifications. *Proceedings 10th European Conference on Artificial Intelligence*, B. Neumann, editor, Vienna, Austria, John Wiley & Sons, pages 119-123, 1992.

[16] J. Lloyd. Foundations of Logic Programming. Second edition. Springer–Verlag, 1987.

[17] J. Lloyd and J. Shepherdson. Partial evaluation in logic programming. *Journal of Logic Programming*, Vol. 11, No. 3 & 4, pages 217–242, 1991.

[18] D. Miller. A logical analysis of modules in logic programming. *Journal of Logic Programming*, 6:79–108, 1989.

[19] D. Sahlin. The Mixtus Approach to Automatic Partial Evaluation of Full Prolog. In S. Debray and M. Hermenegildo, editors, *Proc. NACLP*, pages 377–398. The MIT Press, 1990.

[20] A. Takeuchi, and K. Furukawa. Partial Evaluation of Prolog Programs and its Application to Meta Programming. In *Proceedings 10th World Computer Congress IFIP86*, pages 415–420. North-Holland, 1986.

[21] H. Tamaki, and T. Sato. Unfold/Fold Transformation of Logic Programs. In *Proceedings 2nd Int.l Logic Programming Conference*, pages 127–138. Uppsala, 1984.

[22] M.H. van Emden and R.A. Kowalski. The semantics of predicate logic as a programming language. *Journal of the ACM*, 23(4):733–742, 1976.

Intensional Query Answering: An Application of Partial Evaluation

Giuseppe De Giacomo

Dipartimento di Informatica e Sistemistica

Università di Roma "La Sapienza"

Via Salaria 113, 00198 Roma, Italia

e-mail: degiacom@assi.ing.uniroma1.it

Abstract

We consider intensional answers to be logical formulas expressing sufficient conditions for objects to belong to the usual answer to a query addressed to a knowledge base. We show that in the SLDNF-resolution framework, complete and procedurally complete sets of intensional answers can be generated by using partial evaluation. Specific treatments of recursion and negation are also presented.

1 Introduction

Intensional answers are responses that provide an abstract description of the conventional answer to a query addressed to a knowledge base. They are expected to "provide compact and intuitive characterizations of sets of facts, making explicit *why* a specific set of facts answers the query instead of just *which* facts belong to the answer" ([PR89]). Various research studies have investigated this kind of answers (e.g., [CD86], [CD88], [Corella84], [Demolombe92], [DFI91], [Imielinski87], [Motro89], [Motro91], [MY90], [PR89], [PRZ91], [SM88], etc.). Following [CD86], [PR89], [PRZ91], we consider intensional answers to be logical formulas expressing *sufficient conditions* for objects to belong to the conventional answer to a query.

We assume knowledge bases to be, essentially, programs whose proof procedure is the SLDNF-resolution, as in [Lloyd87]. Partial evaluation (PE) for programs in the SLDNF-resolution framework is defined in [LS91]. Although it is usually considered an optimization technique, we use it for quite a different aim in this paper.

We show that given a program Γ and a query $Q(X)$, a new program $\Gamma' = P \cup \{q(X) \leftarrow Q(X)\}$ (where q is a predicate symbol not occuring in P) can be defined such that for every PE of $q(X)$ in P' there corresponds a *complete set of intensional answers* to $Q(X)$ in P. Furthermore, each set S_{IA} of intensional answers computed in this way is procedurally equivalent to the original query $Q(X)$, i.e., the conventional answers that can be computed from S_{IA} in P are exactly those that can be computed from $Q(X)$ in P.

Having pointed out this correspondence we have a tool to produce intensional answers for a very general class of queries and programs, i.e., for every query in every program intended to run under SLDNF-resolution. Therefore, in principle, we can deal with function symbols, recursion and negation, something usually ruled out by other approaches to intensional query answering.

Specifically, we suggest a simple but quite effective way to return intensional answers when recursion is involved. Notice first of all that by PE we can obtain recursion-free intensional answers for a query involving recursive predicate symbols. On the other hand, if we cannot remove a recursive predicate symbol p from an intensional answer, then we return, together with the intensional answer, an *auxiliary definition* for p. This is a specialized definition that is general enough to cover the meaning of p in the context of the intensional answers in which it appears. Note that, if a recursive predicate symbol p' other than p shows up in the auxiliary definition for p, then we return an auxiliary definition for p' as well.

The pair $< S_{IA}, AD >$, where S_{IA} is a set of intensional answers to a query $Q(X)$, and AD is a set of auxiliary definitions for S_{IA}, can be interpreted as the implicit representation of the infinite set of all the intensional answers to $Q(X)$, which can be inferred from S_{IA}, using the axioms corresponding to AD.

With regard to negation, we remind the reader that if a negative literal is found at a certain point of the PE process, then either it is completely evaluated, or the atom in the negative literal is partially evaluated and the definition obtained is added to the PE to be returned (e.g. see [BL90]).

We could follow a similar approach in the generation of intensional answers, returning auxiliary definitions for the atoms in the negative literals that cannot be evaluated. Yet, this would be quite unsatisfactory, because we would lose the "interactions" between the positive part and the negative part of an intensional answer. To avoid this problem, we make some additional logical transformations. Roughly, we consider the completions of such auxiliary definitions, negate both sides of the equivalences, perform some logical manipulations on the right sides, and replace the negative literals in the intensional answers by the proper instances of the corresponding right parts of the equivalences obtained.

The rest of the paper is organized as follows. After recalling some preliminary notions in the next section, the basic results are presented in Section 3. Our treatments of recursion and negation are described in Sections 4 and 5, respectively. Conclusions and further work end the paper. Due to lack of space only sketches of the proofs are reported. The full proofs appear in [DeGiacomo92].

2   Preliminaries

In this section we introduce some basic definitions, the knowledge bases considered, intensional answers and partial evaluation.

We assume that the reader is familiar with the standard theoretical results of logic programming (cf. [Lloyd87]).[1]

As usual, a *program* is a finite set of statements of the form $A \leftarrow W$, where A is an atom and W is a first order formula. All the statements of a program P, which have the same predicate symbol p in their head, form the *definition* of p in P. Statements whose bodies are conjunctions of literals are called *program clauses* or just *clauses*. A program whose statements are program clauses is called a *normal program*.

---

[1] We mainly use the same notation as [Lloyd87] except that we denote sequences of terms by a single capital letter. Few other differences are pointed out when encountered.

The *completion* of a program P, denoted as $comp(P)$, is the collection of *completed definitions* of the predicate symbols in P together with Clark's equality theory.

Definition Let P and P' be two programs, G and G' two goals with the same free variables. We say that $P \cup \{G\}$ and $P' \cup \{G'\}$ are *procedurally equivalent* if the following holds:

1. $P \cup \{G\}$ has an SLDNF-refutation with computed answer θ iff $P' \cup \{G'\}$ does.

2. $P \cup \{G\}$ has a finitely failed SLDNF-tree iff $P' \cup \{G'\}$ does.

□

When we talk about SLDNF-resolution for non-normal programs we refer to the corresponding normal forms obtained by applying Lloyd & Topor's transformations (cf. [LT84], [Lloyd87]).

Definition Let S be a set of predicate symbol definitions. We call $comp'(S)$ the set of the corresponding completed definitions together with Clark's equality theory. □

Notice that, given a program P, $comp'(P)$ is the subset of $comp(P)$ formed by the completed definitions of the predicate symbols explicitly defined in P (i.e., the predicate symbols appearing in the head of a statement of P). To further clarify the concept let us see an example.

Example Consider the following program $P = \{p(x) \leftarrow r(x) \land s(x), r(a) \leftarrow\}$, $comp(P)$ is $\{\forall x(p(x) \leftrightarrow r(x) \land s(x)), \forall x(r(x) \leftrightarrow (x = a)), \forall x(\sim s(x))\}$ while $comp'(P)$ is $\{\forall x(p(x) \leftrightarrow r(x) \land s(x)), \forall x(r(x) \leftrightarrow (x = a))\}$. □

We consider a knowledge base KB essentially constituted by a program divided in two strata IDB and EDB.

- IDB is a program such that the predicate symbols defined therein may depend upon predicate symbols defined in EDB. We call such a program the *intensional program* of the knowledge base KB.

- EDB is a program such that *no* predicate symbol defined therein depends upon predicate symbols defined in IDB. We call such a program the *extensional program* of the knowledge base KB.

Typically, IDB and EDB are intended to model the intensional knowledge and the extensional knowledge of KB respectively.[2]

We say that an intensional program IDB is a *normal intensional program* if it is a normal program. In the same way, we say that an extensional program EDB is a *normal extensional program* if it is a normal program.

---

[2]Note that, there are no restrictions on the form of the statements neither in IDB nor in EDB.

A *query* to a knowledge base can be any first order formula.[3]

We now turn our attention to intensional answers. We adopt the same definitions as in [CD86], [PR89], [PRZ91], etc, adapting them to the SLDNF-resolution framework. Let IDB be the intensional program of a knowledge base KB, and $Q(X)$ a query whose free variables are X. Since in the present paper we do not use integrity constraints to generate intensional answers, we are actually considering a special kind of intensional answers defined as follows.

Definition A first order formula $A_i(X)$, whose free variables are X, is an *intensional answer* for $Q(X)$ (wrt KB) if

$$comp'(IDB) \models \forall X(A_i(X) \rightarrow Q(X)).$$

□

Obviously not all the intensional answers are interesting, e.g. we can drop intensional answers which are variants of the query, those inconsistent wrt $comp'(IDB)$, and those subsumed by other ones.

Definition A set S_{IA} of intensional answers for $Q(X)$ (wrt KB) is *complete* if

$$comp'(IDB) \models \forall X((\bigvee_{A_i \in S_{IA}} A_i(X)) \leftrightarrow Q(X)).$$

□

Since, SLDNF-resolution is sound but not complete in general, it makes sense to introduce the notion of a set of intensional answers, *complete from the procedural point of view*.

Definition A set S_{IA} of intensional answers for $Q(X)$ (wrt KB) is *procedurally complete* if for every possible extensional program EDB of KB,

$$IDB \cup EDB \cup \{\leftarrow \bigvee_{A_i \in S_{IA}} A_i(X)\} \text{ and } IDB \cup EDB \cup \{\leftarrow Q(X)\}$$

are procedurally equivalent.

□

We finish the preliminary section introducing *partial evaluation (PE)*.[4] The formal notion and result described here are from [LS91]. We refer to normal programs and normal goals only. It is convenient to use slightly more general definitions of SLDNF-derivation and SLDNF-tree than those given in [Lloyd87]. In [Lloyd87], an SLDNF-derivation is either infinite, successful or failed. We also allow it to be *incomplete*, in the sense that at any step we are allowed

---

[3] In [Lloyd87] a query is a goal. Let $\leftarrow W$ be a goal, we call "query" the first order formula W.

[4] Recently, in the context of logic programming, it has been proposed to replace the name *partial evaluation* with the name *partial deduction*, leaving the original name to denote the optimization oriented use of such a machinery. In this paper we stick to the name *partial evaluation* in conformity with [LS91] and [BL90] whose results are extensively used.

simply not to select any literal and terminate the derivation. Likewise, in an SLDNF-tree we may neglect to unfold a goal.

Definition A *resultant* is a first order formula of the form $Q_1 \leftarrow Q_2$, where Q_i, $(i = 1, 2)$, is either absent or a conjunction of literals. Any variables in Q_1 or Q_2 are assumed to be universally quantified in front of the resultant. □

Definition Let P be a normal program, G a normal goal $\leftarrow Q$, and $G_0 = G, G_1, \ldots, G_n$ an SLDNF-derivation $P \cup \{G\}$, where the sequence of substitutions is $\theta_1, \ldots, \theta_n$ and G_n is $\leftarrow Q_n$. Let θ be the restriction of $\theta_1 \ldots \theta_n$ to the variables in G. Then we say the derivation has *length* n with *computed answer* θ and *resultant* $Q\theta \leftarrow Q_n$.[5] □

Definition Let P be a normal program, A an atom, and T a (not necessarily complete) SLDNF-tree for $P \cup \{\leftarrow A\}$. Let $G_1, \ldots, G_r$ be a set of (non-root) goals in T such that each non-failed branch of T contains exactly one of them. Let R_i $(i = 1, \ldots, r)$ be the resultant of the derivation from $\leftarrow A$ down to G_i associated with the branch leading to G_i.

- The set of resultants $\pi = \{R_1, \ldots, R_r\}$ is a *PE of A in P*. These resultants have the following form $R_i = A\theta_i \leftarrow Q_i$ $(i = 1, \ldots, r)$, where we have assumed $G_i = \leftarrow Q_i$.

- Let $\mathbf{A} = \{A_1, \ldots, A_s\}$ be a finite set of atoms, and π_i $(i = 1, \ldots, s)$ a PE of A_i in P. Then $\Pi = \pi_1 \cup \ldots \cup \pi s$ is a *PE of $\mathbf{A}$ in P*.

- Let P' be the normal program resulting from P when the definitions therein of the predicate symbols in $\mathbf{A}$ are replaced by a PE of $\mathbf{A}$ in P. Then P' is a *PE of P wrt $\mathbf{A}$*.

□

The next two theorems are the main results on partial evaluation.

Definition Let S be a set of first order formulas and $\mathbf{A}$ a finite set of atoms. We say S is $\mathbf{A}$-*closed* if each atom in S containing a predicate symbol occurring in $\mathbf{A}$ is an instance of an atom in $\mathbf{A}$. □

Definition Let $\mathbf{A}$ be a finite set of atoms. We say $\mathbf{A}$ is *independent* if no pair of atoms in $\mathbf{A}$ have a common instance. □

Theorem 1 (Lloyd Shepherdson) *Let P be a normal program, W a closed first order formula, $\mathbf{A}$ a finite set of atoms, and P' a PE of P wrt $\mathbf{A}$ such that $P' \cup \{W\}$ is $\mathbf{A}$-closed. If W is a logical consequence of $comp(P')$, then it is a logical consequence of $comp(P)$, i.e., $comp(P') \models W \Rightarrow comp(P) \models W$.*

Theorem 2 (Lloyd Shepherdson) *Let P be a normal program, G a normal goal, $\mathbf{A}$ a finite, independent set of atoms, and P' a PE of P wrt $\mathbf{A}$ such that $P' \cup \{G\}$ is $\mathbf{A}$-closed.[6] Then $P \cup \{G\}$ and $P' \cup \{G\}$ are procedurally equivalent.*

---

[5]Note that, if $n = 0$, the resultant is $Q \leftarrow Q$.

[6]In this theorem, the closedness condition can be replaced by the *coveredness condition* (cf. [LS91]).

Note that the PE of a program wrt a goal is not directly defined. Anyway, there are procedures (e.g. [BL90]) that, given a program P and a goal G, compute a set of atom $\mathbf{A}$ and a PE of the program P wrt $\mathbf{A}$ such that the original program and the partially evaluated program are procedurally equivalent wrt the goal G.

3 Intensional query answering by partial evaluation

The intensional program IDB of a knowledge base KB is an "open program", i.e., a program for which some predicate symbol definitions are missing, hence it should be considered more as a collection of predicate symbol definitions than as a running program. It is clear that for IDB, the completion $comp(IDB)$ does not make sense, while $comp'(IDB)$ does.

The partial evaluation theorems seen in the previous section are not directly useful in dealing with intensional programs. Here, we give analogous theorems more suitable for such programs. First, we need the next definition reported from [BL90].

Definition Let L be a set of predicate symbols. We say that a literal is *L-selectable* if its predicate symbol is in L. We say that an SLDNF-tree is *L-compatible* if the predicate symbol of each selected literal in the tree (including subsidiary refutations and trees) is in L. □

Let IDB be a normal intensional program of a knowledge base KB, L_{IDB} the set of predicate symbols defined in IDB, $\mathbf{A}$ a finite set of L_{IDB}-selectable atoms, and IDB' a PE of IDB wrt $\mathbf{A}$ obtained from a L_{IDB}-compatible SLDNF-tree, such that IDB' is $\mathbf{A}$-closed. The following two theorems hold.

Theorem 3 *Let W be a first order formula which is $\mathbf{A}$-closed. Then*

$comp'(IDB') \models W \Rightarrow comp'(IDB) \models W.$

Sketch of the proof By Theorem 1, for every normal extensional program EDB: $comp(IDB' \cup EDB) \models W \Rightarrow comp(IDB \cup EDB) \models W$. Now, the thesis is proved by contradiction, showing that there exists an EDB, namely $EDB^* = \{A \leftarrow A :$ the predicate symbol in A is not defined in IDB, and an instance of A occurs in the body of a program clause in $IDB\}$, such that Theorem 1 would not hold. □

Theorem 4 *Let G be a normal goal which is $\mathbf{A}$-closed. If $\mathbf{A}$ is independent, then for every possible normal extensional program EDB of KB: $IDB \cup EDB \cup \{G\}$ and $IDB' \cup EDB \cup \{G\}$ are procedurally equivalent.*

Sketch of the proof From the definition of PE it is obvious that $IDB' \cup EDB$ is a PE of $IDB \cup EDB$ wrt $\mathbf{A}$. By Theorem 2 the thesis follows. □

We are now ready to describe the first results on generating intensional answers by using partial evaluation.

1) Let $\leftarrow W$ be a normal goal. We define a new predicate symbol (i.e., a predicate symbol not appearing in P or W), as

$$q(X) \leftarrow W$$

where X are the free variables occurring in W, and we add such a new definition to IDB, getting

$$IDB^q = IDB \cup \{q(X) \leftarrow W\}.$$

2) Let L_{IDB^q} be the set of the predicate symbols defined in IDB^q. We *choose* a PE π of $q(X)$ in IDB^q obtained from an L_{IDB^q}-compatible SLDNF-tree for $IDB^q \cup \{\leftarrow q(X)\}$. Let π be

$$q(X)\theta_1 \leftarrow W_1$$
$$\vdots$$
$$q(X)\theta_r \leftarrow W_r$$

where $\theta_i = \{X_i/T_i\}$, X_i are the variables in X instantiated by θ_i, and T_i are terms.

3) The completed definition for q given by these resultants can be written as follows:

$$\forall X(q(X) \leftrightarrow \exists Y_1((X_1 = T_1) \wedge W_1) \vee \ldots \vee \exists Y_r((X_r = T_r) \wedge W_r)) \qquad (1)$$

where Y_i are the free variables in $(X_i = T_i) \wedge W_i$ other than those in X, and $X_i = T_i$ is a loose notation for $(x_{1i} = t_{1i}) \wedge \ldots \wedge (x_{ni} = t_{ni})$ (supposing X_i to be the sequence $x_{1i} \ldots x_{ni}$).

4) The disjuncts in the above formula

$$\exists Y_1((X_1 = T_1) \wedge W_1)$$
$$\vdots$$
$$\exists Y_r((X_r = T_r) \wedge W_r)$$

can be regarded as *intensional answers*. Furthermore the set formed by these intensional answers is *complete* and *procedurally complete*, as the following theorems show.

Theorem 5 *The formulas at step 4 of the process above form a complete set of intensional answers for the query W in the program P.*

Sketch of the proof By Theorem 3 it can be shown that (1) is a logical consequence of $comp'(IDB^q)$. Then, considering the axiom $\forall X(q(X) \leftrightarrow W)$ in $comp'(IDB^q)$, the formula resulting from (1) replacing $q(X)$ with W can be proved to be a logical consequence of $comp'(IDB)$, hence the thesis follows. $\square$

Theorem 6 *The set of intensional answers obtained by the process above is procedurally complete.*

Sketch of the proof Let $IDB^{q'}$ be the PE of IDB^q wrt $\{q(X)\}$. By Theorem 4, for every possible EDB of KB, $IDB^{q'} \cup EDB \cup \{\leftarrow q(X)\}$ is procedurally equivalent to $IDB^q \cup EDB \cup \{\leftarrow q(X)\}$, which, in turn, is procedurally equivalent to $IDB \cup EDB \cup \{\leftarrow W\}$. On the other hand, $IDB \cup EDB \cup \{\leftarrow \bigvee_{i=1}^r \exists Y_1((X_1 = T_1) \wedge W_1)\}$, once transformed into normal form, and assuming for the predicate symbol "$=$" the standard procedural meaning "unifiable", can be shown to be procedurally equivalent to $IDB^{q'} \cup EDB \cup \{\leftarrow q(X)\}$, regardless of EDB. Hence the thesis follows. $\qquad\square$

Example Consider the following fragment of the intensional program IDB of a knowledge base.

$publication\_bonus(x, 50) \leftarrow$
$\qquad conference\_publication(x, y)$
$publication\_bonus(x, 100) \leftarrow$
$\qquad conference\_publication(x, y) \wedge major\_conference(y)$
$publication\_bonus(x, 150) \leftarrow$
$\qquad journal\_publication(x, y)$

$major\_conference(x) \leftarrow sponsor(x, ACM)$
$major\_conference(x) \leftarrow sponsor(x, IEEE)$
$major\_conference(x) \leftarrow accepted\_rate(x, y) \wedge (y \leq 0.2)$
$\ldots$

Suppose we want the answer to the query

$\leftarrow \exists y(publication\_bonus(x, y) \wedge (y \geq 100)),$

i.e., "Which are the papers that get a publication-bonus greater or equal to 100?".

1) We define a new predicate symbol $\dot{q}$ as

$q(x) \leftarrow publication\_bonus(x, y) \wedge (y \geq 100),$

Let IDB^q be $IDB \cup \{q(x) \leftarrow publication\_bonus(x, y) \wedge (y \geq 100)\}$.

2) We choose a PE π of $q(x)$ in IDB^q obtained from an L_{IDB^q}-compatible SLDNF-tree. Let such a tree be the one in Figure 1, and π the PE associated with the non-failing leaves of such a tree, i.e.

$q(x) \leftarrow conference\_publication(x, z) \wedge sponsor(z, ACM)$
$q(x) \leftarrow conference\_publication(x, z) \wedge sponsor(z, IEEE)$
$q(x) \leftarrow conference\_publication(x, z) \wedge accepted\_rate(x, z) \wedge (z \leq 0.2)$
$q(x) \leftarrow journal\_publication(x, z).$

3) The completed definition of q in IDB^q is

$\forall x(q(x) \leftrightarrow \exists z(conference\_publication(x, z) \wedge sponsor(z, ACM)) \vee$
$\qquad\qquad \exists z(conference\_publication(x, z) \wedge sponsor(z, IEEE)) \vee$
$\qquad\qquad \exists z(conference\_publication(x, z) \wedge accepted\_rate(x, z) \wedge (z \leq 0.2)) \vee$
$\qquad\qquad \exists z(journal\_publication(x, z))).$

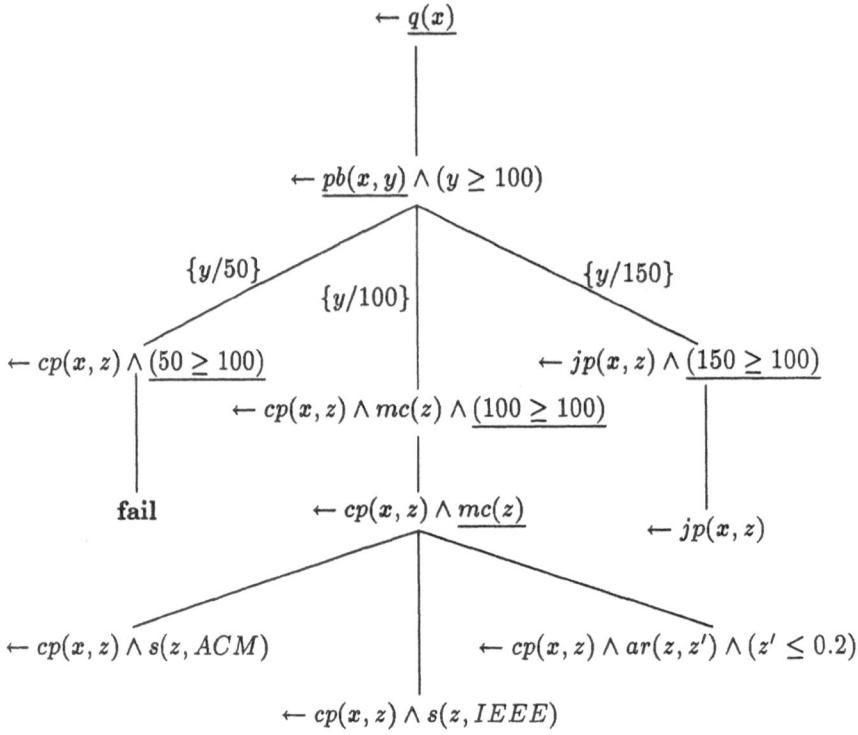

Figure 1: The SLDNF-tree used for the partial evaluation.

4) The disjuncts in the right-hand part of such a formula form a complete and procedurally complete set of intensional answers, that can be read as "Papers published in an ACM conference, papers published in an IEEE conference, papers published in a conference whose acceptance rate is less than or equal to 0.2, and papers published in a journal." □

The process above is *not completely specified* since we are free to choose any PE π of q in IDB^q at step 2.

The *quality* of the intensional answers returned strongly depends on such a choice of π, which in turn substantially depends on the selection rule for the related SLDNF-tree. While we do not directly address such an issue in this paper, the problem of finding a "good" selection rule is one of the most crucial to effectively do intensional query answering by means of partial evaluation.

The *termination* of the above process depends again on the selection rule to be used in the generation of the PE π. Such a selection rule should build finite (incomplete) SLDNF-trees. Conditions on the selection rules, dealing with the termination of the partial evaluation, can be found in the related literature (e.g. [vanHarmelen89]).

4 Dealing with recursion

The basic method presented in the previous section allows one, in principle, to return intensional answers for every query in every logic program. In particular, it does not rule out recursion. Obviously, such intensional answers should be expressed in a language that is known by the user.[7] If recursive predicate symbols (i.e., predicate symbols which appear in a loop in the dependency graph of a program) are allowed to appear in the intensional program of a knowledge base, then it could be impossible to obtain a complete set of intensional answers in which no occurrences of recursive predicate symbols, that are not known by the user, appear. In this case, no satisfying set of intensional answers could be returned.

The next example shows the problem arising when recursion cannot be eliminated, and hints at how it can be tackled.

Example Consider the following fragment of the intensional program of a knowledge base:

$collateral\_line\_relative(x, y) \leftarrow ancestor(x, z) \land ancestor(y, z)$

$ancestor(x, y) \leftarrow parent(x, y)$
$ancestor(x, y) \leftarrow parent(x, z) \land ancestor(z, y)$
. . .

and suppose we want intensional answers for the query:

$\leftarrow collateral\_line\_relative(x, y)$

Possible complete sets of intensional answers are

$\{\exists z(ancestor(x, z) \land ancestor(y, z))\}$

or

$\{\exists z(parent(x, z) \land ancestor(y, z)),$
$\exists z \exists z'(parent(x, z') \land ancestor(z', z) \land ancestor(y, z))\}$

or, also

$\{\exists z(parent(x, z) \land parent(y, z)),$
$\exists z \exists z'(parent(x, z') \land ancestor(z', z) \land parent(y, z)),$
$\exists z \exists z'(parent(x, z) \land parent(y, z') \land ancestor(z', z)),$
$\exists z \exists z' \exists z''(parent(x, z') \land ancestor(z', z) \land parent(y, z'') \land ancestor(z'', z))\}$

etc.

As we can see, we cannot eliminate the predicate symbol *ancestor* in the set of intensional answers returned. Now, if the meaning of *ancestor* is known by the user, then the most intuitive set of answers is probably the first one, being the simplest. But, if the meaning of *ancestor* is not known (e.g., the user may not be clear on whether or not his wife's grandfather is his ancestor), none of the above sets is satisfying, because *ancestor* appears in each of them. We need

---

[7]We assume that the user knows a set of predicate symbols which includes those defined in the extensional program of the knowledge base, and all constants and function symbols.

some kind of definition giving the meaning of *ancestor* in the context of the set of intensional answers returned.

For instance we may return:

$\{\exists z(ancestor(x,z) \wedge ancestor(y,z))\}$

$ancestor(x,y) \leftarrow parent(x,y)$
$ancestor(x,y) \leftarrow parent(x,z) \wedge ancestor(z,y).$

In this way, asking "which are the collateral-line relatives?" we get an answer such as " the individuals that have a common ancestor, *where* an ancestor is a parent or a parent of an ancestor". $\square$

In view of the observations in the above example, we propose to answer a query by a set S_{IA} of intensional answers and a set RD of definitions for the recursive predicate symbols which are somehow marked *unknown*,[8] occuring in the answer. Notice that, if other predicate symbols marked unknown appear in such definitions, then their definitions are included in RD as well.[9] To formalize the set RD we now introduce the notion of a *set of auxiliary definitions*.

Let IDB be the intensional program of a knowledge base KB, L_{IDB} the set of predicate symbols defined in IDB, $Q(X)$ a query whose free variables are X, S_{IA} a set of intensional answers $A_i(X)$ $(i = 1, \ldots, n)$ for $Q(X)$, L a subset of L_{IDB}, and AD a set of definitions for the predicate symbols in L.

Then, let $\mathbf{A}_L$ be a set of atoms, one for each predicate symbol in L,[10] such that S_{IA} is $\mathbf{A}_L$-closed, and let $comp'(AD)_{inst}$ be the instance of $comp'(AD)$ such that the atoms on the left-hand sides of the completed definitions therein coincide (modulo variants) with the corresponding atoms in $\mathbf{A}_L$.

Definition We say AD is a *set of auxiliary definitions*[11] for S_{IA} wrt L if:

1. $comp'(IDB) \models comp'(AD)_{inst}$, and

2. $comp'(AD)_{inst}$ is $\mathbf{A}_L$-closed.

$\square$

---

[8] We may consider a predicate symbol to be marked unknown either generally (e.g., because its meaning is not known by the user) or more specifically, wrt the formulas in which it appears.

[9] In very unfortunate cases, the set of definitions RD may almost coincide with the whole intensional program.

[10] We assume that for each predicate symbol p in L there corresponds just one atom, and hence we have one logical equivalence involving p in $comp'(AD)_{inst}$ which may be thought of as the logical definition of p in the context of S_{IA} and AD. We could also assume that an independent set of atoms corresponds to p. This would entail that in $comp'(AD)_{inst}$ there would be a distinct logical equivalence involving p for each such atom, therefore the idea of a single logical definition of p in the context of S_{IA} and AD should be replaced by the idea of a logical definition of p in the context of a single intensional answer of S_{IA} or statement of AD in which it appears. In this paper we stick to the first assumption; nevertheless the results shown here can be straightforwardly extended to the case where the second assumption is adopted.

[11] Single auxiliary definitions are defined just as elements of AD.

Notice that a set AD of auxiliary definitions always exists. In fact, the IDB definitions of the predicate symbols in L form such a set. But the definitions in AD are not necessarily those in IDB. Intuitively, they can be a "specialized" version of those which are general enough to cover the meaning of each atom occurring in the answer returned (i.e., wrt the atoms in the answer, the definitions in AD retain the same meaning as those in the intensional program).

We could also require the auxiliary definitions in AD to be used, instead of the corresponding definitions in IDB, to evaluate the intensional answers in S_{IA} without losing *correct answers*, or at least *computed answers*. Such a property is quite "severe", since, to enforce it, we should return auxiliary definitions that are not only general enough to cover the meaning of the predicate symbols in L, in the context of S_{IA} and AD, but also to cover their meaning through the whole evaluation of each intensional answer in S_{IA}. Indeed, if a predicate symbol $p \notin L$, which depends on predicate symbol $p' \in L$, appears in some atoms of $S_{IA} \cup AD$, then in choosing the generality of the auxiliary definition for p' we should consider the occurrences of p' arising from the evaluation of these atoms as well.

On the other hand, the formalization of the notion of set of auxiliary definitions above is sufficient to give a nice characterization of the pair $< S_{IA}, AD >$, as shown below.

The intensional answers in S_{IA} have the same status as queries, while the set AD of auxiliary definitions is an (open) program. How does the pair $< S_{IA}, AD >$ relate to the original notion of intensional answers?

The pair $< S_{IA}, AD >$ can be interpreted as the implicit representation of the infinite set of all the intensional answers for $Q(X)$ which can be inferred from the intensional answers in S_{IA} using the axioms of $comp'(AD)_{inst}$.

Indeed, the pair $< S_{IA}, AD >$ may be thought of as representing the infinite set of all the formulas $\chi_{ij}(X)$ $(i = 1, \ldots, n; \ j = 1, 2, \ldots)$ such that

$$comp'(AD)_{inst} \models \forall(\chi_{ij}(X) \to A_i(X)). \tag{2}$$

Note that $\chi_{ij}(X)$ $(j = 1, 2 \ldots)$ are intensional answers to $A_i(X)$ wrt the intensional program AD.

By definition of a set of auxiliary definitions, the following holds

$$comp'(IDB) \models comp'(AD)_{inst}. \tag{3}$$

From (2) and (3) we get

$$comp'(IDB) \models \forall(\chi_{ij}(X) \to A_i(X)). \tag{4}$$

Now, for $A_i(X)$ we have

$$comp'(IDB) \models \forall(A_i(X) \to Q(X)). \tag{5}$$

Hence, from (4) and (5)

$$comp'(IDB) \models \forall(\chi_{ij}(X) \to Q(X)), \tag{6}$$

that is, $\chi_{ij}(X)$ $(i = 1, \ldots, n; \ j = 1, 2, \ldots)$ are intensional answers to $Q(X)$ wrt KB.

Turning to the problem of how to compute a set of auxiliary definitions, assuming IDB to be normal, it can be shown that a PE Π of $\mathbf{A}_L$ in IDB, obtained from an L_{IDB}-compatible SLDNF-tree, and such that $S_{IA} \cup \Pi$ is $\mathbf{A}_L$-closed, is a set of auxiliary definitions for S_{IA} wrt L.

When AD is computed by PE, unfolding the intensional answers in S_{IA} using program clauses in AD leads to new sets of intensional answers S'_{IA} which preserve the completeness and the procedural completeness, as the following theorem shows.

Theorem 7 *Let S_{IA} be a complete and procedurally complete set of intensional answers, and AD a set of auxiliary definitions for S_{IA} wrt L obtained as a PE of $\mathbf{A}_L$. Then every set S'_{IA} of intensional answers derived by SLDNF-resolution from S_{IA} using program clauses in AD, is complete and procedurally complete.*

Sketch of the proof By the sub-derivation lemma in [LS91], and lemma 4.12 in [LS91], it follows that an SLDNF-tree built using resultants in AD can be expanded into an SLDNF-tree built using only program clauses in IDB. Now, consider the query given by the disjunction of the intensional answers in S_{IA}, and let $ans(X)$ be the query introduced by its transformation into normal form. It can be shown that every S'_{IA} can be computed as a PE of $ans(X)$ in the transformed intensional program. Hence, by Theorem 5 and Theorem 6, the thesis follows. □

Now that we have characterized the notion of a set of auxiliary definitions, we can employ it to clarify the idea presented at the beginning of the section.

We answer a query with a set S_{IA} of intensional answers and a set RD of auxiliary definitions for the recursive predicate symbols marked unknown appearing in S_{IA} or in RD itself.

Notice that, by Theorem 7, if an auxiliary definition $D \in RD$ of some predicate symbol p is not recursive in reality, then (assuming, for now, that p does not occur in a negative literal) we may unfold the corresponding positive literals in S_{IA} and RD, and drop D from RD.

An algorithm to compute S_{IA} and RD, based on partial evaluation, can be adapted from the one in [BL90]. The underlying idea is to build the set of atoms that is partially evaluated "run-time" while computing S_{IA} and RD.

5   More about negation

The notion of PE is directly derived from the notion of SLDNF-tree. Therefore, negation during the PE process is treated in a somewhat limited way. In fact

1. A negative literal can be selected only if it is *ground*.

2. If a ground negative literal is selected, then it is either completely evaluated (if possible), or not evaluated at all.

Adopting what has been proposed in the literature on partial evaluation (e.g. [BL90]), we can generate an answer to a query W, constituted by a set S_{IA} of intensional answers, and a set of auxiliary definitions for predicate symbols marked unknown occurring in the answer, partitioned into two subsets RD and ND. RD concerns recursive predicate symbols occuring in either positive or negative literals of the answer, whereas ND concerns those non-recursive occurring in negative literals. Supposing IDB and W to be normal, partial evaluation can be used to generate such an answer. Actually the algorithm, mentioned in the previous section, can easily be modified to compute S_{IA}, RD and ND.

The problem with such an approach is that, in the formulas of S_{IA}, RD and ND, the "interactions" (i.e., possible simplifications) between the part of information in the positive literals and the one in the negative literals is lost, because the latter is embedded in separate definitions. We need to recover such interactions if the answer is to be effective.

Now, for each predicate symbol p in a negative literal there is an auxiliary definition in ND to which corresponds a logical equivalence in $comp'(ND)_{inst}$ of the form:

$$\forall X(p(T(X)) \leftrightarrow \exists Y(F(X,Y))), \tag{7}$$

where $T(X)$ denotes a tuple of terms, X the variables therein, and Y the variables, other than those in X, which are free in F. We may negate both sides of such an equivalence getting:

$$\forall X(\sim p(T(X)) \leftrightarrow \sim \exists Y(F(X,Y))). \tag{8}$$

The literals of $S_{IA} \cup RD \cup ND$ in which p occurs, must be instances of $p(T(X))$, so we may replace them with the proper instances of the right-hand side of (7) or (8). Obviously, when such an expansion of a negative literal is applied, the formulas obtained are logically equivalent to the original ones, but they may not be procedurally equivalent, hence while no correct answers are lost or gained, the same is not true for the computed answers, in general.

The idea of negating both sides of the completed definitions and replaceing the negative literals by the right-hand side of the equivalences obtained is related to *constructive negation* ([Chan88], [Chan89], [Przymusinski89]), and has been used to treat negation during the partial evaluation process in [CW89]. Here we want to apply such a treatment of negation off-line wrt the partial evaluation process, so as to retain the notions and the results in [LS91]. Moreover, our aim is to expand the negative literals in such a way as not to lose computed answers. We now present a method for such an expansion.

For every formula in S_{IA} and RD we recursively apply expansion steps, defined by the following sequence of transformations, until no more expansion steps are possible.

1. We substitute atoms in the positive and negative literals of the formula, with the right-hand sides of the corresponding instances of the completed definitions in $comp'(ND)_{inst}$.

2. Equalities in the formula are treated as follows.

   (a) We substitute equalities whose terms unify by the equality corresponding to their *mgu* (if the mgu is the empty substitution then the equality is eliminated), and we eliminate the conjunctions in which there is an equality whose terms do not unify.

The result of such a transformation is logically equivalent to the original formula, by Clark's Lemma (cf. [Clark78], also Lemma 15.2 in [Lloyd87]).

(b) We eliminate the equalities in which one of the terms is an existentially quantified variable, by means of the following logical equivalence: $\exists y((x = y) \wedge B) \leftrightarrow B\{y/x\}$.

3. We push the (existential) quantifiers to the right as much as possible, eliminating the redundant ones.

4. We move negation all the way inwards, stopping in front of the existential quantifiers, by means of the usual logical equivalences.

A few things must be pointed out. First, a formula resulting from the above process is logically equivalent to the original one. Second, such a process always terminates, since the definitions in ND are non-recursive. Third, at the end of such a process, ND is not needed any more and can be eliminated. Furthermore, although we do not yet have the complete proof, it seems that a kind of procedural containment holds, that is, if G is a goal, and G' the goal resulting from processing G as above, then for every extensional program EDB

1. If $IDB \cup EDB \cup \{G\}$ has an SLDNF-refutation with computed answer θ, then so does $IDB \cup EDB \cup \{G'\}$.

2. If $IDB \cup EDB \cup \{G\}$ has a finitely failed SLDNF-tree, then so does $IDB \cup EDB \cup \{G'\}$.

Notice that, if the intensional program of the knowledge base is not a normal program, then by normalizing it using Lloyd & Topor's transformations to apply partial evaluation, we introduce new predicate symbols[12] that are obviously *unknown* (i.e., they are meaningless to the user). By the method sketched here, such predicate symbols can always be replaced by a meaningful formula.

Example Consider the following intensional program IDB:

$should\_visit(x, y) \leftarrow serves(y, z) \wedge likes(x, z)$

$happy(x) \leftarrow frequents(x, y) \wedge should\_visit(x, y)$

$very\_happy(x) \leftarrow \forall y(frequents(x, y) \rightarrow should\_visit(x, y))$

$unhappy(x) \leftarrow \forall y(frequents(x, y) \rightarrow \sim should\_visit(x, y)),$

the following extensional program EDB (schema):

$frequents(DRINKER, PUB)$
$serves(PUB, BEER)$
$likes(DRINKER, BEER),$

---

[12]New predicate symbols are introduced to eliminate the negated existentially quantified (universally quantified) formulas.

and the query "Who are the drinkers that neither are unhappy nor very happy ?",
that is:

$$\leftarrow \sim unhappy(x) \wedge \sim very\_happy(x).$$

First notice that the last two statements must be transformed into normal form.

$$very\_happy(x) \leftarrow \sim np1(x)$$

$$np1(x) \leftarrow frequents(x,y) \wedge \sim should\_visit(x,y)$$

$$unhappy(x) \leftarrow \sim np2(x)$$

$$np2(x) \leftarrow frequents(x,y) \wedge should\_visit(x,y).$$

The only possible set of intensional answers computed by the basic method is
the one constituted by the query itself. To it we may add the following set ND
of auxiliary definitions.

$$very\_happy(x) \leftarrow \sim np1(x)$$
$$np1(x) \leftarrow frequents(x,y) \wedge \sim should\_visit(x,y)$$
$$unhappy(x) \leftarrow \sim np2(x)$$
$$np2(x) \leftarrow frequents(x,y) \wedge serves(y,z) \wedge likes(x,z).$$

Now we proceed to the expansions. We expand (in parallel, for the sake of
brevity) both $\sim unhappy(x)$ and $\sim very\_happy(x)$:

$\sim unhappy(x) \wedge \sim very\_happy(x)$ (original goal)

$np2(x) \wedge np1(x)$ (first expansion step)

$\exists y(frequents(x,y) \wedge should\_visit(x,y)) \wedge$
$\exists y(frequents(x,y) \wedge \sim \exists z(serves(y,z) \wedge likes(x,z)))$ (second expansion step)

$\exists y(frequents(x,y) \wedge \exists z(serves(y,z) \wedge likes(x,z))) \wedge$
$\exists y(frequents(x,y) \wedge \sim \exists z(serves(y,z) \wedge likes(x,z)))$ (third expansion step)

The last formula is a nice intensional answer, i.e., "The drinkers who visit at
least both a pub where a beer they like is served, and a pub where no beer they
like is served." □

6   Conclusions

In this paper we have presented a set of tools, based on PE, to generate intensional answers in the SLDNF-resolution framework, allowing function symbols,
recursion, and negation.

The results stated on the application of PE techniques to the generation
of intensional answers and auxiliary definitions do not refer to any particular
PE. It would be interesting to investigate ways to choose PE, specific to intensional answering, such as heuristics that make the resulting intensional answers

more "intuitive", or selection rules that use integrity constraints to prune away inconsistent goals.

Regardless of the PE chosen, the PE process tends to destroy the structure of the program to which it is applied. Now there are no reasons to preserve the structure of the original program. In fact, such a structure is normally hidden from the user, and is too general, in the sense that it does not reflect the particular query asked. Nevertheless, if the structure of the user's knowledge is at hand, it could be used to re-express the intensional answers in a language that is more familiar to the user. Hence, another issue to explore is the use of additional components, usually considered for modelling structural aspects of a knowledge base (e.g., taxonomies and integrity constraints), to improve the quality of the intensional answers.

Finally, our work may be considered a first step towards a program transformation approach to intensional answering, and it could be naturally extended using other program transformation techniques. Moreover such an approach can be applied to other kinds of non-conventional query answering. For instance, PE can be used for both "Knowledge query answering" [MY90] and, adding folding techniques, "Intelligent query answering" [Imielinski87].

Acknowledgements

I am grateful to J. W. Lloyd who supervised me during the early stages of this research, and to M. Lenzerini who gave me precious advice and supported me throughout the work.

References

[BL90]   K. Benkerimi and J. W. Lloyd. A Partial Evaluation Procedure for Logic Programs. In *Proc. of North American Conf. on Logic Programming*, S. K. Derbray and M. Hermenegildo eds., pp.343-358, Austin, MIT Press, 1990.

[Clark78]   K. L. Clark. Negation as Failure. In *Logic and Data Bases*, H. Gallaire and J. Minker eds., pp.293-322, Plenum Press, 1978.

[CD86]   L. Cholvy. and R. Demolombe. Querying a Rule Base. In *Proc. 1st Int Conf. on Expert Database Systems*, pp.365-371, Charleston, South Carolina, April 1986.

[CD88]   F. Cuppens and R. Demolombe. Cooperative Answering: A Methodology to Provide Intelligent Access to Databases. In *Proc. 2nd Int. Conf. on Expert Database Systems*, pp.333-353, Tysons Corner, Virginia, April 1988.

[Chan88]   D. Chan. Constructive Negation Based on the Completed Database. In *Proc.of 5th International Conference and Symposium on Logic Programming*, R. A. Kowalski and K. A. Bowen eds., pp.111-125, MIT Press, 1988.

[Chan89]   D. Chan. An Extension of Constructive Negation and its Applica-
             tion in Coroutining. In *Proc. of North American Conf. on Logic Pro-
             gramming*, E. Lusk and R. Overback eds., pp.477-493, MIT Press,
             1989.

[Corella84] F. Corella. Semantic Retrieval and Levels of Abstraction. In *Proc.
             1st Int. Workshop on Expert Database Systems*, pp.397-420, Kiawah
             Island, South Carolina, October 1984.

[CW89]   D. Chan and M. Wallance. A Treatment of Negation During Partial
             Evaluation. In *Meta-Programming in Logic Programming*, H. D.
             Abramson and M. H. Rogers eds., pp.299-317, MIT Press, 1989.
             (*Proc. Meta88*).

[Demolombe92] R. Demolombe. A Strategy for the Computation of Conditional
             Answers. In *Proc. ECAI'92*, to appear.

[DFI91]   R. Demolombe, L. Farinas del Cerro, T. Imielinski (eds.). *Proc.
             Workshop on Nonstandard Queries and Answers*, Toulouse, France,
             July, 1991.

[DeGiacomo92] G. De Giacomo. Intensional Query Answering by Partial Evalu-
             ation. *Technical Report*, Dipartimento di Informatica e Sistemistica,
             Università di Roma "La Sapienza". In preparation.

[Imielinski87] T. Imielinski. Intelligent Query Answering in Rule Based Sys-
             tems. In *The Journal of Logic Programming*, 4(3):229-257, Septem-
             ber 1987.

[Lloyd87]   J. W. Lloyd. *Foundations of Logic Programming* (2nd edition).
             Springer-Verlag, 1987.

[LS91]   J. W. Lloyd and J. C. Shepherdson. Partial Evaluation in Logic
             Programming. In *The Journal of Logic Programming*, 11(3&4):217-
             242, October/November 1991.

[LT84]   J. W. Lloyd and R. W. Topor. Making Prolog More Expressive. *The
             Journal of Logic Programming*, 1(3):225-240, 1984.

[Motro89]   A. Motro. Using Integrity Constraints to Provide Intensional An-
             swers to Relational Queries. In *Proc. 15th Int. Conf on Very Large
             Data Bases*, pp.237-246, Amsterdam, August 1989.

[Motro91]   A. Motro. Intensional Answers to Database Queries. *Technical Re-
             port*, Department of Information and Software Systems Engineer-
             ing, George Mason University, Fairfax, Virginia, 1991.

[MY90]   A. Motro and Q. Yuan. Querying Database Knowledge. In *Proc. of
             ACM SIGMOD-90*, pp.173-183, 1990.

[PR89]   A. Pirotte and D. Roelantes. Constraints for Improving the Gener-
             ation of Intensional Answers in a Deductive Database. In *Proc. 5th
             Int. Conf. on Data Engineering*, pp.652-659, Los Angeles, Califor-
             nia, February 1989.

[PRZ91] A. Pirotte, D. Roelantes, E Zimanyi. Controlled Generation of Intensional Answers. In *IEEE Trans. on Knowledge and Data Engineering*, Vol 3, No.2, pp.221-236, June 1991.

[Przymusinski89] T. C. Przymusinski. On Constructive Negation in Logic Programming. In *Proc. of North American Conf. on Logic Programming*, E. Lusk and R. Overback eds., pp.1-19 (addendum), MIT Press, 1989.

[SM88] C. Shum and R. Muntz. Implicit Representation for Extensional Answers. In *Proc. 2nd Int. Conf. on Expert Database Systems*, pp.257-273, Tysons Corner, Virginia, April 1988.

[vanHarmelen89] F. van Harmelen. The Limitations of Partial Evaluation. In *Logic-Based Knowledge Representation*, P. Jackson, H. Reichgelt, F. van Harmelen eds., pp.87-111, MIT Press, 1989.

Deletion of Redundant Unary Type Predicates from Logic Programs *

J. Gallagher
D.A. de Waal
Department of Computer Science
University of Bristol
Bristol
United Kingdom
{john,andre}@uk.ac.bristol.compsci

Abstract

In this paper, program transformation is proposed as a way of handling type information efficiently. A typed program is translated to an untyped program, with regular unary predicates replacing the types, and then an attempt is made to eliminate as many of the unary type literals as possible. The method is as follows: first a query-answer transformation of the program with a given goal is made. This gives a specification of the calls to each literal in the program arising in the computation of the goal. The set of calls defines the *context* of the literal in the computation. Any literal can be eliminated if its answers are implied by its context. We define a procedure for eliminating literals defined by regular programs, a class which includes the type literals. A regular approximation of the query-answer program is made, and then decidable properties of regular programs are used to check for the elimination of the literal. The method can be compared with type-checking, since the elimination procedure also shows whether some type literal fails, indicating a "badly-typed" clause. Our aim however is not to construct a type system, but rather to show that simple types can be handled using a general framework of program analysis and transformation.

1   Introduction

Type information is desirable for capturing the intended interpretation of logic programs. The advantages of types from the point of view of writing correct programs is clear. On the other hand, the question of how to handle types computationally has several possible answers. In this paper, program transformation is proposed as a way of treating type information efficiently. This can be contrasted to various type-checking schemes.

Our aim is not to construct a type system, but rather to show that simple types can be handled using a general framework of program analysis and transformation. Types need not be distinguished from any other relation in the intended interpretation. Our point of view is to try to regard the analysis of types as being the same as the analysis of any other part of a program.

*Work supported by ESPRIT Project PRINCE (P5246)

In the long term, type checking should merge with a general theory of program analysis and transformation, and the work presented here is a step in this direction.

1.1 Specification of Types

Several type systems for logic programs have been proposed [18], [21], [7], [10], [19]. There are differences in the way in which types are specified. (Only simple types, without polymorphism, are treated here.)

(i) The first approach is based on many-sorted logic; the programmer declares basic types (or sorts), as well as types for all non-logical constants (predicates, functions and constants) in the language. Types are interpreted as subsets of the domain of interpretation of the language. A formula that is not consistent with the types of its symbols is ill-typed and has no interpretation. Type systems using this approach are described in [18] and [10].

(ii) The second approach is not based on semantics as approach (i) is. The constants and functions of the language are used as constructors of the types, which are considered as sets of terms of the language of the program. A set of recursive definitions of the types is given, and types are declared for predicates only, not for functions and constants. The predicate types are intended as restrictions on the terms that can occur in the arguments of the predicates. The type systems described in [21], [7] and [19] are in this style. In contrast to approach (i), an ill-typed formula is not meaningless, but rather has unintended meanings.

There is a well known correspondence between many-sorted logic and unsorted logic [6], which involves introducing unary predicates in place of sorts. A many-sorted theory can be translated to an unsorted theory. Interestingly, an intermediate stage of the translation yields a typed theory in the style of approach (ii), in which types are sets of terms.

1.2 Simple Types as Unary Predicates

The first stage of the transformation is to obtain explicit definitions of unary type predicates from the declarations of the constants and functions. For brevity, treat constants as 0-ary functions. For each declaration of an n-ary function symbol f/n of form

$$f : T_1 \times \ldots \times T_n \to T_{n+1},$$

where $T_1, \ldots, T_n, T_{n+1}$ are base sorts, define a clause

$$T_{n+1}(f(x_1, \ldots, x_n)) \leftarrow T_1(x_1), \ldots, T_n(x_n).$$

The resulting set of clauses can be regarded as the definition of the types. The remaining type declarations for predicates, along with the clauses for the types, now give a typed program in the style of [21], [7] or [19]. In fact, the set of unary clauses obtained by the above scheme is a canonical Regular Unary

Logic (RUL) program, as defined in [21]. Consider for example the following declaration in the notation of Gödel [10]. [1]

$BASE$ $Day, ListOfDay$
$CONSTANT$ $Nil : ListOfDay$
                  $Monday : Day$
                  $Tuesday : Day$

                  . . .
                  $Sunday : Day$

$FUNCTION$ $Cons : Day * ListOfDay \rightarrow ListOfDay$

$PREDICATE$ $Append : ListOfDay * ListOfDay * ListOfDay$

The following type clauses and predicate definition are obtained.

$ListOfDay(Nil) \leftarrow$
$ListOfDay(Cons(x, y)) \leftarrow Day(x), ListOfDay(y)$

$Day(Monday) \leftarrow$
$Day(Tuesday) \leftarrow$
. . .
$Day(Sunday) \leftarrow$

$PREDICATE$ $Append : ListOfDay * ListOfDay * ListOfDay$

The second stage of the translation to unsorted form is to introduce the unary type predicates into the clauses of the program. There are several similar ways to do this. The simplest is to take each program clause of form

- $P(t_1, \ldots, t_n) \leftarrow B$

and translate it to

- $P(t_1, \ldots, t_n) \leftarrow B, T_1(t_1), \ldots, T_n(t_n)$

where the predicate P/n has declared type $T_1 \times \ldots \times T_n$. This set of clauses defining the types is added to the program.

For example, the procedure for $Append$ becomes:

$Append(Nil, y, y) \leftarrow$
         $ListOfDay(Nil),$
         $ListOfDay(y),$
         $ListOfDay(y).$
$Append(Cons(x, u), v, Cons(x, w)) \leftarrow$
         $Append(u, v, w),$
         $ListOfDay(Cons(x, u)),$
         $ListOfDay(v),$
         $ListOfDay(Cons(x, w)).$

---

[1] We follow standard Prolog conventions for variables and constant symbols except where explicitly noted.

Note that there may be variables in the body B that do not occur in the head. However, the transformation ensures that if B succeeds, it succeeds only for arguments of the correct type, so it is not necessary to add unary type predicates to restrict local variables.

An alternative used in [19] is to define a clause for each predicate type declaration using a new predicate symbol for each program predicate. For instance, a clause

$$AppendType(x, y, z) \leftarrow ListOfDay(x), ListOfDay(y), ListOfDay(z)$$

could be defined for the example above. The clauses for *Append* would then become

$$Append(Nil, y, y) \leftarrow$$
$$\qquad AppendType(Nil, y, y).$$
$$Append(Cons(x, u), v, Cons(x, w)) \leftarrow$$
$$\qquad Append(u, v, w),$$
$$\qquad AppendType(Cons(x, u), v, Cons(x, w)).$$

Clearly, unfolding the calls to *AppendType* would yield the same result as before. Further unfolding of the calls to *ListOfDay* and elimination of duplicate calls gives the following clauses.

$$Append(Nil, y, y) \leftarrow$$
$$\qquad ListOfDay(y).$$
$$Append(Cons(x, u), v, Cons(x, w)) \leftarrow$$
$$\qquad Append(u, v, w),$$
$$\qquad Day(x),$$
$$\qquad ListOfDay(u),$$
$$\qquad ListOfDay(v),$$
$$\qquad ListOfDay(w).$$

Typed goals are also translated to unsorted form in a similar way. Given an atomic goal $\leftarrow P(t_1, \ldots, t_n)$, it is translated to $\leftarrow P(t_1, \ldots, t_n), T_1(t_1), \ldots, T_n(t_n)$, where the predicate P/n has declared type $T_1 \times \ldots \times T_n$.

The untyped program corresponding to a typed program will be called a *type-restricted program*.

1.3 Computing With Types

Translation schemes such as the one sketched above do not immediately suggest practical ways of handling types. Indeed, an unsorted program obtained is likely to be inefficient when executed directly, and many redundant type checks will be done.

The usual approach in type systems is to give some definition of a "well-typed" program, and a procedure for checking that a program is well-typed. If a program is well-typed it means, ideally, that a computation of a well-typed goal gives well-typed answers without any run-time checking of the types. Some type systems are used to identify potential bugs related to ill-typed clauses and are not intended to guarantee well-typed answers.

Rather than discuss different definitions and properties of well-typed programs, we now concentrate on taking the unsorted type-restricted programs obtained above, and trying to make them run efficiently by removing redundant type-checks. The aim is to obtain a program which performs as little run-time type checking as possible.

1.4 Example of Type Check Elimination

Suppose we have a typed version of *append*, translated to type-restricted form, which we want to incorporate in a user program. The version below is typed so as to handle arbitrary lists. The predicate $any(X)$ succeeds for any X in the Herbrand universe.

Example: Append with types

$append([\ ], Ys, Ys) \leftarrow list(Ys).$
$append([X|Xs], Ys, [X|Zs])) \leftarrow$
$\qquad append(Xs, Ys, Zs),$
$\qquad any(X),$
$\qquad list(Xs),$
$\qquad list(Ys),$
$\qquad list(Zs).$

$list([\ ]).$
$list([X|Xs]) \leftarrow$
$\qquad any(X),$
$\qquad list(Xs).$

Consider two different cases of calls to *append*. We show how different occurrences of the type checks can be eliminated in each case.

First suppose that some user program or query contains the goal

$\leftarrow intlist(Y), append(X, Y, Z).$

where *intlist* is defined by

$intlist([\ ]) \leftarrow true.$
$intlist([X1|X2]) \leftarrow int(X1), intlist(X2).$
$int(0) \leftarrow true.$
$int(s(X)) \leftarrow int(X).$

As the context in which $append(X, Y, Z)$ may be called is determined by $intlist(Y)$, it is possible to show that all the list-checks may be deleted from the definition of *append* without affecting the answers to the above call.

Secondly, suppose there is a direct query

$\leftarrow append(X, Y, Z).$

In this case it is not possible to delete all the list-checks. The check in the base case of *append* must be kept to ensure that the program still gives well-typed answers. We therefore obtain the following transformed program

$append([\ ], Ys, Ys) \leftarrow list(Ys).$
$append([X|Xs], Ys, [X|Zs])) \leftarrow$
$\qquad append(Xs, Ys, Zs).$

In the rest of the paper we will justify the removal of such checks.

2 Context of a Program Literal

Let P be a program and G a goal. Let $A \leftarrow B_1, \ldots, B_j, \ldots, B_n$ be a clause in P. We wish to analyse the possible calls to B_j $(1 \leq j \leq n)$ that arise in the computation of $P \cup \{G\}$. To distinguish B_j from other body literals having the same predicate symbol as B_j, we introduce a labelling.

Let the clauses in P be numbered from 1 to m. Attach a label (i, j) to the jth literal in the body of the ith clause. This labelling allows us to identify the original program point of any literal occurring in the computation of $P \cup G$.

Definition 2.1 *context*
  Let $A \leftarrow B_1, \ldots, B_j, \ldots, B_n$ be the ith clause in P. Let G be a goal. Define the context of B_j wrt the computation of $P \cup \{G\}$ as the set of instances of atoms labelled (i, j) selected in the computation tree for $P \cup \{G\}$.

The context of B_j is the set of queries to B_j in the computation. If we assume a left-to-right computation rule, and definite clauses, the context of each body literal can be defined using a query-answer transformation, as defined in the next section.

3 Query-answer transformation

This transformation is based on the "magic set" and "Alexander" transformations introduced as recursive query evaluation techniques and later adapted for use in program analysis [2], [4], [12] and [16]. We use here a variation of these transformations incorporating the labels described above.

Usually in program analysis we are not interested in the complete success set of a program, but only in the answers to certain calls. By transforming the program with the query-answer transformation, we can restrict attention to computations of given goals, rather than analyse the complete meaning of the program.

The general form of the query-answer transformation can be described by the following meta-program:

$$query(I, J, B_J) \leftarrow clause(I, H \leftarrow Bs),$$
$$conj(B_{Left}, (B_J, -), Bs, J),$$
$$answer(B_{Left}),$$
$$query(-, -, H).$$
$$query(0, 1, B).$$

$$answer(true).$$
$$answer((B, Bs)) \leftarrow answer(B),$$
$$answer(Bs).$$
$$answer(B) \leftarrow B \neq (-, -), B \neq true,$$
$$clause(B \leftarrow C),$$
$$query(-, -, B),$$
$$answer(C).$$

where $clause(I, H \leftarrow Bs)$ states that $H \leftarrow Bs$ is the Ith clause in the program, B_{Left} represents the goals to the left of B_J in the body of a clause and $conj(P, Q, R, J)$ is true if the conjunction of P and Q is R and J is the position of the leftmost literal in Q. Given the atomic goal $\leftarrow B$ we add the unit clause $query(0, 1, B)$ to the transformed program.

This program defines all queries generated during an SLD computation of a goal with a left to right computation rule and answers computed during a successful computation.

Consider the following simple program (with numbered clauses):

$$p(X) \leftarrow q(X), r(X). \qquad (1)$$
$$q(a). \qquad (2)$$
$$q(b). \qquad (3)$$
$$r(c). \qquad (4)$$

In the first clause, assuming a left-to-right computation rule, for $r(X)$ to be queried, $q(X)$ must be answered and $p(X)$ must be queried. For $q(X)$ to be answered, $q(X)$ must be queried, and for $q(X)$ to be queried $p(X)$ must be queried.

This information about the queries and answers to atoms in the above program can be expressed by the following query-answer transformed program:

$$answer(p(X)) \leftarrow$$
$$\qquad query(\_,\_,p(X)),$$
$$\qquad answer(q(X)),$$
$$\qquad answer(r(X)).$$
$$answer(q(a)) \leftarrow$$
$$\qquad query(\_,\_,q(a)).$$
$$answer(q(b)) \leftarrow$$
$$\qquad query(\_,\_,q(b)).$$
$$answer(r(a)) \leftarrow$$
$$\qquad query(\_,\_,r(a)).$$
$$query(1, 2, r(X)) \leftarrow$$
$$\qquad query(\_,\_,p(X)),$$
$$\qquad answer(q(X)).$$
$$query(1, 1, q(X)) \leftarrow$$
$$\qquad query(\_,\_,p(X)).$$

We now have, for each body literal B_J in clause I, a predicate $query(I, J, B_J)$ defining its context.

Note that the calls and answers produced are not in general identical to those arising in SLD computations, since some spurious instances of calls and answers may be produced. But since we are interested in a safe approximation of the ground success set of the program, this does not matter.

4 Deletion of Redundancy

We now define the rule which allows the elimination of redundant type predicates. The rule is formulated in a general way for the elimination of any body literal.

Consider any positive body literal B_J. Let $query(I, J, B_J)$ be its context wrt the computation of $P \cup \{G\}$. We define a transformation rule:

- If $\forall(query(I, J, B_J) \rightarrow B_J)$ then eliminate B_J from the Ith clause.

Intuitively, if the condition holds then the literal has already been established by the context. In general it is not decidable if $\forall(query(I, J, B_J) \rightarrow B_J)$. However, if we can define sufficient conditions for deciding the implication then the rule can be applied. In particular, in the case where B_J is defined by a regular program, we show that we can use operations on regular programs to decide whether B_J can be eliminated.

The elimination is justified informally by considering the procedural semantics. Suppose B is a program literal labelled (i, j), which is called during a computation of $P \cup \{G\}$ with substitution θ. That is, a literal $B\theta$ is selected in the computation. We know, therefore, that $\forall(query(i, j, B\theta))$ holds. If the implication $\forall((query(i, j, B) \rightarrow B$ has been established, $\forall(B\theta)$ also holds. Hence the call to $B\theta$ is "bound to succeed" and can be omitted, since the empty substitution is a correct answer for $B\theta$.

But all computed answer substitutions are not in general preserved. For instance, if a predicate $p/1$ is defined by the procedure $\{p(X) \leftarrow true, p(a) \leftarrow true\}$, then a call to $p(Z)$ is redundant since it succeeds immediately with the empty substitution by the first clause. However, the second clause would yield an answer $\{Z/a\}$.

In our application this is not a problem, if our types are defined by a canonical RUL program. In this case such subsumed answer substitutions are not possible. Other suitable restrictions on eliminated literals could be defined.

5 Regular Programs

Regular structures can be used to approximate programs as shown, for example, in [11], [17] and [21]. Regular programs have desirable qualities that make them attractive as a means of expressing an approximation of a logic program, namely:

- Regular programs have a number of decidable properties and associated computable operations [1], so that approximations of program meanings expressed as regular programs can conveniently be analysed and manipulated.

- Simple types can be expressed as regular unary logic programs. This relation between types and regular unary logic programs has been clarified in [21]. A type system using regular unary logic programs was also developed.

- Algorithms exist for computing a regular approximation (to be defined below) of a logic program. One such algorithm is described in [9].

The class of Regular Unary Logic (RUL) programs was defined by Yardeni and Shapiro [21]. A slightly more restricted class, called canonical RUL programs in [21], is defined below, but we will still refer to this class as RUL programs. RUL programs contain only unary predicates whose definitions are restricted to the form below.

Definition 5.1 *regular unary clause*

A **regular unary clause** *is of the form* $t_0(f(x_1, \ldots, x_n)) \leftarrow t_1(x_1), \ldots$, $t_n(x_n)$, *where* $x_1, \ldots, x_n$ *are distinct variables.*

Definition 5.2 *regular unary logic program (RUL program)*

A **regular unary logic program** *is a finite set of regular unary clauses, in which there are no two different clauses both of which have the same predicate and function symbol in their heads.*

We are now ready to define a *safe approximation* and an *regular approximation* of a program P. The usual definitions of definite and normal programs, and SLD and SLDNF derivations are used [14].

Definition 5.3 *safe approximation*

Let P, P' *be normal programs. Then* P' *is a* **safe** approximation *of* P *if for all ground atoms* A, $P \cup \{\leftarrow A\}$ *has an SLDNF refutation implies* $P' \cup \{\leftarrow A\}$ *has an SLDNF refutation.*

This definition states that the success set of a logic program is being approximated, that is, P' has a greater success set than P. Therefore, any property that holds for all elements of the success set of P' holds also for all elements of the success set of P.

Definition 5.4 *regular definition of predicates*

Let P *be a normal program containing predicates* $\{p^1/n^1, \ldots, p^m/n^m\}$. A **regular definition** *of the predicates in* P *is a set of clauses* $R \cup Q$, *where* Q *is a set of clauses of form* $p^i(x_1, \ldots, x_{n^i}) \leftarrow t_1(x_1), \ldots, t_{n^i}(x_{n^i})$, *where* $x_1, \ldots, x_{n^i}$ *are distinct variables and* R *is an RUL program defining* $t_1, \ldots, t_{n^i}$. *If* $R \cup Q$ *is a safe approximation of* P *it is called a* **regular approximation** *of* P.

For convenience, abusing notation, an RUL program can be obtained from a regular definition of predicates by replacing each clause $p^i(x_1, \ldots, x_{n^i}) \leftarrow B$ by a clause

$$approx(p^i(x_1, \ldots, x_{n^i})) \leftarrow B$$

where *approx* is a distinguished unary predicate not used elsewhere. Strictly, each predicate p^i/n^i should be replaced by a corresponding function symbol. This transformed program will also be referred to as a regular definition (or approximation), though strictly the original form without the *approx* predicate is meant. This allows us for the remainder of the paper to restrict attention to RUL programs.

We now define $success_R(t)$ of a set of regular unary clauses and a predicate t.

Definition 5.5 $success_R(t)$

Let R *be a set of regular unary clauses containing a predicate* t. *The set of terms* $success_R(t) = \{s \mid s \text{ a ground term}, R \cup \{\leftarrow t(s)\} \text{ succeeds}\}$

The following definition is also needed for the procedure for eliminating redundant literals.

Definition 5.6 *inclusion*

Let R be an RUL program, and let t_1 and t_2 be unary predicates defined in R. Then we write $t_1 \subseteq t_2$ if $success_R(t_1) \subseteq success_R(t_2)$.

The property $t_1 \subseteq t_2$ is true if:

for every clause $t_1(f(x_1, \ldots, x_n)) \leftarrow s_1(x_1), \ldots, s_n(x_n)$ in R there is a clause
$t_2(f(x_1, \ldots, x_n)) \leftarrow r_1(x_1), \ldots, r_n(x_n)$ in R, and $s_i \subseteq r_i$, $1 \le i \le n$.

This can be checked finitely.

5.1 Computation of Regular Approximations

Let B_P be the Herbrand base of P. We can consider a regular program R as representing a subset of B_P, namely $success_R(approx)$.

The approximation algorithm is based on the function $T_P : 2^{B_P} \rightarrow 2^{B_P}$, whose least fixed point is the minimal model of a definite program P [14]. An *abstraction* of T_P is some function $T_\alpha : 2^{B_P} \rightarrow 2^{B_P}$ such that T_α is monotonic, and for all $I \in 2^{B_P}$, $T_\alpha(I) \supseteq T_P(I)$. If these properties hold, then it can be shown that the least fixed point of T_α exists and includes the least fixed point of T_P.

A function T_α is defined, mapping one regular program to another. T_α can be considered to be of type $2^{B_P} \rightarrow 2^{B_P}$ since a regular program represents a subset of B_P. If T_α is an abstraction of T_P, then its fixed point is represented by a regular program whose success set includes the success set of P.

A naive algorithm for computing the fixed point of T_α is as follows:

```
BEGIN
    i := 0;
    R[0] := {};
    REPEAT
        R[i+1] := T_alpha(R[i]);
        i := i+1
    UNTIL success_R[i](approx) = success_R[i-1](approx)
END
```

Thus the algorithm computes a sequence of regular programs R[0], R[1], R[2],.... The algorithm terminates when it reaches some element of the sequence which is a fixed point of T_α, (with respect to the subset of B_P represented by the regular programs). A much more efficient form of the above algorithm is actually used in our safe approximation procedure.

The termination of the algorithm depends on the definition of T_α. The crucial part of T_α affecting termination is a *normalisation* operation, which restricts the structure of regular programs. Different versions of normalisation are possible. Our current version is given by the two following definitions.

Definition 5.7 $D(t, s)$

Let R be an RUL program containing predicates t and s ($t \neq s$). Then the relation $D(t, s)$ is true if t depends on s and the set of function symbols *appearing in the heads of clauses in the procedure for t is equal to the set of function symbols appearing in the heads of clauses in the procedure for s.*

Definition 5.8 *normalised RUL program*

*A **normalised** program R is one in which there are no two predicates t and s such that $D(t, s)$ holds.*

With this definition of normalisation incorporated in T_α it can be shown that the fixed point is reached in a finite number of iterations of the algorithm, since the number of distinct normalised programs over a fixed finite signature of constants and functions is finite.

In practice, the right normalisation operation is crucial to the quality of the safe approximations. Termination can be ensured by relatively crude normalisations, but as always in program analysis, there are trade-offs between precision and efficiency. This is further discussed in Section 7.

5.2 Procedure for Eliminating Redundant Type Checks

We now have defined all the components for presenting the procedure for checking whether a given occurrence of a type predicate in a program is redundant. The steps of the procedure are as follows. Given a program P and a goal G;

1. Compute the query-answer transformation for P with G.

2. Compute a regular approximation of the transformed program, using the algorithm described in Section 5.1. This yields a regular program containing (among others) clauses of the form

$$query(i, j, p(x_1, \ldots, x_n)) \leftarrow t_1(x_1), \ldots, t_n(x_n)$$

In particular, if the type literal labelled (i, j) is $p(s)$, its context is defined by the formula

$$query(i, j, p(s)) \leftarrow t(s)$$

3. If the predicate p is a regular unary predicate (for instance, one of the type predicates), we can check whether $t \subseteq p$ using the procedure in Definition 5.6. Note that the type *any* is treated specially, and we assume that $any \not\subseteq p$, for all p.

4. If $t \subseteq p$ then $\forall(query(i, j, p(s)) \rightarrow p(s))$ holds, and we can eliminate the occurrence of $p(s)$ labelled (i, j).

6 Extended Example

Consider the following typed Towers of Hanoi procedure taken from [21] with regular unary logic programs *nat, peg, move* and *moves* defining the types. Our aim is to delete as many type-checks as possible from the program.

Example: Towers of Hanoi with types

$hanoi(N)\leftarrow$
$\qquad hanoi(N, X),$
$\qquad nat(N).$
$hanoi(N, X) \leftarrow$
$\qquad hanoi(N, a, c, X),$
$\qquad nat(N),$
$\qquad moves(X).$

$hanoi(0, From, To, m(From, To)) \leftarrow$
$\qquad nat(0),$
$\qquad peg(From),$
$\qquad peg(To),$
$\qquad moves(m(From, To)).$
$hanoi(s(N), From, To, ms(Before, m(From, To), After)) \leftarrow$
$\qquad free(From, To, Free),$
$\qquad hanoi(N, From, Free, Before),$
$\qquad hanoi(N, Free, To, After),$
$\qquad nat(s(N)),$
$\qquad peg(From),$
$\qquad peg(To),$
$\qquad moves(ms(Before, m(From, To), After)).$

$free(a, b, c) \leftarrow peg(a), peg(b), peg(c).$
$free(a, c, b) \leftarrow peg(a), peg(b), peg(c).$
$free(b, a, c) \leftarrow peg(a), peg(b), peg(c).$
$free(b, c, a) \leftarrow peg(a), peg(b), peg(c).$
$free(c, a, b) \leftarrow peg(a), peg(b), peg(c).$
$free(c, b, a) \leftarrow peg(a), peg(b), peg(c).$

The types are defined by the following regular procedures:

$nat(0).$
$nat(s(X)) \leftarrow$
$\qquad nat(X).$

$move(m(X, Y)) \leftarrow$
$\qquad peg(X),$
$\qquad peg(Y).$
$moves(m(X, Y)) \leftarrow$
$\qquad peg(X),$
$\qquad peg(Y).$
$moves(ms(X, Y, Z)) \leftarrow$
$\qquad moves(X),$
$\qquad move(Y),$
$\qquad moves(Z).$
$peg(a).$
$peg(b).$
$peg(c).$

The query-answer transformation is now applied to the above program and the following top level query added:

$query(hanoi(\_))$.

The result of the query-answer transformation, which is too long to include here, is now approximated with the algorithm described in section 5.1. The approximation of the queries is the following program.

$query(nat(A1)) \leftarrow t1(A1)$.
$t1(0) \leftarrow true$.
$t1(s(A1)) \leftarrow t1(A1)$.
$query(peg(A1)) \leftarrow t2(A1)$.
$t2(a) \leftarrow true$.
$t2(c) \leftarrow true$.
$t2(b) \leftarrow true$.
$query(moves(A1)) \leftarrow t3(A1)$.
$t3(ms(A1, A2, A3)) \leftarrow t3(A1), t4(A2), t3(A3)$.
$t3(m(A1, A2)) \leftarrow t2(A1), t2(A2)$.
$t4(m(A1, A2)) \leftarrow t2(A1), t2(A2)$.
$query(move(A1)) \leftarrow t5(A1)$.
$t5(m(A1, A2)) \leftarrow t2(A1), t2(A2)$.
$query(hanoi(A1, A2)) \leftarrow any(A1), any(A2)$.
$query(hanoi(A1, A2, A3, A4)) \leftarrow any(A1), t2(A2), t2(A3), any(A4)$.
$query(free(A1, A2, A3)) \leftarrow t2(A1), t2(A2), any(A3)$.

From the above approximation the following holds:

$\forall X(query(peg(X)) \rightarrow peg(X))$ since $t2 \subseteq peg$.
$\forall X(query(nat(X)) \rightarrow nat(X))$ since $t1 \subseteq nat$.
$\forall X(query(move(X)) \rightarrow move(X))$ since $t5 \subseteq move$.
$\forall X(query(moves(X)) \rightarrow moves(X))$ since $t3 \subseteq moves$.

All calls to peg, nat, $move$ and $moves$ can therefore be deleted from the program.

Note that we used a simplified version of the query-answer transformation in which we did not include the label distinguishing different body literals. This is sufficiently precise for this example. Even when "collapsing" the different calls to different occurrences of the same literal into one call-pattern, we still get useful information. In general, it is neccessary to use the "labelled" query-answer transformation to get precise information about complex programs.

Also consider the typed version of $append$ described in the introduction. The approximation of the queries in the query-answer transformed version of $append$ with call

$\leftarrow append(X, Y, Z)$.

given by our implementation is

$query(0, 1, append(X, Y, Z)) \leftarrow any(X), any(Y), any(Z)$.
$query(1, 1, list(Y)) \leftarrow any(Y)$.
$query(2, 1, append(X, Y, Z)) \leftarrow any(X), any(Y), any(Z)$.

$query(2, 2, list(X)) \leftarrow t1(X).$
$query(2, 3, list(X)) \leftarrow t1(X).$
$query(2, 4, list(X)) \leftarrow t1(X).$
$t1([\,]).$
$t1([X|Xs]) \leftarrow any(X), t1(Xs).$

From the above approximation the following holds since $t1 \subseteq list$:

$\forall X(query(2, 2, list(X)) \rightarrow list(X)).$
$\forall X(query(2, 3, list(X)) \rightarrow list(X)).$
$\forall X(query(2, 4, list(X)) \rightarrow list(X)).$

The second, third and fourth occurrences of *list* can therefore be deleted from the *append* procedure and we are left with one list-check, namely the check in the first clause for *append* as given in the introduction.

Note that in this example it was necessary to use the labelling procedure in the query-answer transformation to distinguish between the different occurrences of *list*. If this was not done, only one approximation would be computed for all the different occurrences of *list*, which would not allow us to delete any list-checks ($\forall X(any(X) \subseteq list(X))$ does not hold).

7 Discussion

7.1 Accuracy of the Approximation

The effectiveness of the procedure for eliminating literals partly depends on the accuracy of the regular approximation of the query-answer transformed program. One problem that can arise is that the normalisation procedure abstracts away too much during regular approximation. In particular, if the original types are themselves not normalised, the result of analysis is likely to be too general.

For example, consider the following types describing the structure of a matrix, represented as a list of rows, each of which is a list of integers.

$matrix([\,]) \leftarrow true.$
$matrix([X|Xs]) \leftarrow row(X), matrix(Xs).$

$row([\,]) \leftarrow true.$
$row([X|Xs]) \leftarrow integer(X), row(Xs).$

Both *matrix* and *row* have the same functors in the head of their respective procedures, and *matrix* depends on *row*, so the program above is not normalised. The approximations of the contexts, on the other hand, would be normalised, and are thus defined by regular predicates that are more general than both $row(X)$ and $matrix(X)$; hence the conditions needed to eliminate the type literals are unlikely to be established.

An answer to this problem is to introduce better normalisations. Deeper properties can be used for normalisation, instead of just the functors in the clause heads. Current work involves experimenting with other normalisations.

7.2 Relation to Program Specialisation

The elimination of redundant literals is part of logic program *specialisation*. Given a program and a goal, the aim of specialisation is to derive a program that gives the same results for the given goal as the original program does, but more efficiently. Partial evaluation is the usual procedure for program specialisation.

The idea of contexts, as developed in this paper, can be applied to give a generalisation of partial evaluation [15], [8], [20], called *specialisation in context*. In partial evaluation, a program P is specialised with respect to a goal $\leftarrow G$. The generalisation of partial evaluation is obtained by formulating $\leftarrow G$ as $\leftarrow C(x_1, \ldots, x_n), G'$ where $C(x_1, \ldots, x_n)$ is $x_1 = t_1, \ldots, x_n = t_n$, and $G = G'\{x_1/t_1, \ldots, x_n/t_n\}$. In general, $C(x_1, \ldots, x_n)$ is any formula with free variables $x_1, \ldots, x_n$. We call $C(x_1, \ldots, x_n)$ a *context* for $\leftarrow G'$. In this paper, we considered contexts defined by RUL programs, but in general, arbitrary contexts could be used.

The use of regular contexts to improve partial evaluation has been investigated in [5], where we showed that infinite failed computation trees could be detected and eliminated using regular approximations. In future research we aim to combine these ideas and present a specialisation system that allows both the elimination of redundant literals and powerful partial evaluations based on analysis of contexts.

7.3 Treatment of Normal Programs

Although we have discussed a procedure for analysing definite programs, it can be extended to normal programs. Simply, before applying the query-answer transformation, all negative literals are removed from the program. The transformed program obtained defines approximations of the contexts of each positive literal, (that is, more general contexts than actually occur in computations) but the results are still correct. Negative literals in normal programs do not contribute anything to answer substitutions, and so the type structure of the program is hardly affected by their removal.

7.4 Related Work

We have already discussed our ideas in relation to type systems for logic programs. The elimination of type literals from a program is by no means the same as type-checking, but it can in some cases achieve similar ends. If the analysis for literal elimination derives an empty context for some type literal, this is an indication of a "badly-typed" clause. We have not yet made a detailed comparison between type-checking and our approach. However we note two aspects in which our approach seems more flexible than conventional type-checking.

- We analyse types with respect to computations of given goals, rather than checking the whole program. This allows more precision. A full program could be checked in our method by doing the query-answer transformation with respect to every program predicate.

- Our method allows selective elimination of type checks. In the *append* example, the base case check was retained but the others were eliminated.

This allows some run-time type-checking to be retained where needed.

A paper by Dart and Zobel [3] referred to in [19] appears to adopt a similar approach to ours. They also explicitly aim to analyse a program containing unary type literals in order to eliminate them where possible. Their type inference method (as presented in [22]) gives polymorphic types , which are more informative, but on the other hand, our method gives useful approximation where theirs gives the equivalent of the type "any".

Their method of deleting redundant type literals differs from ours in that it does not take into account the goal, whereas ours detects redundancy with respect to particular computations. However, we would be interested to compare further the power of the two methods.

Our work has some relation to other work on proving properties of logic programs. It has been pointed out (e.g. by [13]) that given a clause $H \leftarrow A, B$, then B can be eliminated if $A \rightarrow B$ holds in all models of P. Our approach uses the idea of approximating A to prove such statements. On the other hand, we obtain more powerful transformations of this kind, since we only require $A \rightarrow B$ to hold in the context of a specific computation, rather than all models of the program. Our motivation is also somewhat different in that we use safe approximations to prove program properties, since this suggests practical proof methods.

Some of our transformations could be achieved by unfold/fold methods. However, unfold/fold transformations do not take into account the answers to literals, as our method does, since they are based only on transforming the text of the program.

Acknowledgements

We thank participants at LOPSTR'92 where an earlier version was presented, and we also thank the referees for constructive remarks.

References

[1] A.V. Aho, J.E. Hopcroft, and J.D. Ullman. *The Design and Analysis of Computer Algorithms*. Addison-Wesley, 1974.

[2] M. Codish. *Abstract Interpretation of Sequential and Concurrent Logic Programs*. PhD thesis, The Weizmann Institute of Science, 1991.

[3] P.W. Dart and J. Zobel. *Transforming typed logic programs into well-typed logic programs*. Technical Report 88/11, University of Melbourne, May 1988.

[4] S. Debray and R. Ramakrishnan. *Canonical computations of logic programs*. Technical Report, University of Arizona-Tucson, July 1990.

[5] D.A. de Waal and J. Gallagher. *Regular Approximations Applied to the Specialisation of a Proof Procedure*. Technical Report CSTR-92-19, University of Bristol, May 1992.

[6] H.B. Enderton. *A Mathematical Introduction to Logic.* Academic Press, New York, 1972.

[7] T. Frühwirth. Type inference by program transformation and partial evaluation. In H. Abramson and M.H. Rogers, editors, *Meta-Programming in Logic Programming*, 1988.

[8] J. Gallagher. *A System for Specialising Logic programs.* Technical Report TR-91-32, University of Bristol, November 1991.

[9] J. Gallagher and D.A. de Waal. *Regular Approximations of Logic Programs and Their Uses.* Technical Report CSTR-92-06, University of Bristol, March 1992.

[10] P.M. Hill and J.W. Lloyd. *The Gödel report.* Technical Report TR-91-02, University of Bristol, March 1991. (preliminary version).

[11] N. Jones. Flow analysis of lazy higher order functional programs. In S. Abramsky and C. Hankin, editors, *Abstract Interpretation of Declarative Languages*, Ellis-Horwood, 1987.

[12] T. Kanamori. *Abstract interpretation based on Alexander templates.* Technical Report TR-549, ICOT, March 1990.

[13] T. Kanamori and H. Seki. Verification of Prolog programs using an extension of execution. In E. Shapiro, editor, *Lecture Note in Computer Science, 225*, pages 475–489, Springer-Verlag, 1986.

[14] J.W. Lloyd. *Foundations of Logic Programming: 2nd Edition.* Springer-Verlag, 1987.

[15] J.W. Lloyd and J.C. Shepherdson. *Partial Evaluation in Logic Programming. Journal of Logic Programming*, 11(3&4):217–242, 1991.

[16] C.S. Mellish. *Using specialisation to reconstruct two mode inference systems.* Technical Report, University of Edinburgh, March 1990.

[17] P. Mishra. Towards a theory of types in prolog. In *Proceedings of the IEEE International Symposium on Logic Programming*, 1984.

[18] A. Mycroft. A polymorphic type system. *Artificial Intelligence*, 23:295–307, 1984.

[19] L. Naish. *Types and the Intended Meaning of Logic Programs.* Technical Report, University of Melbourne, 1990.

[20] D. Sahlin. *An Automatic Partial Evaluator for Full Prolog.* PhD thesis, The Royal Institute of Technology, 1991.

[21] E. Yardeni and E. Shapiro. A type system for logic programs. *Journal of Logic Programming*, 10(2):348–375, 1991.

[22] Zobel. *Analysis of Logic Programs.* PhD thesis, Technical Report 47, University of Melbourne, September 1990.

Automatic Termination Analysis

Kristof Verschaetse   Stefaan Decorte

Danny De Schreye

Department of Computer Science, K.U.Leuven,

Celestijnenlaan 200A, B-3001 Heverlee, Belgium.

e-mail : {kristof,dannyd}@cs.kuleuven.ac.be

August 19, 1992

Abstract

Proving termination of programs is important in any approach to program development. In logic programming, where the logic and the control component of a program can very easily be dealt with in two separate phases of the development, the termination issue is solely addressed in the second phase. Both formal, theoretical frameworks for reasoning about termination, and automatic techniques for termination analysis have recently obtained considerable attention in the logic programming community. Unfortunately, in current work, these two types of approaches to termination have been rather orthogonal. It would be desirable if automatic techniques could rely directly on general frameworks for their correctness proofs.

We recently presented a new, practical framework for termination analysis of definite logic programs with respect to call patterns. In the current paper, we describe an automated technique, which is directly based on the framework. The main advantages are: the generality of the approach (analysis can be performed for any given set of top-level goals), the clear theoretical underpinning provided by the framework and full automation.

1 Introduction

It is widely accepted that one of the great strengths of logic programming languages is the ease with which one can reason about the logic expressed in a program independently from its operational semantics. Following the Algorithm = Logic + Control equation of [13], this invites to a programming style in which one first focuses on the logic component of the program, providing a correct specification for the problem at hand, and in a separate phase, adds the control to tune the algorithm in view of the operational semantics of the specific underlying language.

Systematic approaches to program development in logic programming (see e.g. [10]) strongly build upon this separation of concerns, the main advantage of the logic programming context being that the specification language (e.g. first order logic) and the implementation language (e.g. Prolog) are very closely linked. In particular, this close link between the two languages facilitates automated or semi-automated tools for program synthesis and/or transformation to be exploited in the development steps leading from specification to implementation. As stated above, these steps are tightly connected with the control component for the target program. As a result, the issue of termination requires considerable attention within them.

Termination issues are important at two different levels. One is related to (automated) control generation itself (see e.g. [15]). Here, termination analysis is implicit, in the sense that a minimal requirement for the generated control rule is that the target program will terminate. However, due to the undecidability of the halting problem, termination can not in general be guaranteed by the automated approaches and often heuristics are applied instead of formal, safe techniques. So, the second role for termination analysis is situated on the level of program verification. Independent of the approach used in the control generation, verifying the termination properties of the resulting program is desirable.

In recent years, termination analysis for logic programs has attracted much attention. We distinguish between two approaches. Some works (e.g. [4], [2]) provide general and formal frameworks expressing elegant necessary and sufficient conditions for termination. Rather orthogonal to these, automatic techniques for termination analysis have been proposed in e.g. [19] and [16]. These works only provide sufficient (but decidable) conditions for termination, which are often formulated at a much lower conceptual level (making correctness of these approaches much harder to grasp).

In [8] a new, more practical formal framework for termination analysis is proposed. It extends the works of Apt, Bezem and Pedreschi. The main goal of this work is to provide a framework that is sufficiently practical to allow for automatic approaches to build on it directly. It is shown through several examples that the degree of creativity needed from a user, to fill in the parameters that yield the termination proof for a program at hand, seems significantly lower than in previous frameworks. It was claimed that this feature would at the same time allow automatic techniques to build on it, so that better theoretical support for automatic approaches could be provided.

In this paper, we describe such an automatic termination analysis, directly based on [8]. Our main result consists of two practical sufficient conditions for termination, which are extracted from the framework. The techniques are presented for definite programs, but can be extended to normal programs along the same lines as done in [1] and [3]. An extended version of both [8] and the current paper is available in [7].

The next section contains a short overview of the framework in [8]. In section 3 we formulate all remaining concepts needed for the automation and we present the two sufficient conditions for termination. Section 4 contains some detailed examples. In section 5 we briefly describe the analysis system itself. We end with a discussion.

2 A theoretical characterisation of terminating programs

Throughout this paper, we work with atoms from the extended Herbrand base, B_P^E. This notion was introduced in [11] and is defined as the set $Atom_P/\approx$, where $Atom_P$ is the set of all atoms that can be constructed from the language underlying to the program P, while $\approx$ denotes the variant relation. An element

$\bar{A}$ of B_P^E is actually an equivalence class of atoms, where for every $A, A' \in \bar{A}$, one has that A and A' are variants.

Definition 2.1 (termination with respect to a set of atoms)
Let $S \subseteq B_P^E$ denote a set of atoms that are considered as top level queries. We say that P is *terminating with respect to* S, if for any representant A' of any element $\bar{A}$ of S, every SLD-tree for $(P, \leftarrow A')$ is finite.

In the above definition, the choice of the computation rule is not made explicit. Instead, it says that — whatever this choice may be — all SLD-trees must be finite in order for a program to be terminating. A specialised version is obtained by restricting the attention to Prolog's left-to-right computation rule. Following [2], we call this LD-resolution.

Definition 2.2 (left-termination with respect to a set of atoms)
Let $S \subseteq B_P^E$. We say that P is *left-terminating with respect to* S, if for any representant A' of any element $\bar{A}$ of S, the LD-tree for $(P, \leftarrow A')$ is finite.

Proving termination (or left-termination) will be accomplished by verifying a condition for all possible calls (i.e. selected atoms) in the SLD-trees (LD-trees) that are constructed when one of the atoms in S is used as top-level query. A safe approximation of this set of selected atoms is obtained by means of the following fixpoint characterisation.

First, for any $S' \subseteq B_P^E$, define $T_P^{-1}(S') = \{\overline{B_i\theta} \in B_P^E \mid A'$ is a representant of $\bar{A} \in S'$, $H \leftarrow B_1, \ldots, B_n$ is a clause in P, $\theta = mgu(A', H)$ and $1 \leq i \leq n\}$. Take a fixed set S and let S^c denote its closure under $\leq$. Denote $\mathcal{H}_S = \{S' \in 2^{B_P^E} \mid S^c \subseteq S'\}$. $\mathcal{H}_S$ is a complete lattice with bottom element S^c. We now define the following operator on $\mathcal{H}_S$.

Definition 2.3

$$R_S : \mathcal{H}_S \to \mathcal{H}_S : R_S(S') = S' \cup (T_P^{-1}(S'))^c$$

The ordinal powers of R_S are defined as usual. In [7], it is proved that $R_S \uparrow \omega$ is the least fixpoint of R_S, and that P terminates with respect to S if and only if P terminates with respect to $R_S \uparrow \omega$. Also, $R_S \uparrow \omega$ contains all atoms that can occur as selected atom in any SLD-tree for any representant of any atom in S.

In case one considers a fixed computation rule (in particular: Prolog's left-to-right computation rule), a similar result is obtained by first defining for any $S' \subseteq D_P^E$, $\mathcal{P}_P^{-1}(S') = \{\overline{D_i\theta\sigma_1\cdots\sigma_{i-1}} \in D_P^E \mid A'$ is a representant of $\bar{A} \in S'$, $H \leftarrow B_1, \ldots, B_n$ is a clause in P, $\theta = mgu(A', H)$, $1 \leq i \leq n$, $\exists\sigma_1, \ldots, \sigma_{i-1}, \forall j = 1, \ldots, i-1$: σ_j is a computed answer substitution for $(P, \leftarrow B_j\theta\sigma_1\cdots\sigma_{j-1})\}$, by denoting $\mathcal{H}_S^{l-r} = \{S' \in 2^{B_P^E} \mid S \subseteq S'\}$, and by defining the following operator on $\mathcal{H}_S^{l-r}$.

Definition 2.4

$$R_S^{l-r} : \mathcal{H}_S^{l-r} \to \mathcal{H}_S^{l-r} : R_S^{l-r}(S') = S' \cup \mathcal{P}_P^{-1}(S')$$

Again, $R_S^{l-r} \uparrow \omega$ contains all atoms that can occur as selected atoms in an LD-tree for a representant of an element in S.

Atoms are measured by means of a level mapping.

Definition 2.5 (level mapping)
A *level mapping with respect to a set* $S \subseteq B_P^E$ is a function $|.| : R_S \uparrow \omega \to I\!N$.

A similar definition is again obtained by replacing $R_S \uparrow \omega$ with $R_S^{l-r} \uparrow \omega$. The latter mapping is used when proving left-termination.

A nice theoretical characterisation of respectively termination and left-termination (with respect to a set S) is provided by the respective notions of a *recurrent* program and an *acceptable* program (with respect to a set S). Both notions make use of the concept of a resultant of an incomplete derivation (see [14]). Below, we use the more specialised concept of a *recursive resultant*. A resultant $A'\theta \leftarrow B_1, \ldots, B_m$ for A' is *recursive* if at least one of the atoms B_i has the same predicate symbol as A'.

Definition 2.6 (recurrency with respect to a set of atoms)
Let $S \subseteq B_P^E$. A program P is *recurrent with respect to S*, if there exists a level mapping, $|.|$, with respect to S, such that:

- for any A' representant of $\bar{A} \in R_S \uparrow \omega$,

- for any recursive resultant $A'\theta \leftarrow B_1, \ldots, B_m$, for A',

- for any atom B_i $(1 \leq i \leq m)$ with the same predicate symbol as A':
  $|A'| > |B_i|$.

Definition 2.7 (acceptability with respect to a set of atoms)
Let $S \subseteq B_P^E$. A program P is *acceptable with respect to S*, if there exists a level mapping, $|.|$, with respect to S, such that for any $p(s_1, \ldots, s_n)$, representant of an element in $R_S^{l-r} \uparrow \omega$, and for any recursive resultant $p(s_1, \ldots, s_n)\theta \leftarrow p(t_1, \ldots, t_n), B_2, \ldots, B_m$:

$$|p(s_1, \ldots, s_n)| > |p(t_1, \ldots, t_n)|.$$

In [7], the following notions are shown to be equivalent.

Theorem 2.8
P is recurrent with respect to S if and only if it is terminating with respect to S.

Theorem 2.9
P is acceptable with respect to S if and only if P is left-terminating with respect to S.

As a trivial consequence of the above equivalence results, we can state that recurrency and acceptability are undecidable properties for a logic program.

3 Practical conditions for verifying termination

In the previous section, the equivalence between the theoretical notions of recurrency and acceptability, and our topic of interest — termination and left-termination — has been established. The former notions are of purely theoretical value, in the sense that they rely on the verification of an inequality for a potentially infinite number of syntactical objects. Indeed, both the sets $R_S\uparrow\omega$ and $R_S^{l-r}\uparrow\omega$ are in general infinite sets, and an infinite number of recursive resultants may be constructed for every representant of an element in $R_S\uparrow\omega$ (or $R_S^{l-r}\uparrow\omega$).

The first issue when talking about automation is the computation of $R_S\uparrow\omega$ and $R_S^{l-r}\uparrow\omega$. The set of queries S will in general not be given by explicitly enumerating all its atoms. Instead, it will be specified in terms of some abstract descriptions. Examples of such descriptions are mode information ([9]), rigid types ([12]) and integrated types ([12]). Abstract interpretation allows then to infer similar abstract descriptions for all other atoms in the program. The set of concrete atoms that is denoted by these abstract descriptions can be shown to include $R_S\uparrow\omega$ (or $R_S^{l-r}\uparrow\omega$), i.e. it forms a safe approximation (see [7] for more details).

The second issue that must be addressed by an automatic technique is the problem of the potentially infinite number of recursive resultants. We have addressed this problem by formulating sufficient conditions for recurrency and acceptability, which rely only on the verification of a finite set of representants of minimal cyclic collections.

Definition 3.1 (minimal cyclic collection)
A minimal cyclic collection of P is a finite set of clauses of P, say $\{cl_1, \ldots, cl_m\}$, such that:

- for each pair of clauses $\{cl_i, cl_j\}$ $(1 \le i < j \le m)$, the heads of the clauses have distinct predicate symbols, and

- there exists an order on the elements of the set, say $cl_{i(1)}, cl_{i(2)}, \ldots, cl_{i(m)}$, and an associated m-tuple of atoms, $(A'_1, A'_2, \ldots, A'_m)$, such that for all k $(1 \le k \le m)$,
    - A'_k is an atom in the body of $cl_{i(k)}$,
    - denoting the head of $cl_{i(k)}$ as A_{k-1}, A'_k has the same predicate symbol as $A_{k \bmod m}$.

We say that any m-tuple of pairs, $((cl_{i(1)}, A'_1), (cl_{i(2)}, A'_2), \ldots, (cl_{i(m)}, A'_m))$ satisfying the above conditions, is a *representant* of the minimal cyclic collection $\{cl_1, \ldots, cl_m\}$. Such representants can — more elegantly — be denoted as

$$
\begin{aligned}
A_0 &\leftarrow B^1_1, \ldots, A'_1, \ldots, B^1_{n_1} \\
A_1 &\leftarrow D^2_1, \ldots, A'_2, \ldots, D^2_{n_2} \\
&\vdots \\
A_{m-1} &\leftarrow B^m_1, \ldots, A'_m, \ldots, B^m_{n_m},
\end{aligned}
$$

where, by definition, all A_i have distinct predicate symbols, all A'_i have the same predicate symbol as the corresponding A_i and A'_m has the same predicate symbol as A_0. This representation for representants of minimal cyclic collections also explains the seemingly unnatural shift in the subscripts on the A_i in definition 3.1.

Observe that there can be several representants for any given minimal cyclic collection. In particular, any cyclic permutation of a representant is also a representant. In addition, there can be several atoms in the body of a clause $cl_{i(k)}$, all having the same predicate symbol as $A_{k \bmod m}$. Each gives rise to a different representant. But since the number of clauses in P is finite, only a finite number of minimal cyclic collections (and representants of such collections) exist.

Several other issues must be addressed as well when aiming at a fully automatic technique. The choice of a level mapping is not made explicit in the recurrency and acceptability conditions. Hence, we will provide a procedure for automatically generating level mappings, which will depend on the *rigid* argument positions of an atom (see further). Our practical conditions are expressed as conditions ranging over all "sizes of instantiations of the rigid argument positions". The size of a term will be measured by using *semi-linear norms* (see [6]). A concrete term will be abstractly represented by means of a so-called *size expression*, which is essentially a term in the language $\mathcal{L}_{<0,1;+;\leq>}$, consisting only of the constants $\{0,1\}$, the functor $\{+/2\}$ and the predicate $\{\leq/2\}$.

Before presenting our two practical conditions for verifying recurrency and acceptability, we briefly recall the above mentioned machinery.

A *norm* maps a term to a natural number. Of special interest are semi-linear norms, which were introduced in [6], and are defined as follows.

Definition 3.2 (semi-linear norm; see [6])
A norm $||.||$ is *semi-linear* if it is recursively defined by means of the following schema:

$$\begin{aligned}
||V|| &= 0 \text{ if } V \text{ is a variable, and} \\
||f(t_1,\ldots,t_n)|| &= c + ||t_{i_1}|| + \cdots + ||t_{i_m}|| \\
&\text{with } c \in I\!N, \{i_1,\ldots,i_m\} \subseteq \{1,\ldots,n\} \\
&\text{and } c, i_1,\ldots,i_m \text{ depend only on } f/n.
\end{aligned}$$

Usually, the following two instances of the above definition suffice to prove termination.

Definition 3.3 (list-length)
The *list-length* norm, denoted $||.||_l$, is defined in the following way:

$$\begin{aligned}
||[x|y]||_l &= 1 + ||y||_l \quad \text{with } x \text{ and } y \text{ any term} \\
||x||_l &= 0 \quad \text{otherwise.}
\end{aligned}$$

A more general norm is *term-size*, which counts the number of function symbols in a term.

Definition 3.4 (term-size)
The *term-size* norm, denoted $||.||_t$, is defined in the following way:

$$\begin{aligned}
||f(t_1,\ldots,t_n)||_t &= 1 + \sum_{i=1}^{n} ||t_i||_t \quad \text{with } f \text{ any function symbol} \\
&\qquad\qquad\qquad\qquad \text{and } n > 0 \\
||x||_t &= 0 \quad \text{otherwise.}
\end{aligned}$$

Another important notion (again introduced in [6]) is *rigidity with respect to a (semi-linear) norm*.

Definition 3.5 (rigid term; see [6])
Let $||.||$ be norm and t be a term. We say that t is *rigid* with respect to $||.||$ if for any substitution σ, $||t\sigma|| = ||t||$.

On the basis of these concepts, we propose a generic definition of a natural level mapping.

Definition 3.6 (natural level mapping)

Given is a set of atoms $S \subseteq B_P^{\mathcal{E}}$. A *natural level mapping induced by S*, denoted $|.|_{nat}$, is defined as:

$$\forall p(t_1,\ldots,t_n) \in R_S\uparrow\omega : |p(t_1,\ldots,t_n)|_{nat} = \sum_{i \in I_n^p} \|t_i\| \quad \text{if } I_n^p \neq \emptyset$$
$$= 0 \quad \text{otherwise,}$$

- with $\|.\|$ a semi-linear norm,

- $I_n^p \subseteq \{1,\ldots,n\}$ is a set of argument positions depending only on p/n, and

- $\forall p(u_1,\ldots,u_n) \in R_S\uparrow\omega$ and $\forall i \in I_n^p$: u_i is rigid with respect to $\|.\|$.

The above definition is used when analysing recurrency with respect to S. In the case of acceptability, the same definition can be used, provided that all occurrences of $R_S\uparrow\omega$ are replaced by $R_S^{l-r}\uparrow\omega$.

It is important to notice that the above definition defines again *generic* level mappings. A particular instance is obtained by choosing a *fixed* semi-linear norm and for each predicate symbol a set of properly defined argument positions.

A nice way of expressing the relation between the sizes (norms) of (all instantiations of) two terms is by using size expressions. The variables in these expressions are interpreted in the domain of the natural numbers and represent sizes. We use the notation $S_{<0,1;+;\leq>}$ to denote the set of all terms in the language $\mathcal{L}_{<0,1;+;\leq>}$.

Definition 3.7 (size expression)

Let $\|.\|$ be any semi-linear norm. A term t is mapped to the *size expression* $abs_{\|.\|}(t)$ by means of the function $abs_{\|.\|} : Term_P \rightarrow S_{<0,1;+;\leq>}$, which is defined as:

$$abs_{\|.\|}(V) = V \text{ if } V \text{ is a variable}$$
$$abs_{\|.\|}(f(t_1,\ldots,t_n)) = c + abs_{\|.\|}(t_{i_1}) + \cdots + abs_{\|.\|}(t_{i_m}) \text{ otherwise,}$$

where $c \in \mathbb{N}$, $\{i_1,\ldots,i_m\} \subseteq \{1,\ldots,n\}$, the $c, i_1,\ldots,i_m$ depend only on f/n and are the same as in the definition of $\|.\|$ (see definition 3.2).

An order relation is readily defined on the set of size expressions. Given are two size expressions $\mathcal{E}_1$ and $\mathcal{E}_2$. We say that $\mathcal{E}_1 \leq \mathcal{E}_2$ iff for every substitution

$$\theta = \{(X_i \leftarrow n_i) \mid X_i \in vars(\mathcal{E}_1) \cup vars(\mathcal{E}_2) \text{ and } n_i \in \mathbb{N}\}$$

one has that $\mathcal{E}_1\theta \leq \mathcal{E}_2\theta$. Observe that as a consequence, $vars(\mathcal{E}_1) \subseteq vars(\mathcal{E}_2)$. We will also use the following shorthand forms.

$$\mathcal{E}_1 \geq \mathcal{E}_2 \equiv \mathcal{E}_2 \leq \mathcal{E}_1$$
$$\mathcal{E}_1 < \mathcal{E}_2 \equiv \mathcal{E}_1 + 1 \leq \mathcal{E}_2$$
$$\mathcal{E}_1 > \mathcal{E}_2 \equiv \mathcal{E}_2 + 1 \leq \mathcal{E}_1$$

The following definition extends size expressions, by defining them on atoms and taking a natural level mapping into account.

Definition 3.8

Let $S \subseteq B_P^E$ and let $|.|_{nat}$ denote a natural level mapping induced by S. Let $RelevantAtoms = \{A \in Atom_P \mid A$ is unifiable with at least one representant of an element of $R_S \uparrow \omega\}$. We define a mapping $abs_{|.|_{nat}} : RelevantAtoms \rightarrow S_{<0,1;+;\leq>}$ as follows:

$$abs_{|.|_{nat}}(p(t_1, \ldots, t_n)) = abs_{||.||}(t_{i_1}) + \cdots + abs_{||.||}(t_{i_k})$$

with $\{i_1, \ldots, i_k\} = I_n^p$, the set of argument positions associated to p/n by $|.|_{nat}$ and $||.||$ is the semi-linear norm of $|.|_{nat}$.

Obviously, the corresponding definition for acceptability is found by replacing each occurrence of $R_S \uparrow \omega$ by $R_S^{l-r} \uparrow \omega$. Notice that $abs_{|.|_{nat}}$ is defined on a superset of (the set of representants of elements from) $R_S \uparrow \omega$ (or $R_S^{l-r} \uparrow \omega$). Defining this function on $Atom_P$ would (in general) not be useful, since $|.|_{nat}$ is (in general) not defined on all atoms. On the other hand, restricting the domain of $abs_{|.|_{nat}}$ to the set $R_S \uparrow \omega$, does not allow to compute (again in general) abstract representations for (e.g.) the heads of clauses unifying with elements from $R_S \uparrow \omega$.

At last, we are in a position to formulate the practical condition that we propose to use when (automatically) proving termination.

Proposition 3.9

Given is $S \subseteq B_P^E$. Let $|.|_{nat}$ denote a natural level mapping induced by S. Suppose that for any representant of a minimal cyclic collection of P, say

$$A_0 \quad \leftarrow \quad B_1^1, \ldots, A_1', \ldots, B_{n_1}^1$$
$$\vdots$$
$$A_{m-1} \quad \leftarrow \quad B_1^m, \ldots, A_m', \ldots, B_{n_m}^m,$$

in which all clauses are standardised apart and every A_i $(0 \leq i \leq m-1)$ unifies with at least one representant of an element of $R_S \uparrow \omega$, the system

$$
\begin{cases}
abs_{|.|_{nat}}(A_1') & \geq & abs_{|.|_{nat}}(A_1) \\
& \vdots & \\
abs_{|.|_{nat}}(A_{m-1}') & \geq & abs_{|.|_{nat}}(A_{m-1}) \\
abs_{|.|_{nat}}(A_m') & \geq & abs_{|.|_{nat}}(A_0)
\end{cases}
$$

is not solvable over the domain of natural numbers, then P is recurrent with respect to S and $|.|_{nat}$.

Proof The idea of the proof is that both minimal cyclic collections and recursive resultants can be directly related to the predicate dependency graph for P. Minimal cyclic collections correspond to *elementary* cycles in the predicate dependency graph, while recursive resultants correspond to (not necessarily elementary) cycles. The proof consists of decomposing the cycle associated to a recursive resultant into elementary cycles (and therefore connecting minimal cyclic collections to the recursive resultants). The condition expressed in the proposition is then used to guarantee that in each traversal of an elementary cycle, the level will strictly decrease. As a result, the level decreases for each recursive resultant. We refer to [7] for a full proof. $\qquad\qquad\square$

The counterpart of proposition 3.9 (for the case of left-termination) needs to take additional information about the computed answer substitutions into account, since computed answer substitutions for one atom serve as call substitutions for the next atom, and hence, we have to be able to relate to each other the sizes of the arguments in such intermediate atoms.

Such information is provided by the *linear size relations*, which express a linear relationship between the sizes of the arguments of an atom. A linear size relation is represented as a linear system of equations, $\bar{A} \cdot \bar{X} = \bar{c}$, where $\bar{A}$ is an $m \times n$ matrix of rational numbers, $\bar{X}$ is an $n \times 1$ vector of variables taking values in $\mathbb{N}$, and $\bar{c}$ is an $m \times 1$ vector of rational numbers.

Definition 3.10 (linear size relation of an atom)
A linear size relation $\bar{A} \cdot \bar{X} = \bar{c}$ for an atom $p(t_1, \ldots, t_n)$, is a linear system of equations of the above type, such that

$$
\bar{A} \cdot \begin{bmatrix} abs_{||.||}(t_1\theta) \\ \vdots \\ abs_{||.||}(t_n\theta) \end{bmatrix} = \bar{c}
$$

is solvable for any computed answer substitution θ.

Hence, linear size relations express linear relationships between the sizes of the arguments of atoms in the minimal Herbrand model (success set) of a program. Linear size relations can also be extended to compound goals. In this case, they are a safe approximation (as the solutions to a system of linear equations) of the relation over $\mathbb{N}^m$, which holds between the sizes (under the given norm) of the terms that are substituted for the variables $X_1, \ldots, X_m$ occurring in the compound goal, by *any* computed answer substitution. For more details about this, and for an automatic derivation procedure (based on abstract interpretation) we refer to [20].

The next proposition gives the practical condition that we propose for verifying acceptability.

Proposition 3.11
Given is $S \subseteq B_P^E$. Let $|.|_{nat}$ denote a natural level mapping induced by S and with respect to a semi-linear norm $||.||$. Suppose that for any representant of a minimal cyclic collection of P, say

$$
A_0 \quad \leftarrow \quad B_1^1, \ldots, B_{i_1}^1, A_1', \ldots, B_{n_1}^1
$$
$$
\vdots
$$
$$
A_{m-1} \quad \leftarrow \quad B_1^m, \ldots, B_{i_m}^m, A_m', \ldots, B_{n_m}^m
$$

in which all clauses are standardised apart and every A_j unifies with at least one representant of an element of $R_S^{l-r} \!\uparrow\! \omega$, and where $(\overline{M}_j \cdot \overline{X}_j = \bar{c}_j)$ denotes the linear size relation that is obtained for the goal $B_1^j, \ldots, B_{i_j}^j$ ($\overline{X}_j$ contains all variables occurring in $B_1^j, \ldots, B_{i_j}^j$), the system

$$\begin{cases} \overline{M}_1 \cdot \overline{X}_1 & = & \bar{c}_1 \\ & \vdots & \\ \overline{M}_m \cdot \overline{X}_m & = & \bar{c}_m \\ abs_{|.|_{nat}}(A_1') & \geq & abs_{|.|_{nat}}(A_1) \\ & \vdots & \\ abs_{|.|_{nat}}(A_{m-1}') & \geq & abs_{|.|_{nat}}(A_{m-1}) \\ abs_{|.|_{nat}}(A_m') & \geq & abs_{|.|_{nat}}(A_0) \end{cases}$$

is not solvable over the domain of natural numbers, then P is acceptable with respect to S and $|.|_{nat}$.

Proof See [7]. □

4 Some examples

A number of examples are now worked out in the hope that they will make the reader more familiar with the definitions and the practical propositions introduced in the previous sections.

Example 4.1 (Simple arithmetic expressions)
This program recognises simple expressions that are built up from integers and the function symbols $+/2, */2$ and $-/1$.

cl1	$e(X + Y)$	$\leftarrow$	$f(X), e(Y)$
cl2	$e(X)$	$\leftarrow$	$f(X)$
cl3	$f(X * Y)$	$\leftarrow$	$g(X), f(Y)$
cl4	$f(X)$	$\leftarrow$	$g(X)$
cl5	$g(-(X))$	$\leftarrow$	$e(X)$
cl6	$g(X)$	$\leftarrow$	$integer(X)$

Suppose we analyse termination with respect to the set $S = \{e(x) \mid x$ is ground$\}$.

A safe approximation for $R_S \uparrow \omega$ is $\{e(x), f(y), g(z), integer(n) \mid x, y, z, n$ are ground $\}$.

By selecting the termsize norm and fixing the sets of argument positions to the singleton $\{ 1 \}$ for all four predicates, we obtain the following natural level mapping:

$$\begin{aligned} |e(x)|_{nat} & = \|x\|_t \\ |f(y)|_{nat} & = \|y\|_t \\ |g(z)|_{nat} & = \|z\|_t \\ |integer(n)|_{nat} & = \|n\|_t \end{aligned}$$

Notice that for each atom in $R_S\uparrow\omega$, its argument is rigid with respect to $\|.\|_t$. There are 14 representants of minimal cyclic collections in the program. They are :

$$
\begin{array}{ll}
(1) & (\,(cl1, e(Y))\,) \\
(2) & (\,(cl3, f(Y))\,) \\
(3-5) & (\,(cl1, f(X)), (cl3, g(X)), (cl5, e(X))\,) \text{ and its 2 cyclic permutations.} \\
(6-8) & (\,(cl1, f(X)), (cl4, g(X)), (cl5, e(X))\,) \text{ and its 2 cyclic permutations.} \\
(9-11) & (\,(cl2, f(X)), (cl3, g(X)), (cl5, e(X))\,) \text{ and its 2 cyclic permutations.} \\
(12-14) & (\,(cl2, f(X)), (cl4, g(X)), (cl5, e(X))\,) \text{ and its 2 cyclic permutations.}
\end{array}
$$

As an example, we pick out representant number three. After standardising apart, we can represent it as

$$
\begin{array}{rcl}
e(X + Y) & \leftarrow & f(X), e(Y) \\
f(X' * Y') & \leftarrow & g(X'), f(Y') \\
g(-(X'')) & \leftarrow & e(X'')
\end{array}
$$

Applying the condition in proposition 3.9 yields :

$$
\left\{
\begin{array}{rcll}
X & \geq & X' + Y' + 1 & (1) \\
X' & \geq & X'' + 1 & (2) \\
X'' & \geq & X + Y + 1 & (3)
\end{array}
\right.
$$

The unsolvability of this system should be proved. By using inequality (3) in (2) and the resulting inequality in (1), we obtain the following inequality, $X \geq X + Y + Y' + 3$, which clearly does not hold in the domain of the natural numbers.

Similar results are obtained for the other representants. As a result of proposition 3.9, we may conclude that the program is recurrent with respect to the set of atoms S and a level mapping $|.|_{nat}$ or, equivalently, that it is terminating with respect to S.

Example 4.2 (permutation)

The second example concerns the permutation program :

```
p1   perm([], []).
p2   perm([X₁|X], [Y₁|Y])  ←  delete(Y₁, [X₁|X], Z),perm(Z, Y).

d1   delete(X₁, [X₁|X], X).
d2   delete(Y₁, [X₁|X], [X₁|Z])  ←  delete(Y₁, X, Z).
```

For this program, we will prove acceptability with respect to the set
$S = \{\text{perm}(x, y) \mid x \text{ is ground and } y \text{ is free}\}$.

The following set is an approximation for $R_S^{l-r}\uparrow\omega$:

$$\{\,\text{perm}(x, y) \mid x \text{ is ground and } y \text{ is free}\,\}$$
$$\cup$$
$$\{\,\text{delete}(x, y, z) \mid x \text{ and } z \text{ are free and } y \text{ is ground}\,\}$$

A level mapping is then constructed as an instance of the generic level mapping by selecting the list-length norm and the following sets of argument positions :

$$I_2^{\text{perm}} = \{\, 1 \,\}$$
$$I_3^{\text{delete}} = \{\, 2 \,\}$$

Again, these sets incorporate all possible ground argument positions. This results in the following level mapping :

$$|\text{perm}(x, y)|_{\text{nat}} = \|x\|_l$$
$$|\text{delete}(x, y, z)|_{\text{nat}} = \|y\|_l$$

There are two representants of minimal cyclic collections :

(1) $(\,(p2, \text{perm}(Z, Y))\,)$
(2) $(\,(d2, \text{delete}(Y_1, X, Z))\,)$

Let's examine the first representant. In order to be able to apply the condition expressed in proposition 3.11, we must compute the linear size relation that holds immediately before $\text{perm}(Z, Y)$. Such a size relation for $\text{delete}(x, y, z)$ is :

$$\{\, (x, y, z) \in I\!N^3 \mid y = z + 1 \}$$

It says that whenever the call to the delete predicate succeeds, the size of the second argument is one more than that of the third argument. Hence, the matrix $\bar{M}$ of proposition 3.11 is equal to $[\, 0\; 1\; -1\,]$ and $\bar{c}$ to $[\, 1\,]$. This size relation establishes a model for the delete predicate: an atom $\text{delete}(Y_1, [X_1|X], Z)\theta$ is contained in the model if the system

$$[\, 0\; 1\; -1\,] \cdot \begin{bmatrix} abs_{\|.\|_l}(Y 1\theta) \\ abs_{\|.\|_l}([X_1|X]\theta) \\ abs_{\|.\|_l}(Z\theta) \end{bmatrix} = [\, 1\,] \text{ is solvable.}$$

We are now able to verify the condition of proposition 3.9: the system

$$\begin{cases} X + 1 & = & Z + 1 \\ Z & \geq & X + 1 \end{cases}$$

must be unsolvable. It can be reduced to

$$\begin{cases} X & = & Z \\ X & \geq & X + 1 \end{cases} .$$

which is indeed unsolvable.

For the second representant, one can easily verify the unsolvability of the inequality:

$$X \geq X + 1.$$

As a result, the permutation program is acceptable with respect to the set S and $|.|_{\text{nat}}$. Hence, it is also left-terminating.

5 Automatic termination analysis

In section 3, a proof procedure for showing (left-)termination of a definite logic program is proposed. The method is automation oriented because it requires the verification of a condition for only a finite number of syntactical objects.

The proposed proof procedure has been implemented. For the moment, the system is restricted to the use of mode information to approximate $R_S \uparrow \omega$ ($R_S^{l-r} \uparrow \omega$) and to induce a (natural) level mapping. A mode of a predicate p/n is a function $m_p : \{1, \ldots, n\} \to \{g, f, a\}$. A mode m_p denotes a set of atoms $\{p(t_1, \ldots, t_n) \mid t_i \in D(m_p(i))\}$ where $D(g) = Ground_P, D(f) = Vars_P$ and $D(a) = Term_P$.

The input of the system consists of (1) the choice between verification of either termination or left-termination, (2) the choice of the norm used in the level mapping, and (3) the mode for the top-level goal.

The implementation embodies several hierarchically structured modules. Some of the important ones are :

- A module taking care of the computation of $R_S \uparrow \omega$ ($R_S^{l-r} \uparrow \omega$) by adopting an abstract interpretation approach.

- A module aimed at generating a natural level mapping.

- A module concerned with the generation of the size relations for the occurring predicates. Again, this is based on abstract interpretation (see [20]).

- A module in which the construction of the systems of equations and inequalities is handled.

- A module for checking whether a system of equations and inequalities is solvable.

The system basically behaves as follows. After inputting the abstract call pattern (which represents the set of atoms S with respect to which (left-)termination must be proved), the computation of $R_S \uparrow \omega$ or $R_S^{l-r} \uparrow \omega$ is handled. This results in a mode m_p for each predicate p (at least for these predicates which are reachable in the predicate dependency graph). The union of the denotation of each mode then determines a safe approximation of $R_S \uparrow \omega$ or $R_S^{l-r} \uparrow \omega$. A natural level mapping is constructed as an instance of the generic one (see definition 3.6) using the norm selected by the user. However, also a set of appropriate argument positions I_n^p must be assigned to each predicate p/n. In the program the set I_n^p is constructed using the previously generated mode m_p: $I_n^p = \{i \mid m_p(i) = ground\}$. Thus, the level mapping takes all arguments appearing on ground input positions into account. Another option is to allow the system to infer a set of argument positions. This can be done by using *symbolic natural level mappings* (see the discussion).

Next, the predicate dependency graph is built up and all representants of all minimal cyclic collections can be derived from it. Proving the conditions of propositions 3.9 and 3.11 for each representant is quite inefficient. However, it can be shown that when one representant of a minimal cyclic collection satisfies the condition, all other satisfy it as well. As a result, in the implementation, only one representant is retained for each minimal cyclic collection.

For these representants, the respective conditions are constructed. These conditions are then solved by calling the consistency checker. At present, no special purpose predicate to perform the checking has been implemented. Instead, a message is sent to PrologIII[1] ([17]) to solve these conditions (the equations and inequalities are there considered as imposing constraints on the domain of each single variable). This solution was preferred because PrologIII has a well-established constraint solving environment. Because our current implementation is only intended to perform some experiments with the framework, the loss of efficiency caused by starting up PrologIII is not so dramatic. When PrologIII has finished examining the conditions, it sends a message back, containing the results (solvability or unsolvability) for each system of constraints.

6 Discussion

By default, the natural level mappings that are generated by the system take as much argument positions as possible into account. Sometimes it happens that it is not possible to prove recurrency (or acceptability) with respect to such an automatically generated level mapping, although the program is recurrent (or acceptable) with respect to some other natural level mapping, which takes less argument positions into account. Example 6.1 illustrates this problem.

Example 6.1

$$\texttt{reverse}(X, Y) \quad \leftarrow \quad \texttt{rev}(X, Y, [\,]).$$

$$\texttt{rev}([\,], A, A).$$
$$\texttt{rev}([X1|X], Y, A) \quad \leftarrow \quad \texttt{rev}(X, Y, [X1|A]).$$

Suppose one wants to prove termination (recurrency) with respect to $S = \{\texttt{reverse}(x, y) \mid x$ is ground and y is free$\}$. In that case, $R_S \uparrow \omega$ may be safely approximated by means of

$$\{\texttt{reverse}(x, y) \mid x \text{ is ground and } y \text{ is any term}\}$$
$$\cup \quad \{\texttt{rev}(x, y, z) \mid x \text{ and } z \text{ are ground and } y \text{ is any term}\}.$$

The following natural level mapping is generated by default:

$$|\texttt{reverse}(x, y)|_{nat} \quad = \quad ||x||_l$$
$$|\texttt{rev}(x, y, z)|_{nat} \quad = \quad ||x||_l + ||z||_l,$$

where $||.||_l$ is the *list-length* norm. It does not allow to prove recurrency using proposition 3.9, since $X + A + 1 \geq X + 1 + A$ is solvable.

This problem is solved by allowing natural level mappings of the form

$$|\texttt{rev}(x, y, z)|_{nat} \quad = \quad a||x||_l + b||z||_l,$$

where $a, b \in \{0, 1\}$. This yields the inequality $aX + bA + b \geq aX + a + bA$, whose unsolvability must be established. For this particular example, it is easy

---

[1] The main system is implemented using Prolog by Bim [5].

to see that the above inequality reduces to $b \geq a$. Hence, by taking $a > b$ — or equivalently $a = 1, b = 0$ — an appropriate level mapping is obtained. In general, this comes down to solving a nonlinear integer programming problem (see also [18]). In our implementation, we have addressed this issue by again using the constraint solver of PrologIII.

To conclude, we believe that modularity is one of the major advantages of our approach. This modularity is due to the formal framework that underpins the technique. Practical experiments show that the abstract domain and the size relations determine the precision of the analysis. The current implementation uses mode information to specify sets of goals, but several other abstract domains could be incorporated — thereby augmenting the precision of the analysis — by simply plugging in the appropriate modules. The size relations form another important module. The current implementation uses systems of linear equations. Previously proposed size relations are a.o. the *interargument inequalities* of Ullman and Van Gelder ([19]), which take only two argument positions into account (i.e. $p_i + c \geq p_j$ where p_i and p_j denote the list-length of the ith and jth argument of a predicate and c is an integer constant), and the *linear predicate inequalities* of Plümer ([16]), which take general sets of argument positions into account, but whose coefficients are either 0 or 1 (i.e. $\sum_{i \in I} p_i + c \geq \sum_{j \in J} p_j$ where $a_i, a_j \in \{0, 1\}$ and I, J denote respectively a set of input and a set of output positions). Obviously, the use of inequalities as compared with equalities can sometimes enhance precision, whereas on the other hand, taking $a_i, a_j \in \mathbb{Z}$ may yield some extra precision as well. One of the directions for further extensions is taking the best of both approaches, and working directly with systems of fully linear inequalities.

7 Acknowledgements

Kristof Verschaetse is supported by DPWB contract RFO/AI/02 (Belgium). Danny De Schreye is supported by the Belgian *National Fund for Scientific Research*.

References

[1] K.R. Apt and M. Bezem. Acyclic programs. *New Generation Computing*, 9:335–363, 1991.

[2] K.R. Apt and D. Pedreschi. Studies in pure Prolog: termination. In *Proceedings Esprit symposium on computational logic*, pages 150–176, Brussels, November 1990. Springer-Verlag.

[3] K.R. Apt and D. Pedreschi. Proving termination of general Prolog programs. In *Proceedings International Conference on Theoretical Aspects of Computer Science*, Sendai, Japan, 1991.

[4] M. Bezem. Characterizing termination of logic programs with level mappings. In *Proceedings NACLP'89*, pages 69–80, 1989.

[5] BIM. *Prolog by BIM, release 3.0.*

[6] A. Bossi, N. Cocco, and M. Fabris. Norms on terms and their use in proving universal termination of a logic program. Technical Report 4/29, CNR, Department of Mathematics, University of Padova, March 1991.

[7] D. De Schreye and K. Verschaetse. Termination analysis of definite logic programs with respect to call patterns. Technical Report CW 138, Department Computer Science, K.U.Leuven, January 1992.

[8] D. De Schreye, K. Verschaetse, and M. Bruynooghe. A framework for analysing the termination of definite logic programs with respect to call patterns. In *Proceedings FGCS'92*, Tokyo, June 1992.

[9] S.K. Debray. Static inference of modes and data dependencies in logic programs. *ACM transactions on programming languages and systems*, 11(3):418–450, July 1989.

[10] Y. Deville. *Logic Programming: Systematic Program Development*. Addison-Wesley, 1990.

[11] M. Falaschi, G. Levi, M. Martelli, and C. Palamidessi. Declarative modeling of the operational behaviour of logic languages. *Theoretical Computer Science*, 69(3):289–318, 1989.

[12] G. Janssens and M. Bruynooghe. Deriving descriptions of possible values of program variables by means of abstract interpretation. Technical Report CW 107, Department of Computer Science, K.U.Leuven, March 1990. To appear in Journal of Logic Programming, in print.

[13] R.A. Kowalski. Algorithm = logic + control. *Communications of the ACM*, 22:424–431, 1979.

[14] J.W. Lloyd and J.C. Shepherdson. Partial evaluation in logic programming. *Journal of Logic Programming*, 11(3 & 4):217–242, October/November 1991.

[15] L. Naish. *Negation and control in Prolog*. Lecture Notes in Artificial Intelligence 238. Springer-Verlag, 1986.

[16] L. Plümer. *Termination proofs for logic programs*. Lecture Notes in Artificial Intelligence 446. Springer-Verlag, 1990.

[17] PrologIA. *Prolog III, release 1.1*.

[18] K. Sohn and A. Van Gelder. Termination detection in logic programs using argument sizes. In *Proceedings 10th symposium on principles of database systems*, pages 216–226. Acm Press, May 1991.

[19] J.D. Ullman and A. Van Gelder. Efficient tests for top-down termination of logical rules. *Journal ACM*, 35(2):345–373, April 1988.

[20] K. Verschaetse and D. De Schreye. Automatic derivation of linear size relations. Technical Report CW 139, Department Computer Science, K.U.Leuven, January 1992.

Applications of Unfolding in Prolog Programming

John Jones

Department of Computer Science

University of Hull

Hull, HU6 7RX, UK

jgj@cs.hull.ac.uk

Abstract

Programming in Prolog is like programming in any other language, in that much of the difficulty is caused by having to manage the complexity of the development process. The adoption of appropriate programming conventions can help by promoting clearer and more easily maintained programs. However, such conventions often result in inefficient programs. In this paper we demonstrate how partial evaluation can be used to overcome this drawback in the case of three specific programming conventions.

1 Introduction

Prolog has a number of virtues for the production of software and these strengths are particularly evident in exploratory program development. Nevertheless, the problems of software production in Prolog are certainly not solved; issues of complexity arise in the construction of moderately-sized Prolog applications, just as they do in the construction of procedural programs. The adoption of appropriate programming conventions can help manage this complexity.

In this paper we consider three specific programming conventions relating to data abstraction, error handling, and program portability. What characterises programs constructed according to each convention is the inclusion in the source of additional subgoals and/or clauses. Naturally such programs are relatively inefficient in comparison to Prolog programs developed without adopting such conventions. However, in cases where ease of development and maintenance are considered paramount, this penalty does not deter developers from adopting the conventions.

We show in this paper that there is in fact no need to pay such a penalty. Once program development is complete it is possible to optimise the program by removing the additional components using partial evaluation. We believe that this optimisation phase makes conventions such as we describe more attractive, particularly when efficiency of the delivered application is important. In this paper we illustrate use of the three conventions and demonstrate optimisation in two cases using the partial evaluation system ProMiX.

The remainder of the paper is structured as follows. In §2 we describe ProMiX; in §3 we describe three programming conventions and illustrate the optimisation phase; in §4 we reflect on the three examples; in §5 we briefly consider related research; and in §6 we consider how the work can be extended.

2   ProMiX

ProMix[8] is a partial evaluation system for full Prolog particularly designed for
the specialisation of meta-interpreters. While meta-interpreters offer a powerful
way of constructing programs, there is a performance penalty caused primarily by parsing the object program at run-time. ProMiX specialises a meta-
interpreter to a given object program by performing the parsing at partial
evaluation time, thereby resulting in a more efficient run-time system.

In contrast to fully automatic partial evaluation and program specialisation systems[13, 3], partial evaluation in ProMiX is controlled by means of
declarations provided by the user[9]. These declarations determine what partial evaluation goals ProMiX constructs and specify which subgoals encountered
during partial evaluation are to be unfolded further (ProMiX is primarily based
on unfolding). The set of declarations required for a particular application of
ProMiX is called the *meta-knowledge*.

Our presentation of ProMiX will focus on aspects which are relevant to
our applications and so it will not be comprehensive. Readers interested in
further details should consult [8]. For consistency with the ProMiX literature
we retain the standard ProMiX terminology and the mechanisms for invoking
it, even though they are not entirely suited to our applications.

To illustrate the use of ProMiX, we consider an interpreter for push down
automata (based by Lakhotia on an example from [16]):

```
% accept(+SYMBOLLIST)
accept(Xs) :-
    initial(Q),
    accept(Q,Xs,[]).

% accept(+STATE,+SYMBOLLIST,+STACK)
accept(Q,[X|Xs],S) :-
    delta(Q,X,S,Q1,S1),
    accept(Q1,Xs,S1).
accept(Q,[],[]) :-
    final(Q).
```

and a non-deterministic push down automaton accepting palindromes defined
by the following states and transition table:

```
% initial(-STATE)
initial(q0).

% final(+STATE)
final(q1).

% delta(+STATE,+SYMBOL,+STACK,-STATE,-STACK)
delta(q0,X,S,q0,[X|S]).
delta(q0,X,S,q1,[X|S]).
delta(q0,X,S,q1,S).
delta(q1,X,[X|S],q1,S).
```

The interpreter can be specialised by ProMiX to this particular automaton on
the basis of the following meta-knowledge:

```
flavor(npda,accept(_)).
flavor(npda,accept(_,_,_)).

meta_goal(accept(Xs),Xs).
meta_goal(accept(_,S1,_),S1).
```

The *flavor/2* declarations specify two partial evaluation goals, to be based on *accept/1* and *accept/3*. The first argument, *npda*, names this application of ProMiX and is convenient if other applications are being developed at the same time. The *meta_goal/2* declarations define the meta-argument positions for the goals identified by flavor declarations, and this knowledge influences both the construction of partial evaluation goals and the control of unfolding. The precise partial evaluation goals constructed depend on the method of invoking ProMiX. We shall use the *mixv/2* directive, which constructs partial evaluation goals by inserting a variable into the meta-argument position of each of the goals identified by flavor declarations. Thus, in this example the actual partial evaluation goals are simply *accept(_)* and *accept(_,_,_)*. In addition, the effect of these declarations is such that once each partial evaluation goal has been unfolded once, no further subgoals which match *accept(_)* or *accept(_,_,_)* will be unfolded. All other user-defined subgoals in the program will be unfolded, by default. Prolog system calls are evaluated if they are sufficiently instantiated.

To apply ProMiX to this example we proceed as follows:

```
| ?- reconsult_data_files(npda).
Reconsulting data file npda.pro..
.. done

yes
| ?- reconsult_program_files(meta_k).
meta_k.pro reconsulted 192 bytes 0.016667 sec.

yes
| ?- mixv(npda,palindrome).
Reconsulting data file palindrome.pro..
.. done

accept(A) :-
    accept(q0, A, []).

accept(q0, [A|B], C) :-
    accept(q0, B, [A|C]).
accept(q0, [A|B], C) :-
    accept(q1, B, [A|C]).
accept(q0, [A|B], C) :-
    accept(q1, B, C).
accept(q1, [A|B], [A|C]) :-
    accept(q1, B, C).
accept(q1, [], []).

yes
| ?-
```

The first directive loads the interpreter for push down automata from the file *npda.pro*. The second directive loads the meta-knowledge from the file *meta_k.pro*. The third directive loads the definition of the automaton accepting palindromes from the file *palindrome.pro*, invokes partial evaluation and prints out the complete residue.

ProMiX supports partial evaluation of full Prolog. This means, for example, that it properly handles unfolding in the context of cut, subgoals which have side-effects, and meta-logical system predicates. There are further forms of declaration to help in this respect. We shall see that this capability is important in the applications we consider.

3 Three programming conventions

3.1 Data abstraction in Prolog

Data abstraction is well established as a means of managing complexity in the development of applications in procedural programming languages. It is found to promote semantically clearer programs, and independence from the data representation. In this section we examine data abstraction in Prolog.

In Edinburgh Prolog[1], predicates and functors are global. As a result, unification can easily be used to circumvent the interface to a data type, allowing the creation, examination and modification of values of a type without use of the operations defined by that type.

However, there are more fundamental difficulties in the safe implementation of abstract data types in Prolog. The first concerns unification over abstract objects. For example, if the abstract type 'set' is implemented by lists, then the set $\{1, 2\}$ may be represented by either of the lists $[1, 2]$ or $[2, 1]$. However, these two representations do not unify, and are not readily interchangeable.

The second difficulty concerns the order of solutions found by Prolog. With the representation chosen above, membership over sets, *set_member/2*, would be membership over lists. We consider two implementations. The first:

```
% set_member(?ELEMENT,+SET)
set_member(Element,Set) :-
    member(Element,Set).
```

delivers the members in representation order, while the second:

```
set_member(Element,Set) :-
    reverse(Set,SetRev),
    member(Element,SetRev).
```

delivers them in reverse representation order. As a result, the following goal succeeds with the first implementation, but not the second:

```
:- set_member(Element,[1,2]), !, Element=1.
```

Thus the order in which solutions are found must be the same for all implementations of an abstract type. This means that *set_member/2* cannot be defined over the abstract type, because it cannot be abstractly specified in what order the solutions ought to come from the goal :- **set_member(Element,{1,2})**.

Thus, few of the benefits of abstract data types are guaranteed in Prolog. Rather, they depend on the discipline of the programmer. However, we feel there are still benefits to be obtained from exploiting data abstraction in Prolog. In a typical Prolog program the data representation is reflected by non-variable terms as arguments in the heads of clauses. Such terms can be quite obscure, particularly where representations of different data items are nested. Data abstraction, by which we mean interacting with the data only in terms of constructors, discriminators and selectors, limits the appearance of non-trivial terms as arguments to the definitions of the abstractions, with obvious benefits. Lakhotia[10], for example, cites the complexity of their structure as the reason he employs abstraction for residues in ProMiX.

Systematic use of abstraction for a data type throughout a program makes it independent of the representation of that data type. Thus abstraction can also be helpful if the representation of some data may change during program development. However, recalling that the order of solutions generated by an abstraction is significant, the programmer is not free to change the data representation employed by a tested program without subsequently re-testing it.

As a simple example we consider determining the preorder traversal of a binary tree by maintaining a stack of subtrees to traverse. Since data abstraction can be used selectively, of course, we will use abstraction for stacks and trees[1], but not lists. For binary trees we use *leaf/1* and *node/3* as constructors, and we combine discriminating between leaf and non-leaf nodes with accessing the item recorded at the node:

Binary tree data type 1

```
% leafItem(+TREE,-ITEM)
leafItem(leaf(Item),Item).

% nonLeafItem(+TREE,-ITEM)
nonLeafItem(node(_,Item,_),Item).

% subTrees(+TREE,-TREE,-TREE)
subTrees(node(Left,_,Right),Left,Right).
```

For stacks we choose an implementation in terms of lists:

Stack data type

```
% emptyStack(?STACK)
emptyStack([]).

% push(+ITEM,+STACK,-STACK)
push(Item,Stack,[Item|Stack]).

% pop(+STACK,-ITEM,-STACK)
pop([Item|Stack],Item,Stack).
```

---

[1]The definitions we give in this example are limited in their scope. We return to the stack data type in the next section, modifying it to include the detection of some type errors.

Given these data types, a preorder traversal of a binary tree is defined as follows:

```
% traverse(+TREE,-LIST)
traverse(Tree,Traversal) :-
    emptyStack(EmptyS),
    traverse(Tree,EmptyS,Traversal).

% traverse(+TREE,+STACK,-LIST)
traverse(Tree,Stack,[Item|Rest]) :-
    nonLeafItem(Tree,Item),            % visit internal node
    subTrees(Tree,Left,Right),
    push(Right,Stack,NewStack),        % stack right subtree
    traverse(Left,NewStack,Rest).      % traverse left subtree
traverse(Leaf,Stack,[Item|Rest]) :-
    leafItem(Leaf,Item),               % visit leaf node
    pop(Stack,NextTree,NewStack),      % retrieve next subtree
    traverse(NextTree,NewStack,Rest).  % traverse next subtree
traverse(Leaf,EmptyS,[Item]) :-
    leafItem(Leaf,Item),
    emptyStack(EmptyS).
```

This program shows how abstraction emphasises the distinction between the logical structure of a predicate such as *traverse/3* and the representation of the data it utilises.

However, a program using data abstraction is clearly less efficient than an equivalent program which exploits the data representation. We now demonstrate how partial evaluation can be used to overcome this inefficiency in the form of an optimisation phase reminiscent of data reification (or refinement). The optimisation is achieved by unfolding the data abstractions, and so propagating the data representation throughout the program.

In the case of the *traverse/2* program, partial evaluation of the data abstractions is achieved with the following meta-knowledge:

```
flavor(traverse,traverse(_,_)).
flavor(traverse,traverse(_,_,_)).

meta_goal(traverse(T,_),T).
meta_goal(traverse(T,_,_),T).
```

This declares that appropriate partial evaluation goals are *traverse(_,_)* and *traverse(_,_,_)*, and that once these goals are unfolded no further subgoals of this form are to be unfolded. As a result, we obtain the following residue using the *mixv/2* interface to ProMiX:

```
traverse(A,B) :-
    traverse(A,[],B).

traverse(node(A,B,C),D,[B|E]) :-
    traverse(A,[C|D],E).
traverse(leaf(A),[B|C],[A|D]) :-
    traverse(B,C,D).
traverse(leaf(A),[],[A]).
```

This residue is the conventional Prolog program exploiting the data representation and unification to the full. It is clearly equivalent to the original program, but more efficient.

The independence of the *traverse/2* program from the representation of trees and stacks can be demonstrated by taking an alternative implementation of binary trees based on lists:

Binary tree data type 2

```
% leafItem(+TREE,-ITEM)
leafItem([I],I).

% nonLeafItem(+TREE,-ITEM)
nonLeafItem([_,I,_],I).

% subTrees(+TREE,-TREE,-TREE)
subTrees([L,_,R],L,R).
```

Using the same meta-knowledge as earlier we obtain the following residue:

```
traverse(A,B) :-
    traverse(A,[],B).

traverse([A,B,C],D,[B|E]) :-
    traverse(A,[C|D],E).
traverse([A],[B|C],[A|D]) :-
    traverse(B,C,D).
traverse([A],[],[A]).
```

3.2   Error detection

Locating errors in a large Prolog program can be quite difficult. For errors which can easily be defined an obvious approach to this problem is to add clauses to the program that will only be invoked in the erroneous cases and which will report them to the programmer. Errors which can be treated in this manner include type errors and range errors, for example.

Only some of the error reporting required during program development will also be required at run-time. In this section we show how partial evaluation can be used to selectively remove error reporting, so that the run-time version of an application only contains clauses for reporting run-time errors.

The following program reverses a list using a stack:

```
% reverse(+LIST,-LIST)
reverse(List,Reverse) :-
    list(List),
    emptyStack(Empty),
    reverse(List,Empty,Reverse).
reverse(X,_) :-
    not list(X),
    error(runtime,typeError,reverse/2,'not list',X),
    fail.
```

```
% reverse(+LIST,+STACK,-LIST)
reverse([],Stack,List) :-
    stackToList(Stack,List).
reverse([Head|Rest],Stack,List) :-
    push(Head,Stack,NewStack),
    reverse(Rest,NewStack,List).

% list(+LIST)
list(L) :- nonvar(L), L = [].
list(L) :- nonvar(L), L = [_|L1], list(L1).
```

For this example we use a modified stack data type:

```
% stack(+STACK)
stack(S) :- nonvar(S), S = [].
stack(S) :- nonvar(S), S = [_|Rest], stack(Rest).

% stackToList(+STACK,-LIST)
stackToList(S,S) :-
    stack(S).
stackToList(X,_) :-
    not stack(X),
    error(development,typeError,stackToList/1,'not stack',X),
    fail.

% emptyStack(?STACK)
emptyStack([]).

% push(+ITEM,+STACK,-STACK)
push(Item,Stack,[Item|Stack]) :-
    stack(Stack).
push(_,X,_) :-
    not stack(X),
    error(development,typeError,push/3,'not stack',X),
    fail.

% pop(+STACK,-ITEM,-STACK)
pop(Stack,Item,Remainder) :-
    stack(Stack),
    Stack = [Item|Remainder].
pop(X,_,_) :-
    not stack(X),
    error(development,typeError,pop/3,'not stack',X),
    fail.
```

These programs contain systematic error detection and reporting. Error reports which are only needed during program development, such as checking internally generated values of the stack data type, are distinguished from those that are also required at run-time. The former have the value *development* for the first argument of *error/5* subgoals, while the latter have the value *runtime*.

During development of the program *error/5* is defined so as to report all errors, irrespective of their designation as development or run-time:

```
% error(+CLASS,+TYPE,+PREDICATE,+SUMMARY,+ARGUMENT)
error(_,Error,Pred,Message,Arg) :-
    errorDescription(Error,Description),
    writeList([Description,': ',Pred,': ',Message,': ',Arg]),
    nl.

% errorDescription(+TYPE,-DESCRIPTION)
errorDescription(typeError,'type error').

% writeList(+LIST)
writeList([]).
writeList([Head|Tail]) :- write(Head), writeList(Tail).
```

Once program development is complete, however, only the run-time error reporting is needed. We now show how partial evaluation can be used to selectively remove the error reporting which is only necessary during development. The first step is to modify the error reporting so that development errors are not reported. This requires a change to just one predicate:

```
% error(+CLASS,+TYPE,+PREDICATE,+SUMMARY,+ARGUMENT)
error(development,_,_,_,_).
error(runtime,Error,Pred,Message,Arg) :-
    errorDescription(Error,Description),
    writeList([Description,': ',Pred,': ',Message,': ',Arg]),
    nl.
```

Moreover, it would be the same change for any application which adopted this form of error reporting. This modification results in a program with the desired behaviour, but which is clearly inefficient.

Appropriate partial evaluation is specified by the following meta-knowledge:

```
flavor(error,reverse(_,_)).
flavor(error,reverse(_,_,_)).
flavor(error,stack(_)).
flavor(error,list(_)).

meta_goal(reverse(L, ),L).
meta_goal(reverse(L,_,_),L).
meta_goal(stack(S),S).
meta_goal(list(L),L).

side_effect(error(runtime,_,_,_,_)).
side_effect(writeList(_)).

extra_logical(stack(S)) :- var(S).
extra_logical(list(L)) :- var(L).
```

The *side_effect/1* declarations warn ProMiX that all instances of *writeList/1* and instances of *error/5* with *runtime* as the first argument have side effects, so that clauses involving them need appropriate treatment during partial evaluation. Similarly, the *extra_logical/1* declarations warn Prolog that *list/1* and *stack/1* are extra-logical if their arguments are unbound variables, and appropriate treatment is needed during partial evaluation. The residue generated is:

```
reverse(A,B) :-
    list(A),
    C = [],
    reverse(A,[],B).
reverse(A,B) :-
    not list(A),
    write('type error'),
    write(': '),
    write(reverse/2),
    write(': '),
    write('not list'),
    write(': '),
    write(A),
    nl,
    fail.

reverse([],A,A) :-
    stack(A).
reverse([A|B],C,D) :-
    stack(C),
    reverse(B,[A|C],D).

stack(A) :- nonvar(A), A = [].
stack(A) :- nonvar(A), A = [B|C], stack(C).

list(A) :- nonvar(A), A = [].
list(A) :- nonvar(A), A = [B|C], list(C).
```

This program is equivalent to the original, except for side effects. Only errors originally defined as being important at run-time are reported to the user.

The residue generated in this example is not entirely satisfactory. The first clause for *reverse/2* has a superfluous subgoal C = [], apparently because *list/1* is defined as meta-logical and so explicit unifications appearing to the right of it are retained in the residue because their elimination might lead to backward propagation. The clauses for *reverse/3* contain subgoals of the form *stack/1*, which if this program was only invoked with *reverse/2* would not be needed.

Unlike the example with which we illustrated the use of data abstraction, the optimisation in this example also exploits the proper treatment of full Prolog, in particular those predicates which have side-effects. The clauses which do the error detection and reporting all end in *fail*, as befits the logic of the program. During partial evaluation a clause which ends with *fail* will not result in a clause in the residue unless one or more of the goals to the left of *fail* have side-effects. Thus, redefining *error/5* for development-time errors so that it no longer has side effects in this case means that clauses using this form in the original program do not result in corresponding clauses in the residue. That is, development-time error reporting is stripped out of the program.

This example also needs partial evaluation of full Prolog to ensure that the definitions of *list/1* and *stack/1* are treated properly. System goals of the form *nonvar/1* are known to be meta-logical if the argument is a variable, as is the case in the clauses for these predicates.

3.3 Program portability

Since there is as yet no formal standard for Prolog, different Prolog systems tend to be incompatible when it comes to less central aspects, such as built-in predicates, and the interface to the underlying operating system. When faced with developing a portable Prolog application a well-known and effective convention is to first define a suitable virtual interface to the whole class of systems and develop the application assuming that interface. The application can then be ported to a particular Prolog system by defining the interface predicates appropriately.

We can illustrate this convention with a fragment of ProMiX itself, which assumes, among other things, that *consult_program/1* and *copy_hook/1* are defined for loading programs and copying terms, respectively. Fragments of the code required to port ProMiX to various versions of Prolog are then:

C-Prolog

```
consult_program(File) :- consult(File).

copy_hook(X,Y) :- asserta('#$$'(X)), retract('#$$'(Y)).
```

ALSProlog

```
consult_program(File) :- compile(File).

copy_hook(X,Y) :- asserta('#$$'(X)), retract('#$$'(Y)).
```

Sictus Prolog

```
consult_program(File) :- consult(File).

copy_hook(Term1,Term2) :- copy_term(Term1,Term2).
```

It is obvious that a Prolog application built according to this convention could be optimised to a particular version of Prolog by partial evaluation, so we do not illustrate it. Whether the impact of such optimisation will be appreciable depends on the application itself.

4 Discussion

We have considered three programming conventions which rely on the systematic inclusion of additional subgoals and clauses in the source of an application.

We have shown how such applications can subsequently be optimised using partial evaluation. The examples we have considered have necessarily been small, but we feel they are sufficient to illustrate the potential of the optimisation phase. A consequence of basing the optimisation on partial evaluation is that it must be possible to identify the additional subgoals and clauses in a program on a clause by clause basis.

Our interest in programming conventions arises from a wider interest in an appropriate programming methodology for Prolog. We anticipate conventions such as those illustrated being incorporated into a programming methodology, in which optimisation is applied once system development is complete, in order to obtain an application to 'deliver'. The optimisation may be thought of as a compilation phase. Subsequent maintenance of the application would, of course, be carried out on the developed system, not the delivered system.

We have illustrated the optimisation of programs using ProMiX. ProMiX was a convenient choice for a number of reasons: it already existed; it was readily available; and it handles full Prolog. Employing ProMiX allows us to provide a practical demonstration that appropriate optimisations were possible through partial evaluation. The only influence ProMiX has on the work we have presented is the manner in which partial evaluation is specified and controlled, and this matter of detail is orthogonal to the much more significant issue of the optimisations themselves. The requirement for the partial evaluation system to be able to handle full Prolog is explicit in the example concerning handling errors. Such a capability is also necessary in the other two conventions illustrated, of course. For example, unfolding abstractions can lead to inappropriate backward propagation of variable bindings.

Our manner of exploiting ProMiX has the effect that the meta-knowledge for controlling partial evaluation necessarily focuses on what is to be preserved in the residue. It would be more natural to specify what should be partially evaluated, as was the case in preliminary investigations based on an incomplete partial evaluator[5]. Such an approach would be particularly appropriate where abstractions were selected from a library, since the required meta-knowledge could simply be a part of the definition of the abstraction and so need not be provided by the programmer. In such circumstances the optimisation would *appear* to be automatic.

The semantics we take as the basis of program equivalence is the sequence of answer substitutions semantics[14]. Clearly we are not concerned with preserving side-effects in the error handling example. With ProMiX the correctness of the residue depends not only on the correctness of the partial evaluation process, but also on the correctness of the meta-knowledge. In view of this latter uncertainty a formal correctness argument is infeasible, and it will generally be necessary to test the residue. Fortunately, this is not as onerous as it might first appear, since exactly the same testing can be used as for the original program.

From the perspective of a programming methodology in which optimisation is applied once to obtain a deliverable system, the readability of the residue is not important. However, within the scope of this paper it is helpful because it enables the reader to compare the residue with the original. Fortunately, ProMiX produces fairly readable residues in most cases.

The optimisation phases for the three conventions described could be applied manually, of course, in principle. However, text editing is labour intensive and prone to error. The optimisation phases could also be supported, at least in part, by mechanisms other than partial evaluation. For instance, the particular example employing abstraction we have discussed could be handled using the C-Prolog mechanism which supports automatic clause transformation on loading, based on user definitions for *term_expansion/2*. However, such an approach would be far less attractive than that advocated here. Moreover, the Prolog mechanism only allows one solution to a term expansion, and so is fundamentally limited in its suitability for the application we are illustrating because examples naturally arise in which one original clause gives rise to more than one residual clause. Our approach is attractive because all three examples of optimisation are supported by the same mechanism.

5   Related research work

Partial evaluation is well-studied[15], and the technical problems of partially evaluating full Prolog have received considerable attention[17, 12, 8, 13]. It is usually used to specialise programs, such as meta-interpreters. Issues to do with the correctness of partial evaluation are considered in [11, 14].

The observation that data abstractions are good candidates for partial evaluation is not new, although it is only with the availability of partial evaluation systems for full Prolog that its potential can now be realised in a practical manner. Wilk recognised the potential of the idea in 1984[19]. It is applied by hand in [16] (pg. 253) to a *flatten/3* program in which queues are implemented in terms of difference lists. More recently, Komorowski[6] has proposed an elaborate development environment for knowledge-based systems in Prolog which exploits partial evaluation. The methodology it embodies is intended to support the formal development of specifications and their subsequent incremental, interactive refinement using both unfolding and folding.

Technically, the suggestion we have given for optimising programs that use abstraction would be subsumed by Komorowski's proposal, but we feel the emphasis we have adopted and the manner in which a programmer can exploit our suggestion is sufficiently different for our proposal to merit separate attention. By including folding, Komorowski's methodology supports more elaborate program transformations than we considered in our first example. This necessarily means, however, that specifying and controlling program transformation is more difficult, and Komorowski appears to provide the developer with an environment in which they can apply unfolds and folds interactively. In contrast, we have suggested using program transformation as the basis of a single optimisation phase once program development is complete, and we would hope to make it appear as automatic as possible. We feel this perspective is in keeping with common programming practice in Prolog and will thus be attractive to programmers.

Warren[18] cites macro expansion as an application of partial evaluation, and this is similar to our third application. Other work which is similar in spirit to that described here includes the transformation of Prolog programs into more efficient binary programs[2], and specialisation in context[4], which is motivated by the specialisation of programs constructed from modules. In the wider context of programming, Lakhotia[7] shows how programming techniques expressed as schemas can be incorporated into programs using partial evaluation.

6 Future development

The work described in this paper can be developed in a number of different ways. We expect to identify further programming conventions which result in programs that can be optimised by partial evaluation. Within the wider context of a programming methodology for Prolog, we anticipate considering how partial evaluation in support of programming conventions might interact with other aids to program development such as types, modes, and modules.

The support offered for the three conventions we have described could be improved by constructing a more appropriate interface to ProMiX. This interface would declare goals which were to be partially evaluated, rather than goals which were not. This alternative style of control of partial evaluation is likely to be essential when tackling the development of larger applications. Alternatively, it may be useful to consider using an existing automatic partial evaluation system. Finally, experience of tackling larger applications may also suggest appropriate tools to support the developer in applying the conventions and the subsequent optimisation phase.

Acknowledgements

The author is grateful to Arun Lakhotia and Leon Sterling for making ProMiX readily available. Len Bottaci and Mark Millington provided very helpful comments on the direction that this work could take. Mark Millington provided the two examples about the abstract type set which were used to illustrate problems with data abstraction in Prolog. Len Bottaci provided very helpful comments about the presentation of an earlier version of this paper.

References

[1] Clocksin, W. F., and C. S. Mellish, *Programming in Prolog*, Springer-Verlag (1981).

[2] Demoen, B., On the transformation of a Prolog program to a more efficient binary program, *Proceedings of the workshop on logic program synthesis and transformation*, 1992, Springer-Verlag Workshops in Computing (this volume).

[3] Gallagher, J., A system for specialising logic programs, *Report TR-91-32*, Computer Science Department, University of Bristol, UK, 1991.

[4] Gallagher, J., and D. A. de Waal, Specialisation in context, *Proceedings of the workshop on logic program synthesis and transformation*, 1992, Springer-Verlag Workshops in Computing (this volume).

[5] Jones, J., Prolog, data abstraction, and program transformation: a preliminary report, *Research report 91/1*, Department of Computer Science, University of Hull, UK, 1991.

[6] Komorowski, J., Towards a programming methodology founded on partial deduction, *Proceedings of the 1990 European Conference on Artificial Intelligence*, L. C. Aiello (Ed.), Pitman (1990), 404–409.

[7] Lakhotia, A., Incorporating 'programming techniques' into Prolog programs, *Logic programming: Proceedings of the 1989 North American Conference*, E. L. Lush and R. A. Overbeek (Eds.), MIT Press (1989), 426–440.

[8] Lakhotia, A., and L. Sterling, ProMiX: A Prolog partial evaluation system, in *The Practice of Prolog*, L. Sterling (Ed.), MIT Press (1990), 137–179.

[9] Lakhotia, A., and L. Sterling, How to control unfolding when specializing interpreters, *New Generation Computing* **8** (1990), 61–70.

[10] Lakhotia, A., Private communication by email, 13th May, 1991.

[11] Lloyd, J. W., and J. C. Shepherdson, Partial evaluation in logic programming, *Journal of Logic Programming* **11** (1991), 217–242.

[12] Owen, S., Issues in the partial evaluation of meta-interpreters, in *Meta-Programming in Logic Programming*, H. Abramson and M. H. Rogers (Eds.) MIT Press (1989), 319–339.

[13] Prestwich, S., An unfold rule for full Prolog, *Proceedings of the workshop on logic program synthesis and transformation*, 1992, Springer-Verlag Workshops in Computing (this volume).

[14] Proietti, M., and A. Pettorossi, Semantics preserving transformation rules for Prolog, *Symposium on partial evaluation and semantics-based program manipulation*, SIGPLAN Notices **26** (1991), 274–284.

[15] Sestoft, P., and A. V. Zamulin, Annotated bibliography on partial evaluation and mixed computation, *New Generation Computing* **6** (1988), 309–354.

[16] Sterling, L., and E. Shapiro, *The Art of Prolog*, MIT Press (1986).

[17] Venken, R., and B. Demoen, A partial evaluation system for Prolog: some practical considerations, *New Generation Computing* **6** (1988), 279–290.

[18] Warren, D. S., Memoing for logic programs, *Communications of the ACM*, **35 (3)** (1992), 94–111.

[19] Wilk, P. F., Comment in C-Prolog library file 'Unfold', dated May, 1984.

An Unfold Rule for Full Prolog

Steven Prestwich

ECRC GmbH

Muenchen, Germany

steven@ecrc.de

Abstract

Source-level transformation tools for Prolog often use the unfold rule, for example partial deduction systems and some compilers. Although the unfold rule is very simple for pure Prolog, it has many problems when applied to full Prolog. This paper proposes an approach which removes most of these problems, making the design of transformation tools less complex and error-prone. A way of simplifying program structure is described, so that unfolding strategies can be designed in a much more straightforward way. An unfold rule is then specified for programs which have been simplified. This rule is more powerful than the unfold rule for Prolog. Finally, it is shown how to eliminate a class of redundancies typically found in unfolded simplified programs.

1 Introduction

Source-level transformation tools for Prolog often use the *unfold* rule, for example partial deduction systems and some compilers. The unfold rule consists of applying the resolution rule prior to execution, and can improve the efficiency of programs by eliminating resolution steps, propagating variable bindings and discovering dead end computations.

Although this rule is very simple when applied to pure Prolog, it becomes problematic when applied to full Prolog, that is Prolog with the usual control structures: conjunction (,), disjunction (;), the cut (!), negation-as-failure (**not**), if-then-else ($\ldots \rightarrow \ldots;\ldots$) and once-only calls (**once**). We shall not consider less common control features such as catch-and-throw, coroutining, sound and constructive negation, and soft cuts.

This paper proposes a three phase approach to unfolding full Prolog programs:

1. Program simplification, in which all the usual control structures are reduced to conjunction plus a form of cut (the *ancestral cut*), giving a program with a simple structure which can be unfolded more easily.

2. Unfolding the simplified program, for which an unfold rule is specified which avoids various pitfalls. The unfold rule is a tactical rule which can be applied in various ways. It can form the basis for a transformation strategy, defined by a user.

3. Elimination of a class of redundancies which are commonly introduced by unfolding simplified programs.

The problems associated with unfolding full Prolog are described in Section 2. Section 3 describes the program simplification method. Section 4 describes the unfold rule for simplified programs. Section 5 describes how to eliminate some redundancies from unfolded simplified programs. An illustrative example is given in Section 6. An example of the application of the method to unfolding interpreters is given in Section 7. Related work is discussed in Section 8 and conclusions are drawn in Section 9.

Notation: predicate symbols and atoms will be written $\mathbf{x}$, constants X, function symbols and general terms x, a conjunction of atoms (which may be empty) $\mathbf{X}$ and a tuple of terms $\underline{x}$. An expression $\mathbf{a}[x/y]$ will denote an atom $\mathbf{a}$ with each occurrence of the term x replaced by the term y.

2 Problems with unfolding full Prolog

In this section we describe some of the problems encountered when designing a transformer for full Prolog, providing motivation for the subsequent sections. Most of the problems have been mentioned in other papers, for example [1, 6, 7, 11, 19, 20].

2.1 Generating complex control structures

Full (standard) Prolog has several control structures which make unfolding problematic. Complex expressions may be generated by unfolding, and to handle these correctly a transformer must know many rules such as:

- disjunction and if-then-else are transparent to cut, that is the effects of a cut reach outside these control structures;

- negation and metacalls (**call, once**) are not transparent to cut, that is the effects of the cut are local;

- the disjunction operator ';' is associative except when it appears in if-then-else;

- negated atoms cannot be executed until they are ground;

- variable bindings cannot be propagated from one disjunct to another, for example $x=0$ cannot be unfolded in the disjunction $(x=0 \; ; \; \mathbf{a}(x))$.

Correctly implementing all these rules is an error-prone task. Furthermore, it is possible that not all cases will be considered, so that opportunities for unfolding are missed.

2.2 Propagating cut incorrectly

Consider the program

$$\mathbf{p}(x) : - \mathbf{q}(x). \qquad \mathbf{q}(0) : - \; !.$$
$$\mathbf{p}(2). \qquad \mathbf{q}(1).$$

Unfolding **q** naively we get

> **p**(0) : − !.
> **p**(1).
> **p**(2).

which is not equivalent. Given a query ? − **p**(x) the original program returns (x=0 ; x=2) whereas the unfolded version returns only x=0. The incorrectness arises because the scope of the cut has been propagated from **q** to **p**. In general, an atom which matches a clause containing a cut cannot be unfolded. This is serious because a program may be written with many cuts, in which case very little unfolding can be done.

There are cases where atoms which call the cut directly can be unfolded [1, 7, 11, 15] but they are the exception rather than the rule.

2.3 Propagating failure incorrectly

In pure Prolog an atom may be unfolded which is not leftmost in a clause body, and which does not match any clause head. This causes the clause to be deleted, pruning the search space of the program. We refer to this as *failure propagation*. However, in full Prolog this is unsafe. Say we have a clause

> **p** : − **write**($HELLO$), **f**.

where **f** is an atom matching no clauses. Unfolding **f** deletes the **p** clause altogether, which is incorrect because the side effect of the **write** atom is lost with it. As well as **write**, the cut and all other atoms with side effects have this problem.

2.4 Propagating variable bindings incorrectly

Unfolding an atom which is not leftmost in a clause body may cause variable bindings to be propagated backward; that is, variables in preceding atoms (including the clause head) may become bound earlier than they would under the Prolog left-to-right computation rule. This is useful because it may lead to earlier detection of failure but it can be incorrect. Say we have a program

> **p**(x) : − **var**(x), **a**(x).   **a**(0).

A query ? − **p**(v) succeeds with the answer v=0. Unfolding **a** gives

> **p**(0) : − **var**(0).

The same query now fails, and so the unfolding was incorrect. Even with ground atoms backward binding propagation can be incorrect. Consider

> **p**(x) : − **write**($HELLO$), **a**(x).   **a**(0).

A goal ? − **p**(1) instantiates **a**(x) to **a**(1), which causes the same problem as **f** in Section 2.3.

2.5 Changing the order of solutions

The order of solutions is important in full Prolog, because changing the order may make some solutions unreachable even if there are only a finite number of solutions. For example if we have a clause

goal1(x) : $-$ **goal**(x), !.

then the *order* of the solutions $(x=t_1 ; x=t_2 ; ...)$ for **goal** determines the *set* of solutions $\{x=t_1\}$ for **goal1**. In general we must preserve the order of solutions, but simply taking care not to change the order of clauses when unfolding is not sufficient. Consider the program

p(x) : $-$ **q**(x), **r**.   q(0).   **r**.
                              q(1).   **r**.

Calling ? $-$ **p**(v) gives $(v=0 ; v=0 ; v=1 ; v=1)$. Unfolding **r**:

p(x) : $-$ **q**(x).   q(0).
p(x) : $-$ **q**(x).   q(1).

Now calling ? $-$ **p**(v) gives $(v=0 ; v=1 ; v=0 ; v=1)$. The order has changed because **r** was not the leftmost atom in the clause and the choice point of **r** was moved to the left, violating Prolog's left-to-right computation rule. It is not safe in general to unfold a non-leftmost atom in a goal which matches more than one clause head.

2.6 Redundant unfolding

A common programming technique is to use *grue* cuts [10] to avoid computations which will fail anyway. If the effects of grue cuts are ignored then the search space covered by a program transformer will be larger than necessary, and a transformer will waste time exploring branches of this space which would never be reached during run time.

Another common technique is to use *red* cuts [10] to throw away solutions. If the effects of red cuts are ignored then this may affect the termination of the unfolding process, because a red cut may be used to select a solution from an infinite set of solutions.

Even if a program transformer is guaranteed to terminate, ignoring the effect of a cut may affect the quality of the unfolded program. Suppose the transformer ensures termination by taking generalisations of certain atoms (a common technique in partial deduction systems). Ignoring a cut may cause more atoms to be visited, making the generalisation more general than necessary and possibly losing important variable bindings. This effect has been observed when specialising meta-interpreters to object programs by partial deduction. An example is described in Section 7, and similar problems are mentioned in [11].

3 Simplifying Prolog programs

To avoid the problem of Section 2.2, namely the restriction on unfolding atom calling cuts, Venken [19] proposed annotating cuts where necessary during unfolding to make their scope explicit. The annotated cut is sometimes called the *ancestral cut* [10], and it is expressed by two predicates: **mark**(v) succeeds on being called, binds v to a unique value, and fails on backtracking; **!**(v) succeeds on being called and removes all choice points back to **mark**(v).

We use ancestral cuts to avoid the unfolding restriction, but by transforming all cuts into ancestral cuts *before* unfolding begins. At the same time, we eliminate all other control constructs except conjunction. This is done by applying the following rules repeatedly (in any order) until none are applicable:

Negation: replace (**not a**) by (**a** → **fail** ; **true**).

Once-only calls: replace once(**a**) by (**a** → **true**).

If-then-else: replace (**a** → **b**) by (**mark**(v), **a**, **!**(v), **b**) and

$$\mathbf{a}_1 \rightarrow \mathbf{b}_1 \; ; \; \mathbf{a}_2 \rightarrow \mathbf{b}_2 \; ; \; \dots \; ; \; \mathbf{a}_n$$

by

$$\mathbf{mark}(v), (\mathbf{a}_1, \mathbf{!}(v), \mathbf{b}_1 \; ; \; \mathbf{a}_2, \mathbf{!}(v), \mathbf{b}_2 \; ; \; \dots \; ; \; \mathbf{a}_n)$$

where v is a new variable.

Cut: for each predicate **p** which has a clause containing a cut, replace every atom $\mathbf{p}(\underline{x})$ by $\mathbf{p}(\underline{x}, v)$ where v is a new variable, precede each atom $\mathbf{p}(\underline{x}, v)$ in a clause body by **mark**(v), and in each **p** clause replace each cut by **!**(v) where v is the new argument in the clause head.

Disjunction: replace

$$\mathbf{p} \; : - \; \mathbf{L}, (\mathbf{a}_1 \; ; \; \dots \; ; \; \mathbf{a}_n), \mathbf{R}.$$

by

$$\left\{ \begin{array}{l} \mathbf{p} \; : - \; \mathbf{L}, \mathbf{new}(\underline{x}), \mathbf{R}. \\[2mm] \mathbf{new}(\underline{x}) \; : - \; \mathbf{a}_i. \quad (i = 1 \dots n) \end{array} \right.$$

where **new** is a new predicate symbol created for each disjunction (which we shall refer to as an *auxiliary predicate*), and $\underline{x}$ is the set of variables occurring in both the disjunction and **p**, **L** or **R**.

After applying these transformations each clause body consists only of conjunctions of atoms. From a transformation point of view, simplified programs are written in pure Prolog plus some predicates with special properties. This avoids the problems of generating complex control expressions and of propagating variables bindings across disjunctions, described in Section 2.1.

4 Unfolding simplified programs

Now we specify an unfold rule for simplified programs which avoids the problems described in Sections 2.3, 2.4, 2.5 and 2.6, namely the useless unfolding of redundant branches, the incorrect propagation of variable bindings and failure, and changing the order of solutions.

4.1   A predicate classification

Before describing the unfold rule, we make a classification of predicates. A predicate **p** is classed as either:

- **binding sensitive** if $(\mathbf{a}, v_1{=}v_2) \neq (v_1{=}v_2, \mathbf{a})$ for some atom **a** with predicate symbol **p** (where the v_i are variables and $\neq$ denotes different operational semantics). Examples of binding sensitive predicates are **var** and $==$.

- **failure sensitive** if $(\mathbf{a}, \mathbf{fail}) \neq \mathbf{fail}$ for some atom **a** with predicate symbol **p**. The cut and all predicates with side effects are failure sensitive. All failure sensitive predicates are also binding sensitive, because any atom $v_1{=}v_2$ may become equivalent to **fail** during unfolding, if v_1 and v_2 become bound to non-unifiable terms.

- **pure** if it is neither binding nor failure sensitive.

This classification is similar to that of [15]. The system predicates of Prolog must be classified by hand when designing a program transformer. The classification of all other predicates can be deduced by the rule:

any atom matching a clause head whose clause body contains a binding [failure] sensitive atom is itself classed as binding [failure] sensitive, otherwise it is classed as pure.

When in doubt (for example when handling atoms whose clauses are unknown) it is always safe to classify an atom as failure sensitive. A predicate such as **loop** defined by (**loop** : − **loop**) should strictly be classed as failure sensitive, but we shall class it as pure because infinite loops without side effects are rarely used.

The !/1 predicate is failure sensitive. The **mark**/1 predicate is not failure sensitive because $(\mathbf{mark}(v), \mathbf{fail})$ is always equivalent to $(\mathbf{fail}, \mathbf{mark}(v))$: it sets up a mark for subsequent computation, and **fail** has no subsequent computation. Nor is **mark**/1 binding sensitive because $(\mathbf{mark}(v), v_1{=}v_2)$ is always equivalent to $(v_1{=}v_2, \mathbf{mark}(v))$: either $v_1{=}v_2$ succeeds in which case it is equivalent to **true**, or it fails, and **mark**/1 is not failure sensitive.

4.2   The unfold rule

The unfold rule given in this section avoids all the problems mentioned in Section 2 except one, which is partially solved in the next section. It begins with a clause

$$C : \mathbf{p} \; :- \mathbf{a}_1, \ldots, \mathbf{a}_N.$$

Unfolding a chosen atom $\mathbf{a}_i$ is done as follows:

1. If $i = 1$ then we can use the usual unfold rule, replacing C by a set of resolvents using all matching clauses for $\mathbf{a}_1$.

2. If $i > 1$ then instead of directly resolving, we resolve in a safe way by introducing new atoms **fail** or $=$, and then propagate any variable bindings or failure afterward:

a. If a_i matches no clauses then C is replaced by

$$p : - a_1, \ldots, a_{i-1}, \textbf{fail}.$$

and **fail** is propagated back through $a_1 \ldots a_{i-1}$.

b. If a_i matches one clause $(h : - T)$ then C is replaced by

$$C' : p : - a_1, \ldots, a_{i-1}, a_i{=}h, T, a_{i+1}, \ldots, a_N.$$

and $a_i{=}h$ is propagated through C'.

c. If a_i matches more than one clause then make a new auxiliary definition

$$D : \textbf{new} : - a_i, \ldots, a_N.$$

where the arguments of **new** are the free variables of $a_{i+1}, \ldots, a_N$ which also occur in p, a_1. Fold C using D giving

$$C' : p : - a_1, \ldots, a_{i-1}, \textbf{new}.$$

C is replaced by C' and unfolding is applied to a_i in D.

Some notes on the unfold rule follow.

4.2.1 Failure propagation

This is done in (2a) by applying the rule:

replace $(a, \textbf{fail})$ *in a clause body by* **fail**, *if a is not failure sensitive*

repeatedly until either a failure sensitive a_j $(j < i)$ is encountered, or until the clause $(p : - \textbf{fail})$ is reached (which can be deleted in most Prologs).

4.2.2 Variable binding propagation

This is done in (2b) as follows. First split the atom $a_i{=}h$ into several atoms of the form $v{=}t$ where v is a variable and t is a term (this is always possible). Then propagate each $v{=}t$ through T, $a_{i+1} \ldots a_n$ to give $T[v/t]$, $a_{i+1}[v/t] \ldots a_n[v/t]$. Then move each $v{=}t$ in turn as far to the left as possible by repeatedly applying the rule:

replace $\quad p : - X, a, v{=}t, Y.$
by $\quad\quad p : - X, v{=}t, a[v/t], Y.$

if either

(1) **a** *is binding or failure sensitive and*

    (*i*) v *does not occur in* p, X *or* **a**

    (*ii*) *or* t *is a variable which does not occur in* p, X *or* **a**

(2) *or* **a** *is pure.*

The condition that v (or t) is a variable which does not occur anywhere to the left of $v{=}t$ ensures that $v{=}t$ always succeeds so that it can be safely swapped with failure sensitive **a**. It also ensures that v (or t) cannot occur in **a** even by aliasing so that $v{=}t$ can be safely swapped with binding sensitive **a**. The condition is sufficient to ensure safety, but could be weakened by abstract interpretation to detect aliasing and freeness of variables. This is outside the scope of this paper.

4.2.3 System calls

If a_i is a system call then instead of using clauses the program transformer must simulate its execution. System calls cannot always be unfolded: those with side effects, and some without sufficient bindings on their arguments. For example, $a<b$ can only be finitely unfolded if a and b are both bound to numbers. A program transformer must therefore know when system predicates can be unfolded and how to unfold them.

4.2.4 The effects of folding

The introduction of the auxiliary predicate by folding in (2c) negates any direct advantage gained by the unfolding of a_i. However, it propagates all the variable bindings gained from unfolding a_i to the atoms $a_{i+1} \ldots a_N$, which is likely to lead to directly useful unfolding later.

4.3 Executing ancestral cuts

We have not yet addressed the problem in Section 2.6: that a transformer may explore branches of a program which will never be reached during execution, by ignoring the effects of the cut. If enough is known at unfolding time about the status of predicate arguments, then some cuts can be executed to prune the program as it is being unfolded. This idea is used in [1, 11, 15]. We can adapt the standard cut execution rule to the ancestral cut as follows.

Say we have chosen $a_i = p(\underline{x}, v)$ for unfolding, and the clauses for p are

$$C_j : \; p(\underline{x}_j, v_j) :- X_j. \qquad (j = 1 \ldots k)$$

where $X_i = (!(v_i),\, R)$ for some i. If the unifier of $p(\underline{x}, v)$ and $p(\underline{x}_i, v_i)$ does not bind any variables of $p(\underline{x}, v)$ then only clauses $C_1 \ldots C_i$ need be used for unfolding, and clauses $C_{i+1} \ldots C_k$ can be discarded. In fact by analogy with standard Prolog, if we have a mode analysis of the program then we only need to ensure that the unifier does not bind any *input variables* of $p(\underline{x}, v)$. For further details on this idea see [1, 11, 15].

In the standard cut execution rule the executed cut can be removed, but this is not generally possible with ancestral cuts. For example, say we have a program

$$p(x) :- \text{mark}(v),\; q(x),\; r(x, v).$$

$$r(x, v) :- !(v).$$
$$r(2, v).$$
$$\qquad\qquad\qquad\qquad q(0).$$
$$\qquad\qquad\qquad\qquad q(1).$$

A query $? - p(v)$ would give $v=0$. If we prune r using $!(v)$ to give

$$r(x, v) :- !(v).$$

the answer is the same. But if we also delete $!(v)$ to give

$$r(x, v).$$

then there are two answers ($v=0$; $v=1$) because the cut did not refer to its parent predicate r. Hence it is incorrect to remove $!/1$ in general when pruning, unlike the standard cut. However, in Section 5.2 we show that it is possible under certain circumstances.

5 Post-unfolding optimisations

Mechanically generated programs often contain redundancies of various kinds, and it is usually profitable to apply some simple tidying up rules after unfolding. For example [4] provides rules for the removal of redundant function symbols, [13] describe how to eliminate certain variable arguments, and some general optimisation techniques are given in [16].

Unfolding simplified programs creates a special class of redundancies associated with the ancestral cut predicates, and we now describe some new ways of eliminating these redundancies. These are intended to be applied automatically after unfolding.

5.1 Reintroduction of standard cuts

The standard cut can be implemented more efficiently than ancestral cuts, and so it is beneficial to replace ancestral cuts by standard cuts after the unfolding where possible. This can be done as follows. First we make a definition:

Definition 1 (local cut argument) *Argument i of a predicate p/n ($1 \leq i \leq n$) is a* local cut argument *of p/n if:*

- *it is a variable in every p/n atom in the program,*

- *every p/n atom is immediately preceded by an atom* **mark**(v) *where v is the ith argument of the atom,*

- *in every p/n clause, every occurrence of the ith argument v of the head occurs only in atoms of the form* $!(v)$.

Now if we have a predicate $\mathrm{p}(a_1, \ldots, a_n)$ where a_i is a local cut argument of p/n then we can replace all corresponding atoms $!(v)$ by $!$ in the clauses for p/n. Moreover the atoms **mark**(a_i) preceding each p/n atom can be deleted, and the ith argument can be dropped from every p/n atom in the program. This is the inverse of the transformation in Section 3 which replaced standard cuts by ancestral cuts.

5.2 Removal of ancestral and standard cuts

Figure 1 shows some rules for removing both standard and ancestral cut atoms. The last rule can be applied much more often if redundant arguments are first removed from predicates. A simple rule which is sufficient to detect unused local cut arguments is:

> *an argument of a predicate is redundant if in each clause head for the predicate it is a variable and does not appear in any other argument, nor in any atoms in the clause body.*

The next to last rule is a generalisation of a rule in [3] which optimises contiguous "functional" atoms, and is related to intelligent backtracking strategies.

In Section 4.3 it is noted that an "executed" $!(v)$ cannot in general be deleted. However, if v is a local cut argument then $!(v)$ is replaced by $!$ using the cut reintroduction rule of Section 5.1. We can then apply the well known rule:

replace	$\mathbf{p} : - \mathbf{L}, \mathbf{mark}(v), \mathbf{mark}(v'), \mathbf{R}.$
by	$\mathbf{p} : - \mathbf{L}, \mathbf{mark}(v), \mathbf{R}[v'/v].$
replace	$\mathbf{p} : - \mathbf{L}, \mathbf{mark}(v), !(v), \mathbf{R}.$
by	$\mathbf{p} : - \mathbf{L}, \mathbf{mark}(v), \mathbf{R}.$
replace	$\mathbf{p} : - \mathbf{L}, !(v), !(v'), \mathbf{R}.$
by	$\mathbf{p} : - \mathbf{L}, !(v'), \mathbf{R}[v/v'].$
replace	$\mathbf{p} : - \mathbf{L}, !, !(v), \mathbf{R}.$
by	$\mathbf{p} : - \mathbf{L}, !(v), \mathbf{R}.$
replace	$\mathbf{p} : - \mathbf{L}, !(v), !, \mathbf{R}.$
by	$\mathbf{p} : - \mathbf{L}, !, \mathbf{R}.$
replace	$\mathbf{p} : - \mathbf{L}, !(v), \mathbf{mark}(v'), \mathbf{R}.$
by	$\mathbf{p} : - \mathbf{L}, !(v), \mathbf{R}[v'/v].$
replace	$\mathbf{p} : - \mathbf{L}, \mathbf{mark}(v), \mathbf{R}.$
by	$\mathbf{p} : - \mathbf{L}, \mathbf{R}.$
	(if v does not occur in $\mathbf{R}$)

Figure 1: Eliminating redundant cut predicates

delete any cut at the start of the last clause for a predicate.

6 A simple example

To illustrate our program simplification, unfold rule and optimisation rules, consider the program:

$\mathbf{p}(x) : - \mathbf{q}(x), \mathbf{r}(x).$
$\mathbf{p}(2).$

$\mathbf{q}(1) : - !.$ $\mathbf{r}(1) : - !.$
$\mathbf{q}(3).$ $\mathbf{r}(4).$

We would like to perform some unfolding on this program to make **p** more efficient, but neither **q** nor **r** can be unfolded in the **p** clause because they both call a cut. Nor is a cut execution rule applicable. Hence no improvement by unfolding is possible by the program in this form.

We now apply our method. The simplified program is:

$\mathbf{p}(x) : - \mathbf{mark}(v_1), \mathbf{q}(x, v_1), \mathbf{mark}(v_2), \mathbf{r}(x, v_2).$
$\mathbf{p}(2).$

$\mathbf{q}(1, v_1) : - !(v_1).$ $\mathbf{r}(1, v_2) : - !(v_2).$
$\mathbf{q}(3, v_1).$ $\mathbf{r}(4, v_2).$

To unfold **q**, create an auxiliary predicate:

$\mathbf{p}(x) : - \mathbf{mark}(v_1), \mathbf{new}(x, v_1).$
$\mathbf{p}(2).$

$\mathbf{new}(x, v_1) : - \mathbf{q}(x, v_1), \mathbf{mark}(v_2), \mathbf{r}(x, v_2).$

q can now be unfolded in the **new** clause:

> **new**$(1, v_1)$ $: -$ $!(v_1)$, **mark**(v_2), **r**$(1, v_2)$.
> **new**$(3, v_1)$ $: -$ **mark**(v_2), **r**$(3, v_2)$.

r can be unfolded in both these clauses. The first clause becomes

> **new**$(1, v_1)$ $: -$ $!(v_1)$, **mark**(v_2), $!(v_2)$.

and the second clause is deleted via failure propagation. Now **new** can be unfolded in the first **p** clause:

> **p**(1) $: -$ **mark**(v_1), $!(v_1)$, **mark**(v_2), $!(v_2)$.
> **p**(2).

Finally, the conjunction (**mark**(v_1), $!(v_1)$, **mark**(v_2), $!(v_2)$) has no effect and can be deleted using the rules of Section 5:

> **p**(1).
> **p**(2).

7 Application to meta-interpreters

The example of Section 6 does not illustrate the ancestral cut execution rule of Section 4.3, which has been found particularly useful in meta-interpreter specialisation. A common interpretation strategy is to split up a conjunction of atoms, process these separately, join the results and continue:

> $\vdots$
> **int**$((a, b))$ $: -$ **p**(a, a'), **p**(b, b'), **join**(a', b', c), **int**(c).
> $\vdots$

> **join**(T, b, b) $: -$ $!$.
> **join**(a, T, a) $: -$ $!$.
> **join**$(a, b, (a, b))$.

where T stands for **true** at the object level. Now consider the case where the two **p** atoms are unfolded and bind a, b, a' and b' to T. The **int** clause then becomes

> **int**$((T, T))$ $: -$ **join**(T, T, c), **int**(c).

The **join** of T and T is T, and the last atom in the clause will become **int**(T). But if the pruning effect of the cut is ignored then **join** gives this answer twice, plus an extra answer **int**$((T, T))$. These cases are never reached during execution, and unfolding time is wasted. Worse, in some interpreters the effects may propagate to give atoms

> **int**(T)
> **int**$((T, T))$
> **int**$((T, T, T))$
> $\vdots$

This either prevents the transformer from terminating, or forces it to replace all these atoms by the more general atom $\mathbf{int}(v)$, sacrificing specialisation.

A cut execution rule can avoid this. If we simplify the program then after unfolding we have

$$\mathbf{int}((T, T)) \; :- \; \mathbf{mark}(v), \; \mathbf{join}(T, T, c, v), \; \mathbf{int}(c).$$

where

$$\mathbf{join}(T, b, b, v) \; :- \; !(v).$$
$$\mathbf{join}(a, T, a, v) \; :- \; !(v).$$
$$\mathbf{join}(a, b, (a, b), v).$$

Now to unfold $\mathbf{join}$ we create an auxiliary predicate

$$\mathbf{int}((T, T)) \; :- \; \mathbf{mark}(v), \; \mathbf{new}(v).$$

$$\mathbf{new}(v) \; :- \; \mathbf{join}(T, T, c, v), \; \mathbf{int}(c).$$

then unfold $\mathbf{join}$:

$$\mathbf{new}(v) \; :- \; !(v), \; \mathbf{int}(T).$$
$$\mathbf{new}(v) \; :- \; !(v), \; \mathbf{int}(T).$$
$$\mathbf{new}(v) \; :- \; \mathbf{int}((T, T)).$$

Now the ancestral cut execution rule applies and the second and third **new** clauses can be pruned, avoiding redundant clauses.

8   Related work

We identify three basic approaches for handling control structures when unfolding full Prolog programs.

Firstly, the problems of unfolding full Prolog can be minimised by a variety of techniques. This has the advantage of operating directly on standard Prolog programs, but the disadvantages that unfolding requires complicated rules and is not always applicable. Thus it tends to lead to conservative unfold strategies. The partial deduction systems of Bugliesi & Russo [1], Levi & Sardu [7], Owen [11] and Sahlin [15] follow this approach. They show that the restriction on unfolding atoms which call cuts can be lifted under certain circumstances; also that even when an atom cannot be unfolded, variable bindings can sometimes be propagated by taking the least common generalisation of the matching clause heads. The latter technique recovers some of the benefits of unfolding, but it is only applicable if the bindings on the clause heads are mutually exclusive [1]. The unfolding restriction can also be avoided by removing cuts, and Debray [2] shows that many common uses of the cut can be removed by static analysis.

Secondly, the programmer can be forced to write programs in a more easily unfoldable style. The partial deduction system of Takeuchi & Furukawa [17] is restricted to programs written in if-then-else style. O'Keefe [9] advocates replacing most uses of the cut by if-then-else which can be unfolded easily, and the few cases which cannot be replaced will not greatly restrict the application of unfolding. However, it sometimes takes considerable skill to reorganise a program so that cuts can be replaced by if-then-else. In particular, disjunctions containing cuts cannot be directly mapped to the if-then-else form.

Thirdly, new pruning operators can be introduced, moving away from standard Prolog to languages which behave better under unfolding. This is the approach we follow, by eliminating all Prolog control constructs leaving only conjunction and ancestral cuts. Full Prolog can also be *augmented* with ancestral cuts, as done by Venken [19], which removes an unfolding restriction but not the complications of unfolding full Prolog. Part of Van Roy's Aquarius Prolog system [14] transforms Prolog into a simpler form called Kernel Prolog with ancestral cuts, eliminating if-then-else and cut in the same way as our approach. Kernel Prolog programs have a slightly different form to our simplified programs, using disjunctions and unification made explicit by introducing equalities. The Prolog implementation of Taylor [18] also has a mapping to a simpler form called normalised Prolog. Again, normalised Prolog programs are slightly different to simplified programs. They contain disjunctions, explicit unification and a version of the cut localised to disjunctions. Both these systems map programs to a simpler form to obtain efficient Prolog compilation. The Gödel language has a new pruning operator described by Hill, Lloyd and Shepherdson [5] which, like the ancestral cuts, has the property that unfolding does not change the meaning of programs.

9 Conclusion

We have described an approach which greatly simplifies the writing of program transformers for Prolog, and avoids many of its problems. In the process, we adapted an existing cut execution rule to the ancestral cut and proposed new rules for improving programs containing ancestral cuts. The method relies upon the use of ancestral cuts, which are not available in all Prologs. However, this is not really a problem because they are available in some well known implementations, for example Sepia and BIM Prolog.

Our approach has been successfully applied in a partial deduction system [12] for Sepia Prolog [8], by imposing a terminating transformation strategy on top of our unfold rule. The system was much easier to write because of the program simplification phase, and it performed well on programs written in full Prolog where there was significant program specialisation or unfolding to be done. It performed less well on carefully written programs with no special query to be optimised, because the program simplification phase involves a slight loss of performance — the ancestral cut is less efficient (at least in Sepia Prolog) than the standard control structures.

We intend to solve the problem of loss of performance for carefully written programs by reintroducing more standard control structures after transformation. In particular, replacing some reintroduced standard cuts by if-then-else would enhance performance. We also intend to refine the rather crude predicate classification system by abstract interpretation, which could exploit sharing and aliasing information.

Acknowledgements

I would like to thank Mireille Ducassé, Alexander Herold and Micha Meier for their helpful comments.

References

[1] M.Bugliesi, F.Russo, Partial Evaluation in Prolog: Some Improvements About Cut, *Proceedings of the North American Conference on Logic Programming,* 1989, pp.645–660.

[2] S.K.Debray, Towards Banishing the Cut from Prolog, *Proceedings of the International Conference on Computer Languages*, Miami, October 1986, pp.2–12.

[3] S.K.Debray, D.S.Warren, Detection and Optimization of Functional Computations in Prolog, *Proceedings of the International Conference on Logic Programming,* 1986, pp.490–504.

[4] J.Gallagher, M.Bruynooghe, Some Low-Level Source Transformations for Logic Programs, *Proceedings of META'90* pp.229–244.

[5] P.M.Hill, J.W.Lloyd. J.C.Shepherdson, Properties of a Pruning Operator, *Journal of Logic and Computation* 1(1), 1990, pp.99–143.

[6] A.Lakhotia, L.Sterling, ProMiX: a Prolog Partial Evaluation System, The Practice of Prolog, ed. L.Sterling, MIT Press 1991.

[7] G.Levi, G.Sardu, Partial Evaluation of Metaprograms in a 'Multiple Worlds" Logic Language, *New Generation Computing* 6, 1988, OHSMHA LTD. and Springer-Verlag, pp.227–247.

[8] M.Meier et al, SEPIA — An Extendible Prolog System, *Proceedings of the 11th World Computer Congress IFIP'89,* San Francisco, August 1989, pp.1127–1132.

[9] R.O'Keefe, On the Treatment of Cuts in Prolog Source-Level Tools, *Proceedings of the Symposium on Logic Programming,* IEEE 1985, pp.68–72.

[10] R.O'Keefe, The Craft of Prolog, MIT Press 1990.

[11] S.Owen, Issues in the Partial Evaluation of Meta-Interpreters, *Proceedings of the Workshop on Meta-Programming in Logic Programming,* 1988, pp.241–254.

[12] S.D.Prestwich, The PADDY Partial Deduction System, Technical Report ECRC-92-6.

[13] M.Proietti, A.Pettorossi, Unfolding-Definition-Folding, in this Order, for Avoiding Unnecessary Variables in Logic Programs, *Symposium on Program Language Implementation and Logic Programming,* 1991, pp.347–358.

[14] P.L.Van Roy, Can Logic Programming Execute as Fast as Imperative Programming? Report no.UCB/CSD 90/600 Dec.1990, Computer Science Division (EECS), University of California, Berkeley, California 94720.

[15] D.Sahlin, The Mixtus Approach to Automatic Partial Evaluation of Full Prolog, *Proceedings of the North American Conference on Logic Programming,* 1990, pp.377–398.

[16] H.Sawamura, T.Takeshima, A.Kato, Source-Level Optimization Techniques for Prolog, ICOT Technical Report TR-91, January 1985.

[17] A.Takeuchi, K.Furukawa, Partial Evaluation of Prolog Programs and its Application to Meta Programming, ICOT Technical Report TR-126, July 1985.

[18] A.Taylor, High Performance Prolog Implementation, PhD thesis, Basser Department of Computer Science, University of Sidney, June 1991.

[19] R.Venken, A Prolog Meta-Interpreter for Partial Evaluation and its Application to Source to Source Transformation and Query Optimisation, *ECAI'84*: Advances in Artificial Intelligence, ed. T.O'Shea, Elsevier Science Publishers B.V. (North-Holland), pp.91–100.

[20] R.Venken, B.Demoen, A Partial Evaluation System for Prolog: some Practical Considerations, *New Generation Computing* 6(2,3), 1988, pp.279–290.

Logimix: A Self-Applicable Partial Evaluator for Prolog*

Torben Æ. Mogensen
DIKU, Department of Computer Science,
University of Copenhagen
Copenhagen, Denmark
e-mail: torbenm@diku.dk

Anders Bondorf
DIKU, Department of Computer Science,
University of Copenhagen
Copenhagen, Denmark
e-mail: anders@diku.dk

Abstract

We present a self-applicable partial evaluator for a large subset of full Prolog. The partial evaluator, called Logimix, is the result of applying our experience from partial evaluation of functional languages to Prolog. Great care is taken to preserve the operational semantics of the partially evaluated programs, including the effects of non-logical predicates and side effects.

At the same time, we also want the partial evaluator to handle large programs in reasonable time. This has led us to use simple strategies whenever possible, in particular we let most of the choices made during partial evaluation depend on the results of a prior binding time analysis. We have successfully applied Logimix to interpreters, yielding compiled programs where virtually all interpretation overhead is removed. Self-application of Logimix yields stand-alone compilers and a compiler generator.

To obtain a clear distinction between the different meta-levels when doing self-application, input programs to the partial evaluator are represented as ground terms (as in e.g. [4]). Nevertheless, we implement unification in the partial evaluator by unification in the underlying Prolog system. This significantly improves upon [4] which use explicitly coded meta-unification.

We show the text of the central parts of the partial evaluator.

*This work was partly supported by ESPRIT Basic Research Actions project 3124 "Semantique"

1   Introduction

Partial evaluation of Prolog has in the eighties been investigated by several people, primarily as a tool for compiling by partially evaluating interpreters.

Self-applicable partial evaluation of Prolog is investigated in [5] [6] [4]. [5] extends the classical three line meta-interpreter to perform partial evaluation. This gives a very short partial evaluator, but as noted in [4] the operational semantics are not always preserved when self-application is attempted.

Fuller uses a different approach [6]: the source program is represented as a ground term, which is given as input to the partial evaluator. The language is restricted to pure logic and care is taken to preserve semantics. Unification is simulated by meta-unification on ground terms that represent run-time terms with variables. Though self-application is performed, the resulting programs are very large and slow.

The first efficiently self-applicable and semantically safe partial evaluator for Prolog appears to the one reported in [4]. The source program is represented as a ground term as in Fuller's work, but by using *binding time annotations* [8], efficient self-application is achieved: compiling by using a stand-alone compiler generated by self-application is several times faster than by specializing an interpreter.

In this paper we improve upon [4] in several ways. (1) Most importantly, we avoid using meta-unification by simulating unification meta-circularly by unification of the underlying system. This gives significant efficiency improvements. (2) We make more thorough use of binding time information, in particular to decide unfolding; this results in smaller and faster compilers. (3) The binding time requirements are less restrictive: more variables become static, that is, more work can be done at partial evaluation time. (4) More of Prolog's control features are treated.

Our idea of partial evaluation differs somewhat from that of [9], as ours is not solely based on unfolding: we generate new predicate names derived from predicate names in the original program and the values of some of their arguments. Thus, a single predicate in the original program can yield several differently named predicates in the residual program, each corresponding to a particular set of values for the arguments. This is called *polyvariant specialization* [8]. In the framework of [9], all argument values are present in the residual (partially evaluated) programs, causing unification at run-time.

To get maximum benefit of polyvariant specialization, we want the data with respect to which we specialize (the *static data*) as arguments to the goal predicate rather than as extra clauses appended to the program. When the partial evaluator is self-applicable, its static data is the program to be specialized. Thus this too is a parameter rather than a part of the data base. This is as in [6] and [4], but as opposed to [5].

1.1   Example

Let us illustrate some points by an example: compiling regular expressions into deterministic finite automata by partial evaluation. This example was originally developed for use in the Scheme partial evaluator Similix by the two authors in collaboration with Jesper Jørgensen [2].

The program in figure 1 takes as input a regular expression and a string (a list of characters) and tests whether the string is accepted by the regular expression. The program uses the predicates accepts_empty, first, and next Their definitions have not been included, but let us explain what they do.

The predicate accepts_empty tests if a regular expression accepts the empty string. The predicate first tests if a particular symbol can begin a string which is accepted by the regular expression. next(R,S,R1) is used to move step forward in a regular expression: R1 is a regular expression that accepts the rest of the string (after the symbol S) if and only if R accepts the complete string. next(R,S,R1) thus tests if the strings accepted by the regular expression R1 are exactly the tails of the strings beginning with the symbol S that R accepts.

The three predicates are logical in the sense that they can be run with any or all parameters unbound. The variable S1 is used to *improve binding times* [7]; it is necessary for the partial evaluation to give good results (cf. section 3).

Figure 2 shows the result of using Logimix to specialize the program in figure 1 with respect to the regular expression $(a \mid b) * a\,b\,a$. The predicate accepts occurs in four different specialized versions, accepts_0 ... accepts_3. This illustrates polyvariant specialization: each predicate is specialized according to different values of the static (known) input (the regular expression). The remaining parameter (the string) is dynamic (not known at partial evaluation time), and is thus still present as a parameter in the residual program. All calls to accepts_empty, first and next have been fully evaluated and are thus not present in the residual program. The use of ; in the residual rules stems from different results of calls to first. The residual program is equivalent to a deterministic finite automaton, in fact it is identical to the automaton derived for the same regular expression in [1]. We will later refer to details in this example to explain points in the partial evaluator.

```
accepts(R,[]) :- accepts_empty(R).
accepts(R,[S|Ss]) :- first(R,S1), S=S1, next(R,S1,R1), accepts(R1,Ss).
```

Figure 1: *Program for testing string acceptance by regular expressions*

```
accepts_0([]) :- fail.
accepts_0([S|Ss]) :- S=a, accepts_1(Ss) ; S=b, accepts_0(Ss).

accepts_1([]) :- fail.
accepts_1([S|Ss]) :- S=a, accepts_1(Ss) ; S=b, accepts_2(Ss).

accepts_2([]) :- fail.
accepts_2([S|Ss]) :- S=a, accepts_3(Ss) ; S=b, accepts_0(Ss).

accepts_3([]).
accepts_3([S|Ss]) :- S=a, accepts_1(Ss) ; S=b, accepts_2(Ss).
```

Figure 2: *Residual program*

1.2 The partial evaluator

The partial evaluator consists of two parts: a meta-circular self-interpreter to perform the static parts of the program, and a specializer that unfolds non-static goals or specializes them with respect to their static arguments. The specializer calls the interpreter to execute the static subgoals. This division of the partial evaluator reflects the different behaviours of interpretation and specialization: interpretation can fail or return multiple solutions, whereas specialization should always succeed with exactly one specialized goal.

2 The Interpreter

The meta-circular interpreter has the program as a ground parameter, but simulates unification, backtracking and other control directly by the same contructs in the underlying Prolog system. We have included only those control features that are possible to interpret in this way, that is (_,_), (_;_), (\+_), (_->_;_),..., but not ! (cut). Cut could in most cases be handled (though we do not do so) by pre-transforming uses of ! to uses of (_->_;_). Predicates that are not defined in the program are assumed to be basic (predefined) predicates.

Program	::=	program(*Decls*,[*Pred*])	
Pred	::=	pred(*Name*,*Arity*,[*Clause*])	
Clause	::=	clause([*Name*],[*Term*],*Goal*)	
Goal	::=	basic(*Name*,[*Term*])	— predefined predicates
	|	call(*Name*,[*Term*])	— user defined predicates
	|	true	
	|	fail	
	|	*Goal*, *Goal*	
	|	\+ *Goal*	— negation by failure
	|	*Goal*; *Goal*	
	|	ifcut(*Goal*,*Goal*,*Goal*)	— (...-> ...; ...)
	|	if(*Goal*,*Goal*,*Goal*)	
Term	::=	var(*Name*)	
	|	*Name*. [*Term*]	

Figure 3: Abstract syntax for Prolog programs

2.1 Representation of programs

The abstract syntax (as ground terms) of Prolog programs is shown in figure 3; [*N*] means "list of *N*". Figure 4 shows the regular expression program in abstract syntax.

```
program([],
        [pred(accepts,2,
              [clause([0],[var(0),[[]]],
                      basic(accepts_empty,[var(0)])),
               clause([0,1,2,3,4],[var(0),[.,var(1),var(2)]],
                      (basic(first,[var(0),var(3)]),
                       basic(=,[var(3),var(1)]),
                       basic(next,[var(0),var(3),var(4)]),
                       call(accepts,[var(4),var(2)])))])])
```

Figure 4: *Example of program in abstract syntax*

2.2 Interpreter text

The full self-interpreter is shown in Appendix A.

The predicate `eval/4` solves a goal. It takes as arguments the goal, the entire program, a list of names of the variables in the goal and a list of the values that are bound to these variables. During interpretation, the first three of these arguments will be ground. Calls to basic (predefined) predicates are handled by converting the abstract syntax of the call to normal Prolog syntax, and then passing this term to `call/1`. The predicate `decode_list/4` uses the name and variable lists to convert a list of terms from abstract syntax to concrete syntax. A call to a user defined predicate is handled by decoding the argument terms, and then calling `call_pred/4` with the decoded terms and the functor and arity of the predicate. Control primitives are handled completely meta-circularly.

The predicate `call_pred/4` finds the definition of the predicate in the program and calls `call_clauses/3`. This predicate tries each clause in turn, first making new variables for the clause, then decoding the patterns on the left-hand side, unifying these with the arguments and then, if the unification succeeds, solving the right-hand side.

3 The Specializer

The specializer requires annotation of variables as *static* or *dynamic* (i.e. *non-static*) and annotation of whether or not to unfold calls to user defined predicates. Static variables are neither *more* nor *less* bound than they would be during normal (full) evaluation. This ensures that even meta-logical predicates (like `var/1`) have the same behaviour at specialization time as during a normal evaluation. Goals are considered static if they can be fully evaluated at partial evaluation time, while preserving semantics. The non-static goals are called *dynamic*. This means that they contain only static variables and that they do no side-effects, nor depend on a state that can be modified by side-effects. Dynamic goals are specialized with respect to the values of the static variables. This involves evaluating static subgoals and unfolding some user defined predicates (depending on their annotation) and creating specialized predicates for the calls that aren't unfolded.

Binding of static variables happen only when evaluating static goals, and these bindings will only be visible to later static goals (which may be parts of dynamic goals). This means: no backward unification. Such backwards unification could change the behaviour of non-logical predicates like var/1. Additionally, static goals are annotated by the potential number of solutions ("at most one" or "any number"). This is not essential, but allows the cases with at most one solution to be handled by a simpler procedure.

We use the following specialization strategy:

1. Variables in the program are always considered either static or dynamic. That is, a variable cannot change status from static to dynamic (or vice versa) during its life-time. This decision greatly simplifies the handling of variables, as we otherwise would have to insert explicit substitutions at the points where a variable changes status. If a particular program should require such a change to get good results from partial evaluation, this can be simulated by introducing new variables. This was done in the regular expression example where the variable S1 is a static copy of S. S1 remains static after unification with S, as it is ground at this time. Note that, when we say that a variable is non-ground, we mean that a variable from the program text has been instantiated with a non-ground value (and is thus no longer a free variable).

2. Static subgoals are evaluated by the meta-circular interpreter. The specializer needs the solution set of the static subgoals in a list and thus uses an equivalent of findall/3 when calling the interpreter. The remaining subgoals are specialized according to each solution, and the resulting residual goals are combined with (_;_). This is done by special treatment of (_,_) when the first subgoal is static. The regular expression example shows this: the call to first(R,S1) yields two substitutions for S1, namely a and b. The remaining goal is specialized in two versions, separated by (_;_).

   Note that this means that forward unification only happens across commas: no bindings go "up" the syntax tree. This can have the effect that (s1,(d1,s2)) will pass bindings from s1 to s2, but ((s1,d1),s2) will not since the goal before the second comma is not fully static. Again, this strategy is chosen to simplify the specializer so it need only return residual goals and not bindings of static variables. The limitation can to some extend be overcome by simple modifications to the program prior to specialization, but it is rarely a problem. Indeed, parsing s1,d1,s2 will yield the better of the two forms. If the specializer returned bindings, then we would risk exponential code explosion, as each set of bindings would cause a new specialization of the remaining subgoals.

3. When user defined predicates are not unfolded, they are *suspended*. Suspension replaces the call by a call to a renamed (*residual*) version, which is specialized with respect to the static parameters. In the example, calls to the goal accepts are suspended and specialized with respect to the value of R, yielding the specialized predicates accepts_0 ... accepts_3. The definition of the residual predicate will be added to the residual program at a later time if a previous call to the same residual predicate has

not already caused this. We use side effects to record which specialized predicates we have already added to the residual program. Suspension of user defined predicates does not change the bindings of static variables, but static variables in the parameters have to be ground. It is assumed that the annotation of variables ensures this.

4. Unfolding non-static user defined predicates does not change the bindings of static variables either. This is related to the fact that static values are propagated only through commas, cf. item 2 above.

5. During unfolding, if the unfolded predicate has several matching clauses, the specialized right hand sides of these are combined with (_;_) into a single goal which is inserted in place of the call. This avoids the duplication problem that pure Horn-clause unfolding has. Note that, had we allowed backwards unification, we might be forced to do backwards unification with respect to several substitutions produced by matching against several clauses during unfolding. This would force us to copy the entire right hand side in which the unfolding took place, just like in pure Horn-clause unfolding. Figure 5 shows the difference between Horn-clause unfolding and unfolding using (_;_).

6. If a predicate call is not fully executed by the interpreter, all non-ground variables occurring in it are treated as dynamic. This is because they after the call could be less ground than they would have been, had the call been evaluated. As variables cannot change binding time status during partial evaluation, such variables are dynamic throughout their scope cf. item 1 and 2.

7. If a basic predicate has side effects or depends on global state, it is not evaluated during partial evaluation, even if all its parameters are fully ground. This ensures that side effects occur in the same order when running the residual program, as when running the original program. Other meta-logical predicates (var/1, ==/2, etc.) are performed if their arguments are static. Note that static parameters to basic predicates can be non-ground.

Given the program

```
p(X,Y) :- q(Y), r(X).
r(a) :- s.
r(b) :- t.
```

we unfold r using normal Horn-clause unfolding:

```
p(a,Y) :- q(Y), s.
p(b,Y) :- q(Y), t.
```

Note that q will be executed twice in the unfolded program. Using (_;_) we instead obtain the following program, where q is executed only once.

```
p(X,Y) :- q(Y), (X=a, s ; X=b, t).
```

Note that the second method is only valid if no instantiations of variables are propagated back to the left hand side. This is handled by the explicit substitutions X=a and X=b.

Figure 5: Comparison of different unfolding methods

When a residual goal has been generated, some post-reductions on it are performed. This includes some forward unification of dynamic variables and conversion of `call/1` to a direct call if the functor/arity of the called goal is known. The conversion of `call/1` is mainly to get better results from specialization of interpreters and from self-application. An effect of the forward unification is reduction of long chains of explicit unifications, e.g.

`X=[A|B], B=[C|D], D=[E|F], F=[].`

which is folded to

`X=[A,C,E].`

The binding time analysis is a combination of a dependency analysis, a groundness analysis, a determinacy analysis and a side effect analysis. The dependency analysis is used to trace which variables will depend on others by unification. Combined with groundness analysis this is used to determine in which cases the unification of a static and a dynamic variable should cause the static variable to be reclassified as dynamic, *i.e.* when the static variable is non-ground. The determinacy analysis is used to find out whether a static goal has one or more solutions in order to annotate it with either `static1` or `static`. The side effect analysis is used to classify arguments to side effecting primitives as dynamic. Presently the binding time analysis is not fully implemented (only the side effect analysis is), so some of the annotations are done by hand. Also the decision of when to unfold or specialize (fold) non-static predicates is by way of hand-made annotations. An automatic call unfolding strategy based on static/dynamic control flow, similar to the one in [3], would be suitable.

The regular expression program is annotated with respect to the user supplied information in figure 6 to yield the annotated program in figure 7, which is used as input to Logimix to make the residual program in figure 2. Dynamic variables and patterns and predicate calls that are not to be unfolded are underlined. In addition to this, static goals that can return at most one solution are marked with a superscript "1". The abstract syntax version of the annotated program is shown in figure 8. Automating the binding time analysis would eliminate most of the user supplied information. Note that it will still be necessary to specify the binding times of the goal predicates parameters and the properties of basic predicates. The latter could to some extent be handled by a standard library.

```
pred(accepts,2,suspend,several,patts([s,d]),[bodyvars([]),bodyvars
                                                        ([s,s])]).
basic(accepts_empty,1,meta_logical,single).
basic(first,2,meta_logical,multiple).
basic(next,3,meta_logical,single).
basic(=,2,logical,single).
```

Figure 6: Binding time information for regular expression program

```
accepts(R,[]) :- accepts_empty¹(R).
accepts(R,[S|Ss]) :- first(R,S1), S=S1, next¹(R,S1,R1),
                      accepts(R1,Ss).
```

Figure 7: Annotated regular expression program

```
program([],
       [pred(accepts,2,ann(suspend,several,[s,d]),
            [clause([0],[s],[var(0),[[]]],
                      static1(basic(accepts_empty,[var(0)]))),

clause([0,1,2,3,4],[s,d,d,s,s],[var(0),[.,dvar(1),dvar(2)]],
                    (static(basic(first,[var(0),var(3)])),
                     basic(=,[var(3),dvar(1)]),
                     static1(basic(next,[var(0),var(3),var(4)]))),
                     call(accepts,[var(4),dvar(2)])))])])
```

Figure 8: Annotated regular expression program in abstract syntax

We have not taken possible non-termination of the specialization process into account. There are basically two possible causes for non-termination in Logimix: infinite unfolding and infinite polyvariant specialization. The first problem occurs if the call unfolding annotation allows unfolding of a dynamically controlled recursive predicate, and can normally be solved by a stricter annotation, with a risk of turning it into an instance of infinite specialization. This second problem occurs when the static parameters to a suspended predicate can take on infinitely many values during specialization. The usual solution to this is to reclassify the offending parameter as dynamic, with the cost that less specialization can be done. These decisions would ideally be done automatically. This can be done by monitoring the calls made during specialization, but this is both costly and against our basic strategy of statically annotating the programs prior to specialization.

A part of the specializer is shown in appendix B. It shows how goals are specialized. The part handling unfolding and specialization of predicates is not shown.

The predicate peval/5 handles specialization of dynamic goals. It will *always* succeed and return a residual goal in the variable Rg. Dynamic goals may contain static subgoals. These are marked by embedding them in the functor static/1 or static1/1. The functor static1/1 states that there will be at most one solution to the static goal. A single solution is generated by one_eval/5 which calls eval/4. Note that the value list is copied to avoid backward unification.

General case static goals are handled by all_eval/5 which returns a list of value lists, corresponding to each solution of the goal. It simulates the effect of findall/3 by using side effects. We could have used findall/3 instead, but then, because of self-application, we would also have to extend the interpreter and the specializer to handle findall/3 too. This is not difficult to do, but it would complicate the specializer more than it would save.

Calls to dynamic basic predicates are simply suspended. This involves instantiating static variables and renaming dynamic variables. Calls to user defined predicates are handled according to annotations. The annotations describe whether the call should be unfolded, whether there might be more than one clause that matches, and the binding times of the parameters to the clause. If the call is suspended, the arguments are divided into static and dynamic according to the binding time annotation. The original predicate name and the static parameters are used to make a new name for the specialized predicate. This is handled by suspend/4, which also ensures that the definition of the specialized predicate will be added to the residual program. The residual goal for the call is a call to the specialized predicate with the dynamic arguments of the original call as arguments.

When specializing a _,_, a special case is made when the first subgoal is static and the second is not. All the solutions of the static goal are found, and the second subgoal is specialized according to each solution. The solutions are combined with _;_ to form the residual goal. Again, static goals with at most one solution are given special treatment. If the first subgoal is dynamic, a residual _,_ goal is produced.

Negation (\+/1) just gives rise to a residual \+/1 and _;_ to a residual _;_. The two if-then-else constructs reduce to one of their branches when their condition is static. They differ in what happens if there is more than one solution to the condition.

4   Experiments

The specializer and the self-interpreter have been implemented. Logimix has been successfully applied to interpreters (including the self-interpreter), yielding compiled programs where virtually all interpretation overhead is removed. Self-application of Logimix yields stand-alone compilers and compiler generators. See the table in figure 9; the figures are for execution under SICStus Prolog version 0.6 on a SPARCstation 2. The size of the generated compiler generator *cogen* is approximately 30KB. Generating *cogen* required more than 12MB heap/stack space. Early versions used twice that, but after elimination of unnecessary backtrack points in the specializer, we obtained the present result.

Even though our partial evaluation strategy is quite conservative, we get quite good results, e.g. from specializing interpreters. This can, however, require attention to binding times when writing the interpreter. We are not likely to get good results from off-the-shelf interpreters without modifying them to improve binding times. With the presented self-interpreter our residual programs are similar to the original programs. Thus we have essentially removed all of the interpretation overhead.

The speedup (about 56%) from using a generated compiler rather than compiling by specializing the self-interpreter is modest compared to our experiences from the functional world [8]. This is mainly because a substantial part of the specialization time is spent on reductions of the residual goals, something that

job	time/s	speedup
$output = sint(sint, data)$	2.25	13.7
$output = target(data)$	0.16	
$target = mix(sint^{ann}, sint)$	19.2	1.78
$target = comp(sint)$	10.8	
$comp = mix(mix^{ann}, sint^{ann})$	19.3	1.35
$comp = cogen(sint^{ann})$	14.4	
$cogen = mix(mix^{ann}, mix^{ann})$	172.	1.14
$cogen = cogen(mix^{ann})$	152.	

Figure 9: Logimix performance

is dependent on the programs that are compiled and thus not available at compiler generation time. Compiler generation by using a compiler generator is about 26% faster than specializing the specializer directly. The reduction time is used mainly for folding chains of explicit unifications caused by unfolding recursive calls. The self-interpreter and the partial evaluator (which uses the interpreter) generate many such chains through calls to decode and make-vars. Other programs like the regular expression example generate virtually no such chains, so the speedup of their corresponding "compilers" are better.

5   Conclusion

We have presented a simple and efficient self-applicable partial evaluator for a non-trivial subset of Prolog. We have shown that the simple minded strategy can yield good speed-ups of even fairly large programs and that self-application can be done with fair results. We have had great use of our experience from partial evaluation of functional programs.

References

[1] A.V. Aho, R. Sethi, and J.D. Ullman. *Compilers: Principles, Techniques, and Tools.* Addison-Wesley, 1986.

[2] A. Bondorf. *Self-Applicable Partial Evaluation.* PhD thesis, DIKU, University of Copenhagen, Denmark, 1990. Revised version: DIKU Report 90/17.

[3] A. Bondorf and O. Danvy. Automatic autoprojection of recursive equations with global variables and abstract data types. *Science of Computer Programming,* 16:151–195, 1991.

[4] A. Bondorf, F. Frauendorf, and M. Richter. *An Experiment in Automatic Self-Applicable Partial Evaluation of Prolog.* Technical Report 335, Lehrstuhl Informatik V, University of Dortmund, Germany, 1990. 20 pages.

[5] H. Fujita and K. Furukawa. A self-applicable partial evaluator and its use in incremental compilation. *New Generation Computing,* 6(2,3):91–118, 1988.

[6] D.A. Fuller. *Partial Evaluation and Mix Computation in Logic Programming.* PhD thesis, Imperial College, London, England, February 1989. 222 pages.

[7] C.K. Holst and J. Hughes. Towards binding-time improvement for free. In S.L. Peyton Jones, G. Hutton, and C. Kehler Holst, editors, *Functional Programming, Glasgow 1990*, pages 83–100, Springer-Verlag, 1991.

[8] N.D. Jones, P. Sestoft, and H. Søndergaard. Mix: a self-applicable partial evaluator for experiments in compiler generation. *Lisp and Symbolic Computation*, 2(1):9–50, 1989.

[9] J.W. Lloyd and J.C. Shepherdson. *Partial Evaluation in Logic Programming.* Technical Report CS-87-09, Department of Computer Science, University of Bristol, England, 1987. Revised version in [10].

[10] J.W. Lloyd and J.C. Shepherdson. Partial evaluation in logic programming. *Journal of Logic Programming*, 11:217–242, 1991.

Appendix A

```
% meta_int(++Program,++Name,++Arity,?[Value])
meta_int(program(_,P),N,Arity,Args) :- call_pred(P,N,Arity,Args).

call_pred(P,N,Arity,Args) :-
  is_member(pred(N,Arity,Clauses),P), call_clauses(Clauses,P,Args).

call_clauses(Clauses,P,Args) :-
  member(clause(Vars,Patts,Rhs),Clauses),
  make_vars(Vars,Vs),
  decode_list(Patts,Vars,Vs,Patts1),
  Args = Patts1,
  eval(Rhs,P,Vars,Vs).

% eval(++Goal,++Program,++[Name],?[Value])
eval(basic(N,Args),_,Ns,Vs) :-
  decode_list(Args,Ns,Vs,Nargs), G =.. [N|Nargs], call(G).
eval(call(N,Args),P,Ns,Vs) :-
  length(Args,Arity),
  decode_list(Args,Ns,Vs,Nargs),
  call_pred(P,N,Arity,Nargs).
eval(true,_,_,_).
eval(fail,_,_,_) :-
  fail.
eval((G1 , G2),P,Ns,Vs) :-
  eval(G1,P,Ns,Vs), eval(G2,P,Ns,Vs).
eval((\+ G),P,Ns,Vs) :-
  \+ eval(G,P,Ns,Vs).
eval((G1 ; G2),P,Ns,Vs) :-
  eval(G1,P,Ns,Vs) ; eval(G2,P,Ns,Vs).
eval(ifcut(G1,G2,G3),P,Ns,Vs) :-
  eval(G1,P,Ns,Vs) ->
  eval(G2,P,Ns,Vs) ; eval(G3,P,Ns,Vs).
```

```
eval(if(G1,G2,G3),P,Ns,Vs) :-
  if(eval(G1,P,Ns,Vs),eval(G2,P,Ns,Vs),eval(G3,P,Ns,Vs)).

make_vars([],[]).
make_vars([_|Ns],[_|Vs]) :- make_vars(Ns,Vs).

decode(var(N),Ns,Vs,V) :- lookup(N,Ns,Vs,V).
decode([N|Args],Ns,Vs,V) :-
  decode_list(Args,Ns,Vs,Nargs), V =.. [N|Nargs].

decode_list([],_,_,[]).
decode_list([T1|Ts],Ns,Vs,[Tn1|Tns]) :-
  decode(T1,Ns,Vs,Tn1), decode_list(Ts,Ns,Vs,Tns).

lookup(N,[M|Ns],[W|Vs],V) :- (N = M) -> V = W ; lookup(N,Ns,Vs,V).

is_member(X,[Y|L]) :- X = Y -> true ; is_member(X,L).

member(X,[X|_]).
member(X,[_|L]) :- member(X,L).
```

Figure 10: Meta-circular interpeter

Appendix B

```
% one_eval(++Goal,++Program,++[Name],?[Value],?[Value])
one_eval(G,P,Ns,Vs,Vs1) :- copy_term(Vs,Vs1), eval(G,P,Ns,Vs1).

% all_eval(++Goal,++Program,++[Name],?[Value],?[[Value]])
all_eval(G,P,Ns,Vs,Vss) :-
  all_eval_init(Key),
  (if(eval(G,P,Ns,Vs), (recordz(Key,Vs,_), fail), true) ->
    fail ; key_to_list(Key,Vss)).

% peval(++Goal,++Program,++[Name],?[Value],?Rgoal)
peval(static1(G),P,Ns,Vs,Rg) :-
  one_eval(G,P,Ns,Vs,_) -> Rg = true ; Rg = fail.
peval(static(G),P,Ns,Vs,Rg) :-
  all_eval(G,P,Ns,Vs,Vss) -> make_true_list(Vss,Rg) ; Rg = fail.
peval(basic(N,Args),_,Ns,Vs,basic(N,Rargs)) :-
  residualize_term_list(Args,Ns,Vs,Rargs).
```

```
peval(call(N,Args),P,Ns,Vs,Rg) :-
  length(Args,Arity),
  is_member(pred(N,Arity,ann(Unf,Match,Pbts),Clauses),P),
  (Unf = unfold ->
   (build_actuals(Pbts,Args,Ns,Vs,Nargs),
    unfold_list(Match,Clauses,P,Pbts,Nargs,Rg)) ;
   (find_statics_and_dynamics(Pbts,Args,Ns,Vs,Sargs,Dargs),
    suspend(N,Arity,Sargs,Newn),
    Rg = call(Newn,Dargs))).
peval((G1 , G2),P,Ns,Vs,Rg) :-
  G1 = static1(G) ->
   (one_eval(G,P,Ns,Vs,Vss) -> peval(G2,P,Ns,Vss,Rg) ; Rg = fail) ;
   (G1 = static(G) ->
    (all_eval(G,P,Ns,Vs,Vss) ->
      peval_or_list(G2,P,Ns,Vss,Rg) ; Rg = fail) ;
    (peval(G1,P,Ns,Vs,Rg1), peval(G2,P,Ns,Vs,Rg2), Rg = (Rg1 , Rg2))).
peval((\+ G),P,Ns,Vs,(\+ Rg)) :-
  peval(G,P,Ns,Vs,Rg).
peval((G1 ; G2),P,Ns,Vs,(Rg1 ; Rg2)) :-
  peval(G1,P,Ns,Vs,Rg1), peval(G2,P,Ns,Vs,Rg2).
peval(ifcut(G1,G2,G3),P,Ns,Vs,Rg) :-
  G1 = static1(G) ->
  (one_eval(G,P,Ns,Vs,Vs1) ->
    peval(G2,P,Ns,Vs1,Rg) ; peval(G3,P,Ns,Vs,Rg)) ;
  (G1 = static(G) ->
   (all_eval(G,P,Ns,Vs,[Vs1|_]) ->
     peval(G2,P,Ns,Vs1,Rg) ; peval(G3,P,Ns,Vs,Rg)) ;
   (Rg = ifcut(Rg1,Rg2,Rg3),
    peval(G1,P,Ns,Vs,Rg1), peval(G2,P,Ns,Vs,Rg2),
peval(G3,P,Ns,Vs,Rg3))).
peval(if(G1,G2,G3),P,Ns,Vs,Rg) :-
  G1 = static1(G) ->
  (one_eval(G,P,Ns,Vs,Vss) ->
   peval(G2,P,Ns,Vss,Rg) ; peval(G3,P,Ns,Vs,Rg)) ;
  (G1 = static(G) ->
   (all_eval(G,P,Ns,Vs,Vss) ->
    peval_or_list(G2,P,Ns,Vss,Rg) ; peval(G3,P,Ns,Vs,Rg)) ;
   (Rg = if(Rg1,Rg2,Rg3),
    peval(G1,P,Ns,Vs,Rg1), peval(G2,P,Ns,Vs,Rg2),
peval(G3,P,Ns,Vs,Rg3))).

peval_or_list(G,P,Ns,[Vs|Vss],Rg) :-
  peval(G,P,Ns,Vs,Rg1),
  (Vss = [] ->
    Rg = Rg1 ; (Rg = (Rg1 ; Rg2), peval_or_list(G,P,Ns,Vss,Rg2))).
```

Figure 11: Part of the specializer

Towards Optimization of Full Prolog Programs Guided by Abstract Interpretation

Anne Parrain, Philippe Devienne, Patrick Lebègue *

Laboratoire d'Informatique Fondamentale de Lille

Université de Lille I

59655 Villeneuve d'Ascq   France

{parrain,devienne,lebegue}@lifl.fr

Abstract

In this paper, we propose a partial evaluation system for full Prolog programs based on abstract interpretation. As we deal with non-logical features, we present an elimination method of side-effect predicates preserving the monotonicity of termination, determinism and success set. Abstract interpretation (proposed by [10]) provides to our system information about call and solution patterns arising during resolution, and computes relevant call patterns to have determinism or termination property.

As we add this information directly into programs, we obtain typed programs, and our program transformations can specialise rules. To terminate, we present a clause-indexing method, to deal with our typed logic programs.

1   Introduction

The usual transformations (folding/unfolding techniques) preserve the semantics with respect to the least Herbrand model of the logic programs ([15, 8]). These transformations cannot be applied directly to full Prolog programs, since they do not preserve the operational equivalence (with a standard interpreter) of programs. So, the transformations that we use, take into account full Prolog programs, considering the standard strategy (depth first, leftmost atom).

Some works have been studying transformations preserving a similar operational equivalence [13, 12], considering full Prolog programs [14], without extra-information. Other systems propose transformations of recursive logic

---

*partially supported by the G.D.R. Greco de la Programmation

programs [1], some of them transform only certain recursive predicates to obtain more precise but less general results [2]. In all cases, they use the knowledge (about predicates) of properties like associativity. [3] considers Prolog programs with **cut**, using mode information about predicates. The algorithm for source specialisation of logic programs proposed by [7] is actually based on abstract interpretation, but do not consider full Prolog.

In this paper, we use an abstract interpretation based on OLDT resolution, which gives to our system the set of call and solution patterns arising during the resolution. In a first section, we precise our framework; then, we propose to eliminate side-effect predicates in order to preserve the monotonicity of abstract properties, and to provide the abstract interpreter with pure Prolog programs. In the third section, we propose some program transformations, which lead us to deal with typed rules. That is, if a literal unifies with two rules, only the rule with the same call pattern as the literal has to be selected. So, to conclude, we present an extended WAM indexing method, to take into account such programs.

2 General framework

2.1 An operational equivalence for full Prolog programs

Our aim is to preserve an equivalence in the sense of standard interpreters (unfair, depth first and leftmost atom) between Prolog programs. Two programs are equivalent if they have the same solutions (in the sense of answer-substitutions), in the same order. That extends the logical and denotational semantics for standard interpreters.

To have such equivalence, we have to define an operational semantics for the input/output. So, they are considered to be done with a right-infinite linear tape for each stream (keyboard, screen, files, ...). The user and the program access in mutual exclusion to the read-head, which moves after any reading or writing to the infinite direction.

We call Prolog program an ordered set of Horn clauses, which can have side-effect predicates, and pure Prolog program an ordered set of Horn clauses without side-effect predicates. The order relation on clauses is necessary to preserve solution ordering. We consider SLD-derivation trees in which substitutions are replaced by systems of equations. Thus, any branch in a SLD-tree is labeled by systems of equations such that their union is solvable. To preserve operational equivalence in the sense of standard interpreters, only the first infinite derivation needs to be preserved in the transformed program. The set SSP defined in [5] represents the set of atoms for which there exists a derivation tree containing the empty clause, without any infinite derivation tree at its left-hand side. All solution-nodes that we consider correspond to an atom in SSP.

Definition 1 Strong Operational Equivalence
Let $(\Pi_1, Goal_1)$ and $(\Pi_2, Goal_2)$ be two program-goal couples, they are strongly operationally equivalent if and only if, considering their derivation-tree, there exists a bijection θ:
   $\theta : Solution\text{-}Nodes(\Pi_1, Goal_1) \longrightarrow Solution\text{-}Nodes(\Pi_2, Goal_2)$
   such that θ is compatible with the following points:

1. *let us denote mgu(soln) the answer-substitution of the solution-node soln,*
   $\forall soln \in Solution\text{-}Nodes(\Pi_1, Goal_1)$

$$mgu(soln) = mgu(\theta(soln))$$

2. *the order relation on solution-nodes, considering the depth-first search of the derivation-tree:*

   $\forall soln_1, soln_2 \in Solution\text{-}Nodes(\Pi_1, Goal_1),$

   $soln_1 \leq soln_2 \Leftrightarrow \theta(soln_1) \leq \theta(soln_2)$

Remark: Strong operational equivalence can be defined over a set of variables, denoted by V. The only modified point is 1), where the restriction of the answer-substitution to V is considered:

$$mgu(soln) \uparrow V = mgu(\theta(soln)) \uparrow V$$

2.2 Which non-logical features ?

As we preserve an operational equivalence, we accept non-logical features of Prolog. Even if we have restricted our study to **cut**, **read**, **write**, **assert** and **retract** for at least two reasons:

1. many predefined predicates like **bagof**, **if-then**, **if-then-else**, the disjunction, ..., can be simulated with **cut**, **assert** and **retract**,

2. the predicates like **var**, **functor**, **arg**, ...are deterministic and their behaviour is, in our sense, similar to the behaviour of the **read** predicate.

this study can be simply extended to predicates which delay unification like **freeze**, **dif**, **wait**, ...Nevertheless, we do not deal with programs containing literals as **assert(X)** where **X** is a variable.

In the same way, we consider the negation as failure like a meta-predicate **not**, as it can be simulate with one **cut**:

```
not(X) :- X, !, fail.
not(X).
```

If the behaviour of the **cut**, **read** and **write** is similar in any standard Prolog, there are some differences about the **assert** and **retract** predicates. So, we have chosen languages like Sicstus Prolog and Quintus Prolog, where the **retract** is non-deterministic and the behaviour of the **assert** does not modify the choice points of the ancestor-nodes.

2.3 Which abstract interpretation ?

Generally, abstract interpretation is a partial checking procedure for a program and a property. It is a sound algorithm for properties like termination and determinism:

$$Abs(\Pi, Prop) \longrightarrow yes/unknown$$

The abstract interpretation described in [9, 10] computes information about recursive behaviour of logic programs. It enumerates all solution and call patterns arising during the resolution, and computes relevant call patterns to get termination or determinism property.

This abstract interpretation is based on the OLDT resolution ([16]), and call and solution patterns are seen as typing. So, the usual algebra is extended by considering the variable types. In the following, usual notion of substitution is replaced by systems of equations, disequations, inequations over typed variables.

We present our partial evaluation system with respect to this abstract interpretation, but we could associate it with any other abstract interpretation which is:

- sound for the properties of termination and determinacy;

- complete for the call and solution patterns.

3   Elimination of side-effect predicates

When considering a full Prolog program P and G a goal, the properties of termination, determinism and success set are not preserved by instanciation and abstract interpretation of non-monotonic logic programs is meaningless.

Example 1
```
p(X,b):-!.
p(0,a).
p(s(X),a) :- p(X,a).
```
`:-p(X,Y)` has one solution.
`:-p(X,a)` does not terminate and has an infinity of solutions.

We want both to prune away from Prolog programs non-logical features in order to provide pure Prolog programs for abstract interpretation, and we want to preserve some properties about termination, determinism and success set (a literal is deterministic if its SLD-derivation tree is composed of only one branch).

Let P be a Prolog program, G be a goal and θ be a substitution. We transform P and G in a more general pure Prolog program P' and in a more general pure Prolog goal G', such that:

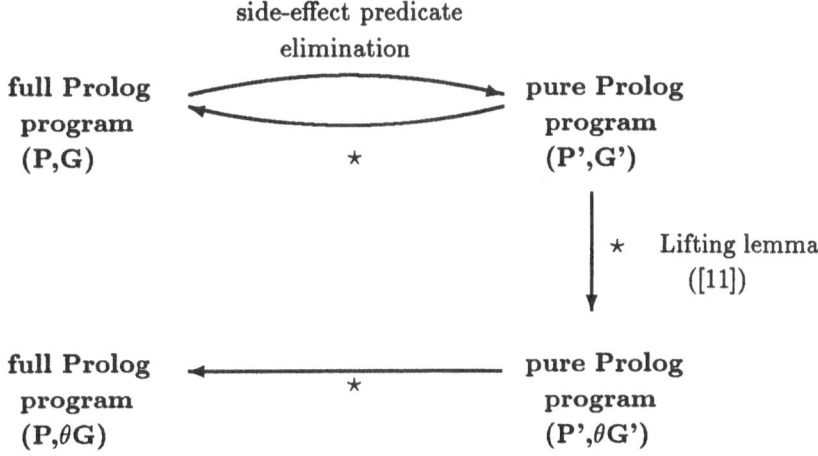

⋆: the properties are preserved.

We now formalize the relation we want to preserve between pure Prolog programs and full Prolog programs. We use the classic definition of a success set of a program P, denoted $SS(P)$ (set of goal-substitution pairs (A, σ) for which there exists a proof tree for A with answer-substitution σ), but we restrict it to a goal (we denoted it $SS(P, A)$).

Definition 2 Strong inclusion relation

Let P_1, P_2 be Prolog programs, G_1 be a goal for P_1, G_2 be a goal for P_2. (P_1, G_1) is strongly included in (P_2, G_2), denoted $(P_1, G_1) \sqsubseteq (P_2, G_2)$ if and only if:

1. (P_2, G_2) terminates $\Rightarrow$ (P_1, G_1) terminates;

2. (P_2, G_2) is deterministic $\Rightarrow$ (P_1, G_1) is deterministic;

3. $SS(P_1, G_1) \subseteq SS(P_2, G_2)$

The weak inclusion relation (denoted $\sqsubset$) is defined in the same manner, but the determinism is not preserved.

The set of Prolog programs is divided in three parts:

- $\Pi_{pur} = \{$pure Prolog programs$\}$

- $\Pi_{ass} = \{$pure Prolog programs $+$ **assert** predicate$\}$

- $\Pi_{nlf} = \{$Prolog programs with **cut**, **read/write**, **assert/retract**$\}$

The **assert** predicate is not considered in the following transformation.

Definition 3 Transformation

$\varphi_1 : \Pi_{nlf} \times \text{Goal} \longrightarrow \Pi_{ass} \times \text{Goal}$
where φ_1 is an homomorphism which adds facts:

1. **cut** $\leftarrow$.

2. **read(_)** $\leftarrow$.

3. **write(_)** $\leftarrow$.

4. each rule of the program is duplicated in a fact:
   retract(rule) $\leftarrow$.

This transformation cancels the behaviour of the **cut**, **read** and **write**: it is similar as replacing them by **true** predicate. The copy of each rule in a fact allows to simulate the non-determinism of the **retract**. It is easy to verify that, given a Prolog program P and a goal G, $(P, G) \sqsubseteq \varphi_1((P, G))$.

Now, the **assert** predicate is considered by the following transformation.

Definition 4 Transformation

$\varphi_2 : \Pi_{ass} \times \text{Goal} \longrightarrow \Pi_{pur} \times \text{Goal}$
where φ_2 is an homomorphism which adds rules:

1. for each literal **assert(X)** in the program (or in the goal), the rule **X** is added to the program.

2. **assert(_)** $\leftarrow$.

We show that for $\forall P \in \Pi_{ass}$, G goal for P, $\varphi_2((P, G)) \sqsubset (P, G)$.

4 Specification and program transformations

Given a program and a goal for this program, abstract interpretation provides, for each predicate, call patterns, solution patterns, properties of determinism and termination.

4.1 Rule specification

The step of specification consists in applying this information to the original full Prolog program. Call and solution patterns for a goal are given as equation and disequation sets over each free variable.

We use these systems of equations as set of lists of equations (each list of equations corresponds to a system of equations, which corresponds to a call-pattern). The $\times$ operator over sets of lists of equations is the cartesian product of the two sets if their union is solvable. The $\times_s$ operator is similar but operates only over lists of equations corresponding to the same call pattern. $A(\Pi) \uparrow H$ is the restriction of the set of call patterns of Π (Prolog program) to the predicate of H, which are compatible to the literal H. $Sol(\Pi) \uparrow H$ is analogous for solution patterns. The restriction of $A(\Pi)$ and $Sol(\Pi)$ to a set of literals is defined too.

$\oplus$ denotes the simple concatenation operator over two lists.

Definition 5 Specification
For any rule $H \leftarrow B_1, B_2, \ldots, B_n$, this transformation can be executed:

- *over the head of the rule:*

$$(A(\Pi) \uparrow H) \ H \leftarrow ((A(\Pi) \uparrow H) \ \times \ (A(\Pi) \uparrow B_1)), B_1, \ldots, B_n$$

- *over the body of the rule (from left to right), this rule:*

$$\leftarrow \ldots (\sigma_i)_{i \in [1,m]}, B_k, B_{k+1}, \ldots, B_n$$

(where $(\sigma_i)_{i \in [1,m]}$ denotes the set of call patterns for B_k computed as follows from the left-hand side of B_k and from the information provided by the abstract interpretation), is replaced by:

$$\leftarrow \ldots (\sigma_i)_{i \in [1,m]}, B_k, (\theta_j)_{j \in [1,n]}, B_{k+1}, \ldots, B_n$$

where

$$(\theta_j)_{j \in [1,n]} = ((\sigma_i)_{i \in [1,m]} \times_s Sol(\Pi) \uparrow (\sigma_i(B_k)_{i \in [1,m]})) \times A(\Pi) \uparrow B_{k+1}$$

- *when all the body of the rule has been specified, the last solution pattern is duplicated behind the head of the rule:*

$$(A(\Pi) \uparrow H) \ H \ ((\sigma_i)_{i \in [1,m]} \times_s Sol(\Pi) \uparrow (\sigma_i(B_n)_{i \in [1,m]})) \uparrow Var(H)$$

Example 2

```
1.      add(0,X,X).
2.      add(s(X),Y,s(Z)) :- add(X,Y,Z).

3.      mul(0,X,0).
4.      mul(s(X),Y,Z) :- mul(X,Y,ZZ), add(Y,ZZ,Z).

        :- mul(X,Y,Z)
```

The following tree and tables present the results of an abstract interpretation applied on this program. We consider an information on terms of the form X:g if the variable X is known ground. (The abstract interpretation defined in [9, 10] provides more precise information, for example branch boundedness on terms with respect to some function symbols).

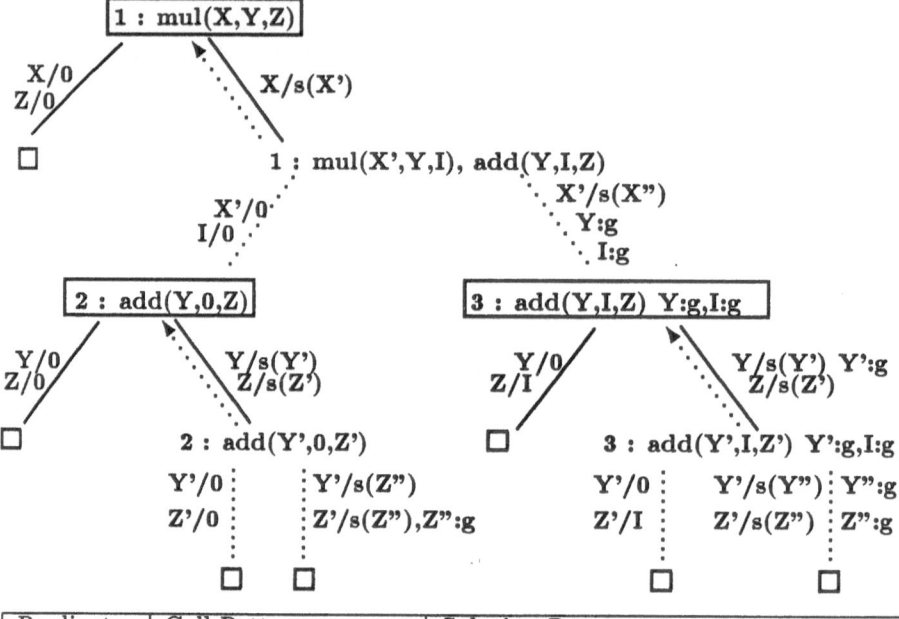

Predicates	Call Patterns	Solution Patterns
add	add(Y,0,Z)	add(0,0,0)
		add(s(Y'),0,s(Y')) Y':g
	add(Y,I,Z) Y:g,I:g	add(0,I,I) I:g
		add(s(Y'),I,s(Z')) Y':g,I:g,Z':g
mul	mul(X,Y,Z)	mul(0,Y,0)
		mul(s(X'),Y,Z) X':g,Y:g,Z:g

Deterministic Call Patterns

add	add(Y,0,Z) Y:g
	add(Y,0,Z) Z:g
	add(X,I,Z) X:g,I:g
mul	mul(X,Y,Z) X:g,Y:g
	mul(X,Y,Z) X:g,Z:g

The result of the specification is:

1. `{[X=0],[X:g]}` `add(0,X,X).` `{[X=0],[X:g]}`
2. `{[Y=0],[X:g,Y:g]}` `add(s(X),Y,s(Z))` `{[Y=0,X=0,Z=0],`
   `[Y=0,X/s(X'),`
   `Z/s(X'),X':g],`
   `[X=0,Y:g,Y=Z],`
   `[X=s(X'),Z=s(Z'),`
   `X':g,Y:g,Z':g]}`

   `:-{[Y=0],[X:g,Y:g]}` `add(X,Y,Z).` `{[Y=0,X=0,Z=0],`
   `[Y=0,X/s(X'),`
   `Z/s(X'),X':g],`
   `[X=0,Y:g,Y=Z],`
   `[X=s(X'),Z=s(Z'),`
   `X':g,Y:g,Z':g]}`

3. `mul(0,X,0).` `{□}`
4. `mul(s(X),Y,Z){...}` `:- mul(X,Y,ZZ),` `{[X=0,ZZ=0],` (1)
   `[X:s(X'),`
   `X':g,Y:g,ZZ:g]}` (2)

   `{(1),(1)⊕[Y:g],`
   `(2)⊕[ZZ=0],(2)}` `add(Y,ZZ,Z).` `{...}`

All abstract information we add in the program does not correspond to the conditions required to get a success, but simply to conditions which will be verified during the execution. An instanciation step after specification allows a simplification of call patterns. Let $((\theta_i)_{i\in[1,m]}, B_j)$ be a literal. If the antiunified of $(\theta_i)_{i\in[1,m]}$ exists and if it can be associated to a concrete substitution σ, then the literal is replaced by $((\theta'_i)_{i\in[1,m]}, \sigma(B_j))$, where $(\theta_i)_{i\in[1,m]} = (\theta'_i)_{i\in[1,m]} \oplus \sigma$.

4.2 Specif operator

The clearing step erase all call and solution patterns. The result is a full Prolog program (it allows to outline the instanciation known by specification for the **read, write, assert** and **retract**).

Intuitively, the Specif operator, denoted by S, is defined by

$$S = \text{clearing} \circ \text{instanciation} \circ \text{specification} \circ \text{abstract interpretation} \circ \varphi_2 \circ \varphi_1$$

The OLDT resolution of $S(S(\Pi))$ and $S(\Pi)$ are quite similar for pure Prolog programs, that is, S is idempotent for pure Prolog programs with respect to OLDT resolution. The predicates **read, write**, and **retract** can be associated to pure Prolog predicates, because of the way they are simulated. On the other side, the transformation φ_2 for the predicate **assert** can be improved by iteration of the Specif operator.

Example 3
Π:
```
p(X):-q1(Y),assert(r(Y)),q2(X).
q1(a).
q2(X):-r(X).
:-p(X)
```

$\varphi_2 \circ \varphi_1(\Pi)$:
```
p(X):-q1(Y),assert(r(Y)),q2(X).
q1(a).
q2(X):-r(X).
r(X).
:-p(X)
```

spec(Π)
```
p(X):-q1(Y),{Y=a},assert(r(Y)),q2(X).
q1(a).
q2(X):-r(X).
:-p(X)
```

clear(inst(spec(Π)))
```
p(X):-q1(Y),assert(r(a)),q2(X).
q1(a).
q2(X):-r(X).
:-p(X)
```

In this example, one iteration of the Specif operator would provide more information: links between `r(X)` and `q1(Y)` are hidden for the abstract interpretation, and that is the specification and instanciation which allow to point it out. If there was a literal like `assert(r(X):-assert(...)...)`, three applications of the Specif operator would be necessary.

There exists a fixpoint for S, which is obtained after a finite number of steps, bounded by maximal overlapping of assert predicates.

4.3 Program transformations

We have studied ([12]) the usual program transformations preserving the strong operational equivalence. These transformations are restrictions of classical folding and unfolding ([15]), but they can be applied on specified programs in a more general manner than on Prolog programs.

Transformations considered are:

- definition of new predicates;

- unfolding on the leftmost atom: a literal can be unfolded only if it is the leftmost non deterministic literal in the body of the rule;

- deterministic unfolding: a literal can be unfolded only if it is deterministic;

- folding: this transformation is the opposite of the deterministic unfolding;

- the transformation proposed in [6]: it is a kind of clearing transformation, which removes from literals useless function symbols, (or equality constraints).

Some additional hypotheses are required concerning side-effects predicates occurring in the (un)folding/(un)folded rules.

A transformation process is a non-deterministic series of considered elementary transformations. That is, from the original program, P_0, a sequence of programs, $P_1, \ldots, P_n, \ldots$, can be built.

In specified programs, a literal has several call patterns. Some of these call patterns may be deterministic. To apply deterministic unfolding, the rule must be divided in two rules: one with non-deterministic call patterns, other with deterministic ones. So, during the step of program transformations, some rules are duplicated, and specialised for some call patterns: it is a kind of rule typing.

Definition 6 Restriction of a set of lists of equations

Let $(\sigma_i)_{i\in[1,n]}$ and $(\theta_j)_{j\in[1,m]}$ be two sets of lists of equations. $(\sigma_i)_{i\in[1,n]} \uparrow_\sigma (\theta_j)_{j\in[1,m]}$ denotes the restriction of the first list to the second, such that:

$$(\sigma_i)_{i\in[1,n]} \uparrow_\sigma (\theta_j)_{j\in[1,m]} = \left\{ \begin{array}{l} \sigma \in (\sigma_i)_{i\in[1,n]} \mid \exists \theta \in (\theta_j)_{j\in[1,m]}, \\ \theta \text{ is a sublist of } \sigma \end{array} \right\}$$

This notion is extended to the restriction of a rule C to a set of lists of equations A. The call patterns of $C \uparrow_\sigma A$ are those of C restricted to A.

Transformation 1 Rule partition

Let C be a rule, A_c be its call patterns, and A be a set of lists of equations. Two rules C_1 and C_2 are obtained from the partition of C with respect to A, where:

$$C_1 = C \uparrow_\sigma A \text{ and } C_2 = C \uparrow_\sigma (A_c - (A_c \uparrow_\sigma A))$$

Definition 7 *The order relation "is derived by" over lists of equations, written $\succeq$, is defined by*
$\forall \sigma, \theta$ *lists of equations, $\sigma \succeq \theta$ iff $\exists \tau$ list of equations such that $\sigma = \theta \oplus \tau$*
(θ is an initial sublist of σ).

We now present an algorithm to divide one list into two lists, with respect to a subset of call patterns of a literal in this rule.

Transformation 2 Determinisation procedure of a literal

Let C be a rule like:

$$\Theta, H_{ead} \leftarrow B_{efore}, \{\Sigma_{det}, \Sigma_{?det}\}, L_{iteral}, A_{fter}$$

where:

- *Θ is the call pattern for C;*

- *H_{ead} and L_{iteral} are atoms;*

- *$\{\Sigma_{det}, \Sigma_{?det}\}$ is the call pattern for L_{iteral}, with Σ_{det} the set of deterministic call patterns for L_{iteral}, and $\Sigma_{?det}$ the set of non-deterministic call patterns;*

- *B_{efore} and A_{fter} are sequences of literals and call patterns.*

1^{rst} *case* : Θ *is divided into two sets,* $\Theta = \{\Theta_{det}, \Theta_{?det}\}$, *such that:*

$$if \ \forall \sigma \in \Sigma_{det}, \ \exists \theta \in \Theta_{det}, \ \sigma \succeq \theta$$

$$and \ if \ \forall \theta \in \Theta_{det}, \ \not\exists \sigma \in \Sigma_{?det}, \ \sigma \succeq \theta$$

then the partition of C *with respect to* θ_{det} *is computed. Two rules* C_{det} *and* $C_{?det}$ *are obtained, and* $P_i = (P_{i-1} - \{C\}) \cup \{C_{det}, C_{?det}\}$

2nd *case* : $\Sigma_{?det}$ *is the set of non-deterministic call patterns for* C, *but:*

- $\forall \sigma \in \Sigma_{?det}$, *each equation in* σ *appears in a deterministic call pattern for* L_{iteral},

- $\exists \tau$ *such that* $\tau\sigma$ *is a deterministic call pattern for* L_{iteral} *and* $\tau \uparrow Var(H_{ead}) = \tau$

then $P_i = P_{i-1} \cup \{C'\}$, *with* C' *builded from* C :

$$\Theta \times \tau, H_{ead} \ \leftarrow \ B_{efore}, \ \{\Sigma_{det}, \Sigma_{?det} \times \tau\}, \ L_{iteral}, \ A_{fter}$$

This transformation is presented with respect to determinism property, but can be done with any other property.

Example 4

By looking at the deterministic call patterns, we remark that three patterns among the four call patterns (for **add**) of the rule 4 are deterministic. Nevertheless, a simple partition of the rule is not possible, since there is no call pattern for the head of the rule. We must extract a constraint which is common for all the deterministic call patterns, and which concerns only the variables of the head of the rule.

In this case, the constraint is [Y:g]. So, the result of the determinisation of the rule 4 for the literal add(Y,ZZ,Z) is (the other clauses are unmodified):

```
4.1.mul(s(X),Y,Z){...}          :- mul(X,Y,ZZ),    {(1),(1)⊕[Y:g],
                                                     (2),(2)⊕[ZZ=0]}
                                   add(Y,ZZ,Z).     {...}
4.2.{[Y:g]} mul(s(X),Y,Z){...}  :- mul(X,Y,ZZ),    {(1)⊕[Y:g],
                                                     (2),(2)⊕[ZZ=0]}
                                   add(Y,ZZ,Z).     {...}
```

All the call patterns for **add** in 4.2 are deterministic, but there is too many clauses (candidate clauses) which unify with **add** to allow the deterministic unfolding. So, we must apply an other partition, more precise, on the rule 4.2. This algorithm is a little bit more complicated than the previous one, because we must deal with the call patterns of the candidate rules.

Intuitively, a matrix must be built: the first row contains the deterministic call patterns of the literal, the first column contains the most general unifiers between the different candidate rules and the literal. All the other elements are computed by unification between the first element of the current row and that of the current column. If all the elements of the matrix are different, then the rule could be entirely determinised. If only some columns have their elements distinct, then the rule could be determinised only for these cases.

The result of this step is:

Deterministic call patterns → mgus ↓	Y:g
Y=0,ZZ=Z	Y=0
Y=s(X), Z=s(Z')	Y=s(X)

The rule 4.2 can be entirely determinised:

```
4.1.              mul(s(X),Y,Z){...}          :- mul(X,Y,ZZ),
                  {(1),(1)⊕[Y:g],
                  (2),(2)⊕[ZZ=0]}            add(Y,ZZ,Z).
4.2.1. {[Y=0]}    mul(s(X),0,Z){...}          :- mul(X,0,ZZ),
                  {(1)⊕[Y=0],
                  (2),(2)⊕[ZZ=0]}            add(0,ZZ,Z).
4.2.2. {[Y/s(Y'), mul(s(X),s(Y'),Z){...}      :- mul(X,s(Y'),ZZ),
       Y':g]}
                  {(1)⊕[Y':g],
                  (2),(2)⊕[ZZ=0]}            add(s(Y'),ZZ,Z).
```

Then, we can apply the deterministic unfolding:

```
4.1.              mul(s(X),Y,Z){...}              :- mul(X,Y,ZZ),
                  {(1),(1)⊕[Y:g],
                  (2),(2)⊕[ZZ=0]}                add(Y,ZZ,Z).
4.2.1. {[Y=0]}    mul(s(X),0,Z){...}              :- mul(X,0,Z).
4.2.2. {[Y/s(Y'), mul(s(X),s(Y'),s(Z')){...}      :- mul(X,s(Y'),ZZ),
       Y':g]}
                  {(1)⊕[Y':g],
                  (2),(2)⊕[ZZ=0]}                add(Y',ZZ,Z').
```

4.4 Extended WAM indexing method

For each predicate, the set of its call patterns with the usual order relation $\leq$ forms an $\vee$-semi-lattice. To connect the compilation of such typed Prolog programs with the classical WAM compilation, we propose a clause-indexing method based on these lattices. We associate the list of the rules to be applied at each node of the lattice. The depth-first search provides to the compiler the rules to apply.

Example 5

The previous program is a simple example:

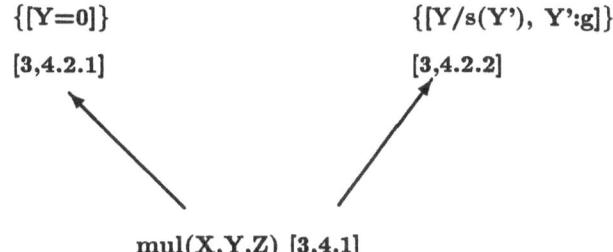

{[Y=0]}   {[Y/s(Y'), Y':g]}

[3,4.2.1]   [3,4.2.2]

mul(X,Y,Z) [3,4.1]

In the usual WAM clause-indexing, there are two levels, as in our representation there are multiple levels: the number of choicepoints that may be created is bounded for each predicate by the depth of its semi-lattice.

5 Conclusion

The figure below summarizes the transformations we have studied (except abstract interpretation).

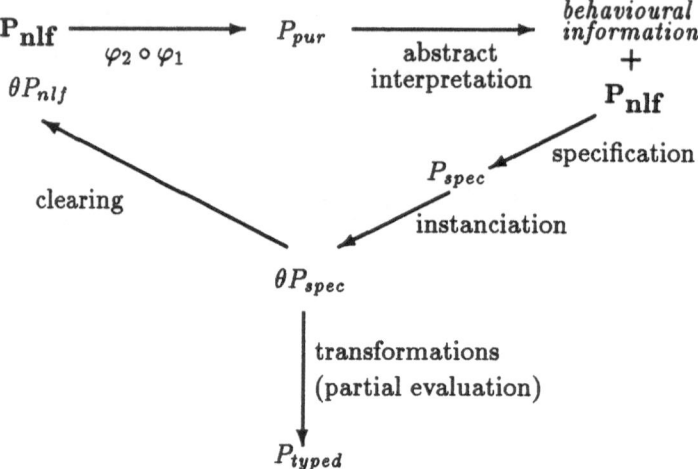

The original program, **P_{nlf}**, after a step of side-effect predicate elimination, is reused to be specificated and transformed with respect to the information provided by abstract interpretation.

We are able to deal with full Prolog programs, and to integrate abstract information. Our aim is now to study and develop some heuristics to provide an algorithm of partial evaluation, using our program transformations.

References

[1] N. Azibi. *TREQUASI : Un système pour la transformation automatique de programmes Prolog récursifs en quasi-itératifs*. PhD thesis, Université de Paris-Sud, December 1987.

[2] D. R. Brough and C. J. Hogger. Compiling associativity into logic programs. *The Journal of Logic Programming*, 4(4):345–360, December 1987.

[3] M. Bugliesi and F. Russo. Partial evaluation in prolog: some improvements about cut. In *Proceedings of the North-American Conference on Logic Programming*, pages 645–660, 1989.

[4] T. Clement and K.-K. Lau, editors. *Logic Program Synthesis and Transformation*, Workshops in Computing, Manchester, July 1991. Springer-Verlag.

[5] J.-P. Delahaye. Sémantique logique et dénotationnelle des interpréteurs Prolog. *Informatique Théorique et Applications*, 22(1):3–42, 1988.

[6] J. Gallagher and M. Bruynooghe. Some low-level source transformations for logic programs. In M. Bruynooghe, editor, *Proceedings of the Second Workshop on Meta-Programming in Logic*, pages 229–244, Leuven, Belgium, April 1990.

[7] J. Gallagher and M. Bruynooghe. The derivation of an algorithm for program specialisation. *New Generation Computing*, 9:305–333, 1991.

[8] T. Kawamura and T. Kanamori. Preservation of stronger equivalence in unfold/fold logic transformation. In *Proceedings of the International Conference on Fifth Generation Computer Systems*, pages 413–421. ICOT, 1988.

[9] C. Lecoutre, P. Devienne, and P. Lebègue. Abstract interpretation and recursive behaviour of logic programs. In Clement and Lau [4], pages 147–166.

[10] C. Lecoutre, P. Devienne, and P. Lebègue. Termination induction by means of an abstract OLDT resolution. In J.-P. Delahaye, P. Devienne, P. Mathieu, and P. Yim, editors, *Premières Journées Francophones sur la Programmation en Logique*, pages 353–373, Lille, May 1992.

[11] J. W. Lloyd. *Foundations of logic programming*. Springer Verlag, 1987.

[12] A. Parrain, P. Devienne, and P. Lebègue. Prolog program transformations and meta-interpreters. In Clement and Lau [4], pages 238–251.

[13] M. Proietti and A. Pettorossi. Semantics preserving transformation rules for prolog. In *ACM Symposium on Partial Evaluation and Semantics Based Program Manipulation*, New-Haven, U.S.A., June 1991.

[14] D. Sahlin. *An Automatic Partial Evaluator for Full Prolog*. PhD thesis, Swedish Institute of Computer Science, Stockholm, March 1991.

[15] H. Tamaki and T. Sato. Unfold/fold transformation of logic programs. In S.-Å. Tärnlund, editor, *Second International Logic Programming Conference*, pages 127–138, Uppsala, 1984.

[16] H. Tamaki and T. Sato. OLD resolution with tabulation. In E. Shapiro, editor, *Proceedings of the Third International Conference on Logic Programming*, Lecture Notes in Computer Science, pages 84–98, London, 1986. Springer-Verlag.

On the Transformation of a Prolog Program to a more efficient binary Program

Bart Demoen   bimbart@cs.kuleuven.ac.be

K.U.Leuven Department of Computer Science
Celestijnenlaan 200 A   B-3001 Leuven Belgium

Abstract. Binary definite programs consist of Horn clauses with at most one negative literal. It is unnatural to program just with such clauses and the naive automatic transformation from a general program to its binary equivalent makes it most often less efficient. Still, sometimes a binary program can solve a problem more efficiently. It is shown that partial evaluation of the alternative binary program, together with the deletion of unnecessary variables and a low level source code transformation, can lead to such an efficient binary program.

1. Introduction

In [Tar], the class of binary definite programs - also called elementary programs - is introduced. The implementation of full Prolog as binary programs is studied in detail in [Dem]: the problem of built-in predicates, cut and in-line optimization is dealt with, so that some disadvantage of binary programs is taken care off. There still remains a quite big space overhead for binary programs, as they construct the continuation on the heap instead of on the local stack and because the heap can't be trimmed on forward execution as can be done with the local stack. Still, [Dem] contains examples which show that both heap consumption and efficiency of a full Horn clause program can be arbitrary better or worse than of its binary equivalent.

Apart from these general facts, binary clauses are attractive from the implementation point of view because they do not need environments on the local stack. Moreover, as their form is so simple, their source level transformation should be easy, in particular, unfolding (see e.g. [Ven]) is very simple for binary programs. Also the temporary register moves optimization (see e.g. [Jan]) is of particular use for binary clauses. Finally, a binary program that is derived from an ordinary program, exposes more clearly the function of some variables in the clauses and it is more natural to take advantage of their function in the binary form.

We will use or discuss three steps in the transformation from a Prolog program to a potentially more efficient binary one: partial evaluation and specialization, deletion of useless variables, register transfer optimization. We are not concerned with changing the control of the original program as in e.g. [Bru]: we believe this is a valuable step, which can be described on the binary program as well, albeit in a somewhat different setting.

The transformation of a Prolog clause to a binary (Prolog) clause is best illustrated by some examples:

	original	binary equivalent
a fact:	a(X) .	a(X,Cont) :- call(Cont) .
a clause:	a(X) :- b(Y) , c(Z) , d(T) .	a(X,Cont) :- b(Y, c(Z, d(T,Cont))) .
query	?- a(X,Y) , b(Y,Z) .	?- a(X,Y,b(Y,Z,true)) .

For clauses with only conjunctions in the body, this transformation can be defined by the predicate bintrans/2:

```
bintrans((H :- B),(NewH :- NewB)) :- ! ,
            bt(H,Cont,NewH) , bintrans(B,Cont,NewB) .
bintrans(H,(NewH :- call(Cont))) :- bt(H,Cont,NewH) .

bintrans((Goal,RestB),Cont,Body) :- ! ,
            bt(Goal,NewC,Body) , bintrans(Body,Cont,NewC) .
bintrans(Goal,Cont,NewGoal) :- bt(Goal,Cont,NewGoal) .

bt(Goal,Cont,NewGoal) :-
            Goal =.. [N|Args] ,
            append(Args,[Cont],NewArgs) ,
            NewGoal =.. [N|NewArgs] .
```

We call this the naive transformation to binary form.

The transformation of full Prolog - i.e. clauses with disjunctions, if-then-else and built-in predicates, in particular cut - as well as the execution of full binary Prolog and how to get rid of the metacall, is treated in [Dem].

We will also make use of an alternative transformation - see also [Dem] - which is illustrated by the transformation of

h(X,Y) :- a(X,I) , b(I,J) , c(J,K) , d(K,Y) .

into its binary form:

h(X,Y,C) :- a(X,I,env1(I,J,K,Y,C)) .
env1(I,J,K,Y,C) :- b(I,J,env2(J,K,Y,C)) .
env2(J,K,Y,C) :- c(J,K,d(K,Y,C)) .

Here the continuation is build up incrementally: it results in general to more heap intensive and less efficient programs. Still, we will use this alternative form as the start for further transformations.

The next section works out some transformations on a particular example and tries to generalize every concrete step. Section 3 lists the results of the measurements on the different transformed programs.

2. A worked out example

Some generally applicable transformations are shown on a sameleaves program:

```
sameleaves(leaf(L),leaf(L)) .
sameleaves(tree(T1,T2),tree(S1,S2)) :-
               getleaf(T1,T2,L,T) ,
               getleaf(S1,S2,L,S) ,
               sameleaves(T,S) .

getleaf(leaf(A),C,A,C) .
getleaf(tree(A,B),C,L,O) :- getleaf(A,tree(B,C),L,O) .

                    program orig
```

It works according to the specification:

tree T and tree S have the same leaves, if
both are a leaf with the same value
or
they are both trees, and they have the same left most leaf and the rests of each tree
(i.e. after removing the left most leaf) have the same leaves

The original program is probably the one any Prolog programmer would naturally write starting from the above specification. But, it is not the most efficient, as the following equivalent hand-written binary program shows:

```
sameleaves(leaf(L),leaf(L)) .
sameleaves(tree(T1,T2),tree(S1,S2)) :- g1(T1,T2,S1,S2) .

g1(leaf(L),T,S1,S2) :- g2(S1,S2,L,T) .
g1(tree(A,B),C,S1,S2) :- g1(A,tree(B,C),S1,S2) .

g2(leaf(L),S,L,T) :- sameleaves(T,S) .
g2(tree(A,B),S2,L,T) :- g2(A,tree(B,S2),L,T) .

                    program target
```

The original program and the target program are equivalent in the Prolog sense.

It is not a natural program to write, but it is about 30% faster than the original sameleaves program ! (the exact amount might depend on the implementation at hand, but was largely confirmed on different implementations) We call it the target program, because we want to transform the original program into this more efficient one, using some general transformation techniques.

Applying the alternative transformation to *orig*, leads to the program *bin1*: as expected *orig* is better than *bin1* (see section 3).

```
sameleaves(leaf(L),leaf(L),Cont) :- call(Cont) .
sameleaves(tree(T1,T2),tree(S1,S2),Cont) :-
                    getleaf(T1,T2,L,T,env(S1,S2,L,S,T,Cont)) .

env(S1,S2,L,S,T,Cont) :- getleaf(S1,S2,L,S,sameleaves(T,S,Cont)) .

getleaf(leaf(A),C,A,C,Cont) :- call(Cont) .
getleaf(tree(A,B),C,L,O,Cont) :- getleaf(A,tree(B,C),L,O,Cont) .

                        program bin1
```

The following transformations are applied successively on *bin1*:

> specialize getleaf/5 and partially evaluate env/6 away
> specialize sameleaves/3: its top-level continuation is true/0
> a variable occurring only once in the body is eliminated
> three variables occurring twice, but only in the body, are eliminated
> register move optimization

2.1. Specialize getleaf/5 and partially evaluate env/6

bin1 contains two non-recursive calls to getleaf/5: this would not have been so apparent if the naive binary transformation would have been used instead of the alternative one. It is then a straightforward step to introduce two copies of getleaf - named g1 and g2 - one for each call. Now we can make the observation that g1 is called with a continuation argument with functor env/6 and g2 is called with a continuation argument with functor sameleaves/3, so that the functors of these arguments can be deleted and the metacall in the base cases can be evaluated. Then, the call to env/6 is unfolded. This leaves us with the program *bin2*. From the results, one sees that *bin2* performs close to the original program, both in space and time.

bin2 can be obtained from *bin1* automatically: in fact, a syntactic variant of *bin2* was produced by a partial evaluation system written by John Gallagher [Gal].

```
sameleaves(leaf(L),leaf(L),Cont) :- call(Cont) .
sameleaves(tree(T1,T2),tree(S1,S2),Cont) :-
                    g1(T1,T2,L,T,S1,S2,L,S,T,Cont) .

g1(leaf(A),C,A,C,S1,S2,L,S,T,Cont) :- g2(S1,S2,L,S,T,S,Cont) .
g1(tree(A,B),C,L,O,S1,S2,L,S,T,Cont) :-
                    g1(A,tree(B,C),L,O,S1,S2,L,S,T,Cont) .

g2(leaf(A),C,A,C,T,S,Cont) :- sameleaves(T,S,Cont) .
g2(tree(A,B),C,L,O,T,S,Cont) :- g2(A,tree(B,C),L,O,T,S,Cont) .

                        program bin2
```

2.2. Specialize sameleaves/3

Assuming that sameleaves is always called with continuation true/0, we can further specialize the program to *bin3*: given a program in which sameleaves is called, one could for every call to sameleaves make a specialized version, so assuming that the continuation is the goal true, is general enough for our purpose.

```
sameleaves(leaf(L),leaf(L)) .
sameleaves(tree(T1,T2),tree(S1,S2)) :- g1(T1,T2,L,T,S1,S2,L,S,T) .

g1(leaf(A),C,A,C,S1,S2,L,S,T) :- g2(S1,S2,L,S,T,S) .
g1(tree(A,B),C,L,O,S1,S2,L,S,T) :- g1(A,tree(B,C),L,O,S1,S2,L,S,T) .

g2(leaf(A),C,A,C,T,S) :- sameleaves(T,S) .
g2(tree(A,B),C,L,O,T,S) :- g2(A,tree(B,C),L,O,T,S) .

                    program bin3
```

An improvement is hardly noticeable, but *bin3* is easier to reason about because it doesn't contain the metacall.

2.3. A variable occurring only once in the body is eliminated

The variable S in the 8th argument of the call to g1 in the body of sameleaves, occurs only once in that clause. So, S is a void variable, conveying no information. Also, its value - after this call to g1 has succeeded - does not contribute to the solution, since S does not appear in the head of the clause. So, we should try to find a way to get rid of it. This is particularly easy in this case, because the 8th argument of g1 in the recursive call is just passed on, and in the base case, it is duplicated and - still free - passed on to g2. And so we arrive at *bin4*:

```
sameleaves(leaf(L),leaf(L)) .
sameleaves(tree(T1,T2),tree(S1,S2)) :- g1(T1,T2,L,T,S1,S2,L,T) .

g1(leaf(A),C,A,C,S1,S2,L,T) :- g2(S1,S2,L,S,T,S) .
g1(tree(A,B),C,L,O,S1,S2,L,T) :- g1(A,tree(B,C),L,O,S1,S2,L,T) .

g2(leaf(A),C,A,C,T,S) :- sameleaves(T,S) .
g2(tree(A,B),C,L,O,T,S) :- g2(A,tree(B,C),L,O,T,S) .

                    program bin4
```

This transformation - getting rid of a void variable in a call - can be automated: one makes a specialized version of the called predicate and deletes the particular argument both in the call and the specialized version. If the specialized version has now a call to the original predicate and a void variable at the same place, then this call to the original predicate can be substituted by a call to the specialized predicate. We show the steps on the example:

the second definition of sameleaves becomes:

sameleaves(tree(T1,T2),tree(S1,S2)) :- gl3(T1,T2,L,T,S1,S2,LT) .

and define gl3:

gl3(leaf(A),C,A,C,S1,S2,L,T) :- g2(S1,S2,L,S,T,S) .
gl3(tree(A,B),C,L,O,S1,S2,L,T) :- g1(A,tree(B,C),L,O,S1,S2,L,S,T) .

now the call to g1 in the body of gl3 has again the void variable in the 8th argument, and can be replaced by a call to gl3.

To be really useful, the conditions for the transformation above should be weakened. Moreover, although this transformation is described at source level, one can relate it easily to the (WAM) execution model for the original program: S in the second clause of sameleaves, is only referred to when at the second call to getleaf, so there is no need to create it before g2 is called.

There is another, more direct way to achieve the deletion of this void variable: the alternative transformation (see [Dem]) could have as a result on

h(X,Y) :- a(X,I) , b(I,J) , c(J,K) , d(K,Y) .

the binary clauses:

h(X,Y,C) :- a(X,I,env1(I,Y,C)) .
env1(I,Y,C) :- b(I,J,env2(J,Y,C)) .
env2(J,Y,C) :- c(J,K,d(K,Y,C)) .

With this transformation, the variable S would never have appeared as a void variable in the body of sameleaves.

2.4. Variables occurring twice, but only in the body, are eliminated

The variable T in the call to g1 in sameleaves, occurs twice (in the 4th and the 8th position), but not in the head of the clause. Again, one can argue that it conveys no information, except that these two argument positions match. Can we find a way to get rid of them? Observe that the 4th and 8th argument of the recursive clause for g1 is just passed along: WAM code for these argument positions is non-existent. In the base case, the 4th argument is bound to C, so the 8th argument has the same binding and the T in the call to g2 could be replaced by C. And this finishes the reasoning on why the 4th and 8th argument in g1 can be deleted. The new program is program *bin5*.

Referring to the original program, we see that T is an output argument in the first call to getleaf. Other authors have suggested that such an output variable could be created only at the moment of the success of the call (see e.g. [Mel]). That is part of what happened here. The other part is that it is clear (syntactically) from the original and the binary program, that the output parameter is only needed in the continuation and therefore, in the binary program, it loses its function as an output argument completely.

```
sameleaves(leaf(L),leaf(L)) .
sameleaves(tree(T1,T2),tree(S1,S2)) :- g1(T1,T2,L,S1,S2,L) .

g1(leaf(A),C,A,S1,S2,L) :- g2(S1,S2,L,S,C,S) .
g1(tree(A,B),C,L,S1,S2,L) :- g1(A,tree(B,C),L,S1,S2,L) .


g2(leaf(A),C,A,C,T,S) :- sameleaves(T,S) .
g2(tree(A,B),C,L,O,T,S) :- g2(A,tree(B,C),L,O,T,S) .

                 program bin5
```

A similar reasoning can be applied to the variable L in sameleaves (resulting in *bin6* - not reproduced here), and the variable S in the non-recursive call to g2 (resulting in *bin7*). *bin7* is actually the *target* program.

Getting rid of variables not occurring in the head, has a wide applicability: many programs have clauses of the form:

$$a(In,Out) :- b(In,O1) , c(O1,O2) , d(O2,Out) .$$

whose binary form is

$$a(In,Out,C) :- b(In,O1,env(O1,O2,Out,C)) .$$
$$env(O1,O2,Out,C) :- c(O1,O2,d(O2,Out,C)) .$$

First one specializes b so that it takes into account that its continuation is always env and one partially evaluates env:

$$a(In,Out,C) :- bspec(In,O1,O1,O2,Out,C) .$$

Then one notices that O2 is a void variable and one deletes it from the specialized version of bspec/6.

$$a(In,Out,C) :- bspec(In,O1,O1,Out,C) .$$

Now, O1 occurs twice, but not in the head, so get rid of it in bspec. And in bspec, there is big chance that O2 occurs twice in some goal, but never in the head, so one can also get rid of this occurrence of O2. Note however that such elimination of variables is not always possible: a notable example is (a binary version of) the naive reverse program.

The above transformation for logic programs (not for Prolog) has been described in [Pro]: the application of this technique to binary clauses is still under investigation.

2.5. Register move optimization

The optimization of the number of register moves, is a low-level issue, not usually dealt with at the source level [Jan]. It is certainly true that a programmer should not care too much about it, but an automatic program transformation tool can easily take it into account at the source level: in WAM, arguments are passed via the argument registers. From this it follows that in a clause like

$$a(X,1) :- b(X) .$$

no code is generated for X, since X arrives in argument register 1, and leaves via argument register 1. On the other hand, a clause like

$$a(1,X) :- b(X) .$$

needs a register move from register 2 to 1.

Also,
$$a(X) :- b(1,X) .$$

needs one more move than

$$a(X) :- b(X,1) .$$

So, the order of the arguments in head and the first call of the body, determine the number of moves needed. Since in a binary program, all bodies have just one goal, it is clear that finding an optimal order is worthwhile. On the other hand, in general, an optimal order might depend on the actual input for the program, because different clauses of the same predicate might have a different local optimal order.

One strategy is bottom-up, reordering the arguments of a goal and propagating this reordering to the goals and heads with the same name/arity: we start by reordering the arguments of the call to g1 in sameleaves: since argument register 2 is occupied still when T2 in the head must be treated, it is better to let T2 switch places with S1 in the body goal. Then, the arguments in the head of g1 have to be reordered, since the order of the arguments of a call to g1 was changed, and the arguments of all the other calls to g1 must be changed as well. Then the arguments in the call to g2 can be reordered. The arguments of the recursive call to g1 are left unchanged, because g1 was treated already: still, by introducing a new version of g1, one could reorder also the arguments of the recursive call, but in this case, the order turns out to be optimal already anyway.

In this way, the program *bin8* was derived and it is even better than the target program.

The top-down strategy - reorder the arguments of the head and propagate the change - leads to program *bin9*, and it leads to better performance in this case. Note that default indexing can be lost by changing the order of the arguments: in ProLog by BIM, an 'index'-directive tells the compiler which argument(s) to index on. Such directives can also be generated automatically.

```
sameleaves(leaf(L),leaf(L)) .
sameleaves(tree(T1,T2),tree(S1,S2)) :- g1(T1,S1,T2,S2) .

g1(leaf(A),S1,C,S2) :- g2(A,S1,C,S2) .
g1(tree(A,B),S1,C,S2) :- g1(A,S1,tree(B,C),S2) .

g2(A,leaf(A),T,C) :- sameleaves(T,C) .
g2(L,tree(A,B),T,C) :- g2(L,A,T,tree(B,C)) .
```

program bin8

```
sameleaves(leaf(L),leaf(L)) .
sameleaves(tree(T1,T2),tree(S1,S2)) :- g1(T2,S2,T1,S1) .

g1(C,S2,leaf(A),S1) :- g2(C,S2,A,S1) .
g1(C,S2,tree(A,B),S1) :- g1(tree(B,C),S2,A,S1) .

:- g2/4 index 4 .

g2(T,C,A,leaf(A)) :- sameleaves(T,C) .
g2(T,C,L,tree(A,B)) :- g2(T,tree(B,C),L,A) .
```

program bin9

In both strategies, one can start with any clause for the reordering.

3. The results

All the above programs have been run on a SPARCstation 1, with ProLog by BIM release 3.0.1 April 1991. It was considered relevant to measure the maximal heap consumption (in number of entries) and the time (in seconds) for a particular query. The measured goal was of the form sameleaves(T,T) or sameleaves(T,T,true)

with T a full tree of depth 15. The generation of this tree is of course not included in the results below.

program	heap	time
orig	294.816	1.22
target	196.515	0.89
bin1	622.486	1.58
bin2	294.816	1.28
bin3	294.816	1.28
bin4	294.816	1.26
bin5	262.049	1.14
bin6	229.282	0.97
bin7 = target	196.515	0.89
bin8	196.515	0.85
bin9	196.515	0.83

4. Conclusion

We have shown that a binary program can be more efficient than the original program it stems from. The final program is arrived at by applying known techniques from partial evaluation and specialization and elimination of variables not occurring in the head of a binary clause. Finally, also register transfer optimization - of particular importance for binary clauses - can be performed at the source level and has a significant impact. All these transformations can be automated.

We believe that the study of binary clauses is interesting not only for performance reasons, but also because transformations on full Prolog have their equivalent in binary programs, and vice versa, but the corresponding transformations might look very different. E.g. partial evaluation and specialization for binary programs amounts sometimes to specialization of a call with respect to its continuation: such a specialization has never been studied as far as we know. Also, techniques of compile time garbage collection when applied to binary programs, are related to the compile time detection of tail recursion optimization for general clauses. And the elimination of unnecessary variables in the binary setting, looks different from the same technique applied to full Prolog.

We conclude that the concept of binary programs can be used as a continuation based implementation technique for full Prolog as in the BinProlog system by Paul Tarau, or as a programming style or as a vehicle to learn more about Prolog implementation and program transformation in general. We advocate strongly the investigation of all three possibilities.

5. Acknowledgment

The author thanks DPWB for support through project RFO/AI/02 and IT/IF/4.

6. References

[Bru]   M.Bruynooghe, D. De Schreye, B.Krekels, 'Compiling Control', Proc. Third Symposium on Logic Programming, Salt Lake City, 1986, pp. 70-77

[Dem]   B. Demoen, A. Marien, 'Implementation of Prolog as binary definite Programs' Proceedings of the Second Russion Conference on Logic Programming, Lecture Notes in Artificial Intelligence, 592, p. 165-176, March 1992

[Gal]   J. Gallagher, private communication, April 1991

[Jan]   G. Janssens, B. Demoen, A. Marien, 'Improving the register allocation in WAM by reordering unification' Proceeding of the International Conference & Symposium on Logic Programming, Seattle, Washington Aug 1988

[Mel]   C.S. Mellish, 'Some Global Optimizations for a Prolog Compiler', Journal of Logic Programming, 2(1):43-66,1985

[Pro]   M. Proietti, A. Pettorossi, 'Unfolding - Definition - Folding, in this Order, for avoiding unnecessary Variables in Logic Programs', Proceedings of PLILP'91, pp. 347-358, (eds) P. Deransart & J. Maluszynski, Springer-Verlag 1991

[Tar]   P. Tarau, M. Boyer, 'Elementary Logic Programs', Proceedings of PLILP'90, pp. 159-173, (eds) P. Deransart & J. Maluszynski, Springer-Verlag 1990

[Ven]   R. Venken, 'A Prolog meta-interpreter for partial evaluation and its application to source-to-source transformation and query optimisation', Proc. ECAI'84, Pisa 1984

[War]   D.H.D. Warren, 'An Abstract Prolog Instruction Set' Technical Report, SRI International, Artificial Intelligence Center, August 1983

Efficient Compilation of Lazy Narrowing into Prolog

José Andrés Jiménez-Martín   Julio Mariño-Carballo

Juan José Moreno-Navarro

LSIIS, Facultad de Informática

Universidad Politécnica de Madrid

Campus de Montegancedo, Boadilla del Monte

28660 Madrid, Spain

{ajimenez,jmarino,jjmoreno}@fi.upm.es

Abstract

The paper presents new techniques for the transformation of lazy narrowing in logic programs. A formalism, called *demand patterns*, is introduced, and used to define a demand driven strategy to compute lazy narrowing. The strategy is used to produce standard PROLOG code from programs written in a functional-logic language. Our method has a number of advantages over other approaches. While it can compute a larger class of programs, it needs less reevaluation effort, and fully uses efficient elements of PROLOG compilers. The gain of efficiency is shown by presenting the execution times of some example programs.

1 Introduction

In the last years, the integration of functional and logic programming languages has been an active area of research (cf. [BL86, dGL86] for surveys). The goal for this integration is to add the advantages of both models (polymorphic typing, lazy evaluation, higher order facilities in the case of functional programming; the expressive power of logical variables, unification, and deductive inference from logic programming).

There are two general approaches to the integration. The so called *functional logic languages* use a functional syntax for the language where predicates are implemented as boolean functions. Narrowing is used as operational semantics. This approach has been taken in [Re85, Re87] and the language BABEL [MR88, MR92]. The alternative approach considers the combination of predicates defined by a set of Horn clauses with functions defined by a set of equations. Examples are EQLOG [GM84], FUNLOG [SY86] and K-LEAF [BGLMP87, BCGMP89]. The operational semantics is SLD resolution guided by semantic unification. Under some conditions, this strategy is equivalent to narrowing and it could be simulated by transforming clauses and equations into a flat form and then using pure SLD-resolution with a dynamic selection function, as is the case for K-LEAF [BGM88].

Lazy evaluation is a key feature in the integration of the two paradigms, making the languages more expressive because it allows us to write highly modular programs [Hu84], to define partial and non strict functions and to use the technique of infinite objects. However, the combination of laziness with logic programming may result in a conflict for a given strategy because of backtracking. The evaluation order in using the rules and evaluating expressions is an important point. On one hand, we have the risk of non-termination. An expression E can be delayed and, when its value needed, evaluated later, but if the expression E has infinitely many answers and all the values are not useful for the computation, it could be very late to use an alternative branch and the infinite values for E can be computed without success. Nevertheless, an eager strategy would yield the result by evaluating first E, and then decide the correct alternative to use, depending on E's value. On the other hand, if the evaluation of an expression is delayed and its evaluation is affected by backtracking, the expression can be computed several times instead of once in an eager strategy. In such cases, efficiency is penalized.

These problems are common to several implementations of functional logic languages. In particular, they cannot compute some simple examples even when they do not need lazy evaluation. Most of these examples deal with the computation of inverse functions, a very useful logic programming technique.

Some authors [BCM89, KLMR90, MKLR90, Ha90, ChL91] have developed direct and efficient implementation techniques based on abstract machines for languages which integrate functional and logic programming. But another way to obtain an easy, portable and relatively efficient implementation is to translate the code to PROLOG and to execute it in a ordinary PROLOG interpreter or compiler. Considerable attention has been devoted to the transformation of term rewriting (in particular, lazy rewriting) in logic programs [Na86, An91a, An91b]. Less effort has been invested in the transformation of narrowing. [vEY87] implements innermost narrowing by a translation to a set of Horn clauses. As far as we know, only [Ch91] treats the problem of lazy narrowing. He developes some techniques for this problem, working with the language K-LEAF. Although the paper contains a lot of interesting ideas, the techniques developed there share some of the problems mentioned above.

In this paper, we present an efficient technique for the implementation of lazy functional logic languages solving some of these problems. The technique is applied to get a compilation of these languages into PROLOG. Only standard features of PROLOG are used, without working on a specific PROLOG implementation or extension (as in [Na91] by using coroutining). Our approach is more efficient than others presented in the literature. We use BABEL as the specific language used to show the transformation. However, it is easy to see that it can be considered as a general scheme for compiling lazy narrowing into PROLOG.

The rest of the paper is organized as follows. Section 2 briefly describes the syntax and the lazy narrowing semantics of the language BABEL. Section 3 discusses the strategies to implement it and points out some problems and solutions. Section 4 contains the definition of the translation of a BABEL program to a PROLOG program. The management of primitive functions, especially equality, is the goal of section 5. Some optimizations are sketched in section 6, while section 7 briefly discusses some related work and presents experimental results. Finally, section 8 summarizes the conclusions and points out future work areas.

2 An Overview of the Language

We will present BABEL in an informal manner. The examples used later in the paper will help in understanding the use of the language.

First of all we will start with a couple of BABEL programs. The first one computes the *fibonacci* function in the straightforward manner. This function is used to calculate fibonacci numbers lesser than 5. The successor representation of natural numbers is used.

```
fun   plus : nat → nat → nat.        fun   fib : nat → nat.
      plus 0 Y := Y.                        fib 0 := s 0.
      plus (s X) Y := s (plus X Y).         fib (s 0) := s (s 0).
                                            fib (s(s N)) :=
                                                plus (fib N) (fib (s N)).
```

```
        %Predicate to decide if X is a fibonacci number
        pred   fib_nb : nat
               fib_nb X := ((fib Y) = X) → true.
        %Rules for less should be added
        eval   (less X 5), (fib_nb X).
```

The second program is equivalent to the previous one but computes the fibonacci function by using an infinite list with all the fibonacci sequence. Only a language with lazy evaluation can compute this kind of programs.[1] Both programs compute sequentially the values 1, 2, 3 for X.

```
%Infinite sequence of fibonacci numbers
fun   fib_nbs:nat→nat→(list nat).      fun   nth:nat→(list nat)→nat.
      fib_nbs X Y :=                         nth 0 [X|Xs] := X.
          [X|fib_nbs Y (plus X Y)].          nth (suc N) [X|Xs] := nth N Xs.
```

```
        %New predicate to decide if X is a fibonacci number
        pred   fib_nb : nat
               fib_nb X := ((nth N (fib_nbs 1 2)) = X) → true.
        %Rules for plus, less should be added
        eval   (less X 5), (fib_nb X).
```

BABEL is a typed language, using a Miranda-like type system [Tu85], where currying is the way to work with higher order functions. However, for the sake of simplicity, the presentation will be based on the first order subset of the language only. Section 5 will discuss this point with respect to the translation to PROLOG.

Let $DC = \bigcup_{n \in \mathbb{N}} DC^n$ and $FS = \bigcup_{n \in \mathbb{N}} FS^n$ be ranked alphabets of *constructors* and *function symbols* respectively. We assume that these alphabets contain some *primitive symbols*, including at least the constructors of types *bool* (with constants 'true' and 'false'), *nat* and *list*, the usual boolean operators, the weak equality operator and conditional operators. In the following,

---

[1] Note that the complexity of this program is $O(n)$ while the previous one needs exponential time.

letters $a, b, c, d, \ldots$ are used for constructors, letters $f, g, h \ldots$ for function symbols and capital letters $X, Y, Z \ldots$ for the elements of the set Var of variables. A PROLOG-like syntax for lists is allowed.

The expressions of the language are the following:

$$
\begin{array}{llll}
Expressions \ M, N \ldots \in Exp ::= & X & & X \in Var \\
& | & (c \ M_1 \ldots M_n) & \text{Construction} \\
& & & \% \ c \in DC^n, n \geq 0 \\
& | & (f \ M_1 \ldots M_n) & \text{Function application} \\
& & & f \in FS^n, n \geq 0
\end{array}
$$

In particular, we get expressions built from the primitive function symbols:

$\neg B$	Negation	$(B \rightarrow M)$	Guarded expression
(B_1, B_2)	Conjunction		**if_then**
$(B_1; B_2)$	Disjunction	$(B \rightarrow M_1 \square M_2)$	Conditional expression
$(M_1 = M_2)$	Weak equality		**if_then_else**

A BABEL *program* consists of a set of defining rules for the non predefined symbols in FS. Let $f \in FS^n$. Each defining *rule* for f must have the form

$$
lhs: \quad f \ t_1 \ldots t_n := \underbrace{\{B \rightarrow\}}_{\text{optional guard}} \underbrace{M}_{\text{body}} \quad : rhs
$$

and satisfy the following restrictions, in order to ensure that BABEL functions are functions in the mathematical sense:

1. *Data Patterns*: t_i's are terms.

2. *Left Linearity*: $f \ t_1 \ldots t_n$ does not contain multiple variable occurrences.

3. *Restrictions on free variables*: Variables occurring in the rhs but not in the lhs are only allowed in the guard.

4. *Nonambiguity*: For two different rules for the same function at least one of the three following cases must hold:

   (a) their left hand sides are not unifiable.

   (b) if the lhs unify with most general unifier σ, the bodies are identical after applying σ

   (c) their guards are incompatible.[2]

BABEL embeds pure PROLOG as a particular case, since relations can be defined as boolean functions and Horn clauses can be expressed as guarded rules with 'true' as body.

BABEL works with a *lazy* narrowing mechanism. Hence, it tries to narrow expressions at outermost narrowable positions. Narrowing at inner positions is performed only if it is demanded (by the pattern in the lhs of some rule) and contributes to some later narrowing step at an outer position. Now we sketch a formal specification of lazy narrowing.

---

[2]Incompatibility [KLMR91] is a decidable syntactical property of two boolean expressions which guarantees that they cannot be reduced to true.

The *Narrowing rule* describes how to apply a BABEL rule through unification. We have

$$f\, M_1 \ldots M_n \longrightarrow_{\sigma_{out}} R\sigma_{in}$$

if there is some variant $f\, t_1 \ldots t_n := R$ of a rule in the program which shares no variables with $f\, M_1 \ldots M_n$ and is such that $f\, t_1 \ldots t_n$ and $f\, M_1 \ldots M_n$ are unifiable with m.g.u. $\sigma = \sigma_{in} \cup \sigma_{out}$ where σ_{in} resp. σ_{out} records the binding variables in $f\, t_1 \ldots t_n$ resp. $f\, M_1 \ldots M_n$.

"M narrows in one step to N with answer substitution σ_{out}", in symbols

$$M \Longrightarrow_{\sigma_{out}} N$$

is specified as follows:

- Narrowing arguments in a construction:

$$\frac{M_i \Longrightarrow_{\sigma_{out}} N_i}{c\, M_1 \ldots M_i \ldots M_n \Longrightarrow_{\sigma_{out}} c\,(M_1\sigma_{out}) \ldots N_i \ldots (M_n\sigma_{out})}$$

- Outermost narrowing by application of a rule:

$$\frac{f\, M_1 \ldots M_n \longrightarrow_{\sigma_{out}} N}{f\, M_1 \ldots M_n \Longrightarrow_{\sigma_{out}} N} \quad (f \in FS^n)$$

- Inner narrowing step (allowed only if it is demanded and contributes to some later narrowing at an outer position):

$$\frac{M_i \Longrightarrow_{\sigma_{out}} N}{f\, M_1 \ldots M_i \ldots M_n \Longrightarrow_{\sigma_{out}} f\,(M_1\sigma_{out}) \ldots N \ldots (M_n\sigma_{out})}$$

Finally, the *Narrowing relation* is defined as follows: "M narrows in several steps to N with answer substitution σ_{out}", in symbols

$$M \overset{*}{\Longrightarrow}_{\sigma_{out}} N$$

is defined inductively by

$$M \overset{*}{\Longrightarrow}_{\{\}} M \qquad \frac{M \Longrightarrow_{\sigma_{out,1}} M_1 \quad M_1 \overset{*}{\Longrightarrow}_{\sigma_{out,rest}} M'}{M \overset{*}{\Longrightarrow}_{\sigma_{out}} M}$$
$$\text{where } \sigma_{out} = \sigma_{out,1}\,\sigma_{out,rest} \mid vars(M)$$

If $M \overset{*}{\Longrightarrow}_{\sigma_{out}} N$ we speak of a *lazy narrowing* computation with *answer* σ_{out} and *result* N. For a practical implementation, we are only interested in results of goals in normal form, i.e. N is a term, and any reduction finishing in a non-reducible expression which is not a term initiates a backtracking.

Lazy narrowing is proved to be sound and complete. A more detailed presentation of BABEL's operational semantics is given in [MR88, MR92], where a discussion of declarative semantics and soundness and completeness issues can be found too.

3   Strategies for the Implementation

As we have said, the lazy narrowing mechanism is sound and complete. However, the concrete definition of a strategy guiding the narrowing process is very important for the practical computation of programs. The usual pure outermost strategy, found in the literature, is the following:

1. Select one rule for the outermost redex.

2. Evaluate the arguments until they have the shape of formal parameters.

3. If they do not match, backtrack to the arguments, trying to get new values that match with the parameters.

Unfortunately, this strategy is not even valid for very simple cases. Consider the following example:

$$
\begin{array}{ll}
\textbf{fun} & \text{one : nat} \rightarrow \text{nat} \\
& \text{one } 0 := \text{s } 0. \qquad\qquad [O1] \\
& \text{one (s X)} := \text{one X.} \quad [O2] \\
\textbf{eval} & \text{one (one Y).}
\end{array}
$$

The previous strategy proceeds in this way, where the redices are underlined:

$one\ (\underline{one\ Y}) \Longrightarrow_{O1}$

$one\ (\underline{one\ Y}) \Longrightarrow_{O1,\{Y:=0\}}$ $one\ (s\ 0) \Longrightarrow_{O1} failure$
     $(discarded\ because\ the\ argument\ is\ not\ 0)$

$one\ (\underline{one\ X}) \Longrightarrow_{\{Y:=(sX)\}}$ $one\ (s\ 0) \Longrightarrow_{O1} failure$
     $(discarded\ because\ the\ argument\ is\ not\ 0)$

. . .

No result can be computed, for (one Y) gives infinitely many answers and none of them is 0. Nevertheless, an innermost strategy can compute the results:

$one\ (\underline{one\ Y}) \Longrightarrow_{O1,\{Y:=0\}}$ $one\ (s\ 0) \Longrightarrow_{O2}$

$\underline{one\ 0} \Longrightarrow_{O1} s\ 0$ $First\ solution;\ backtracking$

$one\ (\underline{one\ Y}) \Longrightarrow_{O2,\{Y:=(sX)\}}$ $one\ (\underline{one\ X}) \Longrightarrow_{O1,\{X:=0\}}$

$one\ (s\ 0) \Longrightarrow_{O2} \underline{one\ 0} \Longrightarrow_{O1} s\ 0$ $Second\ solution;\ backtracking$

. . .

Although the program presented is very simple, the problem can be generalized when inverse functions are computed. For instance, the first program for the fibonacci numbers presented previously cannot be computed with the pure outermost strategy.

Another problem of the strategy is the risk of reevaluation of arguments. Consider the goal one (one 20) for the previous examples. The pure outermost strategy select the rule [O1] and then evaluates the argument (one 20) to get the value 0. However, the result is (s 0) (after 20 narrowing steps) and backtracking to get a new value for (one 20) is performed. No new solution can be reached and [O2] is tried for the outer one call. Now, another computation of (one 20) is done, the result matches with (s X) and the evaluation can be completed. Unfortunately, two computations of (one 20) have been done.

These two drawbacks of the pure outermost strategy suggest finding a different strategy to cope with them. The problem of the pure outermost strategy appears in the evaluation order: it evaluates the function call and then, inside it, the arguments. Any correct strategy must evaluate the arguments (to some degree) and then perform the function call. In order to define more precisely the strategy, let us give some previous definitions

Definition 1 (pattern tree) : *A pattern tree is an or-pattern*

$$or(p_1, \ldots, p_n) \text{ where each } p_i \text{ is an and-pattern.}$$

An and-pattern *is one of the following*

$$\textbf{any} \mid \quad \textbf{nf} \mid \quad \textbf{hnf} \mid \quad c(pt_1, \ldots, pt_m)$$
$$c/m \in DC^m, pt_i \text{ or-patterns} \square$$

Intuitively, a pattern tree can be used to indicate how much an argument needs to be evaluated. An or-pattern enumerates different alternatives. **any** means that no evaluation is needed. **hnf** asks for evaluation to *head normal form*, i.e. evaluation to an expression which is either a free variable or has a constructor on the top. **nf** (for *normal form*) demands evaluation to a term. These last two components are introduced to simplify the patterns. For instance, the pattern $or(c_1 \ (pt_1), \ldots, c_m \ (pt_m))$ could be simplified to $or(\textbf{hnf})$ if each pt_i's is of the form $(\textbf{any}, \ldots, \textbf{any})$ and $c_1, \ldots, c_m$ are all the constructors of the type.

Definition 2 *A demand pattern for a function $f/n \in FS$ is a n-tuple of pattern trees, demanding evaluation for all of the arguments.*

Definition 3 *Every set of rules for a function f defines the* direct demand pattern: *for each of the arguments, the pattern tree is the or-pattern composed of the and-patterns of each rule.* $\square$

More formally, a set of rules:

$$ft_1^1 \ldots t_n^1 := M_1, \ldots, \ ft_1^m \ldots t_n^m := M_m$$

defines the demand pattern $or(and\_pattern(t_1^1, .., t_1^m), .., and\_pattern(t_n^1, .., t_n^m))$, where the function $and\_pattern$ is defined inductively as:

$$and\_pattern \ (X) := \textbf{any}$$
$$and\_pattern \ (c \ s_1 \ \ldots \ s_r) := c \ (and\_pattern \ (s_1), \ \ldots, \ and\_pattern \ (s_r))$$

The direct demand pattern for the fib function defined with rules *[FI1, FI2, FI3]* is the following:

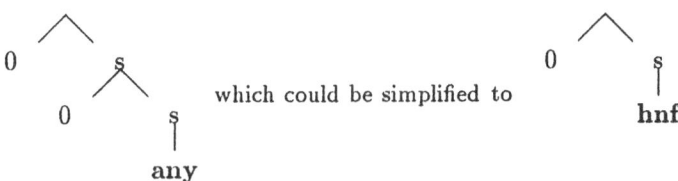

The direct demand pattern for a function is the "minimum" evaluation needed for the arguments. However, the formalism of demand patterns is able to describe more defined evaluation patterns which can be used to optimize the computation, as we will show in section 6.

Now, we are in a position to define a *demand driven strategy* based on a demand pattern for each function of the program. The application of a function to some arguments is done in the following way:

1. Evaluate the arguments as demanded by the demand pattern.

2. Try the rules in textual order. In case of failure, backtrack to next rule.

3. If no rule is applicable, backtrack to the arguments.

The easiest strategy is that based on the direct demand pattern.

4 Translating Lazy Narrowing into Prolog

This section is devoted to describe how a BABEL program can be translated into a PROLOG program by means of a program transformation. We will define the transformation stepwise, starting with a general approach describing a straightforward method. This method can be optimized by compiling the demand patterns. Finally, a technique for doing structure sharing is presented. All the techniques are combined into a translation process, which is formally defined.

4.1 General Approach

In general, a function is translated into a relation and a constructor can be represented by a PROLOG functor with the same name. Inside the PROLOG program, every function symbol f/n now has two meanings: f/n is a functor which represents a function application not yet evaluated, while $f/n+1$ is a relation which reduces f applied to the first n arguments to **hnf** and puts it as the $n + 1$ argument.

The relation $f/n+1$ expects n arguments previously evaluated to the degree required by the pattern. More exactly, a rule

$$f\ t1\ \ldots\ tn := M,$$

is transformed into the PROLOG clause

$$f\ (t1,\ \ldots,\ tn,\ R):-eval(M,R,hnf).\qquad [F]$$

Evaluation of expressions is performed by the predicate **eval** which has three arguments. The first one is the expression to be evaluated, the second one is the result of the evaluation and the third one is the demand tree, which defines the degree of evaluation. Demand trees are represented, in principle, by the constants **any**, **hnf**, **nf**, user-defined constructors for the and-patterns and the functor **or**, which is applied to a list of and-patterns, for the or-patterns.

The rules for **eval** are the following:

```
eval(X,Y,or([P1|LP])):-eval_aux(X,Y,P1).
eval(X,Y,or([P1|LP])):-eval(X,Y,LP).
```

```
% Pattern any
eval_aux(X,X,any).
% Variable expression
eval_aux(X,X,P):-var(X),!.
% Construction: For any c/n ∈ DCⁿ
eval_aux(c(X1,...,Xn),c(X1,...,Xn),hnf).
eval_aux(c(X1,...,Xn),c(Y1,...,Yn),nf):-
              eval_aux(X1,Y1,nf),...,eval_aux(Xn,Yn,nf).
eval_aux(c(X1,...,Xn),c(Y1,...,Yn),c(P1,..Pn)) :-
              eval_aux (X1,Y1,P1),...,eval_aux(Xn,Yn,Pn).
% Function Application: For any f/n ∈ FSⁿ
eval_aux(f(X1,...,Xn),R,P):-
              ...,eval(Xi,Yi,Pfi),...
              f(Y1,...,Yn,Res),
              eval_aux(Res,R,P).
```

where the `Pfi` is the demand pattern for `f`.
Any goal expression M is transformed into a call to `eval (M, N, nf)`, giving N as the result and bindings for M's variables.

4.2 Compilation of Demand Patterns

The treatment of pattern trees as PROLOG terms, with a general predicate `eval`, is not the most efficient solution. Instead of this, a concrete demand pattern for a function f can be "compiled" into PROLOG code. A set of specialized `eval_f_i` predicates are used to get the evaluation of each ith argument as demanded by the concrete pattern tree.

Any `eval_f_i` predicate has two arguments: the first one is the expression to be evaluated and the second the result of the evaluation. An or-pattern is compiled by using different clauses for each of its and-patterns, plus a special clause for the expression being a variable. The compilation of an and-pattern follows these rules:

- **any** does not need to be compiled.

- **hnf** implies the evaluation to head normal form. It is obtained by performing a call to the predicate `tohnf`. An extra clause is needed for the case where the expression is a free variable.

- **nf** can be got by recursively demanding evaluation to **hnf** of all the components of a construction. The predicate `nf` is the responsible for this.

- an and-pattern of the form $c(pt1, \ldots, ptn)$ implies the evaluation of the expression to head normal form (predicate `tohnf`) and then n calls new auxiliary predicates to compute patterns $pt1, \ldots, ptn$. These predicates are compiled with the same rules. If some pattern appears twice, the same predicate could be used. In particular, it allows us to make recursive calls, for regular patterns (see section 6).

A more precise definition will be given in section 4.4, where an example will also appear.

4.3 Structure Sharing

As usual, lazy narrowing has been described syntactically, as a string reduction process. Unfortunately, this leads to potential reevaluation. For instance, consider the rule [$FI3$] in the previous example used to compute fibonacci function. It is clear that, to be efficient, N should get evaluated simultaneously for its two occurrences in the right-hand side.

This gave birth to the concept of graph reduction, where substructures can be *shared* among different expressions. In graph-reduction abstract machines sharing is done via pointer assignments. This is not directly applicable to PROLOG, whose assignments are monotonic. We need a clear and efficient scheme for sharing in PROLOG.

To meet this, all expressions to be evaluated are represented by a pair

expression # pointer

The expression is a PROLOG term showing nested application of functions — possibly to other expressions also represented by terms — and the pointer is a PROLOG variable which is used to hold all the information needed to implement sharing. This implies both containing (partial) results and signalling whether or not to evaluate:

- The pointer remains free while the expression is not evaluated.

- When two expressions are unified, so are the pointers.

- When the expression is evaluated *to the demanded degree*, the pointer is made to point to the (partial) result.

- When evaluating a expression, if the pointer is not free it is followed, instead of doing further reductions.

Sharing can be illustrated with an example. Consider the function

$$\text{stupid } 0 \quad := 0.$$
$$\text{stupid } (s\ N) \quad := s\ (\text{stupid } N).$$

and the goal fib (stupid (s(s(s 0)))). The narrowing steps for the extended terms are shown below, along with the bindings for sharing:

$$\text{fib } (\underline{\text{stupid}(s(s(s(0))))}\#V)\#R$$
$$\text{stupid } (s(s(s\ 0))) \Longrightarrow_{<V/s(s(V1))>} s(s(\text{stupid}(s(0))\#V1))$$
$$\underline{\text{fib}(s(s(\text{stupid}(s(0))\#V1))\#s(s(V1)))\#R}$$
$$\text{fib } (s(s(\text{stupid } (s\ 0)))) \Longrightarrow$$
$$\text{plus}(\text{fib}(\text{stupid}(s(0))\#V1),\text{fib}(s(\text{stupid}(s(0))\#V1)))\#V2$$
$$\text{plus}(\text{fib}(\underline{\text{stupid}(s(0))}\#V1),\text{fib}(s(\text{stupid}(s(0))\#V1)))\#V2$$
$$\underline{\text{stupid } (s\ 0)} \Longrightarrow_{<V1/s(V3)>} s(\text{stupid}(0)\#V3)$$
$$\text{plus}(\text{fib}(s(\text{stupid}(0)\#V3)),\text{fib}(s(\text{stupid}(s(0))\#(s(V3)))))\#V2$$

thus avoiding reevaluation.

A similar technique for sharing is presented in [Ch91].

4.4 The Transformation

The techniques described yield the general program transformation presented in figure 1.

Some minor optimizations can be done by "folding" and "unfolding" clauses. Furthermore, in order to avoid the growth of the PROLOG program some techniques could be used. Predicates tohnf, tonf can be specialized for each type of the program. Another solution is to use the predefined predicate =.., present in most PROLOG implementations, to get separately the functor (constructor or function) and its arguments. The clauses depending on constructors and functions can be unified in a single one.

The resulting PROLOG code for the fib function and the direct demand pattern is the following:

```
tohnf(X,X):-var(X),!.          plus(0,Y,Y).
tohnf(0,0).                     plus(s(X),Y,s(plus(X,Y)#_)).
tohnf(s(N),s(N)).
tohnf(E#P,V):-                  fib(0,s(0)).
    nonvar(P),!,P=V.            fib(s(0),s(s(0))).
tohnf(plus(N,M)#R,R):-          fib((s(s(N))),R):-
    eval_plus_1(N,X),               tohnf(plus(fib(N)#_,fib(s(N))#_)
    plus(X,M,R).                                               #_,R).
tohnf(fib(N)#R,R):-
    eval_fib_1(N,X),            tonf(X,X):-var(X),!.
    fib(X,R).                   tonf(0,0).
                                tonf(s(N),s(X)):-tonf(N,X).
                                tonf(E#P,R):-
eval_plus_1(X,Y):-                  tohnf(E#P,P),
    tohnf(X,Y).                     tonf(P,R).


eval_fib_1(X,Y):-
    tohnf(X,T),
    eval_fib_1_1(T,Y).
eval_fib_1_1(0,0).
eval_fib_1_1(s(X),s(Y)):-
    tohnf(X,Y).
```

and the goal (fib s (s (s 0))) is translated into

```
tonf (fib(s(s(s(0))) # F, R)
```

[JMM92] contains the result of the transformation for the rest of the examples used in the paper.

5 Lazy Equality, Primitive Operations and Higher Order

5.1 Lazy Equality

One of the most important features of BABEL is lazy equality. The semantics of the equality is the following: two terms t_1, t_2 are said to be equal if both are

- Compilation of pattern trees

  if tree $= OR(pt_1, \ldots, pt_n)$
  $\implies$ `tree(X,X):-var(X),!.`
        `tree(X,Y):-pt1(X,Y).`
        `...`
        `tree(X,Y):-ptn(X,Y).`

  if tree $= c(pt_1, \ldots, pt_n)$
  $\implies$ `tree(X,X):-var(X),!.`
        `tree(X,c(Y1,...,Yn)):-tohnf(X,c(X1,...,Xn)),`
                               `pt1(X1,Y1),...,ptn(Xn,Yn).`

  where `pti` are new auxiliar predicates with rules generated with the same method. Predicates for the demand pattern for a function f are named **eval_f_i** and generated by the previous rules.

- Translating expressions to PROLOG terms for sharing:
  $$
  \begin{aligned}
  exptrans(X) &= X \quad X \text{ variable} \\
  exptrans(c\ e_1 \ldots e_n) &= c(exptrans(e_1), \ldots, exptrans(e_n)) \\
  exptrans(f\ e_1 \ldots e_n) &= f(exptrans(e_1), \ldots, exptrans(e_n))\#X \\
  & \quad X \text{ new variable}
  \end{aligned}
  $$

- For each program we generate the following clauses:
  $\implies$ `tohnf(X,X):-var(X),!.`
        `tohnf(E#P,V):-nonvar(P),!,P=V.`
        `tonf(X,X):-var(X),!.`
        `tonf(E#P,V):-`
            `tohnf(E#P,P),`
            `tonf(P,V).`

- For each constructor c/n (n possibly 0):
  $\implies$ `tohnf(c(X1,...,Xn),c(X1,...,Xn)).`
        `tonf(c(X1,...,Xn),c(Y1,...,Yn)):-`
                          `tonf(X1,Y1),...,tonf(Xn,Yn).`

- For each function f/n:
  $\implies$ `tohnf(f(X1,...,Xn)#R,R):-`
            `...,`
            `eval_f_i(Xi,Yi),`
            `...,`
            `f(Y1,...,Yn,R).`

- For each defining rule:
  f t1...tn:=M $\implies$ `f(t1,...,tn,R):-tohnf(`*exptrans*`(M),R)`

- A goal expression is translated by
  eval M $\implies$ `tonf (`*exptrans*(M)`, R).`

Figure 1: Translation process

finite and equal, and are said to be non equal if they are different at any finite level (even if they are infinite). [Ch91] shows a way to compute the truth value for equality: Both terms are evaluated to hnf and then checked for equality. If one of them is a variable, a binding is done (if the occur check succeeds). If both have the same constructors, equality of the arguments is performed sequentially. However, to compute the falsity of equality the method is not always valid, since the first two arguments of the terms could be infinite and equal but the second arguments could be different. One safe way to implement equality is by means of a queue. The queue contains pairs of terms in head normal form to be checked equal. The lazy equality checks the top level constructor of the terms and, if they are equal, their arguments are introduced in the queue. A well known technique for an efficient implementation of queues in PROLOG is the use of difference lists.

```
eq(X,Y,res):-tohnf(X,U),tohnf(Y,V),
             eq_queue (dif ([(U, V)|Q1], Q2)), res).


% empty queue
eq_queue (dif (Q1, Q1), true) :- !.
% Checking variables
eq_queue (dif ([(X, Y)|Q1],Q2)', res) :-
                          var(X), var (Y), !, X = Y,
                          eq_queue (dif (Q1, Q2), res).
eq_queue (dif ([(X, Y)|Q1], Q2), res) :-
                  var (X), eval (Y, V, nf),
                  ((occur (X,Y)) -> (res == false);
                                    (eq_queue (dif (Q1, Q2), res))).
% Similar rules but being Y the variable
% Checking constructions
eq_queue (dif ([(c (X1, ..., Xn), c (Y1, ..., Yn))|Q1],
                [((U1,...,Un),(V1,...,Vn)|Q2]), res) :-
                          tohnf (X1, U1), ..., tohnf (Xn, Un),
                          tohnf (Y1, V1), ..., tohnf (Yn, Vn),
                          eq_queue (dif (Q1, Q2), res).
                  % for each constructor c/n ∈ DCⁿ
eq_queue (dif ([(c (X1, ..., Xn), d (Y1, ..., Ym))|Q1], Q2), false).
                  % for each c/n ∈ DCⁿ, d/m ∈ DCᵐ,
                  % of the same type and different
```

The predicate **occur** is any implementation of the occur-check in PROLOG.

5.2 Primitive Operations and Higher Order

The rest of BABEL primitives can be handled in two ways. BABEL primitives can be defined by some *predefined rules* [MR88, MR92], so, we can treat them as user-defined functions and the previous rules are valid for them. Of course, more efficient code should be generated to manage primitive symbols. For instance, the logical connectives (and ",", or ";") can be compiled into the equivalent PROLOG ones, the guard and the conditional operator fit into PROLOG "if_then_else", and so on. [JMM92] contains a full description.

Higher order facilities of BABEL can be simulated in PROLOG too. The transformation uses the idea introduced by Warren [Wa82] for coding higher order programming features into first order PROLOG. Due to the lack of space, we omit the definition, which can be found in [JMM92].

6 Optimizations

One of the key points of our construction is to avoid reevaluation from one rule to another. The previous techniques ensure that the evaluation of the arguments is done once and no further evaluation is needed to use a rule. But, the problem can appear even when the evaluation of arguments is not required to perform the rule application. Consider the following example:

> **fun** f: nat → nat → nat.
> f 0 X := g X.
> f 1 X := g' X.
> %*Some rules for g, g' demanding evaluation for the first argument*

The second argument of f does not need to be evaluated in order to use f's rules. However, for a goal like f X (fib 20), both rules are applicable and the evaluation of fib 20 will be needed later. In case of backtracking from the first rule to the second rule, a reevaluation of fib 20 will be done. Some techniques of strictness analysis could be used to detect such possibility of reevaluation, and this information can be incorporated into the demand pattern for f.

Consider, for instance, the function *len*, length of a list:

> **fun** len: list T → num.
> len [H|T] := 1 + len T.
> len [] := 0.

Its direct demand pattern is or([],[**any**|**any**]). However, the demand pattern expressed as the solution to the equation DP=or([],[**any**|DP]) is also correct. The latter requires evaluation till a list of expressions ended by *nil* is constructed. This is obvious, for a full list will eventually be constructed to compute its length. This pattern is usually called **spine normal form**. If we are capable of inferring this at compile time, execution can be substantially improved for some programs. A more detailed description of the abstract interpretation framework can be found in [MM92b]

7 Related Work and Experimental Results

As we have said in the introduction, only a few authors have worked on the transformation of narrowing into PROLOG. [vEY87] presents two approaches to this problem: the interpretative one and the compilational. The second one translates innermost narrowing into a set of Horn clauses. This eager strategy cannot cope with infinite objects as in our second fibonacci program.

The most interesting approach appears in [Ch91]. Cheong's transformation applies a pure outermost strategy. Roughly speaking, and using our terminology, a rule

program	Cheong's	ours	*ratio*
$one^2(4000)$	6840	3300	2.1
$one^2(5000)$	9218	4190	2.2
$subsets(6)$	889	390	2.3
$subsets(7)$	1980	800	2.5

Table 1: Execution times

f t1 ... tn := M.

is transformed (replacing rules F, $F of our approach) into:

f (X1, ..., Xn, M) :- eval (X1, t1),..., eval (Xn, tn).   [F']

where predicate eval has similar rules to those described here, but with the second (and last) argument the result of the computation and the demand tree as the same time. He also uses a different (although equivalent) technique for sharing.

Reevaluation of the arguments could be done for each rule. Furthermore, it makes less use of the efficient features of PROLOG: all the unifications are performed in the eval predicate and no indexing of f's rules is performed, because all of them have the same head.

A comparison of the two methods based on the the execution times of some examples can be found in table 1. We used two examples: one^2 applies function one twice. *subsets* calculates all the subsets of the first N natural numbers. The times are in milliseconds. Our method provides a speed up at of least twice Cheong's. It is well known that lazy evaluation can run faster than innermost evaluation when full evaluation of some subexpression is not needed. Table 2 shows the comparison of PROLOG and BABEL running the well-known *naivesort* example. The success of the lazy strategy is due to the fact that permutations are partially generated and then the *sorted* check used to prune further evaluation. It is a good example of the important role of laziness in typical search programs.

Finally we can show the impact of strictness analysis. The effect of reevaluation on efficiency can be shown with the following example: computing the

naivesort				sublists		
	PROLOG	BABEL	*speedup*	*without* abst.int.	*with* abst.int.	*ratio*
[3...0]	9	59	0.152			
[4...0]	60	159	0.377	[1...3]	41	36	1.138
[5...0]	330	439	0.751	[1...4]	88	72	1.222
[6...0]	2300	1279	1.798	[1...5]	183	141	1.297
[7...0]	18270	3760	4.859	[1...6]	374	275	1.36
[8...0]	163940	11459	14.30	[1...7]	757	538	1.407
[9...0]	1631430	34679	47.04	[1...8]	1524	1058	1.44

Table 2: Benchmarks

sublists of some reversed list nondeterministically. The *sublist* function generates the same equations as *len*. If the reversing is done lazily, partial reevaluation will occur when constructing the different sublists. The result is displayed in table 2.

8 Conclusions and Future Work

We have provided some techniques to compile lazy narrowing to PROLOG in a clean and efficient way. The paper could also be seen as some techniques for handling infinite objects in PROLOG.

Our approach has a number of advantages with respect to the existing ones. The method is more complete, in the sense that a larger class of programs can be managed. In particular, every program that can be computed with an eager strategy can also be executed with our technique. Moreover, programs with non-strict functions and infinite objects can be handled.

The resulting code is very efficient because reevaluation is highly avoided. Furthermore, full use is made of the elements of PROLOG implementations which provide efficiency. (In the Warren Abstract Machine [Wa83]) these are: unification, indexing, fewer choice points, etc.)

Another advantage comes from the order of solution generation. With our approach, the solutions are generated in the same way as in an eager strategy. In other words, the order in which constraints are imposed on variables during execution is the same as in eager evaluation. This gives the programmer the possibility of organizing the control of the program as convenient, as can be done in PROLOG. For instance, a *generate and test* program is translated into a real generate and test PROLOG program with our transformation, which need not be the case in other approaches using a pure outermost strategy.

We plan to investigate in more detail global flow analysis techniques to avoid reevaluation by inferring more accurate demand patterns. Abstract interpretation, strictness analysis, mode inference, partial evaluation techniques, etc. can help us in this goal. A key point for this purpose is to establish a theoretical framework to work with demand trees, which we have sketched in [MM92].

We also plan to incorporate some of these techniques in the current abstract machine implementation (LBAM [MKLR90]). In particular, the compilation of demand patterns could be done more efficiently in a direct implementation.

References

[An91a]   S. Antoy: Lazy Evaluation in Logic, Proceedings PLILP'91, Springer Verlag, 1991, LNCS 528, pp. 371-382.

[An91b]   S. Antoy: Non-Determinism and Lazy Evaluation in Logic Programming, LOPSTR'91.

[BL86]   M. Bellia, G. Levi: The Relation between Logic and Functional Languages, Journal of Logic Programming 3, 1986, pp. 217-236.

[BGLMP87] G.P. Bosco, E. Giovanetti, G. Levi, C. Moisso, C. Palamidessi: A complete semantic characterization of K-LEAF, A logic language with partial evaluation, Symposium on Logic Programming, S. Francisco, 1987.

[BGM88]   P.G. Bosco, E. Giovannetti, C. Moiso: Narrowing versus SLD-resolution, Theoretical Computer Science 59, 1988, pp. 3-23.

[BCGMP89] P.G. Bosco, C. Cecchi, E. Giovannetti, C. Moiso, C. Palamidessi: Using Resolution for a Sound and Efficient Integration of Logic and Functional Programming, in: J. de Bakker (ed.), Languages for parallel architectures: Design, Semantics, Implementation Models, Wiley, 1989.

[BCM89] P.G. Bosco, C. Cecchi, C. Moiso: An Extension of WAM for K-LEAF: A WAM-based Compilation of Conditional Narrowing, Procs. Int. Conf. on Logic Programming, The MIT Press, 1989, pp. 318-333.

[ChL91] M. Chakravarty, H. Lock: The Implementation of Lazy Narrowing, Symp. on Progr. Language Impl. and Logic Progr (PLILP'91), Springer Verlag, 1991, LNCS 528, pp. 123-134.

[Ch91] P.H. Cheong: Compiling Lazy Narrowing into Prolog, to appear in: New Generation Computing, 1992.

[vEY87] M. van Emden, K. Yukawa: Logic Programming with Equations, Journal of Logic Programming 4, 1987, pp. 265-288

[GM84] J.A. Goguen, J. Meseguer: EQLOG: Equality, Types and Generic Modules for Logic Programming, Journal of Logic Programming 1(2), 1984, pp. 179-210; also in [dGL86].

[dGL86] D. DeGroot, G. Lindstrom (eds.): *Logic Programming: Functions, Relations, Equations*, Prentice Hall, 1986.

[Ha90] M. Hanus: Compiling Logic Programs with Equality, Symp. on Progr. Language Impl. and Logic Progr (PLILP'90), Springer Verlag, 1990, LNCS 456, pp. 387-401.

[Hu84] J. Hughes: Why Functional Programming Matters, Technical Report 16, Programming Methodology Group, University of Goteborg, November 1984.

[JMM92] J.A. Jiménez-Martín, J. Mariño-Carballo, J.J. Moreno-Navarro, Efficient Compilation of Lazy Narrowing into PROLOG, Technical Report, Facultad de Informática de Madrid, 1992 (to appear).

[KLMR90] H. Kuchen, R. Loogen, J.J. Moreno Navarro, M. Rodríguez Artalejo: Graph-Based Implementation of a Functional Logic Language, European Symp. on Prog. (ESOP) 1990, LNCS 432, 1990, pp. 271-290.

[KLMR91] H. Kuchen, R. Loogen, J.J. Moreno-Navarro, M. Rodríguez-Artalejo: Graph Narrowing to Implement a Functional Language, Technical Report, Facultad de Informática de Madrid.

[MM92] J. Mariño-Carballo, J.J. Moreno Navarro, Some notes on lazy evaluation, 1st Compulog-Network Meeting on Programming Languages, Pisa 1992.

[MM92b] J. Mariño-Carballo, J.J. Moreno-Navarro, Strictness Analysis for Lazy Narrowing, Technical Report, Facultad de Informática de Madrid, 1992 (to appear).

[MKLR90] J.J. Moreno Navarro, H. Kuchen, R. Loogen, M. Rodríguez-Artalejo: Lazy Narrowing in a Graph Machine, 2nd Int. Conf. on Algebraic and Logic Programming (ALP), LNCS 456, 1990, pp. 298-317.

[MR88] J.J. Moreno Navarro, M. Rodríguez-Artalejo: BABEL: A Functional and Logic Programming Language Based on Constructor Discipline and Narrowing, Conf. on Algebraic and Logic Programming (ALP), LNCS 343, 1989, pp. 223-232.

[MR92] J.J. Moreno Navarro, M. Rodríguez Artalejo: Logic Programming with Functions and Predicates: The Language BABEL, Journal of Logic Programming,12, 1992, pp. 189-223.

[Na91] L. Naish: Adding Equations to NU-Prolog, Symp. on Progr. Language Impl. and Logic Progr (PLILP'91), Springer Verlag, 1991, LNCS 528, pp. 15-26.

[Na86] S. Narain: A technique for doing lazy evaluation in logic, Journal of Logic Programming 3, 1986, pp. 259–276.

[Re85] U.S. Reddy: Narrowing as the Operational Semantics of Functional Languages, IEEE Int. Symp. on Logic Progr., IEEE Computer Society Press, 1985, pp. 138–151.

[Re87] U.S. Reddy: Functional Logic Languages, Part I, Workshop on Graph Reduction, LNCS 279, 1987, pp. 401–425.

[SY86] P.A. Subrahmanyan, J.H. You: FUNLOG:A Computational Model Integrating Logic and Functional Programming, in [dGL86],pp.157-198.

[Tu85] D.A. Turner: MIRANDA, a Non-strict Functional Language with Polymorphic Types, Procs. Int. Conf. on Functional Programming Languages and Architectures, Springer Verlag, LNCS 201, 1985, pp. 1-16.

[Wa82] D.H.D. Warren: Higher-order Extensions to PROLOG: Are they Needed?, in J.E. Hayes, D. Mitchie, Y.H. Yao (eds.), Machine Intelligence 10, Ellis Horwood Ltd., John Wiley&Sons, 1982, pp. 441-454.

[Wa83] D.H.D. Warren: An Abstract PROLOG Instruction Set, Technical Note 309, SRI International, Menlo Park, California, October 1983

Author Index

Published in 1990–91

AI and Cognitive Science '89, Dublin City University, Eire, 14–15 September 1989
A. F. Smeaton and G. McDermott (Eds.)

Specification and Verification of Concurrent Systems, University of Stirling, Scotland, 6–8 July 1988
C. Rattray (Ed.)

Semantics for Concurrency, Proceedings of the International BCS-FACS Workshop, Sponsored by Logic for IT (S.E.R.C.), University of Leicester, UK, 23–25 July 1990
M. Z. Kwiatkowska, M. W. Shields and R. M. Thomas (Eds.)

Functional Programming, Glasgow 1989
Proceedings of the 1989 Glasgow Workshop, Fraserburgh, Scotland, 21–23 August 1989
K. Davis and J. Hughes (Eds.)

Persistent Object Systems, Proceedings of the Third International Workshop, Newcastle, Australia, 10–13 January 1989
J. Rosenberg and D. Koch (Eds.)

Z User Workshop, Oxford 1989, Proceedings of the Fourth Annual Z User Meeting, Oxford, 15 December 1989
J. E. Nicholls (Ed.)

Formal Methods for Trustworthy Computer Systems (FM89), Halifax, Canada, 23–27 July 1989
Dan Craigen (Editor) and Karen Summerskill (Assistant Editor)

Security and Persistence, Proceedings of the International Workshop on Computer Architecture to Support Security and Persistence of Information, Bremen, West Germany, 8–11 May 1990
John Rosenberg and J. Leslie Keedy (Eds.)

Women into Computing: Selected Papers 1988–1990
Gillian Lovegrove and Barbara Segal (Eds.)

3rd Refinement Workshop (organised by BCS-FACS, and sponsored by IBM UK Laboratories, Hursley Park and the Programming Research Group, University of Oxford), Hursley Park, 9–11 January 1990
Carroll Morgan and J. C. P. Woodcock (Eds.)

Designing Correct Circuits, Workshop jointly organised by the Universities of Oxford and Glasgow, Oxford, 26–28 September 1990
Geraint Jones and Mary Sheeran (Eds.)

Functional Programming, Glasgow 1990
Proceedings of the 1990 Glasgow Workshop on Functional Programming, Ullapool, Scotland, 13–15 August 1990
Simon L. Peyton Jones, Graham Hutton and Carsten Kehler Holst (Eds.)

4th Refinement Workshop, Proceedings of the 4th Refinement Workshop, organised by BCS-FACS, Cambridge, 9–11 January 1991
Joseph M. Morris and Roger C. Shaw (Eds.)

AI and Cognitive Science '90, University of Ulster at Jordanstown, 20–21 September 1990
Michael F. McTear and Norman Creaney (Eds.)

Software Re-use, Utrecht 1989, Proceedings of the Software Re-use Workshop, Utrecht, The Netherlands, 23–24 November 1989
Liesbeth Dusink and Patrick Hall (Eds.)

Z User Workshop, 1990, Proceedings of the Fifth Annual Z User Meeting, Oxford, 17–18 December 1990
J.E. Nicholls (Ed.)

IV Higher Order Workshop, Banff 1990
Proceedings of the IV Higher Order Workshop, Banff, Alberta, Canada, 10–14 September 1990
Graham Birtwistle (Ed.)